Inside Iran

Also by John Simpson:

The Disappeared and the Mothers of the Plaza
(with Jana Bennett)

Inside Iran

Life Under Khomeini's Regime

John Simpson

St. Martin's Press
New York

To all the good friends in London, Paris and Tehran
who know that this is addressed to them.

INSIDE IRAN. Copyright © 1988 by John Simpson.
All rights reserved. Printed in the United States of
America. No part of this book may be used or
reproduced in any manner whatsoever without
written permission except in the case of brief
quotations embodied in critical articles or reviews.
For information, address St. Martin's Press, 175 Fifth
Avenue, New York, N.Y. 10010.

Library of Congress Cataloging-in-Publication Data

Simpson, John, 1944–
          Inside Iran : life under Khomeini's regime /
by John Simpson.
              p.   cm.
      ISBN 0-312-01448-1 : $16.95
      1. Iran—Description and travel—1979–
   2. Iran—Politics and government—1979–
   3. Simpson, John, 1944–   —Journeys—Iran.
I. Title.
DS259.2.S58 1988
955'.054—dc19   87-27484
                                                    CIP

First published in Great Britain by Robson Books
Ltd., under the title *Behind Iranian Lines: Despatches
from Khomeini's Regime.*

First U.S. Edition

10 9 8 7 6 5 4 3 2 1

Contents

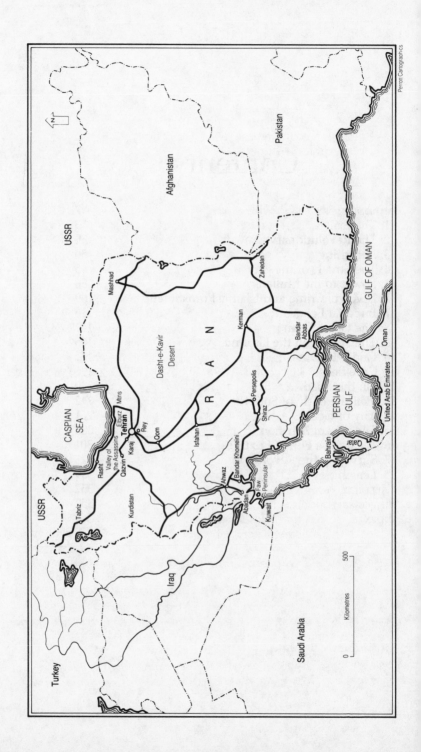

Introductory

> I do not wish to intrude myself unnecessarily on the attention of my readers, and one can hardly be auto-biographical without running the risk of being egotistical. But....[i]t is too late now to turn squeamish about the use of the pronoun of the first person. I will be as sparing of its use as I can, but use it I must.
>
> Edward Granville Browne, *A Year Amongst The Persians: Impressions as to the Life, Character and Thought of the People of Persia, Received during Twelve Months' Residence in that Country in the Years 1887-1888*

On the western side of Tehran University, in what is now the centre of the city but a century ago was part of the bare plain outside it, is a short street called *Kuche Porofesor Brown:* Professor Browne Street. The name appears twice: on an old marble plaque, of a kind which is gradually disappearing from Tehran, and on a less attractive modern plate installed just after the Revolution of 1979. Professor Browne Street has retained the imprimatur of the revolutionary authorities.

All around the area, the larger streets have been renamed: Shah Reza Avenue has become Revolution Avenue; Los Angeles Road is now Islamic Dress Road; Queen Elizabeth Boulevard has been turned, with a particular touch of irony, into Peasant Farmer Boulevard. The Islamic Republic, under the leadership of Ayatollah Khomeini, is determined to wipe out every trace of Iran's subjection to the Shahs, and through them to the British, the Americans, and the Russians. But the name of Professor Edward Granville Browne, the British scholar who spent his year among the Persians at a time when Persia was at its weakest under foreign (and particularly British) influence, has survived in this small street. E.G. Browne was a gentle, pleasant man who never returned to Persia after the year ended in 1888, but who studied its literature all his life and wrote powerfully in support of its efforts to win greater constitutional freedom. Persians reciprocated the affection. Some links, it seems, are too strong to be broken even by revolutions.

There have always been small but distinguished groups of people in the West – particularly in Britain, but in the United

States and France as well – who regard themselves as Irano-philes: diplomats, linguists, connoisseurs, archaeologists, some businessmen, a few journalists. But the majority of them have, understandably, suspended their affection for the country since 1979; while most people, reading only the headlines and watching the television pictures, regard Iran as nothing more than a barbaric place where terrible cruelties are committed by a régime which has wilfully returned to the Middle Ages.

Dreadful things have indeed occurred in Iran as a result of the Revolution. British people, American people, French people, Lebanese people, Iranian people have died as a direct result of the terrorism which the revolutionary authorities in Tehran have deliberately adopted as a settled part of their foreign policy. Inside the country, thousands of Iranians have been executed for the crime of disagreeing with their government's views. The rigid approach of an eye for an eye, not merely in legal terms but in political ones, has brought death and injury to innocent men on board ships in the Persian Gulf – attacked simply because Iraqi planes have attacked other ships carrying Iranian oil. It is not the purpose of this book to attempt to justify the unjustifi-able; instead its purpose is to look a little beyond the headlines and the television pictures to the kind of place the country has become under its Islamic Republic. If Iran has become the leading enemy of Western society (a view which is fairly gener-ally held), it is important to understand why it behaves as it does, and what sort of place it is.

It is not, for instance, another version of Colonel Qadafy's Libya: a small, posturing, cowardly régime which swings from one policy to another according to the whim of a single dictator. Iran is large and powerful, and possessed of an ideology with a proven force to it. It is also a country with a history of political and cultural achievement reaching back, relatively unbroken, for three millenia. Herodotus recorded the first intervention by religious leaders in the government of Persia, fifteen hundred years before the emergence of most European nations. But examining the character of the Islamic Republic of Iran is not easy. The régime is chronically suspicious and deeply isolatio-nist. Leading political figures are rarely willing to talk to a Westerner for any length of time about the nature of the society they are trying to create. Few Western journalists have been permitted to go to Iran, and their visits rarely last longer than a few days.

I spent a good deal of time in the country in the months before the fall of the Shah in 1979, and I was a passenger on Ayatollah

8

Khomeini's triumphant flight from Paris to Tehran which ushered in the Revolution. I was, however, barred from returning until seven years later, when the authorities in Tehran invited me on a brief trip to cover the war. I was determined, after that, to go back for a longer visit, together with my companion Tira Shubart, who works as a freelance producer of television news. For months she and I made a persistent nuisance of ourselves at the Iranian embassy in London, Tira in full *hejab* or Islamic dress, until we received the kind of visa which only a handful of foreign journalists have been accorded: one which allowed us to stay in Iran for several weeks, and to go where we wanted, on our own and without an escort. It was this that decided me finally to write a book, with Tira Shubart's help, which would contrast my visits to Iran before and during the Revolution with what has happened there since then.

For that reason there is no avoiding the first person singular. These are my impressions, and I do not claim anything more for them than that: they constitute a kind of travel-book with political overtones, anecdotal and impressionistic rather than analytical. It is still too soon to write the definitive account of the Islamic Republic in Iran. But Edward Granville Browne's genial explanation of his approach in *A Year Amongst The Persians* has encouraged me more than a little in mine:

> I might, indeed, have given to this book the form of a systematic treatise on Persia, a plan which for some time I did actually entertain; but against this plan three reasons finally decided me. *Firstly*, that my publishers expressed a preference for the narrative form, which, they believed, would render the book more readable. *Secondly*, that for the more ambitious project of writing a systematic treatise I did not feel myself prepared and could not prepare myself without the expenditure of time only to be obtained by the sacrifice of other work which seemed to me to be of greater importance. *Thirdly*, that the recent publication of the Hon. G. N. Curzon's encyclopaedic work on Persia will for some time to come prevent any similar attempt on the part of anyone else who is not either remarkably rash or exceedingly well-informed.

All three reasons apply strongly in my case; with the addition that instead of one encyclopaedic work on the Revolution of 1979, and the type of government and society which it ushered in, there are now a number, several of which are excellent. I have resisted as much as possible the temptation to stray into areas which are personally unknown to me or to the people we met: and for that reason some of the most significant events of the past eight or nine years have received scant attention here. There will be little mention of the hostage crisis of 1979-81, or of the political convulsions which resulted in the flight of President Bani-Sadr.

The disinguished historian Roy Mottahedeh, whose book *The Mantle Of The Prophet* is one of the works of excellence which have persuaded me to keep my ambitions modest, writes feelingly:

> the non-Iranian reader should be aware that no presentation of the history of Iranian culture, and, in particular, no presentation of its religious traditions, can please all Iranians.... Any consensus on the meaning of the Iranian past has been torn up by the deeply felt disagreement among Iranians over the meaning of the Iranian present.

When we returned from our visit to Iran and I reported on radio and television about what we had found there, I experienced a little of that deeply felt disagreement. Threats, physical and moral, arrived by post and telephone. I was denounced in the newspaper of one émigré faction and shouted at in the streets by its supporters. A well-known broadcaster was chased and threatened by an Iranian in the otherwise quiet English city of Salisbury simply because he was recognized as being a colleague of mine. And yet on the very day that a woman from Isfahan rang to accuse me of accepting the flatteringly large bribe of half a million pounds from Ayatollah Khomeini, I received a letter, immensely long, from the government press department in Tehran listing all the errors I had made and the prejudices I had shown in my reporting. Whatever reception this book may have in general, I am not anticipating rapturous praise either from the Iranian authorities or from many Iranian émigrés.

When the first-known English visitors to Persia arrived at the end of the sixteenth century, it was a difficult and dangerous country to get to, and its ways seemed very strange to them. By the end of the nineteenth century, when Edward Granville Browne spent his year there, the West regarded Persia as a degenerate, weak, backward country where Europeans could behave like conquerors. The fact that Browne did not share this attitude goes a long way towards explaining why there is still a street named after him in Tehran. But a hundred years later, Iran is feared and hated rather than despised, and it has receded into the impenetrability of its sixteenth century self; when Tira

Shubart and I were there, we were greeted with something of the curiosity which must have been accorded to the earliest Europeans who walked the streets of Isfahan, Qazvin and Tehran. I felt, therefore, a little like a traveller from an earlier period, and have accordingly chosen as my texts throughout this book the words not just of Edward Granville Browne and George Nathaniel Curzon (the author whose work persuaded Browne to restrict himself to the anecdotal), but of other intrepid explorers for whom Persia was *terra incognita*.

It is customary, in an introductory chapter like this, to list all the people to whom thanks are due for help in writing the book, and especially the particular friends who provided information and checked the manuscript. But in this case I shall omit their names, since printing them here would in the circumstances be a poor way of returning their thoughtfulness and generosity. To quote Browne again, 'I received much hospitality and kindness, which I shall not soon forget, and on which I would gladly dwell did I feel justified in so doing.' Part of my gratitude to them, I should warn the reader, involves changing any details in my narrative which might help to identify those people who should not be identified.

I can however express my gratitude to Ron Neil, the BBC's Deputy Director of News and Current Affairs, and to Nick Guthrie, the Foreign Editor of the BBC's 'Newsnight' programme, for encouraging me to travel to Iran and for assigning the two of us to make a television film there; to the London Library and the Cambridge University Library and their staffs; and to the friends who put us up, and put up with this enterprise, at their houses in Dorset, the French Alps, and Devonshire. Finally, much more than thanks is due to Tira Shubart, who shared the pleasures and the problems of our joint trip to Iran with courage, patience and enthusiasm. She supplied a great deal of the research that has gone into this book, conducted many interviews for it in Iran and in Britain, and drafted the chapters on women and on the American involvement in Iran. Without her, the entire project would have been unthinkable.

South Kensington,
September 1987.

Note

At 1987 rates, the Iranian *rial* was officially valued at 117 to the pound sterling, and 72 to the dollar. This, however, does not reflect its purchasing value within Iran itself, which was probably ten times the official rate.

1

The Exile

Sir/Anthony Sherley/His/Relation of his Travels/into
Persia/The Dangers and/Distresses, which befell him
in his passage, both by sea/and land, and his strange
and unexpected deliverances
                    Title-page of *Sherley's Travels*, 1613

IT WAS ALL faintly familiar, as I drove out of Paris and took the
road to Dreux, then branched off to the right into the valley of the
Mauldre; just as, when you chance upon a poem you learned as a
child, you remember each word or each stanza as you read it, but
have no clear idea where it takes you after that. It was brilliant
December weather, and as I saw the sign for Neauphle-le-
Château and turned up into the wooded hillside, the leaves still
hung on the beeches and the oaks and gave them a faint gilding
that was wearing thin, like a cheap wedding-ring from a long,
successful marriage. It was only twenty miles out of Paris, and if
this had been London or New York it would still have been outer
suburbia. Here it was deep countryside.

I drove through the Place du Marché, past the stalls of the
butchers and fishmongers, and the early shoppers looking for
something to take back for lunch. Somehow I had lost the thread:
the next line of the poem had slipped from my mind. I ranged
around, remembering other isolated landmarks, and suddenly
found myself back on course, in a street with high walls on either
side; and at the end of the street was a café I had forgotten for
seven years. Le Café des Trois Communes, it said in large letters
above the glass façade. It was nearly midday, and the windows
were encouragingly steamed up.

For sixteen weeks, from October 1978 to the following January,
this café, with its mildly bogus claim to represent the meeting-
point of three local communities, had been the operations centre
for the journalists and camera crews who had gathered in
Neauphle-le-Château to report the exotic presence in this small,
unremarkable village of Ayatollah Haj Sayyed Ruhollah Mussavi

Khomeini, and his return from exile to triumph in Iran. Neauphle was not entirely unused to fame: Brigitte Bardot had once lived here, and so had the American singer and actress Deanna Durbin. But it had never seen anything like the thousands of enthusiastic Iranians who flooded in to join their leader.

The café was largely unchanged inside: the red vinyl seats of the bar stools sagged a little more, the brown melamine on the tables was more chipped, the prices in the *Tarif des Consommations* had no doubt increased. Three men in city suits who would never have thought of setting foot in here seven years ago were sitting at a table, waiting for lunch; the Ayatollah's stay had clearly done no damage to property prices in the village. But the regulars were the same: four vinous old men in greasy flat caps and *bleu de travail* were propping up the bar, each with a small glass of something powerful in front of him.

It was not particularly easy to make light conversation with them about the events of seven years before, and I was left, inevitably, with the village joker. 'The Iranians? They were all mad. I'll tell you why. First, because they went back to Iran when they could have stayed in France. And second, because they didn't drink this.' He held up his glass of Ricard, and pointed to it with his chin. The other regulars roared obediently.

The proprietor was a little more forthcoming; he had moved into the café only after the Ayatollah had left. 'At the time, we thought it was a dreadful thing for the village, but afterwards we realized that it put us on the map. People come here quite often nowadays, like yourself, to see the place where the Iranians lived.' He paused. 'Except, of course, that it got blown up.'

I was not prepared for that: the news of the explosion must have passed me by. I thanked him for his excellent lunch, and headed off immediately for the Route de Chevreuse to see for myself. The familiar green gate with its slightly oriental lintel was still there, though brambles had grown up through the wire fence. But behind that, up the slope of the garden, there was nothing but a heap of rubble. On the third anniversary of the Iranian Revolution, in February 1982, someone had placed a bomb beside the foundations of the empty house, and it had been destroyed.

I walked through the gate, and into the neglected garden. The grass was up to my calves: no one had lived here since the Ayatollah left. On the trees in the straggling little orchard a few apples still hung at the end of the twigs, very brown and very dead. The brick steps up to the front door had survived, but everything else had collapsed in a pile of masonry and charred wood. A couple of decaying mattresses lay on the ground, and fragments of broken crockery. I looked at them carefully: I had eaten here several times. A dog barked violently in the garden next door, the noise echoing off the hillside in the silence.

The house that had been blown up was an ugly 1930s affair, no loss to France's architectural heritage. It was owned by Khomeini's organization, but he had not lived there; it had simply been his headquarters building. Knowing that, no doubt, and knowing too that it was empty, some group of Iranian exiles had decided to destroy it at a significant moment. The house where Khomeini had lived lay on the other side of the road, and had been left untouched.

As I walked out through the green gate the door of the house opposite opened, and a man emerged. He was not anxious to speak to me. 'Certainly this is my house. I rented it out to the Iranians. I had to spend quite a lot on it when they left, I can tell you.'

'Do they still own the land?'

'Yes, as far as I know they still own it, though the house may have been sold. There are so many legal problems no one has been able to sort them out.'

He climbed into his car and drove away, glad to shake me off. I had been told that people in the village blamed him for letting the Iranians come there in the first place, and by extension for everything that happened as a result. In the small world of Neauphle-le-Château, one of the great turning-points in history is ascribed to the desire of a neighbour to make a quick *centime*.

When he came to France, Ayatollah Khomeini had been an exile for fourteen years. He had first been imprisoned for leading a campaign against the Shah's attempts to redistribute land to the peasants, allow greater freedom to women, and open posts in local government to non-Muslims; then, after a period of house arrest, he was forced to leave Iran. He settled at first in Turkey, and then in Iraq, in the Shi'ite holy city of Najaf. After the Shah's triumphant diplomatic *rapprochement* with Iraq over the Shatt-el-Arab waterway dispute in 1975, when he cynically stopped his support overnight for the Iraqi Kurds, the flow of Iranian pilgrims wanting to see the holy places of Najaf and visit Khomeini greatly increased; and when the pilgrims returned home they took with them tapes of Khomeini's sermons. But as long as Khomeini stayed in Najaf he did not represent a revolutionary threat to the imperial power in Tehran.

15

Some autocrats who are overthrown are the passive victims of events; not so the Shah. He was the engineer of his own downfall, and his greatest diplomatic triumphs made the Revolution against him possible. His success in persuading the Arab members of the Organization of Petroleum Exporting Countries to raise the price of oil to unprecedented heights in 1973 brought a flood of sudden wealth pouring into Iran; that created corruption and social dislocation on such a scale that the political system he had created could not withstand it. And he presented the incipient Revolution with its leader when, in the aftermath of the diplomatic success with Iraq, he decided to do something about Khomeini. He was characteristically unable to leave well enough alone.

In the summer of 1978, when crowds of demonstrators boiled onto the streets of his cities chanting '*Dorud bar Khomeini!*' – 'Long live Khomeini!' – in obedience to the commands issued by the Ayatollah in Najaf, the Shah asked President Saddam Hussein of Iraq to expel him; and Saddam Hussein, anxious to keep on good terms with the Shah, agreed. By making the request, the Shah was expediting the Revolution against himself, and Saddam Hussein, by acceding to it, was adding to a chain of events which led to his disastrous invasion of Iran two years later and the beginning of the Gulf War. It is not necessary to share Ayatollah Khomeini's views of his destiny to see that everything his enemies did, for whatever motive, was turned to the interests of the Revolution.

Given forty-eight hours to leave Najaf, Khomeini alerted his followers abroad and made his preparations. The message reached a medical laboratory in Texas, where one of his strongest supporters, Ibrahim Yazdi, was carrying out research into the treatment of cancer. Yazdi, a subtle-minded and ambitious man who was by now a naturalized American citizen, left immediately for Najaf, and arrived there before the forty-eight hours were up: if the Revolution were about to begin, he wanted to claim his place in it. At first, he and Khomeini wanted to go to Kuwait; the Kuwaitis, however, refused to accept so difficult a visitor. The refugees went to Baghdad, to search for another place of refuge.

At this point, ambition again played a part. Sadeq Qotbzadeh, another devoted follower of Khomeini, had been living in Paris, and managed to persuade the French Foreign Ministry, the Quai d'Orsay, to issue the Ayatollah with a tourist visa. A third exile, Abol-Hassan Bani-Sadr, had the rather more difficult task of persuading him to accept it. Khomeini had profound doubts about the wisdom of living in a Western country so manifestly full of impurity. But there was no real alternative.

On 6 October 1978, Khomeini arrived at Paris-Orly. His flowing robes and black turban drew a good deal of attention in the airport terminal, but he kept his eyes on the ground the entire time, determined not to allow anything that was evil to impinge on his consciousness. And as Bani-Sadr drove him to his own flat in the featureless suburb of Cachan he resolutely refused to look out of the window. Their route did not take them to the centre of Paris, and Khomeini never visited, let alone saw, the city whose environs provided the spring-board for his return.

They waited at Cachan for several days, while the local building firm in Neauphle belatedly finished the conversion work on the house where the exile was to live. Even nowadays there is a mild sense of scandal in the village about the work that was required. The workmen had, for instance, to dismantle the modern lavatory and replace it with the type that has no seat, just two porcelain steps on either side of a hole in the ground; the same firm had removed precisely that kind of lavatory from a dozen houses in the area over the previous decade. Planning permission for these and other changes, which would normally have taken weeks, was arranged in a day; and four new telephones and two telex lines were installed with extraordinary speed. The hand of the Quai d'Orsay was detected in all of this. Khomeini had always refused to use a telephone, but at the age of 78 he learned the advantages of instant communication. From then on he was in regular, though never daily, contact through his lieutenants with those who were preparing for the Revolution in Iran itself.

But if Neauphle made it easier for him to communicate with his followers in Iran, it also brought him to the attention of the world at large. During the summer a French television team had penetrated to Najaf to try to interview him, only to find that forty Iraqi soldiers were deployed around his house to stop them. In Neauphle there were no barriers of any kind. In the first ten days he was there, he complied with his undertaking to the French government not to make political statements in public. But the French press, radio and television did not give up their efforts to persuade him to speak to them; and on 17 October he talked for the first time directly to a Western audience.

The second French television channel, *Antenne-2*, filmed a rather stilted interview with him that day, in which he said he was prepared to urge his followers towards armed insurrection against the Shah, who was, he said, kept in power by the United States; the central themes of the next few months were present

17

from the beginning of his time in the West. During the 105 days from this *début* to the time of his return, he gave 132 interviews: a remarkable rate of activity for a man in his eighth decade. Much has been made by supporters of the Shah of the effect of these interviews in creating a revolutionary climate in Iran; but their real effect was to bring the confrontation between Shah and Ayatollah to the attention of the outside world. Within Iran, it was the regular telephone calls from Neauphle and the smuggled cassettes of sermons which were of crucial importance.

Not long afterwards, I went to Neauphle myself with a camera crew. My colleagues and I drove out early on a fine cold morning, with the shadows lying long and sharp across the road, and reached the village at about eight-thirty. It was too early to visit the house in the Route de Chevreuse, so we stopped at the Café des Trois Communes for a coffee and croissant. Then, too, the windows were steamed up – eight-thirty is a busy time in French cafés – and the bar was full of regulars; the same regulars, no doubt.

The atmosphere was heavy with tobacco smoke and the noise of conversation as we clattered in, carrying our gear: camera, recorder, lights. The conversation died away, the heavy red faces of the French countryside turning to inspect us, as we scraped our chairs on the wooden floor and filled the sudden silence with a discussion of what we were going to order.

'Iranians,' said one of the regulars dismissively, and turned his back on us. The others followed suit. We were, in their eyes, simply extensions of the Ayatollah's entourage, foreigners, whose generic name was 'Iranian', and who did nothing but take up tables in French cafés which could be put to better use by Frenchmen.

It was not difficult to find the Ayatollah's headquarters: the police had already set up a roadblock outside it. We parked a little way short of it, outside a house with red wooden shutters with the cross-bars picked out in white like large Zs. The lace curtain twitched slightly: either a Neauphlienne had still not been sated by the arrival of strangers, or the French equivalent of the Special Branch and the FBI, the *Renseignements Généraux*, had found themselves a warm billet. An unmarked Simca was parked across the road, and the men in it were watching us speculatively.

'You have an appointment?' The question was directed at me through the Simca's window. A gun lay on the back seat. As it happened, I did not have an appointment; but I used, unknowingly, a technique which had been used for centuries by Shi'ites – *khod'eh*, or the telling of deceptive half-truths if it is necessary to

18

protect the faith, and replied that a Mr Yazdi wanted to see me. I had obtained the name from the previous evening's *Le Monde*, and it would have been truer to say that I wanted to see him. The policeman made a delicate gesture with his gloved hand, which I took to mean that he was letting me past even though he did not entirely believe me.

But by this stage the *Renseignements Généraux*, like the French government itself, had come to a kind of understanding with the difficult visitors; I noticed, as I passed the car, that a small heater was keeping the occupants warm, and that an electrical flex which powered it ran from the car and snaked up the slope into the house.

Inside the gate I talked my way past a fierce-looking but entirely pleasant young man in an open-necked shirt, dark suit and scrubby beard, and went up the steps of the house to the front door. Inside there was an air of undirected bustle. More young men, built along much the same lines as the one by the gate, were speaking into telephones and cutting articles out of newspapers or talking and laughing.

No attention was paid to me, as I stood there adjusting to the warmth and the thick atmosphere. No one, I noticed, was wearing shoes; and anxious not to offend some religious custom I did not understand, I took my own shoes off. I found out later it was to protect the carpets from mud. An old man with one eye came past with a metal tray and two or three cups of unclaimed tea on it, and he courteously offered me one. The action attracted attention, and the name of Yazdi was invoked.

Ibrahim Yazdi, the American cancer researcher who was to become his country's foreign minister, was a pleasant-featured man in his early forties, with a neatly clipped beard and horn-rimmed glasses. His English was perfect, with a slight Texas accent.

'You wish to interview the Imam,' he said. The title surprised me; until then I had heard it applied only to the great figures of the Shi'ite faith from eleven hundred years before. I agreed, and he outlined the rules. All questions were to be submitted in advance, and put to the Ayatollah by him, and no supplementary questions were to be asked. I disliked all this, but saw there was no alternative. 'What are your questions?' I had none prepared, and tore a page from my notebook and wrote the questions out one by one, as I thought of them, in a clearer hand than usual. I still have the paper:

1. Is it your intention to lead a revolution against the Shah, or

do you simply wish to force him to change his policies?

2. What kind of government do you wish to see in Iran, and what form would an Islamic Republic take?

3. What would be the attitude of an Islamic Republic to the United States and the Soviet Union? Or to Britain, which has played an important part in your country's history?

4. Would there be a place for foreign companies in an Islamic Republic?

Looked at in the light of what was to come, these questions seem naïve and misdirected: there were so many better ones, about intolerance and future persecution, or the treatment of racial and religious minorities, that one could have asked. Perhaps it was simply that the Shah still seemed so strong, and the prospect that a revolution could be run successfully from a place like this seemed so distant. The judgment was not mine alone; it was being made by the government of every major country in the world. Yazdi looked at my questions, and said we could have our interview that afternoon. In the meantime, we were free to film the Ayatollah at his prayers.

During my visits to Iran in the previous summer I had seen the face a thousand times, printed on posters, stencilled on walls, embroidered on banners. It was still a shock to encounter the Ayatollah in the flesh. As he walked slowly out of his house and across the road, the posters and stencils and banners came to life. Those heavy black eye-brows, that hawklike nose, the white beard, the still-grey moustache constituted perhaps the most readily identifiable features in the world at that moment.

His black turban, which indicated descent from the Prophet, accentuated the high forehead with its powerful lines which made his face angry, even in repose. He wore a neat grey tunic under black robes, and walked slowly past us, taking no notice of the camera, his eyes as ever on the ground, to avoid the sight of impurity. He looked the very personification of revenge.

A group of about thirty men and twenty women was waiting in the garden outside the blue and white tent where prayers were said. They fell back to allow him to pass, and then followed him in, the men first. The women formed a solid mass of black at the rear of the tent.

Khomeini knelt at the front, a small knot of mullahs in white turbans around him. His quiet, toneless voice was almost lost in the heat and press of the tent, but it was his movements that everyone followed: he was the first to kneel and the first to rise, and late-comers at the very back stood on tiptoe from time to time to catch a glimpse of the back of his head. As always, Khomeini's mastery over himself was complete. He showed no emotion of any kind, then or later. Seventy years of rigid self-control had eradicated everything: anger, hatred, pleasure, happiness, relief. Already, even before he returned to Iran, he was indistinguishable from the icon.

At three o'clock that afternoon we presented ourselves at the Ayatollah's house, and began making the arrangements for the interview. The room where it was to take place was small, almost square, and had only one tiny window. The walls were covered with an incongruous pattern of pink roses and some blue flower unknown to botany. We took off our shoes, not knowing if the room was holy or the presence of the Ayatollah might make it so. Within a few minutes we had the room as well-lighted as a studio set, and all that was required was the arrival of the principal performer. But it was another fifteen minutes before the door opened. I was aware of the rustling of subfusc robes and the manifestation of a powerful presence. Outside, he had been impressive but isolated, a figure in a landscape. In this small, brilliant, overheated room he was overpowering.

I put out my hand, though I was uncertain how one should greet somebody whose followers called him 'Imam'. He ignored it, but in such a way that I might think he was busying himself with his robes; it was not, therefore, an ungracious gesture on his part, simply one that thrust aside as meaningless anything but the essentials of the relationship between us. My rôle, as far as he was concerned, was that of an emissary from a country of which he did not approve, speaking to him for reasons which did not concern him. He would no doubt have preferred to spend the time in religious contemplation. But the pattern had established itself clearly: people came to Ayatollah Khomeini thinking to use him for their own ends, and found themselves serving instead the ends that he himself served.

Any interview between a journalist and a politician represents a balance of interest: the journalist wants strong, enlightening material, the politician wants to present his views to a wider audience. Khomeini was not, of course, a politician in the usual sense, and he did not need to speak to Western journalists in order to ensure that people in Iran heard his views: he had far more effective and immediate means of doing that, chief among them being the cassette recorder. He gave interviews at this time for two reasons: firstly, because his advisers, more worldly than he, had a greater faith in the power of foreign newspapers, radio and television and persuaded him to speak to them; and secondly because it was a way of demonstrating to the governments he regarded as Iran's enemies – Britain, the United States and the Soviet Union – that he could not be deflected from his declared purpose. He was attempting, not without success, to weaken the support which each of those governments gave the Shah.

And so the balance of interest between Khomeini and the journalists who interviewed him differed from the usual one. They came to him because he was exotic yet accessible, a curiosity as well as a figure of menace: he spoke to them to further his revolutionary ends. Who, in Lenin's phrase, used whom? Certainly, Khomeini used his interviewers more than they used him; but the real effect (despite the complaints of Iranian royalists ever since) was less on the people in Iran than on foreign opinion, and on liberal-minded Iranian exiles. Khomeini's ability to play down the fiercer, more reactionary elements in his political programme was impressive. His advisers, once again, had briefed him well; he always gave his interviewers the impression that human rights and the equality of women would be assured – along Western, rather than Islamic, lines.

Now he settled himself down cross-legged on a large square of foam rubber, which rested on a rough blanket on the floor. His back was against the wall with its red and blue flowers. The powerful lighting deepened the furrow between his eyebrows as he stared at the brown Baluchi carpet in front of him. He looked at me only twice during the entire interview: once at the end of his first answer, and once at the end of his last one. On each occasion it was to mark an important point with some force. His voice was quiet and level throughout, and his words were chosen with care:

1. 'The Shah has ruled Iran as though it were his private estate, his property, to do with as he chooses. He has created a dictatorship, and has neglected his duties. The forces of Islam will bring this situation to an end. The monarchy will be eradicated.

2. 'The Islamic Republic will be based on the will of the people, as expressed by universal suffrage. They will decide on the precise form it takes. Every political party which works for the good of the country will be free. But there are aspects of life under the present corrupt form of government in Iran which will have to be changed: we cannot allow our youth to be corrupted and our Islamic culture to be destroyed, and drugs such as alcoholic beverages will be prohibited.

3. 'We are hostile to governments which have put pressure on Iran, which have forced the Shah on Iran, and which have made Iran suffer at their hands. But we are not hostile to the citizens of those countries. We intend to reject a relationship which makes us dependent on other countries. As for the Soviet Union, we are not afraid of it or of its influence. But we have bitter memories of the British, because they ensured that Reza Shah (the Shah's father) came to power, and for half a century we have been under the domination of this man and his son.

4. 'There will be a place for foreigners and their companies if they go about their daily business. But there are many foreigners who work against the interests of our people and help the Shah and his régime. They will not be allowed to remain in our country.'

The audience was over. Yazdi folded up the piece of paper with my questions on it and handed it back to me. The Ayatollah, after his dark, penetrating glance at me, raised his arms slightly. The two men who had sat behind him throughout helped him with reverence to his feet. In its way, it was a significant interview, delivered in the fashion of an oracle: everything in it came true, but not in the way one would have thought at the time; especially the passage about universal suffrage and the freedom of political parties.

Ibrahim Yazdi followed him out, and they were met by Sadeq Qotbzadeh. Abol-Hassan Bani-Sadr came from an inner room to join them. All three represented the more liberal Westernized tendencies within the incipient Revolution. Within a few years the first would become foreign minister, and then be disgraced and forced to remain on the outer fringes of Iranian politics; the second would also be foreign minister, and would later be executed for treason; the third would be elected President, and afterwards be forced into exile. They would have done better to remember the child-devouring habit of revolutions, just as the Carter Administration in Washington would have done better to take notice of the force with which Ayatollah Khomeini said, 'The monarchy will be eradicated', and the powerful look he gave as he said it. So, if the contents of the interview were reported to him, would the Shah himself.

I next went to Neauphle-le-Château in January 1979. The Shah had left Iran and the brief Kerensky-like government of Dr

23

Shahpour Bakhtiar was trying to hold the country together. All that kept Ayatollah Khomeini in France was the lack of a safe-conduct to return. Neauphle itself was in a state of permanent demonstration now. The students who paraded endlessly up and down the street between Khomeini's headquarters and his house did not always have a clear idea of what they expected to happen when he went back. Most defined the future by the past: they wanted a society which was different from the one they had known in Iran, a society where, they claimed, every fourth person was a SAVAK informer, and where you had to stay quiet if you wanted to avoid trouble.

'We want to say what we think without getting locked up,' one student told me. Others pushed their way into the group surrounding us to describe the problems they had had – being spied on, threatened, losing their government grants, fearing reprisals against their families at home if they criticized the Shah abroad. The women were fewer in number than the men, but no less vociferous. All wore some form of *hejab*, even if it were only a headscarf; all believed that women would be freer under the new dispensation. Not many would probably have been religious a year or so before, but they had been attracted by the political philosophy of Dr Ali Shariati, who had demonstrated that Shi'a Islam could be an intellectual force in its own right, as effective as the doctrines of liberal democracy or Marxism. To people who were experiencing the sudden shock of life at a Western university for the first time, Shariati's theories provided a sense of purpose and of moral strength.

The news from Iran was conflicting. As a result, Yazdi and Qotbzadeh twice announced that the Ayatollah was about to return, and both times the journey had to be postponed for lack of assurances about his safety. In the streets of Tehran there were daily clashes between the demonstrators and the military. The government of the country had come almost to a halt. Day by day, Bakhtiar's power decayed, and his last real sanction was to block Khomeini's return. But it could not be done indefinitely; and on January 31st he announced that the Ayatollah's plane would be permitted to land at Tehran airport.

The crowds at Neauphle went wild with joy, and the competition began for seats on the flight. My office did not want me to go, preferring that I should stay in London and 'anchor' the news from Iran every night; but I had decided privately that I would catch the plane no matter what happened, as a kind of broadcasting stowaway if necessary. It was going to be one of the turning-points of modern times, and I did not want to stay at home and read about it in the newspapers. Fortunately my office relented in time.

Air France had agreed to fly Ayatollah Khomeini back to Iran in a Boeing 747 with a volunteer crew, but it could carry only half the normal number of passengers, in case the plane were refused permission to land and had to fly back to Paris. Only two hundred seats would be available: 150 for the journalists and cameramen, fifty for Khomeini's party. The plan was to leave from Charles de Gaulle Airport at 1 am the following morning, and tickets were to be issued at seven o'clock that evening outside the headquarters building in Neauphle. Although it was a little before midday, a ragged queue for tickets began to form immediately.

I decided to join it. I knew that I was on the provisional list for seats, but experience suggested that those who presented themselves and refused to go away almost invariably did better than those who trusted in the promises of officials. I sent my colleagues off to the Café des Trois Communes, and took my place in the queue of hopefuls. It was very cold – several degrees below freezing – and my brand new Loden coat did not altogether keep out the chill. I waited in all for seven hours, unable to move in case the crowd behind me inched me out of my place. I still bear a souvenir of the ordeal: each winter my left shoulder aches unpleasantly in the cold. I ran out of conversation with the Iranian enthusiasts on either side of me very soon. Sometimes the queue would move a few paces; sometimes there was a scuffle as a latecomer tried to force his way in. There was nothing to do, nothing to read, nothing to eat, and nothing much to think about.

The waiting ended in a sudden blaze of action and shouting, for which our seven hours in the cold had scarcely prepared us. Names were called, and those who were not there to answer did not get tickets. It had been dark for some hours, and people had to use cigarette lighters to read the list of favoured names and count out the money: five hundred dollars each, or the equivalent in French francs. There was anger and despair then; several hundred dollar bills and a couple of tickets blew out of someone's hand, and vanished in the mud and darkness. People kept arriving late and shouting out their demands and pleas.

As for me, I took the two tickets we had been allocated and headed off. The waiting and the cold had sapped everything except the desire to get away and eat something. I left the late arrivals to their Hieronymus Bosch experience in the dark, scrabbling on the ground, fighting, and bewailing their losses.

The Café des Trois Communes was exerting an attraction I could no longer resist.

The French are a magnificent people, but sometimes lacking in sensitivity. As our suitcases were weighed and checked in at Charles de Gaulle Airport, and a mysterious blue tag with the figure 2 was stuck across each of them, one of the baggage-handlers called out, 'This way to the death-flight.' We duly laughed, in order to show that we were not scared; though I, for one, certainly was. My throat was dry, and I was prey to a number of sentimental thoughts about home. With some reason: the reports from Tehran indicated that the armed forces were deeply divided. Firstly there was their duty to their current master Dr Bakhtiar; secondly there was the temptation of many of the ordinary soldiers to follow Khomeini and the cause of religion. Thirdly there was their loyalty, still strong, to the Shah. Who knew which tendency we would land among?

I looked around me, and detected the same anxiety among many of my fellow-passengers. There was only one good thing about it, I thought: the office had assigned me a cameraman who was one of the few people I would actually want to be with, in a tricky situation: a short, spry, nautical-looking figure in his fifties called Bill Handford, with a bristly beard that stood him in good stead with the ayatollahs and mullahs we were to meet, and the sharp blue eyes of a sailor. Throughout our experiences of the coming weeks, he never once complained. Bill Handford had filmed in Vietnam, in the Nigerian civil war, in Northern Ireland at its worst; maybe a plane trip to Iran with an ayatollah was nothing very serious, after that.

There was, fortunately, no shortage of space on the plane. Khomeini and his supporters and advisers were taking over the first-class section, which left us with two or three seats each. The discreet curtain dividing first-class passengers from the lower orders was kept firmly drawn. A regular undertone of prayer filtered through it, and those Iranians who had not been able to get seats in first-class stood or knelt in the aisles. I struck up a conversation with a British acquaintance of mine, who was based in Paris. He was not happy to be on the plane. 'I'm their Paris correspondent,' he kept saying. 'The only reason I'm here is because this whole thing is starting from Paris. What do I know about Iran? Nothing. So why did they send me? Because I'm their Paris correspondent.' The litany continued, and I moved away.

A little later in the flight I fell into conversation with a returning Iranian student. 'I am hoping with great sincerity,' he said, 'that this plane will be shot down.' Another student inter-

26

rupted. 'That wouldn't be right at all. I want to sacrifice my life too, but I want us to land and take part in the Revolution. That would be a far better sacrifice.' With such difficult moral choices under discussion, I envied Bill Handford's ability, the inheritance of an old campaigner, to remain firmly asleep.

The Air France steward, an amusing, phlegmatic man, brought us dinner. There was no alcohol on the drinks trolley, by the express wish of the Ayatollah. For me, purely practical anxieties were beginning to take over: assuming that our flight landed safely, some pictures from it would be needed. Television is a literal medium: if you talk about someone flying from Paris to Tehran, you need to show him doing so. I applied at the dividing curtain, and was told that my request, like that of every other television correspondent on board (there were, apparently, fifteen of us) would be considered. I settled down for an uneasy sleep, nervous about what the morning might bring.

Three hours later it was light outside the aircraft, and coffee and croissants had put a little life back into me. There was a stir at the front end of the plane, and Sadeq Qotbzadeh emerged from behind the curtain, like Chorus in a Shakespeare play. He climbed on the foremost row of seats in our section, his back to the place where the film would have been projected if the Ayatollah had permitted such a thing on his flight.

'I have a serious announcement to make,' he said in French, and glanced at a piece of paper he was holding. Everyone went extremely quiet. 'We have just received a warning over the aircraft radio that the Iranian Air Force has orders to shoot us down directly we enter Iranian airspace.' Someone – it may have been the correspondent based in Paris – asked nervously if we would be turning round. 'Certainly not,' said Sadeq Qotbzadeh. 'What's he saying?' I heard Bill's voice ask me, quietly. 'You don't want to know,' I said.

Qotbzadeh, meanwhile, had climbed off his seat and was walking along the aisle with the practised skill of a public relations man, seeking out the television cameraman and the photographers. 'You can film the Imam now. But be brief.' I picked up the sound-recordist's gear and hurried forward with Bill. 'No journalists, just cameramen,' Qotbzadeh said, trying to hold me back. I reminded him that we had been allocated only two tickets, and had been forced to leave our sound-recordist in Paris, to follow us on a scheduled flight. He smiled and let me pass.

The Ayatollah was sitting at the front of the first-class compartment, on the left-hand side, looking out of the window: there were no impurities to be seen at this height. The whirring of the camera – we were still using film then, rather than video – caught his attention, and he turned to face us. He was utterly calm and passionless. I asked him a question, a routine enough one about his emotions on returning; his son Ahmad, sitting next to him, translated it into Farsi. The Ayatollah lowered his head without answering, and looked out of the window again.

A few minutes later, a better-phrased question from a French correspondent elicited the most famous remark of the trip.

'We are now over Iranian territory. What are your emotions after so many years of exile?'

'Hichi,' was the answer: 'Nothing.' Question and answer exemplified a mutual incomprehension. To Westerners, and to westernized Iranians, it sounded as though he cared nothing for the country he was about to plunge into revolution; perhaps we would have preferred him to break down and weep. But weeping was not much in Khomeini's line. He had spent his entire life ridding himself of false, personal, human emotions. It is permissible for a Muslim to express his love for Allah through the love of a person or a place, but not to love them strictly speaking for their own sake. Ayatollah Khomeini did not.

The Prophet Mohammed returned from his Hegira, the flight to Mecca, in order to carry out the first Islamic Revolution; Khomeini, too, was returning from a Hegira. Such moments were not to be debased with common emotions. But news of his reply to the French journalist's question was passed incredulously from one journalist to another at the back of the aircraft, and as we took note of it each of us remembered, no doubt, what Sadeq Qotbzadeh had warned might happen when we reached Iranian territory.

But nobody shot us down, and we continued our flight to Tehran, seeing at last the snowy peaks of the Elburz Mountains below us. Then, indeed, many of the Iranians in our part of the plane gave way to an unIslamic outburst of rejoicing, though some of them may have cast an anxious glance at the curtain to check that they were not being overheard and disapproved of. A thin yellowish sunshine cut through the cloud cover as we descended.

Tehran lay spread out below us, as peaceable and featureless as any city looks from the air. People were crowding together in their hundreds of thousands, their millions even, waiting for us to land; but from this height they were invisible. The pilot's voice came over the loudspeaker: 'We have not received permission to land. Until we receive this permission we shall be obliged to circle over the city. You may experience some discomfort.'

We experienced discomfort in fairly large quantities. A passenger aircraft like a Boeing 747 is stable and pleasant enough when it flies in a straight line, but when it circles at low altitude for half an hour or more it can induce air-sickness and earache in the most seasoned traveller. Bill Handford caught my glance and winked; but the gloomy British journalist of my acquaintance was in an ecstasy of unhappiness. 'I am the Paris correspondent,' I could imagine him intoning. 'What am I doing here?'

At last it was over. The revolutionary welcoming committee on the ground had completed its negotiations with the air force men who were running Mehrabad Airport, and the Boeing's agony of circling was at an end. We set a straight course for the runway, and the wheels touched the ground of the country the Ayatollah felt nothing about returning to. The exile was back, his *Hegira* over; the final phase of the Revolution was about to begin.

2

The Revolutionary Crowds

> The multitude of people were so great that we had
> much ado in six hours to pass three miles, which was
> from the place where we met the King to the market-
> place of the city.   William Parry,
> *A Discourse On The Travels Of Sir Anthony Sherley*
> *To The Persian Empire, 1601*

A REVOLUTION IS perhaps the most enthralling and frightening
event on earth to observe at close hand. Wars, by and large,
generate more confusion and boredom than unalloyed fear, and
from your small patch of hillside or bundu you have no idea of
what is going on anywhere else. The information you gather has
usually been distorted long before you hear it, and censored
when you try to report it. In a revolution, by contrast, the
information comes so fast there is often no time for it to become
seriously distorted, and there is certainly no time to organize an
effective system of censorship. The action takes place before your
eyes; and it is clear almost immediately who has won and lost.
You need have no sympathies whatever with the objectives of
the revolutionaries to find yourself caught up in the violent
excitement of it all: the animal magnetism of the crowd sweeps
you along like a river in flood, and the hundreds of people who
swarm around you, shouting and waving their home-made
weapons in the air, are immediately your devoted friends, ready
to sacrifice their lives to protect you and very happy indeed for
you to record their heroics.

The parallels between what happened in Iran in 1979 and what
happened in Russia in 1917 may be facile, but they are hard to
avoid altogether. For the Winter Palace read the Eshratabad
Barracks in Tehran; for the Tsar's Imperial Guard read the Shah's
Immortals. Kerensky becomes Bakhtiar, and Lenin's sealed train

arriving at the Finland Station becomes Khomeini's Air France Boeing landing at Mehrabad Airport. But finding historical parallels is mostly just a party game: little extra light is shed on either side of the equation. In Iran there was no Trotsky (unless it was Bani-Sadr), no counter-revolutionary Kornilov, no intervention by Western armies, and as yet no Stalin; and the ideologies could hardly differ more.

But the one point which the two revolutions genuinely had in common was crowd behaviour. A revolutionary crowd is awesome: there is nothing so cruel, nothing so courageous, nothing so stupid, nothing so good at improvising solutions to the most impossible problems. Normally intelligent, prudent people abandon their individuality at once when they gather together in large numbers on these occasions; they merge into a wild, unstoppable mob.

I had had experience of near-revolutionary crowds in Iran several times during the last months of 1978. On 5 November, the date when buildings throughout the centre of Tehran were burned and the British embassy went up in flames, we were on the streets early, filming the opening stages of the big demonstration. Shortly before lunch, when nothing very much had happened, I left the camera team in order to telephone a report to London from our hotel, about three miles away. We arranged to meet at two o'clock in the place where we had been filming. 'I'll find you around here somewhere,' I said. It seemed a sensible enough arrangement at the time.

But the telephone call took three hours to come through, and when I was finally able to leave the hotel the sky was black with the smoke of a dozen major fires. The taxi-driver we had hired for the day was old and cowardly, with a face like a lugubrious sheep. He refused to drive me back, on the grounds that I would be murdered and the cab burned; it was the second eventuality which seemed to weigh particularly heavily with him. I cajoled and raged and offered money: a bonus of a hundred pounds sterling plus a written guarantee to indemnify him against any loss. He refused. In a last effort to change his mind I said I would have to walk if he would not take me.

My intention was to make him feel guilty; but having committed myself I felt I had at least to set out, and having set out I found it as difficult to go back as to go on. Besides, the two members of the camera team I was working with were famous for their joint courage: the cameraman, Bernard Hesketh, and the sound recordist, John Jockell, were later to win many awards for their coverage of the Falklands War. I was nervous that they

31

might think I had abandoned them, and that overrode even my fear of walking through the streets.

That fear was not altogether misplaced. There were fires and barricades at every intersection along the way, and a million or more people on the streets. Anyone who could be mistaken for an American could expect rough treatment, and the crowds seemed unlikely to wait while one produced a passport. Foreign television crews were usually safe enough: the camera was the only passport we needed when we were all together. Without it, I felt very alone. I walked with a kind of artificial purpose through the noise and smoke in a conspicuous Austin Reed sports jacket, the stench of burning tyres and burning buildings in my nostrils and the racket of thousands of chanting voices in my ears. If I had known how disciplined the crowds were, in many ways, and how they concentrated solely on attacking buildings that were owned by members of the royal family or were connected with gambling or the liquor trade, or more generally with the government, I might have felt rather better. As it was, I found myself praying quietly and enthusiastically as I walked along. People screamed in my face and threw things at me, but although I must have passed through ten or eleven barricades nobody stopped me. On the two occasions when it looked as though someone might, I glared at them like the Victorian engravings of Sir Charles Napier outstaring the tiger in the Indian jungle. It seemed to work.

But it was a very long three miles; and it soon became obvious that with so many people running through the streets our rendez-vous was unlikely to stand. It was, anyway, three o'clock, and I was an hour late. By now I had to push my way physically through the crowds, which made it rather safer since there was no time for people to see me coming and react to my presence; with the natural politeness of the Persian they made way for me, and I was gone before they had entirely registered my presence and appearance. But I was hopelessly lost; the landmarks had been blotted out by the sheer density of people. I had only one concern: to avoid being swept away by the crowd, and to maintain my individuality of purpose. In the noise and the weight of numbers it was becoming difficult, and I was growing tired.

And then I caught sight of them. It was so unlikely that I shouted out loud – not that it mattered, in that noise. To have come all this way in the largest crowd I had ever seen, and to have stumbled on the only two people in it whom I wanted to meet, was quite extraordinary; but there, ten yards from me, a little above the general level of the crowd, was the outline of our camera, with its absurd Mickey Mouse-eared film magazine on top.

When I fought my way over to where they were, though, I found that Bernard and John had troubles of their own. The crowd was stirred up by something which had been broadcast in Persian from London the night before, and although Bernard had pulled the British stickers off his camera, it was too late. Most people knew exactly who we were.

I have always made it a rule never to deny working for the organization which employs me, regardless of the circumstances. As long as the pay-cheque comes in at regular intervals, it seems the only decent thing to do. But in this case there was no point in trying to deny it. Bernard had obtained some remarkable pictures: soldiers firing on the demonstrators, and other soldiers throwing down their weapons and going over to the side of the crowd, weeping and ripping the insignia from their uniforms, and being carried away shoulder-high by the crowds. Until a few minutes before I arrived, Bernard and John had been surrounded by an entirely friendly group of demonstrators, fifty strong, who had helped them find new things to film. But then a man who was beside himself with violent emotion made his way to the fringe of the group and began screaming that his brother had been shot dead by the army the day before, and that our organization had failed to report it. 'That proves it, my friends,' the man started shouting soon after I arrived, 'they're in the pay of the Shah.'

There was no time to soothe him or to cope rationally with the crowd's emotions. The mood of these people, which had been so friendly a moment before, turned instantly to hatred, and hatred made them violent. A small man who had pinned a picture of Ayatollah Khomeini onto a broom-handle started beating me in the face with it, while others (including a student who had spent a term at a British polytechnic and had been perfectly pleasant until a moment or so before) started pulling us about and wrenching at our clothes. I felt the material of my conspicuous jacket ripping, and I realized that they were going to tear us to pieces. I had seen it happen to others: now it was happening to us. Violent, contorted faces pressed into mine, screaming insults; a dozen powerful hands gripped me. And all the time the little man with the picture of Khomeini on a broomstick carried on beating me about the face.

If it had not been for that, I should probably have succumbed. It is impossible to fight off so many people at such close quarters;

33

not even Sir Charles Napier could have done it. But you can grab hold of a broomstick. I did so first out of instinctive rage, because of the pain the little man was causing me, and I lunged back at him with it, missing him. But when I had it in my hand, and had wrestled my arm free, I waved the stick with its portrait of Khomeini in the air, and did the first entirely intelligent thing I had done all day. I shouted *'Dorud bar Khomeini!'* – 'Long live Khomeini.'

That so simple a device should have worked is an indication of the ease with which the collective emotions of a crowd can be turned. All three of us were released, our equipment was picked up, and we ourselves had some difficulty in persuading them not to carry us shoulder-high, like the soldiers whom we had filmed deserting. We were very shaken and very relieved, and the knowledge that I had contravened all the rules of balance and objectivity worried me not a bit. I have the picture of Khomeini in front of me as I write, complete with the holes from the drawing-pins which fixed it to the broomstick, a few small rust-coloured stains, and the folds I made in it when I put in my pocket, a gift from the little man who had been hitting me with it a few minutes before. I regard it with some affection; I think it may have saved me from the most unpleasant death of my imagining.

The crowds which gathered three months later, on 1 February 1979, to welcome Ayatollah Khomeini at Mehrabad Airport were quite possibly the largest group of human beings ever assembled together in one place on one day for one objective. And in contrast to the angry mood of 5 November and all the other bitter days of confrontation with the army and SAVAK, the mood was solely one of joy. More than joy, indeed: there was a state of near-ecstasy. Central to the Shi'ite faith is the belief in the Missing Imam, Muhammed al-Mehdi, who disappeared in 880 AD and is expected to come again bringing righteousness and judgment to the earth. When Khomeini, whose followers gave him the title 'Imam', returned to sweep away the old, failed political system of Iran and establish an Islamic Republic, the clear blue skies and bright sunlight of that day seemed to them to take on the transcendent quality of a Second Coming. Some days before, a Tehran magazine had carried a poem entitled 'The Day The Imam Returns', which raised the expectations to millenial, chiliastic heights:

The day the Imam returns

No one will tell lies any more
no one will lock the doors of his house;
people will become brothers
sharing the bread of their joys together
in justice and in sincerity. . . .

Such feelings were general, and it was not necessary to be a fundamentalist Muslim to share them. An old system had died and a new one was being born; people invested the moment with every new quality they wanted to see applied to daily life. Those who had flocked to the poor, ugly slums of Iran's cities from the quiet villages, those who had been shocked by the sudden social changes of the five years of oil wealth, those who had been exposed for the first time to the corruption of a Third World country with First World money – for all of them, the coming Revolution seemed to promise a return to decency and sanity. And for the urban middle class, who had benefitted from the oil wealth but had often been disturbed by the effects of it, there seemed to be a chance to start again on a better and more decent basis. If there might be a darker side to the coming Revolution, no one wanted to think about it. For the moment, all was optimism; everyone's wishes, political, social, personal, seemed on the point of coming true.

All through the night, in this highly charged spirit of expectation, volunteers had been at work on the roads the Ayatollah would be taking from the airport, washing and cleansing them as if to make sure that they would be worthy of him. Later, there were reports that among the chants that rose from the enormous crowds as the Ayatollah's car passed were some which made the religious reference explicit: 'The doors of paradise have been opened again!' 'Now is the hour of martyrdom!'

When the Air France Boeing landed at Mehrabad, and Bill Handford and I had filmed the triumphal appearance of the Ayatollah at the top of the aircraft steps, our part in the day's proceedings was over. We made contact with the correspondent and crew who were to take over from us, and were at last able to look after our belongings and relax; we had been working for twenty-six hours.

Khomeini's party swept ahead of us into the special terminal building for passengers making the *Haj*, or pilgrimage to Mecca. By the time we arrived our luggage lay unclaimed and isolated on the carousel. There seemed little point in hurrying anywhere: the

35

roads were all blocked off for the Ayatollah's arrival, and there were no taxis to be had. Bill and I sat side by side on a wooden bench, talking or dozing, and luxuriating in the fact that, for a few hours at least, there was nothing for us to do. On the other side of a pair of thick glass doors the Imam was speaking to a gathering of several hundred mullahs who had come from all over Iran to welcome him. His quiet voice did not penetrate the doors to us, but the fierce applauding with which his words were punctuated did. The heat and emotion of the moment must have been intense.

And then, suddenly, the glass doors opened and Khomeini appeared, almost carried by two mullahs. His arms were over their shoulders and his head hung down on his chest. Several figures in clerical robes followed, and we could hear the cries and murmurs of dismay rising from the hundreds of others who had come to greet him. As for Bill and me, the challenge to our lethargy was such that it took us a little time to react. The group which was half-carrying, half-dragging the Imam with them took no notice of us; and when we had finally gathered up ourselves and our equipment Khomeini was lying on a couch in the waiting-room with a doctor bending over him. We were able to film unhindered.

For a moment or two there was utter silence. The Ayatollah lay on the couch, eyes shut, while everyone stood and watched, frozen. Then the eyes opened. '*Ab,*' he said faintly: 'Water'. Someone put a glass of water tenderly to his lips, and he drank from it. Then very slowly, he sat up and thanked them for the attention he had received. The heat, the tiredness, and perhaps, in spite of himself, the emotion of the return had caused him to faint. It was an uncharacteristic weakness, and one which he must have been determined should not interfere again with this transcendent day. And we, by chance, were the only ones outside the circle of the faithful to have witnessed it.

As he drove away from the airport, no one who watched his blue Mercedes pass can have had any idea of the problem that had briefly arisen. For them, all that was visible was the icon: Khomeini sitting straight-backed, waving only occasionally, and with the fierce, purposeful, unforgiving visage which was reproduced in every one of the tens of thousands of pictures of him along the way. Khomeini knew his Persians well: they are a people who respect firmness and strength. Only posters which showed him in the capacity of the stern avenger were allowed to be displayed.

As the crowds who had waited for eight or more hours for this

36

moment caught sight of the Mercedes, complete with its escort of motorcycle outriders, a roar went up from them and was picked up all along the route: a travelling chain of noise which stretched for half-a-mile or so at any given moment. People were not, by and large, smiling: their feelings went much deeper than that. Their faces were serious and triumphant, and they chanted the words of pre-arranged slogans and waved their fists in time to the chanting with a ferocious confidence. Between two and three million people saw the Mercedes pass. They lined the route twenty deep, they climbed into the boughs of the flimsiest trees, they clung precariously to the steel skeletons of unfinished buildings along the way. Every post and wall had its portrait of him, and a new banner was seen for the first time: a clenched fist in black, with faces representing political prisoners, and the words '*Allahu Akbar*' – 'God is great'. It was the first flag of the Islamic Republic.

Khomeini was determined to stay aloof from the opposition politicians who had remained in Iran during his long exile. He was not going to ally himself with anyone else. Instead of accepting their invitation to attend a meeting at Tehran University, he went instead to pay his respects to those who had given their lives for his cause. The route which the crowds lined led to Behesht-e-Zahra cemetery, eighteen miles away in South Tehran. But long before he reached it the crowds had grown to the point where the blue Mercedes could no longer make its way through in safety. The army, which had scarcely appeared on the streets at all, made its facilities available to Khomeini, and the man who had never made a telephone call until four months earlier completed the last three miles of his journey in a helicopter.

At Behesht-e-Zahra itself the pressure of the crowds was indescribable. The sheer weight of bodies broke up and displaced the gravestones which were set in cement in the ground. There was serious doubt as to whether the Ayatollah's helicopter could put down without injuring or killing someone; and then one of the marshals had the idea of taking off his leather belt and swinging it in an arc round his head, which both cleared a path around him and mimed the action of a helicopter. Soon all the marshals were doing the same thing, over the full extent of the area which had been selected for the helicopter to land, and the necessary clearance was achieved.

Behesht-e-Zahra is vast, and Khomeini could visit only one part of it: section 17, chosen because the seventeenth day of the Persian month of Shahrivar (8 September 1978, by the Western calendar) was Black Friday: the day the Shah's troops shot and killed hundreds of demonstrators in Jaleh Square and other areas of Tehran. As the returning Imam sat on a chair beside section 17, surrounded by people who had each lost at least one member of their family in the campaign against the Shah, his quiet words were relayed by loudspeaker to the hundreds of thousands who had come to the cemetery to hear him:

'I have suffered many difficulties and have witnessed a great deal of pain, and I do not know how to thank these noble people who have sacrificed everything for their revolution.'

He appealed to the army's generals to join the cause of the people, and warned the government of Dr Bakhtiar that he would stop their mouths and appoint a new government with the people's support. 'We will cut off the hands of foreign agents,' he said, to a roar of approval. A mistranslation of this, confusing the word 'agents' for 'correspondents', was nervously passed from one foreign journalist to another, until the mistake was rectified.

In his office in the centre of Tehran, meanwhile, Dr Bakhtiar himself, a forlorn but gallant figure, sat almost alone, with a few guards outside his door but almost no civil servants around him to do his bidding. 'I am going to do my best to have good relations with him,' he said to a passing Western journalist who had stopped in to ask how he was planning to deal with Khomeini.

Bakhtiar was an impressive politician with a long and honourable record of opposition to the Shah, but his moment had passed. Although he still occupied the office of the prime minister, power had long since fled from him – had never, indeed, belonged to him. But it had not yet entirely passed to Khomeini. The army, the sixth most powerful in the world, in terms of numbers and equipment, was still in being; and although it had been depleted by desertions it still had the appearance of a force which could do a great deal of damage if it chose. President Carter had sent General Robert C. Huyser as his personal representative to show support for the Bakhtiar government, but Huyser had been warning the military not to consider a military coup. As events were to show, they would probably not have been able to carry one out if they had tried, but that was not the impression of most people at the time. Bloodshed on a large scale seemed inevitable.

At seven-thirty on the morning of Saturday 3 February, two days after the Ayatollah's return, our taxi (driven by a man called Mahmoudi, who will feature later in this personal history) nosed its way into a narrow street not far from the Majlis, or parliament. The shops in it were closed and shuttered. The external appearance of the houses was deceptively small and mean, though behind the mud-coloured brick walls they were often grand and even magnificent, with fountains playing in the gardens. The street was full of people, all heading in the same direction, and we had to slow down to their speed.

'Just close now, Mr John,' said Mahmoudi, and showed us where he would wait for us. The alley-way into which we had to turn was too narrow for our car, and it was blocked by a group of heavily-armed men, part of a contingent of several hundred, some of them Shi'ites from Lebanon and Iraq. We were still some way from our destination, but the chanting we could hear showed us the way to go. Occasionally the hurrying crowd would pick up the chant as they pushed each other along: *'Allahu Akbar, Khomeini rahbar!'* – 'God is great, Khomeini is our leader'.

There were three of us now: Bill Handford and I, and David Johnson, Bill's sound recordist, who had been separated from us in Paris but had followed by the next available flight. David was also a sailor, like Bill, but was his physical opposite in every way. Where Bill was small and wiry, David was big: so big that people always seemed to think twice about interfering with what we were doing. (They were known among their colleagues as Bill and Bulkhead.)

Here, in particular, David's size and strength were great assets. The alleyway down which we had to pass was entirely packed with chanting, excited people, and the dozens of armed guards whose job it was to guard the approaches had been forced to give way, as powerless as anyone else to stem the sheer weight of numbers. For at the end of the alley was the Alawi Girls' School, which had been selected as the Ayatollah's headquarters; and the Ayatollah himself was to give his first audience there this morning. Slowly, a few inches at a time, we squeezed along the edge of the crowd, pushing our way along beside the wall. David was first, and we moved in his wake; but for someone who suffers, as I do, from the joint distresses of claustrophobia and a dislike of crowds it was a most unpleasant experience. As the masses of people swayed and shifted, we would find ourselves jammed hard against the wall, in constant danger of having the breath knocked out of us. There were times when I was afraid of giving way to my phobias, though in that narrow space and with that noise few people would have noticed.

At last, however, David's strength and our joint determination got us to a narrow gate, and we were pulled in by the guards much as they would have pulled drowning men into a life-boat. We found ourselves in the yard of the school. Before the turbulence of the immediate pre-revolutionary period had closed the schools of Tehran, this one, behind its mud-brick walls, had had three hundred pupils. Now we were shown into the assembly hall, with texts in Farsi on the walls enjoining the girls to quiet and good behaviour, and maps showing the countries of the world. A large group of journalists, gathered together from places all over those maps, were waiting for the Imam's first full news conference on Iranian soil.

It took a long time. Yazdi and Qotbzadeh, looking nervous and unsettled, translated Khomeini's answers into English and French respectively. Most of what he said was intended to weaken Dr Bakhtiar's control, or to make a probing approach to the army leadership:

'Certain talks have taken place, and, should it become necessary, more will take place. We shall call on them to act in their own interests as well as those of the people, for the army is one with the people, it is the people's brother. The army must not use its machine guns against the people. We do not want our soldiers to be under the thumb of foreigners. They should be independent. They are our sons, and we love them as such.'

A Frenchwoman with a harsh voice asked if the Ayatollah's followers had weapons. In the pause while he formulated his answer in his mind the noise of the chanting outside filled the room: 'Allahu Akbar, Khomeini rahbar!'. 'When the moment comes, we will get arms from the proper places,' he said. 'We will work together in the streets.'

And so it was to prove.

During the week which followed, Bill Handford, David Johnson and I were away from Tehran, having decided to find out what was happening elsewhere in the country. It was a difficult decision to take, since no one knew when the moment of revolution might come; but it turned out to be the right one. In places like Isfahan we found that the Revolution had already begun, and the Islamic Republic had established itself without bloodshed. In Tehran, however, the deadlock continued. Khomeini had named his government, as promised, the rival government of Shahpour Bakhtiar continued to crumble, and the strength of the armed forces suffered further and further erosion as group after group of soldiers and airmen marched to the Alawi Girls' School to pledge their loyalty to the Ayatollah.

When we returned to Tehran on the evening of Friday 9 February we found the city in a state of wild confusion and excitement. Road blocks had been set up, cars were burning, and the revolutionaries had guns for the first time. During the day crowds had attacked the air base at Doshan Tapeh, outside Tehran, and air force NCOs with the rank of *homafar* had gone over to them. After a fierce battle the base was captured and large quantities of arms and ammunition were seized. They were carried off to Tehran University, the nerve centre of the Revolution. The revolutionaries already held the streets, and as we drove to the InterContinental Hotel we saw hundreds of people building barricades to protect themselves against the counter-attack which everyone knew would come soon. The Imperial Guard had remained almost totally loyal to what remained of the Bakhtiar government, just as it had remained loyal to its oath of obedience to the Shah.

Saturday 10 February began with a bitter reminder of vulnerability. Joe Alex Morris, a correspondent for the *Los Angeles Times* who was a general favourite at the InterContinental, was out early in the streets that morning. He had taken refuge in an upstairs room, watching a gun battle going on further down the road and was just raising his head to look out of the window when he was hit in the forehead by a stray bullet. He died instantly.

The barricades were everywhere now: usually wretchedly inadequate collections gathered from whatever lay to hand: baulks of timber, the gates of buildings, rocks, cars which had been abandoned by their owners. The Chieftain tanks of the Imperial Guard would ride over such things without noticing them. As we drove slowly round the streets, filming and being stopped by self-appointed vigilantes everywhere we went, I pointed out to the proud constructors the inadequacy of their work, but they just laughed. There was a wildness in the air, a feeling that nothing mattered. The sense that some millennial event was about to take place, cancelling out the past and ushering in a new age, had persisted. Drivers passing the barricades would offer their precious cars for the building of barricades; shop-keepers would open their stores and hand out their stock of food to the revolutionaries, without being asked.

As the morning wore on, the tension grew. Flat-bed trucks

drove past at speed, twenty or more young men holding grimly on at the back or waving white bandages. The smoke from fires was starting to build up over the city roof-tops again: people were setting fire nervously to their barricades to give themselves a feeling of greater security, and the remaining symbols of the Pahlavi government were being attacked yet again. For once the alley leading to the Alawi Girls' School was almost deserted, and the chant of '*Allahu Akbar, Khomeini Rahbar!*' was silenced. We found six or seven youths in blue uniforms, some with their faces blackened as a form of camouflage, guarding the entrance. They had, they said, been on duty there all night. The others were off fighting.

But fighting where? It was proving frustratingly difficult to find the battlegrounds where the brief contacts between army and revolutionaries were taking place. Twice we hurried to the scene of some reported fire-fight, only to find that it had ended half-an-hour before; all that was visible was a pile of cartridge cases from a light machine gun, and traces of blood on the roadway. And, unlikely as it may sound, my greatest fear amid all the other not inconsiderable fears was that we would be present for the Revolution and yet not have a single foot of film to show for what had happened.

An ambulance drove slowly past us, its rear doors open to show the bare stretcher inside drenched with blood, but whoever had been injured had been delivered to the nearby hospital, and the ambulance was out looking for more cases to bring in. Not far away we could hear the stutter of an automatic rifle, and a helicopter gunship appeared a couple of miles away, hovering over a revolutionary strong-point somewhere in the south of the city and pouring machine-gun fire and rockets at it before banking steeply and moving farther away. A truck passed us, the body of a man lying on a bloodstained sheet on the open back, surrounded by red tulips: the symbol of martyrdom. The signs of violent conflict were all about us, but we were unable to track it down. Every decision we took seemed to be the wrong one.

The curfew was extended: anyone found in the streets between four-thirty in the afternoon and five the following morning would be shot on sight, the announcememt said. There was panic then, and Mahmoudi had to pull in to the side of the road to avoid the wild driving of people who had done enough sight-seeing and were desperate to get home in time to save their cars and their lives. Not everyone, it seemed, had millennial expectations now that the Revolution was at hand. Almost every barricade we came across had a portable radio, but at that stage only the orders issued by the Bakhtiar government were being broadcast by the official stations. Some of the revolutionaries had brought out their portable television sets – somehow, a very Persian thing to do – and Khomeini's followers had managed to set up a private transmitting station of their own. I have a photograph of a group of people sitting on the ground beside a white Paykan, watching a small yellow set on which a flickering black-and-white Khomeini was enjoining them in equally strong terms not to obey Bakhtiar's curfew, but to stay on the streets.

We examined the map carefully, and took the advice of Mahmoudi: if and when the tanks came, they would take the road past the InterContinental. It seemed the best place to be, and we settled down with the activists there to await events. Three fires were kept burning all night long, partly to keep the 150 or so diehards warm, and partly, they said, to attract the attention of the Imperial Guard; they took a pride in offering themselves as a target for counter-revolution. A few minutes into the morning of what was to be the culminating day of the Revolution, Sunday 11 February, I grew bored with waiting, and with making light conversation with would-be martyrs, and sat down on the pavement a little to one side in order to jot down some notes by the fitful light of a burning car-tyre. Neither the grammar nor the descriptive power amounts to much, but they give a sense of the atmosphere as the night wore on:

Barricades scarcely strong: 1 large old US car (Buick) dragged up, tipped on side. Other barricades even smaller & mostly composed of rubbish from nearby tip. Unlikely give us much protection. Smoke and sparks go up from fires in streets all round. Smoke hangs over dark streets, stench of burning rubber. Each tyre lasts good hour, and no shortage. Biggest crowd round car with bullhorn inside: symbol of leadership. Owner tempted to use it from time to time to chant 'Allahu Akbar', etc., but as night goes on, instinct fades. Ambulance sirens go, but nothing passes us. Some cars and m/cycles still on streets even now. Gunfire? Rare. Waiting. When will tanks come?

They came, as they always do, at dawn: twenty-six Chieftains by my count, some with rubber treads and some with metal ones which ground their way into the tarmacadam of the roadway, leaving marks which were still there when I went back, seven years later. The noise of clanking, grating metal could be heard half a mile off, and the remnants of the 150 defenders who had lasted out the night fled precipitately, leaving behind the Molotov cocktails they had spent much of the night assiduously filling. I could not blame them, even though they spoiled our chances, once again, of filming a street-battle from close up. The lead tank, finding only an upturned Buick and some skips of rubble across its path, scarcely checked its speed by a single mile an hour. It struck the Buick on the roof with a grinding sound, and flipped it to one side as though it were made of tin-foil; and, like tin-foil, the car crumpled up and lay in the middle of the road, twitching every now and then as another Chieftain passed, slightly out of line with its predecessor, and struck it again.

Now, indeed, there was no shortage of good pictures; and my fear of failing to produce a good story could at last take second place to my fears for our collective safety. As Mahmoudi ferried us through the streets it was obvious that today would see a fight to the finish. The ineffectual barricades had mostly been replaced with sandbags during the night, and the people who were manning them were now armed: mostly, I noticed, with the standard NATO rifle with which the Shah had re-equipped his troops. Everywhere, impromptu lessons in the use of firearms were going on, so that it was impossible to tell whether the constant crack and rattle of gunfire was mostly for practice, or being directed at an enemy. The Revolution now had its own cavalry as well, something never seen at the storming of the Winter Palace: motorcyclists with armed and helmeted men as passengers on the back, driving to the points where fighting was going on. And from them, at last, we obtained hard news about the scene of battle: the Eshratabad garrison.

But although we urged Mahmoudi to hurry, there was a sight I could not pass without stopping to film. We were driving along what was the main Shah Reza Avenue, soon to be renamed Revolution Avenue. Ahead of us lay one of the disfiguring iron overpasses, which carries the road over the crossroads with Hafez Avenue. There was smoke everywhere, and the sound of gunfire and louder explosions; but what attracted my attention was the sight of a crowd of two or three hundred people gathered outside a police station close to the overpass. It was here, during the difficult days of the previous August, during my first visit to Iran, that two of my colleagues and I had been held after we had been arrested by a senior officer of the SAVAK, the Shah's secret police. We had had an unpleasant time in this place: threatened with shooting, and being refused food, water and permission to relieve ourselves, although one of my colleagues was ill with a stomach complaint.

Now the crowd was besieging the police station, and as we ran along the overpass to get a better camera angle, they broke in by the main entrance and made their way through the offices, looting and attacking the detectives and the SAVAK agents who were unfortunate enough to be inside. We could see the crowd clearly through the windows, as they started tipping out the contents of the drawers and showering the street below with three-by-five filing cards of suspects; I caught up a handful as mementos. One of them carries nothing more than the name of a suspect and the words 'Attended a Communist meeting'.

Unpleasant things were going on inside the police station; and as we filmed outside, uniforms, some wet with blood, were thrown out of the windows, catching ludicrously in the branches of a tree outside, like washing hung out to dry. I urged my colleagues to finish their filming; I had no desire to see or to record anything else. As we made our way across the overpass a helicopter gunship came swooping low over the city skyline, attracting desultory and harmless rifle-fire from the ground. I felt unpleasantly vulnerable on our overpass; there was no cover of any kind, and we happened to be the only people on it. A helicopter seems to have omniscience and perfect vision, if you are a small figure cowering underneath it: you feel naked and trapped. I was nervous enough to cross the road, away from the others, in order to provide a less compact target if the helicopter moved in for the kill. It was an impulse I felt ashamed of, later; especially when the helicopter veered away from us, its crew's faces clearly visible, and headed off for more promising targets.

Mahmoudi dropped us at the end of a long street which led towards the Eshratabad barracks. He would probably have driven us further; gunfire did not seem to scare him excessively. But people on the street corner were lying on the ground and making urgent, frightened signals to us to get out of the line of fire, and there seemed no point in offering a target in an otherwise empty street.

'Waiting here, Mr John,' Mahmoudi said, and nodded sympathetically at the nature of our work, which led us to such distasteful places. Absurdly, words from an Irish folksong set to music by Beethoven came to my mind: 'When shall I see thee more?' I nodded, and said he should wait for us, however long it took. We headed up the street.

In some ways it was the most difficult thing we did that entire day. A firefight was going on at the end of the street somewhere, though from this angle it was impossible to say where, and a great many stray bullets were coming down the length of the street. Some splattered against the walls or sang off the brickwork, which was frightening and reassuring at the same time: reassuring, because the sudden white marks they made on the dull grey brick showed that they, at least, were two feet or so above the level of our heads. Some, however, cracked in the air above us in a way that I have always understood meant they were too close for comfort. The words of another Beethoven folksong floated into my mind:

> The pulse of an Irishman ever beats quicker
> When war is the story or love is the theme;

That, at least, was true enough: my pulse was beating extremely fast as we lumbered up the middle of the empty street (the sides of it seemed to take us too close to the smack of the bullets on the brickwork) but what was, alas, not true was the couplet which follows:

> And place him where bullets fly thicker and thicker
> You'll find him all cowardice scorning.

The other two earned my admiration: Bill, striding forward in his tweed jacket, looking as though he were off to make a documentary about country sports, and David, whose size made him a greater target than any of us, keeping up with Bill, and carrying the heavy recorder which was linked to Bill's camera by a thick umbilical cable.

We stopped twice to consider what we should do, but by now the excitement of the thing had taken over: we wanted to know what was going on at the end of the road, even though the bullets were starting, indeed, to fly thicker and thicker. And at the end of the road the layout of the battle finally became clear: at the T-junction, the right-hand bar of the T was occupied by the insurgents, who were keeping up a heavy fire from their positions behind sand-bags at the barracks, which was situated close to the joining-point between the stem of the T and its cross-bar. The bullets which had been fired in our direction emanated from the barracks, and were the wilder shots in what was otherwise a powerful and disciplined barrage.

But we had arrived late in the day: about the time Blücher arrived at Waterloo. The attackers were still being pinned down, and had sustained serious losses, some of whom were being carried past us, under fire, by some of their comrades. But soon after we had stationed ourselves in the open, filming, the fire of the defenders grew weaker and more intermittent, and the revolutionaries charged across the open space and broke their way through the main gate. Within a short time of our arrival it was all over; the military had surrendered and the attackers were driving trucks into the perimeter wall of the barracks in order to force new ways into the barracks. Soon hundreds of men in civilian clothes were streaming out, laden with rifles and hand-guns and ammunition.

'This'll win us an award,' David Johnson said, when we'd shot the last frame and were thinking about going back to find Mahmoudi. I was too new to television to know what constituted good pictures, but Bill Handford demurred. 'You couldn't see it all clearly enough,' he grumbled.

He was, I felt, being too rigorous, but as it happened it didn't matter; the pictures which he and one of his colleagues had shot on the day of the Ayatollah's return later won us the most important international news prize of the year at the Monte Carlo festival.

Vae victis. That evening, a line of men with scarves tied over their eyes was led into the vast complex of houses and store-rooms centring on the Alawi Girls' School, where Ayatollah Khomeini had his headquarters. They were, in spite of their civilian clothes, senior military men, captured in the course of a day which had seen the authority they had wielded, the forces they commanded, and the state they served smashed beyond any hope of recovery. They were led along like blind men, their arms resting on the shoulders of their guards. A group of us, all foreign journalists, was allowed in too; in our way, we were just as bemused by the suddenness of the Revolution's victory as the prisoners were. The store-rooms behind the schoolyard were filled with more weapons and larger amounts of ammunition than I had ever seen in my life.

We had been invited here in order to question for ourselves the most important prisoner who had been captured that day: General Mehti Rahimi, the martial law commander for Tehran. He was the most senior general left in the city. When we were seated around a large table, he and his deputy, General Mohammed Ali Noruzi, were brought in, and their blindfolds removed. In the intense heat of the room, with the occasional noise of gunfire outside as the delighted revolutionaries loosed off their weapons in celebration of the victory they had achieved

47

that day, these two men represented the spoils of victory: physical proof of the Revolution's success. It still seemed unlikely that untutored civilians, who hadn't known the previous night how to build a decent barricade or fire a gun, could possibly have captured men like these two, who had possessed the powers of life and death over a capital city until that morning.

Rahimi, the senior officer, was a heavy-featured man with silver hair and sharp, intelligent eyes. He was dressed in a bush shirt and trousers and had a cut on his right cheek. He bore his sudden change of fortune with remarkable composure; having accepted that he would soon be a dead man, he behaved with quiet dignity.

'My name is Mehti Rahimi. I am the military governor of Tehran. I was arrested this afternoon as I was walking in the street to my office. Someone captured me and brought me here.'

His quiet Farsi was translated into English by the ubiquitous Ibrahim Yazdi. We were invited to put our questions. Some people shouted them out, concerned only with getting precise answers to questions that had been unclear all day. I felt that there was more here than a simple source of information: we were looking at a man who faced execution, perhaps within hours. Even if his orders had sentenced hundreds of people to death during the previous few days, he deserved the decency of being allowed to explain himself and his situation. I interrupted the flow of questions with one of my own: how had he been treated since his arrest?

'In the beginning we were treated very harshly. We were insulted, and people threw stones at us. But I have to say that we also received words of comfort, and orders were given that we should not be hurt.'

His deputy, General Norusi, was smaller and gentler-looking, and was less uncompromising. Rahimi, however, had clearly decided not to dishonour himself in his own eyes: he spoke of the orders he had given during the previous few days:

'All nations need fatherly punishment from time to time, even if it has to be taken to the point of killing people. . . . There was disorder and it was necessary to send in forces to restore order.'

'Whom do you recognize as your overall commander now?'

'My commander-in-chief is His Imperial Majesty, the Shah.'

'Do you believe your life is in danger from the decision of the court which, we understand, will try you?'

General Rahimi smiled slightly, looked up and lifted his hands a little, as though this were all an irrelevance. 'I came into this world once, and once I will leave it,' he said.

The next morning, the last pockets of resistance were dealt with; the Ayatollah's prime minister, Dr Mehti Bazargan, announced the names of his three deputies, and the Shah's last prime minister, Dr Shahpour Bakhtiar, went into hiding. He later escaped to France. 654 people, the new government estimated, had died in the fighting, and 2,804 had been injured.

Bill Handford, David Johnson and I drove out early to the Niavaran Palace, the Shah's residence in the Elburz foothills. We watched as the last remnants of the Imperial Guard, the Shah's 'Immortals', each man chosen for his height and good physical condition, piled up their uniforms on the back of a flatbed truck and stood around in their underwear. Every individual among them had sworn a personal oath to the Shah to defend him with the last blood in their body, but no single drop of blood was shed in the capture of the palace.

Three days later, four generals were found guilty of 'causing corruption on earth' and 'fighting against Allah': crimes that had not existed until that day. Among them was General Rahimi. He was reported to have faced his firing squad with the shout 'Javid Shah!' – 'Long live the Shah'.

3

Returning

[T]he people are very courteous and friendly to
strangers; their apparel very neat and comely. The
men wear long coats to the small of their leg, with
great rolls on their heads, of divers colours, called
turbans. . . . The women are very beautiful, for the
better sort, in regard they wear veils over their heads,
so that the sun never shines on their faces.

George Manwaring,
*A True Discourse Of Sir Anthony Sherley's Travel
Into Persia*, c. 1601

IT WAS SEVEN years before I travelled to Iran again. The Revolution had taken place, had duly devoured its own children, and
had sacrificed hundreds of thousands of other people's children
in the war against Iraq and against internal opposition. The
Revolution had brought about the humiliation of one President
of the United States, and ensured that the administration of his
successor crumbled into weakness and confusion. It had resisted
any efforts from other countries to tame it or render it more
acceptable to the outside world. It had tried to make its own
people pure, and to export its ideas to the rest of the Muslim
world, though it had remained the only example of a truly Islamic
Republic. Above all, it had survived. The one thing it had not done
was to invite visitors in from the West. It remained a country at war:
not just with Iraq and internal opposition, but with the process of
Westernization. It was hostile and difficult and challenging, and I
wanted to go back and see what sort of place it had become.

I did not, fortunately, return alone. My companion, Tira
Shubart, was American by birth and British by nationality; I, by
contrast, was British by birth but was travelling on an Irish
passport. We had been together for two years. Tira, a freelance
television journalist, was representing various television, radio
and print organizations, but she was travelling primarily as my
producer for the television report I intended to make. We had

worked like this several times before: in Nicaragua, in Portugal, in Ireland.

Getting permission to go to Iran had been a difficult business from the start. Virtually the only Westerners who were allowed in were those with something Iran wanted: either trade or arms. The Islamic Republic was not interested in dollars, francs or pounds if they came from the pockets of tourists, because tourism meant the smuggling in of alcohol and the smuggling out of carpets, and a general dilution of religious fervour. Some Westerners were given transit visas in order to make brief overland trips across Iran from Turkey to Pakistan or vice versa; but generally speaking the only people from Western countries who were allowed into Iran were diplomats, businessmen, and one or two journalists. There were perhaps a hundred and fifty Western Europeans in Iran at any one time, and no Americans whatever, with the exception of a small number who had dual citizenship and had always lived there.

It had taken months to persuade the Iranian embassy in London to accept Tira and me; and lucky timing, together with the attacking spirit of the Iranian Revolutionary Guards in the war with Iraq, had played a decisive part in the process. In February 1986, convinced that the Iranian authorities would never allow me in to report on life under the Islamic Republic, I tried to obtain a transit visa from the Iranian embassy in Bonn; only to be told that the waiting period would be months and the visa itself, when it came through, would be valid for a matter of days only. In great depression I returned to London, and rang a close friend of mine at the Foreign Office. 'Only one thing to do,' he said. 'Give the embassy a call and tell them you want to go officially.'

'Ah yes, Mr Simpson,' a polite Iranian voice was saying a few minutes later. 'You are replying to the invitation we sent out by telex this morning.'

'Naturally,' I replied. I had in fact heard nothing about it, but was still employing the Shi'ite tactic of *khod'eh* at moments of uncertainty. 'What exactly was it for?'

'To come to Iran to see the victory our forces have won in the Faw Peninsula, of course.'

'Of course. Yes. Absolutely. Count me in.'

I was on a plane for Tehran forty-eight hours later, but it was scarcely what I had been hoping for. Tira was not allowed to come, and the entire visit lasted only four days; two were spent travelling to and from the front line at Faw, one was devoted to being bombed by the Iraqi air force, and the final day to trying to

51

get on a flight to anywhere in Western Europe before my visa ran out. But my willingness to go was enough to demonstrate my *bona fides* to the Orwellian-sounding Ministry of Islamic Guidance in Iran.

'I must congratulate you on your courage,' said an Iranian official when I returned to London.

Remembering how I had grovelled fearfully in the mud of Faw while the bombing was going on, I found it difficult to answer.

'We saw you on television, shaking your fist at the Iraqi bombers,' he went on, approvingly.

I was thoroughly bewildered, but hurried home to examine the video recording of this unlikely moment. Eventually I found it: a subliminal glimpse, not of me but of a shell-shattered tree with a single knobbly right-angled branch pointing up at the sky. A romantic imagination might just have made it out to be a defiant, fist-shaking correspondent.

The reward for all these benign strokes of fortune and all this hard effort was that Tira and I found ourselves one Sunday evening in August at Heathrow, queuing up to check in for Iran Air flight 710 to Tehran. For us, Iran began there, just as seven years before it had begun for Bill Handford and me in the garden of the Ayatollah's headquarters at Neauphle-le-Château. The everyday assumptions of life in the developed world dropped away, and we were operating under the conditions that any of the great English travellers in Persia, from Sir Anthony Sherley to Edward Granville Browne, would have recognized amid the late twentieth-century confusion of baggage trolleys and loud-speaker announcements.

It turned out to be a matter of who we knew and what pressure we could bring to bear, rather than of our position in the queue. And there were those other indications that one already had left the First World behind: the small acts of attention and kindness from others, the useful bits of advice, the awareness that dead-lines were things that could be bent rather than broken. There was, eventually, order of a kind: imperceptibly we found our-selves moving forward, but it was by an act of common will, not simply because it happened to be our turn next. There was a wide range of types and classes around us; in front was an elderly white-haired man, an archetypal supporter of the Shah by his appearance, who wore an expensive grey suit, and who probably had a house in the northern suburbs of Tehran and an estate somewhere in the country: while behind us was a woman of much the same age, with a brown face as wrinkled as a dead apple on the trees in the Ayatollah's garden in Neauphle-le-

Château, a few broken brown teeth, and the bandy, broad legs of a peasant.

We, as non-Iranians, were the cynosure of all the interested eyes around us. Twice we were asked, in the friendliest way, if we were sure we were in the right queue. 'It's easier to find a drink in Tehran than an Englishman,' said a man in his early thirties.

Everywhere there were mounds of luggage, like a mountaineering base camp. Supplies were being brought back to a country hungry for consumer durables: video cassette recorders, tape decks, electronic keyboards, hair driers, elaborate toys, and any number of smaller items in plastic bags from Harrods and Marks and Spencer. On average, each person in the queue had three pieces of gear apart from personal luggage. Any restrictions about how much hand-baggage could be taken on board seemed to have been set aside; at the Iran Air desk at Heathrow, Iranian rules were played. Lightened of our own burdens, we followed the other passengers through the remaining formalities and exited from the First World.

We boarded the plane twenty minutes after its scheduled departure time, but under Iranian rules the time a plane is due to take off represents more a statement of intent, an advice to passengers, than a hard-and-fast deadline. Maybe this was why the air traffic controllers delayed us a further half-hour, once we were finally aboard, before we were at last allowed to take off. There were as many women passengers as men, but at this stage of the journey few of them were wearing *hejab*, Islamic dress. Many women, indeed, wore the silk dresses and tailored suits they had bought during their time away. The great majority of our fellow-passengers were clearly well-to-do, though there was a sprinkling of unsophisticated, older men and women who had perhaps been visiting their successful sons or daughters in Europe, or had received specialized hospital treatment. The only obvious representatives of the Islamic Republic were the airline stewardesses; they wore black hoods, the official government headgear known as the *maghne'eh*, over their heads and shoulders, accentuating their pale, unmade-up faces. Their dark eyebrows met fiercely in the middle.

The plane was recognizably Iranian territory. The aisles were already turning into boulevards, and older men, in particular, were parading up and down looking for their friends, shaking hands with people, and exchanging notes about their experiences while they were in Europe. One man, younger than the others, showed off a heavy gold watch he had bought, but the older figure he was talking to took care not to seem impressed. The young man moved on down the aisle, reaching across the seats to shake hands with acquaintances. The watch was in evidence every time. In all, he greeted seven people before going back to his own seat and settling down. Persians are perhaps the most sociable nation on earth, and knowing people is a national pastime.

The areas by the emergency exits, by contrast, had become a mosque. Five men were alternately kneeling, bowing their foreheads, and standing up in prayer, led by a young, sallow-faced mullah in fastidiously neat robes. The words came faintly through to us: *'Allahu Akbar . . . Bismillahir rahmanir rahim . . . Alhamdulillahi rabbil-alamin . . .'* A young man, obviously a soldier, trudged painfully past them on crutches, the left leg of his jeans hanging empty.

Women, meanwhile, were starting to prepare themselves for the journey in a different way. Now that they had established themselves in their seats, they were slowly coming to terms with the social and religious change which boarding an Iranian aircraft represents. And whereas most women, on most airlines, would take off whatever they were wearing on their heads when they sat down, here they busied themselves with putting their headscarves on. Few were prepared to challenge the laws on clothing: their headscarves were mostly black, dark brown or grey: dull, nun-like things which deadened their faces immediately. Some women, however – usually the better-dressed of them – had taken a mild risk or two. One, for instance, had a black headscarf with white flowers on it: a small enough gesture, and one that could quickly be disclaimed if necessary, but an attempt to keep a little of the West with her on her return to Islam. Another was much bolder: her scarf was startlingly bright, with big magenta flowers on a bright blue background. There could be no disclaiming this: she was wearing her commitment as strongly as if she carried a lapel-badge with a slogan on it. I am wearing this under protest, her headscarf said, and the women around her, as they covered their unIslamic hair in meek, dull shades, glanced at her with a kind of resignation which in some cases might have indicated admiration.

We, by contrast, made no such statements. Tira, in the seat beside me, had put on the full armour of Islam: black headscarf, black gown with long sleeves, black trousers, black socks, black flat-heeled shoes; it seemed the sensible thing to do, given that we knew so little about the demands of the system or the possible areas of tolerance within it. For my part, it was a great deal easier.

The only concession most men made in terms of clothing was to abandon their ties: the symbol of Westernism. A few of the older men on the plane had ignored that, and were wearing the kind of tie, silver, with diagonal lines, that men of a certain age and income affect throughout the Middle East. They too were making a muted statement of position: a manifesto of their refusal to give up the past and their connexions to it. It struck me as brave at the time, but later I realized that they went unchallenged despite the gesture; still, there was always the possibility that they might be singled out for especially unpleasant attention, so perhaps it took a certain moral courage all the same.

As our plane climbed steeply and headed south-east, England lay opalescent and hazy in the evening air, and people craned for a last look at the greenness below them, anticipating already the subtle browns and yellows of Iran. A stage of the journey was over, and a mild sense of relief seemed to settle on our fellow-passengers. Twenty minutes later there was an announcement: 'Ladies and gentlemen, in honour of the Islamic Revolution in Iran, ladies should please to respect the Islamic dress and head-scarf.' Plainly, we had now left British airspace. The ways of the West had finally to be abandoned. One or two women who had waited until the last moment made the required adjustments, but the great majority had done everything that was necessary to conform long before. Some had wrapped themselves in the *chador*: the figure-encompassing cloak of thin black cotton, which covers the head and body down to the ankles, and has to be held together at the neck with the left hand, or if necessary with the teeth.

By now the stewardesses, in their slightly more convenient alternative, the *maghne'eh* and black tunic, were moving down the aisles offering us food and drink. The choices turned out to be between veal and lamb chops, and between Coca-Cola and Pepsi; there was no effective way of slaking one's thirst and avoiding contact with the Great Satan. The food was standard airline fare: carrots, broccoli, croquette potatoes; there was nothing either Iranian or Islamic about it except the negatives – no pork, and no alcohol. As we ate, a tall, bearded figure in the regulation open-necked shirt and a double-breasted brown jacket sauntered along, looking searchingly at the faces in the rows on either side of the aisle. The Revolutionary Guard smiled faintly as he caught sight of us, but for the most part his glance was impassive and officially severe, and people avoided it if they could.

Several hours passed. Below us in the darkness now lay a

curious pattern of lights: orange, blue, white, without any coherence. There were roads and housing estates and suburbs, but no apparent centre; we were somewhere over the Soviet Union, heading southwards towards the Caspian Sea after sweeping far to the north to avoid getting within range of Iraqi warplanes or ground-to-air missiles. Our precise course was secret and varied from day to day, since Iraq was threatening at that time to regard Iran Air flights as legitimate targets. Beside me, a girl of nine or ten was also looking out at the lights below. She was clutching a folder to her thin chest, as she had done throughout the flight, even during the meal; it was labelled 'Cromwell Hospital, West London', with the words 'Chest Examination' underneath. She was alone on the plane, pale, hollow-cheeked, and wearing a beige headscarf. The folder, presumably, contained the indications of her future life. She turned her face, aware of my gaze, and frowned with the seriousness of the premature, habitual invalid.

I went back to my book, with the accusing green label of the London Library on its front cover: accusing, because the Library rules say that members are not allowed to take books out of the country. *Colloquial Persian*, by L.P. Elwell-Sutton, is not a popular work if the issuing sheet is anything to go by, and it was published in 1941, just before the Shah came to power. It seems to have been designed for use by executives of British companies; the sort of people Ayatollah Khomeini had suggested, in the interview he gave me at Neauphle seven years before, were to be thrown out of the country. Reading the phrases, I could understand why:

Ali Jan, you are the laziest of all the men; why don't you do your work? You are discharged: go to the office and get your money. We don't want men like you here.

I worked my way through the phrases conscientiously, repeating them in a tone low enough not to be overheard: *'Ali Jan, shoma as ham-eye kargan tanbaltar-id: chera karetun-ra namikonid?'* Farsi has a lovely lilt to it, and it is attractive not just to the ear but to the mind. Although it has been jammed into the Arabic script, like a stately woman in a dress made for someone else, it is an Indo-European language with reassuring similarities to our own: Persians being not Semitic but Aryan (a word which is, of course, identical with the name 'Iran'). Mother is *madar*, father is *pedar*, 'brother' is *baradar*; and anyone who has learned Latin or French can feel comfortable with a language in which 'to give' is *dadan* and 'to die' is *mordan*. The lazy Anglo-Saxon can take comfort in the absence of genders, definite or indefinite articles, and case inflections in Persian; though the countervailing difficulties are the Arabic script, which contains letters for which there is no Persian sound and no letters for sounds which Persian does have, and the fact that the human mind, relishing complexity, will always make a simple language difficult by going in for a large degree of colloquialism.

'Why are you visiting our country?' The words were in English, and broke into my linguistic efforts.

I turned my head, to find an elderly man, genteelly dressed, leaning over my seat. My answer was non-committal, but he had identified me as potentially friendly; what might have been termed, under a different kind of revolution, a class-ally.

'You have been there before, I know. Very many things have changed, but now it is easier than it used to be.' His voice dropped a little, and he came closer. 'You can even get a drink now.' Another pause, another glance around, another drop in decibels. 'A week before I left Tehran, I had a drink close to where you-know-who lives.'

'The Imam?' I asked, my voice rather louder than his.

'Shhh!' He nudged me playfully, and doubled up with soundless laughter.

Altogether, six of my fellow-passengers stopped to speak to me. All of them either lived in Britain or had been there for several years, and were able to travel back and forth to Iran without difficulty, having made their peace with the revolutionary authorities. They all appeared to regard the Islamic régime and its laws as a surmountable obstacle – not something they would have chosen, perhaps, but something which, with a little care and discretion, could be got round. They brimmed with hospitality, insisting that we should visit them, dine with them, stay with them. And they all wanted to be told what I thought about Iran, as though I had access to some special information which was hidden from them. I found myself in familiar waters, after a long absence: the confidences, the ability to turn the most difficult of circumstances to advantage, the endless, uncalculating kindness and the sense that secret, complicated things were going on below the surface, which they could only speculate about – all of these were reactions I knew well from the past, and all of them had made Iran exasperatingly delightful to me.

As the plane's undercarriage unfolded, and the lights of Tehran stretched out to the horizon below us, I felt that I was coming, not exactly home, but to a complex, subtle, satisfying place which would repay whatever effort one could put into living and working there.

The aircraft door, which had closed on a cool London summer evening six hours before, was opened to the warmth of the Persian night. It was, with the changes in the time-zones, three-forty in the morning. As we gathered together our things and prepared to leave, the pressurized atmosphere of the cabin was slowly infiltrated by the outside air, and through the smell of aircraft fuel and our own smell of sweat and expensive toiletries there was something else: the warm, dry, brisk savour of Asia, which catches at your throat in the first moments, much as the smell of hops or horse-dung does. I stood at the top of the aircraft steps and took it in, knowing that within a matter of minutes I would have become accustomed to it and might not be aware of it again.

The other passengers were being a great deal more practical; they appreciated that the sooner they reached the airport ter-minal, the quicker would be their passage through the long process of checks and searches which awaited us. Tira and I, by contrast, were slow and far too polite, and each time we tried to get on one of the airport buses we found ourselves elbowed jovially aside and left standing while it moved off. It turned out to be a game played by variegated rules: you could use whatever methods you needed to get on the bus, sparing and being spared by no one; but, once aboard, you could be friendly and helpful, and everyone allowed you whatever small amount of room was available for your bags and cardboard boxes.

Inside the terminal, the people who had been talkative and friendly on the plane and in the bus were noticeably quieter. I looked up and saw why: five or six men, and a couple of women in *hejab*, were looking down at us searchingly as we formed up for the first stage of the arrival process, the passport control desk. For Tira and me, Iran had begun at Heathrow Airport; but for our fellow-passengers, Europe had ended only a matter of minutes before, with the bus-ride from the plane. Until that point, there had been a kind of conspiracy of pleasure, in which almost everyone, except the Revolutionary Guards on the plane and one or two of the stewardesses, was involved. Now they were back under the eyes of people who did not travel to the West and break the rules of Islam, and they did not want to attract unnecessary attention to themselves. Not much hair showed now from under the coloured headscarves, and a marked silence descended on us as we shuffled forward every three or four minutes, our passports in our hands.

IN THE NAME OF GOD, FOR THE ATTENTION OF DEAR IN-COMING PASSENGERS, WELCOME TO OUR COUNTRY, IRAN. The notice greeted us after we had made our way through the passport control – which had taken fifty minutes in all – and passed through another control point where the forms they had just given us were taken away and stamped with relish and determination. Everyone but us had to report at a desk marked, in Farsi only, 'Returning Citizens', and when we stopped in front of it, doubt-fully, we were waved impatiently on. We had plenty of time while waiting for the next stage, therefore, to digest the remainder of the welcoming sign. It was rather more pointed:

DEAR PASSENGERS, IN CASE YOU HAVE FOREIGN EXCHANGE (F.E.) PLEASE GET F.E. DECLARATION FORMS, AS YOU WILL NOT BE PERMITTED TO TAKE OUT ANY F.E. WITHOUT THIS FORM YOU ARE REQUESTED TO TAKE GOOD CARE OF IT. OTHERWISE YOU WILL FACE DIFFICULTIES FOR WHICH THE CUSTOMS OFFICIALS ARE NOT HELD RESPONSIBLE.

All official notices at airports contain a certain hint of menace: the threat of 'difficulties' is, after all, the main sanction any bureaucracy can wield. But we were in Iran, and the menace seemed particularly strong.

At this desk the women did the work, thumbing fast through the wads of pounds and dollars and francs which everyone was thrusting towards them as though it were a market-place. One man, for no reason that I could see, was singled out and searched in the most thorough way, his clothes and his hand-luggage examined with the skill of experts. Perhaps he looked like a smuggler; or perhaps they simply pulled someone out at random from time to time to make sure everyone knew that the 'difficul-ties' were not just something to be read about on posters. But the woman who dealt with me paid no great attention to the money I had with me, and jotted down the amount I had declared without checking it.

I looked back as we passed through: the selected victim was starting to stuff his things back into their plastic bags and wrappers, nothing illicit having been found on him. He did not complain; if he had, perhaps he might have run into more difficulties for which the customs officials would not be held responsible. Much better to regard all this as a form of physical airport tax, extracted from a few passengers in part payment for whatever pleasure they had gained from visiting Europe. As Tira and I reached the top of the escalator which took us to the customs hall he was starting to follow, and the foreign exchange people who had searched him watched him go without exchanging a word with him.

Because we were unfamiliar with the business of arriving at Mehrabad Airport, we thought we had made our way through the system with remarkable speed; the stories about waiting for three or four hours seemed to have been exaggerated. Then we came into the baggage hall. It was a scene of desolation. Luggage in huge quantities piled up around the slowly moving carousels, and five great queues, each a hundred or so long, were waiting for the baggage search which was being carried out in minute detail by a total of three officials. Our jumbo jet had arrived within a few minutes of another which had come in from Turkey, and every seat on that, as on ours, had been filled. There was a remarkable silence in the great hall, but it was the silence of resignation. No one bothered to complain, because this, like the searching of the man downstairs, was another instalment of the price that had to be paid for travelling abroad. If you found the price too high, you shouldn't do it.

But resignation brought an air of great calm. At five o'clock in the morning there were no meetings to go to, no appointments to keep. Waiting here was an alternative to sleeping: not, perhaps, a very pleasant one, but people were prepared to make it as acceptable as they could by being sociable. Outside, when it had been a question of getting through the system as quickly as possible by reaching the airport buses first, they had competed fiercely because competition paid off. Here in the customs hall competition was pointless. With only three people to search our luggage, the process would be quicker if they were allowed to do it in relative calm, without being besieged. The collective Persian will was at work.

I lugged our cases from the ancient carousel to where Tira had prudently established herself in one of the queues. We calculated the likely waiting-time by working out how long it took for each passenger to be searched; depressingly, it seemed to be about seventeen minutes per family, and that was too many hours for us to want to compute. But the friendliness of our fellow-passengers was an important compensation. Men and women were continually coming up to us and commiserating with us for the long delays. 'This is nothing like England,' someone said; and, seeing that I was taking notes, he added dolefully, 'You are writing down how much you don't like it here.' 'Not at all. I just want to make sure I remember the details.' 'No one wants to remember this,' he said, and I remembered then that a kind of self-deprecation about themselves and their country was another feature of the Persian character which I had noticed in the past. In a fine patriotic gloom the man moved off, confident that Iran was being justly condemned.

As it happened, we found it refreshing to sit on our luggage and talk to people; and it was now obvious that we had been wrong in assuming that we were the only Westerners on our plane. An Englishwoman in her early thirties told us in a strong Manchester accent that she and her Iranian husband had lived in North Tehran since before the Revolution. Her Farsi was almost perfect, and when her husband lost his job she had gone out to work and earned enough money to keep both of them. They had, she said, decided to leave Iran the previous year, because of the Iraqi bombing; but now the pull of the place was too strong, and they were back. She was, however, prepared. Taking Tira aside, she showed her an entire suitcase full of Tampax. Another Englishwoman, seeing them together, came across and joined them, but she had never liked living in Iran and the sight of so many people waiting to have their bags searched was almost too much for her.

'I'd forgotten how bad it is here,' she said, the lines of her face accentuating her depression. 'Once I've got through all this, and seen everybody, I'm getting out for good.' 'What about your husband?' I looked around, but couldn't see him. 'That's his problem,' she said, and her mouth closed sharply, her lips thin and colourless. The pattern was clear: adventurous-minded women, often from backgrounds which were restricting and where there was little money, had met and married Iranian students whose own families were frequently extremely wealthy. For most, it was probably too much of a gamble if the husband insisted on going back to Iran to live. Only the most adaptable and lucky of them, like the woman with the case of Tampax, would be likely to make a success of it; and yet if there were two such wives on our plane alone, it was clear that it must happen a good deal.

By this time, I was deep in conversation with a man from Isfahan. 'I am Christian, like yourself,' he said courteously, singling me out from the others about us. 'From Armenia. We also are allowed to drink, you know.' I congratulated him on that, and asked how long he had been in Isfahan; it sounded as though he was a fairly recent arrival. 'My family was invited to come by Shah Abbas.' And he added, assuming that I would not

61

be encumbered by such details, 'In the sixteenth century.' We had now moved forward, by my estimation, ten yards in two hours; and when I remarked on that, he answered, with a joy in discovering hidden reasons that all Iranians appear to share, regardless of their racial origins, their religious beliefs or their drinking habits, 'They do it deliberately to discourage us from buying foreign goods.'

There was one last, important Persian characteristic which I had benefitted from often in the past, and was about to benefit from again: the propensity for doing selfless, purely gratuitous acts of kindness involving a good deal of personal effort. As I was talking to the Armenian, a fellow-passenger whom I had not noticed before came down the line, and called out when he spotted me.

'I have arranged everything. They're waiting for you now.'

I had not the slightest idea what he was talking about, but he shook me by the hand and called me his dear friend. He had seen me, he said, on television in England, and had noticed me at Heathrow Airport. He was a government official, and he wanted to help me now.

'The customs men. I told them you were waiting here, and they say to bring you to them.'

He looked at me, the fire of a generous enthusiasm in his face. He did not altogether look like the kind of man you would want to entrust yourself and your belongings to: he was hollow-cheeked and unshaven, his shirt was open at the neck, his eyes were deep-set and glinting. And yet this man, who never gave us his name, and whose own family stayed firmly embedded, with him, in the depths of the queue, had made it his business to help us through the last and longest of the arriving passenger's ordeals. I looked around for signs of resistance or antagonism from the group we had been talking to, but they, it seemed, approved. If you have an advantage, their faces appeared to say, you must naturally make use of it. What, after all, are contacts for, if not to be used? We said our goodbyes and followed him. It was six-thirty, and we had been travelling for ten hours.

The head customs man greeted us absently – from where he stood, the queue seemed to stretch out to infinity, and the fate of two particular members of it cannot have affected him too much – and handed us over to one of his searchers, a woman. I shook hands with the man who had rescued us, genuinely grateful for his kindness, and so (forgetting the religious instruction which prohibits a Muslim from touching an unknown female) did Tira. He took her hand without hesitation, and vanished back into the queue, to await his own eventual turn. He was, clearly, an idealist who did not believe in taking advantage of the system, and I respected him for it.

It was harder to feel sympathy for the woman who was preparing to search our bags. The light of enthusiasm shone in her eyes too, but it was a harder and more vindictive enthusiasm, which drove her to open everything in our cases that could be opened, and inspect everything regardless of whether it was worth inspecting. Every book we had brought with us, and both of us are invariably weighed down with books, was gone through with care, to see if it might contain some passage offensive to the faith or critical of the Islamic Revolution. Every article of clothing was pulled out and held up, every toiletry was opened and sniffed. The salami we had brought as a gift, two and a half feet long, provoked a good deal of suspicion, in that it was unopenable, powerful-smelling, and of no obvious political or religious use. Our searcher put it on one side for later examination.

Tira's rock-and-roll tapes and my Bartók and Mahler caused a more specific problem. Ever since Ayatollah Khomeini's speeches were smuggled into the Shah's Iran in cassette form, tapes have been a source of suspicion to customs officials. In this case, though, we each had so many that a few moments of Bartók and ZZ Top were more than enough for our heavy-browed, impassive customs official. Pulling off the Walkman headphones Tira had offered her, she swept the entire pile of cassettes aside with distaste. Behind her trestle table, she ignored our remarks and jokes, stolidly filling in the details of the equipment we had brought in on one of the visa pages of our passports, in the swooping hand of the Iranian official. Then we were free, nothing having been found against us, and all that was required was to repack our belongings, remedying the disorder she had wrought, and move to the next check-point: the sixth, by my calculation.

We pushed our way, bewildered, through the crowd of waiting relatives and friends at the exit gate, and into the main hall of the airport building. The noise, the tiredness, and the sense of having had our possessions rifled combined to make us sick of the entire experience. We got through the main doors and let our cases slip to the ground around us. The air was warm and fresh, like the waters of a summer lake, and on the mountains opposite us the topmost peaks were touched with the first rays of the sun. I noticed again the warm, dry savour I had recognized when we arrived: the smell of dust and animals. A journey which had been thought about for seven years and plotted in detail for nine months was over. I looked across in the growing light to the strident signs which officialdom had erected to raise the spirits of the citizenry: 'We are with the innocents of the world', said one. The other read 'Victory is ours'. At that moment, I shared both sentiments.

4

The Streets of the City

> Tyroan [Tehran] is seated...in the midst of a large level or plain; and, albeit at a distance it be environ'd with hills, yet one way it offers a large horizon. The air is temperate in the morning and towards sunset, but in the sun's meridian we found it very hot.
>
> Thomas Herbert, *Travels in Persia*, 1627

THE COUNTRY WE had come to see had endured one of the most extraordinary changes of national direction in the twentieth century. As a result of the Revolution, Iran had rebuilt its social, economic, political and legal life according to the lines laid down in the Holy Koran. The Shah had set Iran the national task of overtaking France economically and militarily by 1993; rejecting him, it had instead found itself governed according to the ordinances of the seventh century.

The Islamic Republic had been created on the basis of a revealed religion: it did not have to justify itself to non-Muslims, and its leaders had no doubts about what they were doing. The outside world and its opinions were irrelevent. The mullahs who controlled the workings of the state had rarely left the closed circle of the Shi'ite Muslim world: the holy cities of Saudi Arabia and Iraq, and Iran itself. They were concerned with exporting their brand of revolution to other Islamic countries, and in particular to Lebanon and the Gulf; but beyond that the only function their foreign ministry needed to perform, in their eyes, was to try to win foreign support and foreign weapons for the war against Iraq. All their other energies and interests were turned inwards.

In the absence of regular, dependable news from inside Iran, Western newspapers frequently printed accounts of what was going on there during the years which followed the Revolution which were entirely speculative, deriving for the most part from émigré sources. On at least eight separate occasions between 1979 and 1987 Ayatollah Khomeini was reported to be dead or

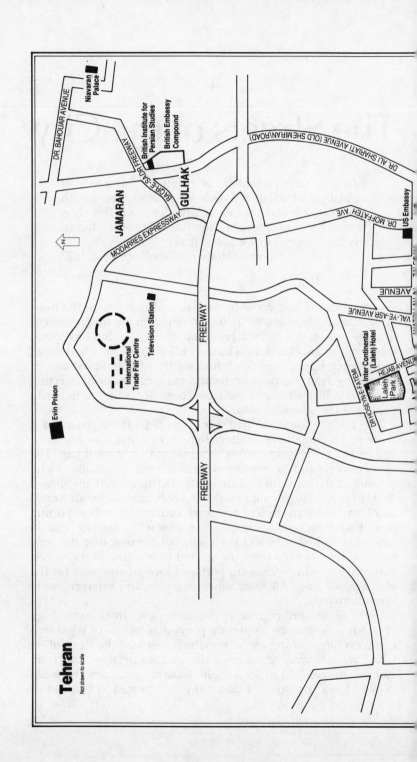

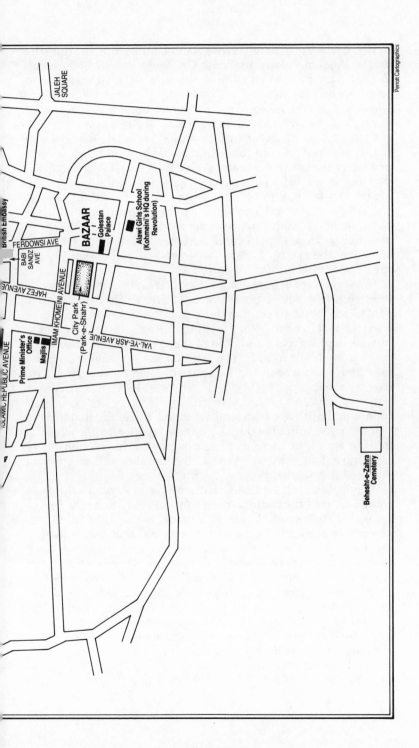

JALEH
SQUARE

British Embassy

FERDOWSI AVE

BABI
SANDZ
AVE

HAFEZ AVENUE

BAZAAR

Golestan
Palace

Alawi Girls School
(Kohmeini's HQ during
Revolution)

IMAM KHOMEINI AVENUE

City Park
(Park-e-Shahr)

VAL-YE-ASR AVENUE

ISLAMIC REPUBLIC AVENUE

Prime Minister's
Office

Majlis

Behesht-e-Zahra
Cemetery

Perrot Cartographics

dying. It was like obtaining news about Lenin's Moscow from the White Russian colony in Paris. On the few occasions when Western cameras and journalists were allowed in, it was often to witness some unguarded act of triumph over the enemies of Islam which convinced Western public opinion all the more strongly that Iran had sunk into mediaeval barbarism.

I felt, from long experience of closed societies, that the real nature of what was going on in Iran would be found in the streets or behind the blank walls and doors of its cities. A city is like a prisoner in the hands of hostage-takers, who will say anything his captors tell him to say, but whose eyes, if watched closely, will tell the real story. The officials of any government which is based on an ideology have a strong tendency to assert that their system is as close to perfection as human beings can reasonably come; but the reality of life in the streets of the cities will always reveal how true, or how false, that is.

Tira and I were to be staying in North Tehran, in the foothills of the mountains whose peaks were starting to glow in the early sunlight as we emerged from the airport terminal. But tired as we were, I felt obliged to get my bearings once again, and see a little of what had happened in Tehran during the years I had been away from it. We found a taxi with far greater ease than I had expected: now, it seemed, the authorities kept a stricter control over what happened at the airport, and the old days, when it was besieged day and night by large crowds of passengers, their friends and relatives, had gone. It helped, no doubt, that instead of forty or more flights a day at Mehrabad Airport to and from the outside world, as there had been before the Revolution, there were now half-a-dozen. At last, the number of taxis almost matched the number of people wanting them.

We piled our luggage into a battered green Paykan – the most common car in the country, built from kits exported by a British car manufacturer, and based on a model of the early 70s called, suitably enough, the Hillman Avenger – and settled ourselves in the back. The seats were rump-sprung, and there was fake orange fur on every available flat surface. A yellow string of *tasbih*, Iranian worry beads, dangled from the driver's rear-view mirror, and clinked at each pothole in the road. The driver himself was scrawny-armed and unshaven, and looked extremely brigandish except for the rare occasions when he broke into a brilliant, gap-toothed grin. His name was Ali.

At first there was little traffic, and within a few minutes we had reached the elegant monument which the Shah erected to himself and his dynasty: the *Shahyad*, a soaring arch of white marble in a square which had been renamed *Azadi* – 'freedom'. It was here that enormous rallies were held in the days of the Revolution, with a million or more well-marshalled people surrounding it, while the more adventurous spirits in the crowd competed to see how high they could climb up its apparently sheer sides and stencil portraits of Khomeini on the stone. Now, I noticed, the marks had been cleaned off, and only the unambitious base of the monument was covered with posters: the official posters which we were to see everywhere, condemning Iraq and calling for further sacrifices in the war. The audio-visual display which had taken place at regular intervals during the day to demonstrate the achievements of the Pahlavi dynasty had been replaced by an exhibition of photographs of the Revolution. It was usually closed, Ali told us with gloomy enthusiasm. He was not a great supporter of the Revolution.

In these outer suburbs to the west of the city the shops were starting to open, lit still by the yellow glare of hurricane lamps or the blue of neon. Inside, the shopkeepers were laying out their stocks of vegetables, or piling up bolts of cloth, or heaving bloody half-carcasses of meat onto slabs while their assistants stood by, yawning. The sun was below the skyline still, and the light in the streets was dull and grey. The lamps shone onto the pavement in front of the shops, throwing its unevenness into relief. Tehran demands careful walking: the paving-stones rear up every now and then, as though some powerful hidden force were starting to exert itself.

There is indeed a powerful pressure within the city: the enormous upward thrust of population. Areas which had been open land when I saw them at the time of the Revolution were now covered with shacks or more permanent buildings. In 1978 Tehran had had a population of six million. Now, although the precise figure was impossible even for census officials to determine, it was thought to be well over ten million. In the country as a whole the population was approaching fifty million, and was increasing at 4% a year: one of the highest rates of growth in the world. Tehran had grown fastest of all. The process had begun in the first decade of the century, but the greatest increase came after 1973, when the Shah was influential in persuading OPEC to raise the oil price; an unprecedented flood of wealth, job opportunities and corruption flowed through the larger cities of Iran. If the Shah had studied the history of his large neighbour to the north a little more carefully, he would have known that Tsar Nicholas II's sudden campaign of industrialization after 1905 had brought social dislocation on an immense scale, followed by revolution. In Iran, the Revolution led to further dislocation. People came to Tehran and the other cities in their hundreds of thousands, searching for work and social benefit payments. Refugees who lost their homes in western and south-western Iran when the Iraqis invaded in 1980 drifted there; and although the one and a half million people who had fled to Iran from Afghanistan after the Soviet invasion in 1979 had not been supposed to settle in the cities, large numbers of them had ended up in Tehran as well.

Most revolutionary régimes practise social engineering on a large scale, and the huge increase in population gave the officials who ran the Islamic Republic of Iran every excuse to control the movement of people and specify the places where they could live. A system of pass-laws was introduced in the Soviet Union soon after the revolution there, for instance. But in many ways the revolutionaries in Iran were not *dirigiste* at all, except along the lines of the Muslim fundamentalist agenda. They did not, for instance, interfere much in economic matters; they did not launch a campaign of birth control; and they did not tell people where to live. There were times when they seemed more like nineteenth-century liberals than like revolutionaries.

Since few planning controls were enforced, the working-class population of Tehran spread out into the plain, colonizing areas which had previously been scrub and near-desert; the middle class had pushed their way up into the cool, wooded foothills of the Elburz mountains, and the rich had sought refuge further up the slopes, taking over the small villages which had once been a day's ride from the city.

And yet, I found, one of the Revolution's achievements had been to ensure that the growth of the city in size and numbers had not overwhelmed it. As we drove through the quiet morning streets, the sweepers were already out with their wide brooms, clearing the gutters and dealing with the overnight piles of refuse, as they always had; and now there were more of them. The *jubs* or channels which carried the streams from the Elburz right down into the heart of the city, cooling it and providing the poor with their water, were no more obstructed than they had always been. The streets seemed for the most part surprisingly clean.

In the slums of Tehran, which we did not visit until later, there was gross overcrowding and conditions were often highly unsanitary, but not noticeably worse than they had been under the Shah in those same areas. The collapse of the urban system, which had often been predicted within Iran, had never happened. The Shah's road-building programme had been continued and extended, and so had his afforestation schemes on the edge of the city. The trees that had been planted after the Revolution had brought about a drop in the mean annual temperature in Tehran itself of approximately half a degree a year.

But as our taxi penetrated deeper into the city itself, there was no mistaking the signs of decay. Among the parades of shops that were just opening for the day there were plenty that had closed down for good, looking like gaps in an uncared-for row of teeth. Plastic signs that advertised bakeries or electrical goods shops or tailors were cracked and broken, and the walls were covered with grafitti and the tattered remnants of posters. Tehran had never been fortunate in its architecture, and the few grand buildings had long since been swallowed up by the sudden expansion after the Second World War.

Now the drab grey stucco façades were cracked and stained by the weather, and criss-crossed with cables which were strung along their fronts to carry power, legally or illegally, to the shops and apartments above them. The metal fixtures rusted, the dirt from the atmosphere lay thick on every surface, and not even the first sunshine of the day could make them look attractive. Sometimes a thin tree, planted by the roadside, would lean in towards the buildings, suffering from a kind of arboreal rickets, and in the branches would hang a birdcage; but the little yellow finch inside would be motionless, its feathers ruffled up, silent in spite of the morning sun. Tehran was dirty and drab under the Shah: but the economic problems of the years of war, and the ban on imports, had made it worse.

The Iranian economy had nevertheless done a great deal better than anyone expected. The disruptive effects of the war on Iran's oil exports, the country's isolation from the outside world and the total inexperience of the revolutionary government had made an economic collapse seem almost inevitable – and yet it had not happened. But it had been averted only at a considerable long-term cost to the country. The decline in the world oil price during the 1980s, which probably had a more damaging effect than the war itself, had led Iran to trade its oil at a discount; while in order to keep up a momentum in the economy and to pay for the war the government had engaged in deficit financing for several years. But Iran draws its underlying economic strength from its oil and gas reserves, which are among the world's biggest; and it represented a secure long term prospect, whatever the problems in the short and medium term. By 1987 the

71

régime estimated that the damage to its economy from the war had amounted to $350 billion; but even that offered an enormous range of contractual opportunities for the time when the war would finally end and the process of reconstruction would begin. Industrial corporations throughout Europe and the Far East were anxious to keep some residual links with Iran, waiting for the time when the opportunities opened up.

By now the streets were filling up with cars and people: men in open-necked shirts, long-sleeved for decency, carrying brief-cases for their day at the office; women, pale and unemotional in their *maghne'ehs;* mullahs, in the crisp grey robes that give them the appearance of contented pigeons, walking past with the rolling gait that so many Persian men adopt: a side-to-side motion, instead of the angular, up-and-down lope of the Euro-pean; older women, their faces masked by their *chadors,* seeming thinner and more bent by the black material. Now that the traffic was building up, filling the entire street with fumes and the sound of car horns, some scooters and motorbikes were taking to the sidewalks, weaving slowly in and out among the crowds of people.

'Traffic is very bad now.' It was said resentfully. Ali, our taxi-driver, disapproved of the sight-seeing tour we were on, and may have been anxious about his fuel-gauge: we had passed enough queues for petrol, each a dozen or more cars long, to know that we did not want to get involved in one ourselves. But there was no escaping the traffic. We were in the middle of three lanes of cars, held up by an ineffectual policeman some way down the road. Between him and us a superannuated set of traffic lights changed intermittently, but no one took any notice of them. An urbane Persian remarked to me, some weeks later, 'Traffic lights are like all the other rules here: we regard them as being purely advisory.'

Certainly life – as represented by the traffic around us – seemed to be concerned with what you could get away with. The standard of driving was not good, but it never had been. Cars insinuated themselves in and out of the lines to gain a little advantage. Beside us, a blue bus lumbered slowly forward, exhaust belching out smoke the colour of its paintwork, brakes shrieking at every touch on the pedal. Several faces looked down at us from behind the blue chintz curtains the owner had thoughtfully supplied, their expressions changing from boredom to a real interest when they saw European faces; Westerners were almost as unfamiliar as unveiled women nowadays.

An ambulance siren wailed, and in the traffic jam something of the common will we had seen displayed by our fellow-passengers from the plane was aroused: cars which had competed for a centimetre of space a short time before now moved aside in order to allow the ambulance through. It slowly manoeuvred its way along, the siren's blaring minor notes echoing off the walls of the buildings. Inside, the outline of the sufferer could just be made out, a para-medic leaning solicitously over him. As it passed, the competition began for the ambulance's wake, and into it, ahead of us, wobbled a Honda motorbike ridden by a thin, oldish man with a face eaten with smallpox. He turned his head riskily as he passed us, shouting something to the woman sitting side-saddle behind him. She was wrapped in a *chador*, and was at least twenty years younger than he. She gripped the handle tightly with both hands, and had to use her teeth to keep the two sides of the *chador* together. What she could not do, for the sake of Islamic decency, was to sit astride the motorbike or hold her husband around the waist. Ali cursed, and had to brake hard: in Iran, if you hit a motorbike, it is legally your fault. That gives them their slight margin of security on the dangerous and competitive roads.

'Before the Americans and English left,' Ali said, his thin arms working hard over the steering-wheel, 'plenty of money, plenty of *an'am*.' He rubbed his finger-tips with his thumb – *an'am* means a tip – and then spread his fingers out sharply, to illustrate a little explosion. 'Now, nothing.'

He flashed his teeth to show he was being friendly, and to celebrate his good luck at having a potential *an'am*-giver in his cab again. But even he accepted that the Revolution had brought one good thing: control over the traffic. Before 1979, the traffic jams in Tehran were among the worst in the world. The fundamental rules of driving on the right were ignored as the jams built up; the traffic would fill the boulevards from side to side, and choke the *kuches*, the side-streets, that linked them to one another.

Faced with the imminent seizing up of the city, the revolutionary authorities had decided to ban all private cars from the centre of Tehran for five days a week: Saturday to Wednesday, from 7.30 am to 1.30 pm. This, indeed, was *dirigiste*, and it worked. Every road into the centre of the city was blocked off during those hours, and the only vehicles the police would allow through were those which carried an official sticker: a stylized map of Tehran with an arrow pointing to its centre. Not long before we arrived, a ring which had been forging these stickers was broken up, and its members harshly punished.

But the authorities were then faced with the lack of any serious public alternative to the private car, and so they introduced a new type of taxi, green in colour, to work alongside the old system of orange ones. The orange taxis operated to and from the city centre, but the green ones worked across the city from suburb to suburb, often avoiding the centre altogether. The taxis in the streets are usually crammed with passengers, each paying five or ten *rials* per stage, but it is rare to wait longer than a few minutes for one that has a seat available. There were still traffic jams, as we saw, but things were better.

A few months after we left, the Tehran authorities relaunched a project which, for a country involved in a fierce and expensive war, showed a remarkable degree of self-confidence. During the Shah's last years the city had begun to plan its own Metro system; it was part of the imperial strategy of modelling Iran on France, and attempting to overtake the model. For years the sites lay abandoned, open to the weather; and then in October 1986, with little ceremony, the work on the Metro began in earnest, with the help of a number of Japanese consortia. It was, if anything, more ambitious now: two lines were to be built in the shape of a cross, one going from the northern suburbs through the centre to the poorer southern suburbs, the other crossing from east to west, and reaching out to the rapidly-growing dormitory suburb of Karaj, more than thirty miles away.

The purpose of the enterprise was clearly to provide Iran's sluggish economy with an injection of public money, but there was considerable opposition to it within the governmental structure itself. In the summer of 1987 the second most powerful politician in the country, Ali-Akbar Hashemi-Rafsanjani, came to inspect the work and to give it his backing. Speaking without notes, Rafsanjani, a witty, quick-thinking man, said he knew there had been a good deal of criticism of the idea that so much money should be spent on the Metro at a time when every *rial* was needed for the war with Iraq.

'But,' he said, looking round at the serious-minded officials with him and grinning suddenly, 'just think how useful it will be as an air-raid shelter.'

'Our fried chicken' declared the sign on a shop beside us: 'The ultimate taste'. Below it was the smiling face of an Iranian. I had seen this shop shortly before the Revolution, and the face on display then had belonged to Colonel Sanders. We happened to be filming it because an angry crowd, understandably confusing

74

Colonel Sanders with Uncle Sam, was tearing the place apart. Afterwards the smiling Iranian in the picture stepped in and took it over. The only boom industries, during the years that followed the Revolution, were fast foods and video rentals: fried chicken, hamburgers (there was a Mac Ali's) and whatever American movies a resourceful owner with a network of friends abroad could copy and bring in through the customs. An entire generation of young, middle-class Iranians had been brought up with American food, American clothes, and American entertainments; the habit could not be broken simply by cutting off the supply.

Beyond cutting off political links with the West, and declaring that harmful Western influences were to be banned, the authorities were curiously relaxed. I watched a young girl walking down the street in full, unexceptionable *hejab*, but carrying a plastic bag with the American Stars and Stripes on it. It did not seem like an act of defiance, and she would not, presumably, have carried it if it had been likely to get her into trouble with the local government authority, the *Komiteh*. Taxis and cars frequently carried stickers with the face of an American Indian and the English words 'Navajo American Marine'. Perhaps if they had been written in Farsi there would have been trouble; but it was curious, nevertheless, to see people sporting the stickers of the force which participated in the attempted rescue of the American hostages in Iran in 1980. Slowly, I felt, the streets of the city were beginning to provide their message: the authorities, having crushed all serious opposition, felt they could afford to be a little more indulgent now. Outward conformity was what they demanded; nothing more.

But by the same token, nothing less than conformity was permitted. When, from time to time, some political dissident would emerge to write an anti-war or anti-Khomeini sentiment on a wall, it would be scrubbed or whitewashed out within hours by the local *Komiteh*, one of whose tasks is specifically to look out for opposition graffiti and deal with it. The ayatollahs are preachers: the word is important to them, and they know the force that anti-Shah slogans had before the Revolution, when SAVAK, the Shah's secret police, had much the same task of keeping the walls of the city ideologically clean.

During the two or three years after the Revolution, the political confusion of the time was reflected in the graffiti everywhere. Opposition groups like the Mojaheddin, the Fedayeen, the Communist Tudeh Party, and even some remaining Royalist elements fought out their political battles with the revolutionary government, in part, with spray-cans of paint and powerful slogans. But with the defeat of the opposition came the desire for uniformity, and the old offending messages were obliterated. An occasional one has survived, usually because its sentiments are bland and acceptable: 'Power to the people!' and 'Freedom is indivisible' are probably Tudeh Party or Fedayeen slogans, but they can be made to fit most political ideologies.

On one wall, I was told, someone had written the extraordinarily nihilistic slogan 'Long live conflict!', which might well have been meant ironically; but that too was left by the *Komiteh*, perhaps on the grounds that it showed a suitably warlike spirit. Nowadays the slogans of Tehran are notable mostly for their skilful workmanship and their entirely loyal sentiments. The *Komitehs*, it seems, are responsible for selecting them from an official list, much as slogans for special occasions are worked out by committees in the Soviet Union; and they are often painted up by professional sign-writers. They rarely touch great heights of creativity: 'Neither east nor west, but Islam!', 'Freedom is obtained through sacrifice', 'If the Revolutionary Guards didn't exist, our country wouldn't exist'; and, more threateningly, 'I recommend women to forget their behaviour under the last régime and accept the Islamic code', 'Death to America, death to England, death to France'. It says something about the absence of political moderation in Iran that the only way to express condemnation of others is to condemn them to death; the relatively mild formula of the West ('Down with . . .', 'A bas . . .,!' Abajo . . .!') does not exist.

But in one or two particularly significant places, a more entertaining approach has been followed. As we left the airport, for instance, and passed the military barracks close beside it, we saw that a splendid sequence of huge political cartoons had been painted on the walls, showing the Iraqi leader Saddam Hussein as a puppet worked by Uncle Sam, and – to provide the political balance which the Iranian government felt was required in the difficult years of 1984 and 1985 – a greedy Russian bear attempting to claw the world in half. Later on our taxi journey we passed another place where I had heard these big cartoons had been painted up: the British embassy. Ali was persuaded to help us find them, somewhere on the wall of the embassy compound, a quiet and restful park the size of a city block in the middle of one of the noisiest and most congested areas of Tehran. It was beginning to get seriously hot now, and the traffic was at its peak.

Seven years before, I had stood here and watched as an angry crowd swarmed over the compound walls and set fire to the main chancery building, but it had been so well restored that no sign of the fire could now be seen. We made our way round the periphery of the compound, and found confirmation of something else I had heard about: the renaming of the street which runs beside the embassy, and had been called Winston Churchill Avenue ever since the Three-Power Conference in Tehran in 1943. Now it was called Neauphle-le-Château Avenue. Homayoun ('Royal') Avenue at the back of the embassy had been renamed too; I spelled out the new name from the Arabic lettering on the street sign: *'Ghiaban Babi Sandz'*. During the IRA hunger-strike in Northern Ireland, the name of the street had been officially changed to that of the best-known of the men who died: Bobby Sands.

The political cartoons were on the fourth side of the embassy compound, and they proved to be the best I saw in Iran. The wall had been built in convenient sections, each one ten feet by fifteen, and the official cartoonist had turned each section into a painting in primary colours, each with a good, identifiable likeness. Suitably enough, so close to Bobby Sands Avenue, Mrs Thatcher, blonde and toothy, is running away from *'Irlanda N.'* pursued by a volley of bottles and rotten fruit. Her arms and legs are unIslamically bare, and she is trailing an inevitable handbag. A nervous Uncle Sam, his arms in the air, is being marched across the desert (marked, helpfully, 'Iran') with a monster fountain pen the length of a gun-barrel pointed at his back: the pen bears the 'Allah' symbol of the Islamic Republic: the moral, presumably, being that Iran's propaganda can rid Iran of American influence.

Further on, the nonchalant figure of the Soviet-imposed leader of Afghanistan smokes a cigar as he lounges on top of a huge time-bomb whose fuse is well alight, and Saddam Hussein of Iraq lurks nervously behind the paunchy figure of the Saudi king, who is holding out a battered dustbin-lid shield with a dollar sign on it. It is all good, clean fun; the kind of cartoons a newspaper might print in a far more moderate country than Iran. And for once there was none of the gore and the obsessive concern with physical wounds which many official posters displayed.

The war with Iraq was the most important and intrusive fact in Iran's national life; and although it was not immediately obvious that Tehran was the capital of a country at war – there was no black-out, and no bombed buildings were to be seen in the city centre – the signs were certainly there. In the small streets near the British embassy I noticed several attractive little structures of

77

wood and metal standing in the roadway, decked out with coloured lights and mirrors, and each bearing a man's photograph at the top. 'Like a grave,' Ali explained in reply to my question. 'To remind people.'

It was a memorial, set up outside the shop or office where the dead man had worked, and left there, its green and red and orange light-bulbs shining gaily, for the forty days of the mourning period: a means by which the neighbours could show respect to a substantial local figure. After that, I began noticing how every available stretch of wall-space was to be plastered over with privately printed death notices for men associated with the area who had been killed in the war. Thousands of pensive faces looked out at us as we drove along, sometimes on clean new white paper, unstained as yet by dust and weather, sometimes on faded paper, sometimes on paper which had been ripped off to make room for someone new. The wording on the posters followed a formula: In the Name of God, such and such a man had been martyred in such and such a place, during such and such an offensive. He was so many years old, had followed this or that calling, and his family and friends expressed their sorrow or their pride at his loss. The poster would stay there until its place would be needed to mark the passing of another local hero.

Once we knew what to look for, signs of the war were everywhere. In front of one of the entrances to the main bazaar a mobile collection centre had been established: a large container had been set down on the pavement, open at one end, and, inside, out of the sun and the noise, a group of men sat at the receipt of custom behind a table. The walls of the container were covered inside and out with the fiercer kind of government publicity: close-ups of wounds and dead bodies, all the work of Iraqi soldiers and, at one remove, of Saddam Hussein himself; and behind him, the Americans, the British, the Israelis. The men were collecting money and goods for the soldiers at the front, and a loudspeaker broadcast encouraging music to the street in general. A sign promised that anyone who contributed would be immune from seventy types of evil. As we watched, I estimated that one passer-by in about twelve stopped to give something, and often it was the poorer people who did the giving.

There were signs too of the shortages which the high cost of the war had created. A saying was going the rounds of North Tehran, I found later, to the effect that the Islamic Republic had achieved a miracle: it had turned the most individualistic people on earth into a nation of queuers.

'Benzin,' said Ali briefly: 'petrol.' I had asked him the reason

78

why a driver had stopped his car by the side of the road, and was tying something onto a long rope. I saw then that it was an empty jerrycan, which was being added to a long line of others. At the far end of the rope a man was filling the cans one by one, hauling them in as he did so. The drivers could come back later, in time to collect their filled cans.

Outside the government meat store in Vali-e-Asr Avenue, a hundred or so women at the other end of the economic scale were waiting. For them, queuing had turned into a social activity, and they sat in line on the steps of the store in the hot sunshine, like so many black crows in their *chadors*, or else took advantage of the shade round the corner in the side street, squatting with their backs to the wall. They were waiting for their meat ration. The basic commodities – rice, meat, butter, bread – were guaranteed by the government in quantities which were just about enough for each individual in a family, at prices which were pegged artificially low. But the ration books were obtainable only from the mullahs or the *Komitehs:* it gave the governmental system an extra degree of control over the lives of ordinary people.

Anyone could buy what they wanted, in whatever quantities they could get it, on the free market; but the price was often very high, and there were constant accusations that shopkeepers manipulated the supplies to keep it that way. Such accusations are always made during periods of high inflation, and in Iran during 1986-7 inflation was estimated at more than sixty per cent. By the middle of 1987 the authorities had introduced an extensive system of price-controls, and were recruiting a corps of several thousand inspectors to police it. But governments had tried to cope with inflation by such means since at least the time of the Roman emperor Diocletian, with little success; and the threat of 'Islamic' punishments seemed insufficient to prevent a general rise in prices which owed far more to the damage done to the Iranian economy by the war, than to the greed of individual shopkeepers. Worse, farmers were beginning to withhold their produce from the markets on the grounds that the price was insufficient to be worth the cost of harvesting.

The women at the Vali-e-Asr store waited cheerfully, chattering to each other with animation, their children playing behind them on the steps or teetering dangerously on the edges of the *jub* that channelled a fitful stream down from the mountains.

'I heard of a place where they're selling butter much cheaper than anywhere else,' one woman was saying as we stood nearby. 'There's nothing that's any cheaper anywhere – it's all the same, and it's all too high,' her friend said. 'Tell me how much.' The first woman, seeing that we were listening, leaned over and whispered something in her ear. 'It's evil,' said the friend, looking at us as though challenging us to report her for what she was saying. 'They ought to do something about the prices. But of course they won't.'

There were always stories of food riots elsewhere in the country, but the tangible sense of war-weariness and the irritation caused by the shortages were certainly not strong enough in Tehran itself, or in the other cities and towns we visited, to force the régime to consider bringing the war to an end. As long as the shortages were bearable, the misery was spread around, and the authorities were prepared to stamp fiercely on any sign of opposition, people put up with their conditions. Not that there was any alternative: the atmosphere of relaxation in the streets showed that the Islamic Republic felt it was firmly in place, and its systems of control were firmly entrenched throughout Iranian society.

Our taxi was caught in another traffic jam now, near the Modarres Expressway, a gridlock that spread across all four arms of an intersection. At the centre of it, two cars had crashed into one another, leaving a small heap of orange and white plastic shards of the kind you can see at almost every crossroads in Tehran. The Islamic Republic, in trying to make people pure, has not yet turned them into good drivers. Ali made a whistling noise, and pointed with some irritation to a white four-wheel drive Nissan jeep which had drawn up alongside. The local *Komiteh* had sent its flying squad to sort out the trouble. Four tough, self-reliant men in olive-green fatigues and beards were inside, and the two at the back cradled machine-pistols of an unfamiliar make: Chinese, perhaps. They were all equipped with walkie-talkies; there was a good deal of expensive equipment riding in this patrol. The *Komiteh* man sitting behind the driver said something into his walkie-talkie and got out, throwing his gun carelessly onto the seat: he wouldn't be needing it to clear the traffic.

He sauntered across with the rolling gait I had already noticed in the mullahs – we came to think of it as the Islamic walk – and threaded his way between the cars, stopping occasionally to speak to the drivers and tell them what he wanted them to do. Then he dealt with the two cars which had collided. The dispute between the two drivers had stopped the moment the *Komiteh* arrived: these were not the kind of people you argued with. The horns had stopped blaring everywhere too, and within three

minutes the entire jam was cleared. It was an impressive performance, and the *Komiteh* man knew it. He walked slowly back
to the Nissan, ignoring the ingratiating thanks of the drivers
around him. The Nissan started up with a roar and made a sharp
U-turn, its tyres squealing as it drove off at speed.

Most successful revolutions have their *Komitehs* – their élite
volunteers whose job is to regulate the behaviour of others in the
interests of the new orthodoxy. They tend to begin in the same
way, as rallying-points for dedicated revolutionaries in the early
stages of the new dispensation, when counter-revolution is a
very real possibility. In Iran, they started as local committees (the
name was taken from the English word) and eventually spread to
ensure that every district, every suburb, every street had its
Komiteh, checking on people's conformity and loyalty, sometimes
carrying out acts of calculated brutality, and taking over many of
the functions which had formerly been performed by the police.
The *Komitehs*, it seemed to me, were feared but not necessarily
always hated; and often, as in the minor matter of clearing a
traffic jam, they came in with the necessary powers and decisive-
ness to get things done. In the early years of the Revolution there
had been an often bitter rivalry between the *Pasdaran* or Revolutionary Guards, the police, and the *Komitehs*. But it had tailed off
by the time of our visit. The Revolutionary Guards were too
involved with the war against Iraq, and the police were too weak
to challenge the authority of the *Komitehs*.

In a North Tehran police station, the local *Komiteh* had the
offices to the left of the main door: the better offices. The
uniformed police and the detectives, more in number, had to
cram together in the other half of the building. Behind the door
marked *KOMITEH* several more of the bearded, tough-looking
young men in olive-green fatigues were sitting round waiting for
something to happen, their feet on the table. They were wary
when the door opened, but not necessarily hostile; as long as
there is no spy-scare at the time, Westerners are not usually
regarded as a threat, since it is assumed that they must have
business in the country to have been allowed to enter it in the
first place. But no one found it necessary to be positively friendly.
The *Komitehs* have an image of themselves that has to be
maintained.

After Khomeini's declaration that people were to be allowed to
do what they wanted in the privacy of their own homes, as long
as it was not offensive to others, the *Komitehs* lost some of their
powers to intrude into people's lives. Nevertheless, it was they
who had ensured that women obeyed the laws on dress with

such care. Every Iranian seems to know the stories of how female *Komiteh* members used razor-blades to slash the faces of women who wore make-up in the streets; and regardless of the literal truth of the story, it is certainly not impossible to believe. The Revolution took place, in part, to reverse the process, begun in the 1930s under Reza Shah, to introduce Western clothes and Western customs for women. The intention of the revolutionary régime was to ensure that women resumed their traditional place in Iranian society; and the outward and visible sign of that is the way they dress. 'Death to unveiled women!' is a slogan that can still be seen on some walls in Tehran. We were to find some women who genuinely welcomed what they regarded as the greater protection that wearing *hejab* gave them in a male-dominated society; but Westernized, middle-class women often felt that they were singled out for unpleasant treatment. One put it this way:

'I tell you frankly, I think we are a kind of target. No one cares what men wear: they can get away with having bare arms or tight trousers, even though they aren't supposed to. But they always watch us. There's only one good thing about it – they're usually too embarrassed to touch us. It's something they can't bring themselves to do. So if we get stopped, they may push my husband around, but they leave me alone. That's really the only advantage, though.'

As we drove down the Modarres Expressway we noticed two cars which had stopped on the hard shoulder. One was a battered private car, the other an unmarked white Paykan with a book with Khomeini's face on it lying on the back seat. The couple from the first car were being questioned by two men in regulation olive-green. The woman was about twenty-five, and was wearing a bright headscarf and a cheap blue smock. The man was a good bit older: forty-five, perhaps. The two *Komiteh* men were going through every piece of identification he had on him. It was clearly going to be a long search. The woman tried to sit down on the grass verge, but a sharp word brought her nervously to her feet again.

In a quiet tree-lined residential area nearby, two young men and two girls had been stopped while they were driving motorbikes. A *Komiteh* patrol was questioning them too. Ali, our driver, skirted the group, and had to be persuaded to drive round in a circle so that we could see what happened. The persuasion had to include a promise to pay him in pounds for the whole journey.

By the time we returned, the two young men were being driven off in the *Komiteh* car; they could expect to be held for several hours, at the very least. Unusually, the girls had been allowed to go home. They did not look particularly upset at what had happened. The two motorbikes, identical BMWs, were left abandoned by the road: two expensive Western imports, driven by people who had forgotten they could not live as though they were in the West.

Elsewhere, rock-and-roll blared from a car stereo, while a *Komiteh* man searched vainly for a way to turn the volume down. A man in his mid-thirties stood looking on, a pile of ten or more audio cassettes on the ground in front of him. He had made the mistake of leaving the music on when he reached a road-block; and the penalty was that the *Komiteh* was insisting on hearing everything that was on these tapes, and would probably confiscate them when they were finished. Rock-and-roll was frowned on, but was not strictly speaking illegal, if it were for one individual only to listen to. But cassettes, as we had found at the airport some hours before, were suspect in themselves. The owner of the potentially dissident material looked on blankly. He, and the *Komiteh*, were going to be listening to a lot of music before he was freed.

In the distance I could see the distinctive T-shape of the old InterContinental Hotel, now called the Laleh, or 'tulip'. I pointed it out to Tira. It had been the headquarters of the international press corps which covered the Revolution and the hostage crisis which followed it, and had a considerable hold on the affections of anyone who was there at that time. The InterContinental was shot up, invaded, raided, searched for illicit alcohol; and yet the staff were unfailingly courteous and helpful in spite of everything. Tira had been bequeathed a bottle of gin by a correspondent who hid it in the air-conditioning duct of Room 617 during a raid by Revolutionary Guards, but it seemed unlikely that she would be able to reclaim it. When we reached the hotel I paid off Ali, who was glad to see the back of us, and I wondered how I would explain the loss of my sterling notes to the customs official at the airport, who (the notice there had warned us) would not be responsible for any difficulties I might face on leaving.

We pushed through the familiar doors into the large open lobby where so much television equipment had once been piled up. It was dark and almost empty: one of the power-cuts which affected most parts of Tehran at least twice a day for a couple of hours at a time had just begun; another effect of the war with Iraq. We sat on the high-backed chairs under the same enormous old colour photograph of a birch wood in autumn, and ordered tea and a moist slab of what Persians call 'English cake'. Apart from two Japanese businessmen and their Iranian contact, we were the only people there. Nothing much had changed since the days when I used to occupy Room 1119 here, though the ever-optimistic sign which used to promise that a garden terrace would be opening there soon had been replaced by huge square raffia-work letters which read 'Down with USA'. But another old fixture was still in place: the board that said 'Wedding arrangement is a fine art, especially when done by Hotel InterContinental Tehran'. A throne had been lost, tens of thousands had died in prisons and hundreds of thousands on the battlefield, but the sign advertising wedding arrangements had scarcely shifted by more than a foot.

I looked round to see if, by any chance, I might remember any of the staff. My eye caught that of a man at the reception desk, and there was something faintly familiar about his face. I walked over to him, and he put out his hand enthusiastically to greet me. He did not, I am sure, remember me as an individual, but for him I was a kind of identikit of all the Western journalists who had been here once. 'Is very quiet here now,' he said, unnecessarily.

After that minor success, we walked over to the taxi desk to order a car which would take us to the place where we were going to stay. A beaten-up white Paykan that we were to come to know extremely well drew up outside, and we handed the driver our luggage and got in. From the angle of the rear passenger seat there was something I seemed to remember about the iron-grey hair and the round, bullet head in front of me.

'Did you ever,' I asked experimentally, 'work for foreign television companies during the time of *Enqelab* – the Revolution?'

'Yes, sir. Working for ABC, CBC, BBC . . .'

The name Mohammed, or perhaps Mehti, floated towards the surface of my memory. I was just about to ask him, when he added:

'Sir, name of Mahmoudi, sir.'

'Name of John, Mahmoudi.'

'Yes, Mr John.' He said it as though he was not surprised. 'Now working for you again, Mr John.'

He put out his hand at a particularly dangerous point as we drove off, and took hold of mine in a dignified, ceremonious manner. It was a splendid moment.

That evening, having hired Mahmoudi for the length of our

visit, established ourselves in the place where we were to stay, and slept off some of our tiredness, we went out for a short walk. The sun was below the peaks of the Elburz mountains now, and the cloud of fumes hanging over the city lay below us like a benevolent haze. Horns blared continually outside, and trucks rasped their way up the steep Shemiran Road in unsuitable gears, but the walls of our compound kept out the worst of the noise. I found myself waiting for something, and at last it began: the amplified voice of the *muezzin*, floating out to us from the blue-domed mosque a little way down the hill: a wailing, sad, clear, comforting noise. Now, for the first time, I felt that I had really returned.

5

Power to the Mullahs

As for their churches, they be very fair, and have high
steeples, but no bells in them; but four times in the day
they have a man which goeth up into the top of the
steeple, and singeth out with a loud voice, that they
may hear him all the town over, and biddeth them
remember Mahomet's laws, which he left them . . .
Their priests go apparelled in white, and preach every
Friday, for that day is their sabbath: they pray with
great devotion, for I myself have seen them at their
prayers with such zeal, that they have fallen into a
swoon.   George Manwaring,
*'A True Discourse Of Sir Anthony Sherley's Travel
Into Persia'*, c.1601

HALF A MILE from the Niavaran Palace, where the Shah once
lived in splendour, lies the village of Jamaran. For the inhabitants
of North Tehran, Jamaran has never had a good name: literally,
since it means 'the abode of snakes'. A roadblock manned by
Revolutionary Guards prevents you from turning left onto the
Jamaran Road as you drive along the Hojat-ol-Eslam Doctor
Bahonar Highway (formerly the Niavaran Road). The reason is
not snakes, but security: virtually the entire village of Jamaran
has been turned into a headquarters for the Imam Khomeini.

Farther along the road, set into the hillside, is an anti-aircraft
battery which has seen action several times. The Iraqi air force
has made several determined but unsuccessful attempts to bomb
Jamaran, and a number of supposed plots have been uncovered
to capture or assassinate Khomeini. None of them, however,
seems to have gone farther than the planning stage, though my
old acquaintance from Neauphle-le-Château, Khomeini's spokesman and later foreign minister, Sadeq Qotbzadeh, was

executed for his alleged involvement in one of them. A passing Western visitor, if he arrives without an invitation and an official escort, will be told politely that he cannot turn into the Jamaran Road, and his bullet-headed driver will laugh sympathetically as their white Paykan continues along the Bahonar Highway.

Almost every day small groups of people are, however, allowed past the road-block and up to the group of houses where the Imam lives. The layout is curiously reminiscent of the Alawi Girls' School which formed his headquarters during the Revolution: the surrounding buildings have been subsumed into the complex, and the area where Khomeini and his family live and pray lies in the very centre of it, protected not just by the large contingent of Revolutionary Guards but also by an expensive electronic security system, with cameras set on the angles of the buildings and corridors and alarm-bells high on the walls. Within the living-quarters Khomeini and his wife Batoul share a few simple rooms, unadorned with pictures and empty of furniture except for cushions on the thick carpets. Batoul, who is twenty-three years younger than her husband (she was born in 1925, the daughter of an ayatollah), prepares each of his meals with her own hands: small portions of vegetarian dishes, together with a little milk and yoghurt. She ministers also to his heart condition, which has troubled him since his late fifties, although his personal physician lives in the complex. Batoul was herself injured in July 1987 when she led the women's section of Iranian pilgrims to the Grand Mosque in Mecca. Shortly before the Saudi Arabian police opened fire on the Iranian group, and several hundred people were killed either by bullets or in the stampede which followed, Batoul Khomeini was struck on the forehead by a stone thrown from an overpass across the road. A group of Saudis had gathered on the overpass, and were angered by the anti-Saudi chanting from the Iranians below.

Visitors to Jamaran are ushered into a bare, open yard, at the very heart of the complex. Some of the windows which look out onto the yard are those of Khomeini's living-quarters. On a fixed platform at the end of the yard is a large outside broadcast camera of the national television: the Islamic Republic of Iran Broadcasting Authority, IRIB. Another camera was installed at the rear of the yard. Almost every audience with the Imam is televised and shown at length on the evening news. On this particular day the favoured group was military, from the regular army, and about a hundred senior officers accompanied by their sons, some of them mere children, settled themselves down on the ground to wait for the Imam to appear. They had to wait about half-an-hour before the french windows of the ugly bungalow slid open, and a small group of clerics processed slowly out, followed by Khomeini himself.

His appearance was a considerable shock to me. Somehow the icon had seemed unchanging, because it had been reproduced so many millions of times around the globe and had become so familiar, and because he had always exuded a granite-like determination which it seemed could not be deflected by anything: not even the passage of time itself. But the figure which presented itself to us now was that of a very old and frail man. The black turban, denoting his status as a descendant of the Prophet, had been replaced by a black skull-cap. He was shrunken and bent, in a way that would have been unimaginable when I had seen him last, at his press conference in the Alawi School in Tehran. His beard and moustache had taken on a soft whiteness, and the angry, disapproving blackness had gone from the fierce eyebrows. He was now faint-voiced, and gentler and more vulnerable than anyone could have thought.

And yet the voice had not lost effectiveness, only volume. His words were still clearly enunciated, and he spoke without notes, never raising his eyes from the microphone in front of him. He was teaching his audience a history lesson about the system they were fighting to protect, and to extend to other countries:

'This Revolution is completely different from any other that has taken place in the world. What usually happens after a Revolution is that people take power from one oppressive régime and give it to another régime, which becomes oppressive in its turn. The French Revolution, the Russian Revolution – you should study them. Nothing happened as a result of them. Before and after, they were the same; they didn't do anything for the nation. In Iran, the greatest change imaginable took place – a change in the attitude of the people.'

He paused for breath, and perhaps for effect as well; and the crowd, seizing their cue, chanted obediently, 'O God, keep Khomeini until the Coming of the Messiah.' He lectured them further, and although his words were allusive and gnomic, he seemed to be rebuking them for the rivalry they had shown towards the Revolutionary Guards, who had been doing most of the really successful fighting in the war with Iraq, and had obtained a far larger share of the credit than the regular army; not least because the régime had never entirely trusted the army.

Nowadays his light grey robes made the Imam seem more like

a wraith than the personification of revenge, as he had once seemed to me, seven years before: on this occasion he was so fragile he looked almost transparent, and he talked more and more about death and the afterlife:

'Everything in this world lasts for a short time only. All that remains is the soul. I am old now, too old. I am already a dead man. You have to take over now, and I know that I have not done enough for you.'

People in his audience were crying unaffectedly and saying, 'No, no.' But soon they broke into another chant:

'You are our soul, you are the breaker of idols, you can do anything. We are ready to give you our blood, for as long as it runs in our veins. Khomeini is our leader.'

One of his acolytes took his hand, reverently, and placed it like some inanimate, holy relic on the rail that separated him from them; and the military leaders, some still with tears of emotion running down their faces, lined up to kiss the shrunken, veined, tendonous object that was presented to them. He seemed scarcely aware of it, as if feeling that his physical hand had nothing to do with either him or them; and he was sunk in his own thoughts, a frail figure who had smashed images and seemed now to be fading away, very slowly, in the presence of people who worshipped him. And over all there hung the memory of his voice, no less compelling than it always had been, telling them that his Revolution had changed the nature of things in Iran, but that now they must prepare themselves to continue without him.

Almost all revolutions, if they last long enough, go through stages of idealism and cruelty, before they reach stability. The Iranian Revolution is striving to reach that level, and its supporters maintained it has already achieved it; but the cruelties continue. There are several thousand political prisoners, from teenagers to people over the age of seventy. Those in prison include members and supporters of the Democratic Party of Kurdistan of Iran, *Komeleh*, the People's *Feda'i*, the People's *Mojaheddin*, *Rah-e Kargar*, the Communist *Tudeh* Party, the Union of Communists, and members of various Monarchist groups, as well as members of the Bahá'í faith.

After the bloodletting of the early 1980s, Iran was mostly

quiescent by the time of my return. Government officials had a noticeable air of self-confidence which, in my experience of countries under siege and with closed political systems, is rare. In such countries foreign journalists tend to be carefully controlled, and are not allowed to move about with any great freedom. In Iran, by contrast, Tira and I were able to move around the country as we chose – though we had to sign an undertaking not to go to the various war-fronts unaccompanied. We went everywhere alone, except for the one occasion when we ourselves asked for someone from the Ministry of Islamic Guidance to go with us to Qom to arrange an interview with a senior cleric. For the rest of the time we did not even tell the Ministry where we were going. We were never once stopped by the police or the *Komitehs*, and we were never, as far as I could tell, followed. It is, of course, perfectly possible that our movements were monitored through our driver, Mahmoudi, though I doubt it. It was always our decision to ask him to drive us somewhere. If we had so decided, we could have flown everywhere or gone by bus, and nobody would have been the wiser. It amused me, when I returned, to receive unsigned or unaddressed letters from angry Iranian exiles containing such phrases as 'I don't know what you were allowed to see, but . . .' or 'You were only shown the places the régime wanted to take you to...' Compared with the wide variety of post-revolutionary countries I have visited, from Angola, Mozambique and Libya to Cuba, Nicaragua and the states of the Soviet bloc, the freedom of movement we were allowed was unusual.

This impression was reinforced by Western diplomats and Iranians alike. There had been, they agreed, a greater sense of relaxation about most things from 1983 and 1984 on. There were, it is true, continual rumours in Tehran about demonstrations and riots in other parts of the country, though when we went to Isfahan – one of the cities specifically named in the rumours – we found from speaking to a range of people, critics of the government as well as supporters of it, that no riots had recently occurred there.

If the Revolution and its bloody aftermath had faded a little in people's minds, so had the fervour which the supporters of the Revolution felt naturally, and everybody else assumed as a matter of self-protection. There were small signs that a degree of corruption had returned to Iranian life: not every Revolutionary Guard was immune, people said, to the offer of money, and if you were a foreign businessman with goods to sell there was usually a government official and sometimes a mullah who would, for a consideration, put you in touch with the right people. It was not as noticeable as it had been before the Revolution, but the atmosphere was there. It was rarer to find people praying five times a day now, and since religion was no longer the badge of an embattled opposition to the existing power, as it had been under the Shah, it had lost some of its hold on the minds of the less committed. Persians had rarely been very intense about religion before the Revolution, and they seemed to be moving back to their old ways.

The air of strained intensity about the war was less noticeable as well. Middle-class people rarely turned out now for rallies supporting the war effort, and even the people who did – mostly working-class people and peasants, who provided the great bulk of the volunteers for the front – took a little time at one such rally, in the south of Tehran, to get into the mood. They chanted the responses, but a Western observer who had been at similar rallies a year before told me there was little of the fire that had character-ized them then. Until, that is, a wild and rather gallant figure in Revolutionary Guard uniform appeared on a motorbike at the end of the field to the accompaniment of great applause. Now, at last, the reason for the presence of seven Honda vans and cars, parked end to end, became obvious.

Four men ran on carrying a large American flag made of paper and set it up at the other end of the line of vehicles, and then, to even greater applause and shouting, the Iranian Evel Knievel revved his motorbike up to a violent roar, and set off up a long wooden ramp. He launched himself off it at about ninety miles an hour, and flew over the Hondas, his front wheel high in the air, while everyone went dramatically silent. He came to earth on the far side with a crash which must have come close to bursting his rear tyre, and drove heroically through the Stars and Stripes, leaving a man-sized rip in it. The flag was then ceremonially burned, and the rider modestly accepted the plaudits of the delighted crowd. That, at least, had cheered them up, and the chanting of slogans about the war and the inevitable '*Marg bar Amrika!*', 'Death to America!' took on a more enthusiastic tone. It was not that they did not agree with the slogans: they, or their sons, were ready to give their lives for them in astonishing numbers; it was just that it took a little more nowadays to get them interested and enthusiastic.

Even the government's strongest supporters were more restrained than they had been. In the early eighties, when huge sacrifices were being made in the war and senior government figures were dying regularly in the attacks of the Mojaheddin, a special watch was manufactured – in Switzerland, inevitably – for sale in Iran: its second hand was painted scarlet, to denote the blood that had been and was being shed, and every thirty seconds part of the watch-face opened to reveal a portrait of the Imam. By the time I returned to Iran it was impossible to find any of these extraordinary objects for sale, and government officials, when asked about them, showed signs of a certain embarrassment. Extreme fervour was no longer in fashion.

In the Majlis, the Iranian parliament, a debate was taking place about agriculture. It was a heated affair, as many Majlis debates often were. Somewhere at the back sat a cleric in a white turban: a man with heavy-rimmed glasses and a knowing smirk on his face. He seemed interested in what was being said, and followed the action carefully, but said nothing himself. Indeed, he rarely spoke now, and the empty places around him might well have indicated that his colleagues in the Majlis were not particularly keen to be associated with him. Hojat-ol-Eslam Sadeq Khalkhali once personified the farthest extremes of fervour. The Western media incorrectly promoted him to the rank of Ayatollah and nicknamed him 'Judge Blood' for the leading rôle he took in ordering the executions of hundreds of victims of the Revolution. A former *talabeh* or student of Ayatollah Khomeini, Khalkhali served his apprenticeship as organizer of often violent protests against the Shah in the early sixties, and of secret groups after Khomeini was exiled.

His loyalty to Khomeini during the years in Iraq stood him in good stead when the Ayatollah returned, and his ruthlessness was placed at the disposal of the Revolution in the first days after the victory in the streets. General Rahimi, whose 'interrogation' I had taken part in on the night of the Revolution itself, was a difficult prisoner to deal with, and so were four other military leaders, including General Nasiri, the former head of SAVAK. For all the completeness of the Revolution's success, there were considerable fears that something might be done, by the Americans or someone else, to free the generals. Rahimi himself spoke of the possibility of such an attempt. At that stage the Ayatollah's followers had usually been punctilious in their treatment of prisoners; it was more often the far left-wing groups which had murdered the people they captured. But Khomeini seems to have wanted Rahimi and the others out of the way, and Khalkhali volunteered to conduct a rapid trial, after which they could be shot.

It was the start of a career which led Khalkhali to order several hundred executions in all, from that of Amir-Abbas Hoveyda, a former prime minister under the Shah, to a one-time senator aged 102 who had made a speech attacking Khomeini sixteen years before, to wounded Kurdish prisoners, shot as they lay on their stretchers, and to a sixteen-year-old boy whose pleas of innocence were dismissed on the grounds that if he were genuinely innocent he would go to Paradise anyway. When he was in charge of Qasr prison in Tehran he used to stage group executions late at night. On one night only eleven out of twelve prisoners whom he had listed for execution could be found, and he told his guards to go and bring him someone else – anyone – in order to make up the required number.

It was Khalkhali who said, 'Human rights mean that unsuitable individuals should be liquidated so that others can live free,' and who, in full view of the television cameras, toyed with the charred corpse of an American serviceman who had died in President Carter's bungled attempt to rescue the American hostages in 1980. There were strong suggestions that Khalkhali was mentally unbalanced; but his fall from grace came not from his eagerness to sentence people to death on flimsy evidence, but from his inability, as the man in charge of the narcotics squad, to account for the sum of $14 million which had been confiscated from the people he had arrested.

Unlike Fouquier-Tinville, the Judge Blood of the French Revolution, Khalkhali has yet to suffer the kind of summary justice he handed out to others; in his case, as in others, the Iranian Revolution has not devoured those of its children who most deserved it. He has managed to keep his seat in the Majlis; but he sits there, shunned by the other members, never making a speech, and always paying great attention to those who do. He has the hurt yet eager look on his face of someone who feels unjustly left out of things; injustice being something he is more used to inflicting than to experiencing.

The debate on agriculture is heating up. A mullah in a white turban and a black gown is making a point about the poor quality of last year's harvest, and he is interrupted furiously by a man in the dull green anorak which is the uniform of the Revolutionary Guards and others. He seems to regard what the mullah has said as an insult to himself and his constituency. Then he sinks into his straight-backed brown leather chair, still muttering angrily to himself. The Majlis is much more like a Western parliament than I had imagined. With its seven or eight semi-circular rows of seats, all turned towards the dais where the Speaker sits, it could be the Bundestag or the Danish Parliament – except that a majority of the members are wearing clerical garb. As the members interrupt and argue with the person who has the floor, and wait impatiently until he (or, just possibly, she: there are four women among the 270 members) has finished, they demonstrate that what is said in debate is politically important.

The Iranian Parliament's proceedings are broadcast live on television (another sign of self-confidence in itself, given the unpredictable and sometimes fiery nature of the speeches), and the debates are followed in the press with considerable interest. Members frequently disagree violently with government policy, gripping their microphones like rock singers and gesturing angrily at whichever minister is trying to make a speech. The public gallery, which runs the full semi-circumference of the hemicycle, is usually packed with people. But the degree of open debate leads inevitably to factionalism; and in June 1987 the hostility between the various groups reached the point where the Imam Khomeini decided to take action. Listeners to Iran Radio heard his faint voice tell them:

'You should think what will happen if at this time the Majlis is blemished. Try to ensure that the Majlis is not blemished. Try to solve agreements in the way that Islam prescribes.'

The solution he prescribed was to close down the Islamic Republic Party, at least temporarily; and although the move seemed to have no effect on the ferocity of debate in the Majlis, a spokesman for the Party obediently agreed that discord and factionalism had damaged the nation's unity.

In the West, the immediate assumption was that the battle to succeed the Imam Khomeini had been joined in earnest. There were certainly signs of some complex political manoeuvring, but the purpose of that manoeuvring was little understood in the West. When I returned to Iran in the summer of 1987, I had an adventitious meeting with a senior figure in the governmental structure which resulted in a seven-hour conversation about the nature of religion and politics under the Islamic Republic. Over dinner in his flat he made the point that disagreements between political leaders were invariably presented by Western observers as symptomatic of a fundamental power struggle if they took place in countries like Iran, whereas if similar disagreements occurred in the West they were simply seen as the normal cut and thrust of politics. He conceded that there was constant argument, which often became heated, over the policies which

94

the leadership of the Islamic Republic should follow; but he claimed that it was economic issues – he seemed to be referring particularly to the strict controls on prices which were introduced during 1987 – which brought about the fiercest disagreements. And he maintained that however strong the disagreements might be, they never brought into question the foundations of the Islamic state.

Under the constitution of the Islamic Republic the system is relatively unstructured: the political hierarchy is determined by the personal significance and prestige of individual figures, rather than by the posts they occupy. This is the point at which political rivalries enter the equation. The leading figures compete, not for positions and titles, but for influence. Everything is available for use as ammunition in this battle, from the conduct of the war with Iraq and the question of a cease-fire, to the tentative links with the Americans, and government policy on food and oil depletion.

Shortly before noon one Friday in May 1987 the doors of one particular mosque in the centre of Tehran opened and a crowd of young mullahs and their supporters burst out and marched along the street chanting 'We must call on the Imam to forgive Saddam.' For Khomeini to 'forgive' Saddam Hussein, the Iraqi leader, would have meant an end to the Gulf War; in other words one of the factions in the complex political interplay was attempting to turn itself into the peace party. Nothing more was heard of the demonstration, and the attempt faded, at least for the time being. But the war had been shown to be a political issue, even though it might be dangerous to call openly for it to end. Clearly, some senior religious figure had decided that there was momentary advantage to be gained from opposing the continuation of the war. His identity was never revealed; but it was an interesting example of the way politics in Iran – or the competition for influence, as it is better understood – can operate.

In the Speaker's chair in the Majlis, presiding over the noise and emotion, is a smiling figure in a brown robe, and a turban which is pushed back slightly raffishly to reveal his hair. He sits in his chair on the dais as alert as a boxer, his eyes darting round continually to see who is about to interrupt and who wants to speak next. Sometimes, when tempers are high, he makes some witty remark, bringing the members to order more by cajoling and manipulating them than by beating his gavel or relying on the rule-book. Hojat-ol-Eslam Ali Akbar Hashemi-Rafsanjani has, indeed, risen to his present position entirely as a result of his forceful personality.

A round-faced, pudgy figure in his early fifties (he was born in 1934), almost beardless and with a sparse moustache that never seems to flourish on the unpromising field of his upper lip, Rafsanjani, like Khalkhali, was a pupil of Khomeini, and was imprisoned under the Shah. He took an active but not particularly prominent part in setting up the revolutionary *Komitehs* which established Khomeini's dominance in Iran in 1978 even before the Shah left. He was one of the founders of the Islamic Republican Party, and became deputy minister of the Interior. But it was in the openness of debate in the Majlis that he emerged from the junior ranks of government and made himself the foremost power in Iran after the Imam himself. In July 1980, his eloquence and his ability to chivvy the other members along were rewarded when he was elected Speaker. After that, with the proceedings of the Majlis being broadcast regularly on television and reprinted in the newspapers, Rafsanjani's rise was assured. His alliance with the top leadership of the Revolutionary Guards made him the spokesman of the most effective military force in the country.

In private, as in public, he is a witty man, perpetually smiling, though not necessarily from friendship: and he can display a sudden irritation which is unnerving, even if it seems never to be directed against the person he is talking to. But although he resorts a good deal to humour, it is not the humour of flippancy. Instead, it gets its force from a kind of grimness: 'I am', he appears to be saying, 'the only person who sees the full absurdity of things, and is prepared to speak out about it.' He can be overconfident about his ability to handle himself in interviews with foreigners; time and again his desire to make a joke about something has led him too far, and he has had either to deny his words or else explain them away. But his position is so strong, and his support so great, that this is rarely difficult.

Rafsanjani has been skilful in using the structures of the Islamic Republic to establish his position further. He is the deputy chairman of the Council of Experts, which has the task of overseeing the succession when the Imam Khomeini dies. He is also Khomeini's representative on the Supreme Defence Council, which controls the policy and conduct of the war. He has the reputation, within the Iranian political hierarchy, of being a man who does not make enemies if he can avoid it, preferring to rely on his positional skills rather than to force confrontations with his political rivals. A personal friend of Rafsanjani's says he often speaks about devoting himself to his library and forgetting about the political life altogether; but that is probably another of his methods of disarming hostility. Essentially Rafsanjani is a pragmatist who knows the value of compromise, rather than an ideologue.

It has been a natural assumption in the West that because Rafsanjani is an intelligent and ambitious man, he must be a rival for supreme power in Iran once Khomeini dies. And when Ayatollah Hosayn Ali Montazeri was chosen by the religious Council of Guardians to succeed Khomeini, this was regarded by most Western observers as a temporary political victory for Montazeri, which would later expose him to powerful counter-attacks by his rivals. But the post of *Wali Faqih,* Religious Leader, was one to which only a senior ayatollah could be appointed; it was not open to all comers. To assume that someone like Hojat-ol-Eslam Rafsanjani, who does not even possess the rank of ayatollah, is a contender with Montazeri for the post of Khomeini's successor, is a little like suspecting the British prime minister of entertaining hopes of becoming the reigning monarch: it is a constitutional impossibility. Furthermore, Khomeini's place as leader of the Revolution and the country is a personal one; it is not something which can be passed on to a successor.

In fact there are indications that Montazeri and Rafsanjani have co-operated together. They both studied under Khomeini, and sharing the same teacher is usually regarded as a powerful bond among mullahs in Iran. They also appear to share many of the same basic opinions about the functions and direction of the state in Iran. Montazeri, who is nine years older than Rafsanjani, has been considerably more outspoken in these views. He is a strong supporter of the concept of free enterprise, which has brought him the allegiance of the bazaar merchants. His photograph appears more frequently than that of anyone else except Khomeini himself in the shops and stalls of the bazaars in Tehran and Isfahan. He has criticized some of the excesses committed by the courts, and has called for a halt to the persecution of opponents of the régime, as well as for permission for exiles to return home. He is also said to have condemned Iran's support for terrorism in other countries.

He is not, however, highly regarded for his intellectual powers. According to one joke going the rounds in Tehran, Iraq's terms for ending the war are two-fold: Rafsanjani has to grow a beard, and Montazeri has to learn the name of the Secretary-General of the United Nations. Montazeri's nickname is 'Gorbechev', '*gorbe*' being the Farsi for 'cat'; his jovial round face is felt to have a feline look to it. After Khomeini himself, Montazeri receives the most attention each night from the official television news broadcasts. His doings for the day are reported in considerable detail, following whatever the Imam himself may have done or said.

There are various other competitors for political influence. The President, Hojat-ol-Eslam Ali Khamene'i, who was born in 1940 and has won two terms in office by overwhelming majorities (though against little-known opponents) does not have an important power-base, and has been reduced to a mostly ceremonial rôle, although he is the chairman of the Supreme Defence Council. The prime minister, Mir Hosayn Mussavi (born in 1944) is a technocrat with a strong belief in the need for strict state control of the economy. It was he who advocated the controls, which were possibly too rigid to be effective, over retail prices; it seems likely that he will receive the blame in the public mind if those controls fail. Neither he nor President Khamene'i are in any way charismatic figures, and have no obvious public following.

But in a society like Iran, public following is not the only criterion of political power. Ayatollah Mohammed Mohammedi-Reyshahri is a studious-looking man with a reputation for courteous and undramatic public speaking. He is head of *Vezarat-e Ettelaat va Amniyat-e Kishvar:* the Ministry of Intelligence and Internal Security. It is a large ministry, which operates from a drab modern office block in the centre of Tehran, and has taken over all the functions of the Shah's SAVAK, and many of those belonging to SAVAMA, the eventually discredited organization set up by Khomeini in 1979 to take SAVAK's place. The Ministry of Intelligence is responsible for dealing with terrorism inside Iran, and with the surveillance of dissidents and exile groups abroad. It maintains strong links with fundamentalist Muslim groups in Lebanon, the Gulf States, Egypt, Tunisia and further afield, and it has a strong interest in the acquisition of weapons for the war against Iraq. Ayatollah Reyshahri is the man responsible for ensuring the survival of the Islamic Republic.

In one sense, the rôle is not a new one for him. He became chief judge of the military revolutionary tribunal in 1979 – an important job in the new régime, since it carried with it the task of purging the armed forces of officers whose loyalty was dubious. In comparison with men like Khalkhali he distinguished himself by sticking to the facts in the cases he tried, and he never screamed insults at the prisoners before him. Nevertheless he dealt severely and summarily with two plots within the armed forces in 1980, 'Operation Overthrow' and 'Operation Red Alert', sentencing more than a hundred officers to death, sometimes on evidence that was dubious or flimsy.

He rose to the topmost levels of the hierarchy in 1984, as a result of his effective destruction of the Tudeh or Communist Party. Two years earlier, in June 1982, Vladimir Andreyevich Kuzichkin, a KGB officer who had worked in the Soviet embassy in Tehran, defected to Britain. His job had been to maintain contact with the Tudeh Party, and he brought with him to London a list of 400 Soviet agents in Iran, most of them covertly or openly members of the Tudeh Party. After a good deal of discussion at Cabinet level the British government instructed the Secret Intelligence Service, MI6, to hand over the list to the Iranian authorities in October 1982.

The following April, Nur al-Din Kianouri, the general secretary of the Tudeh Party, appeared on Iranian television to make an abject confession of guilt. Four days later, on 4 May, Reyshahri dissolved the Party and arrested nearly 1,500 of its members. In December 1983 Reyshahri presided over the trial of 87 of the Party's military organization, drawing heavily on the information received from Britain but without revealing its provenance. It was a show-trial, whose purpose was to gain maximum publicuty for the claim that the Soviet Union had been meddling in Iranian affairs, with a view to establishing a régime which would be favourable to Moscow. Reyshahri did not, however, play the part of a Vyshinsky; his conduct in court was restrained and capable, and the foreign diplomats who were allowed to attend the court found him impressive.

Reyshahri's political rise began almost as soon as the trial closed. His experience in security matters was now considerable: he had helped to safeguard the Islamic Republic from the threat of a military coup, and he had helped to redirect the political and diplomatic alignment of Iran away from the Soviet Union. As a result he was appointed to head the Security Ministry. He had become a figure of considerable political importance; and he was soon to play an important, though not always clear, part in the political scandal which erupted as a result of the secret links between the United States and Iran in 1986 – Irangate.

For several nights running, in September 1986, students from the Sepahsalar Religious College in Tehran posted leaflets on the walls near the college, accusing factions within the government of opening secret negotiations with the Americans, and compromising on the war against Iraq. Reyshahri's Intelligence Ministry investigated the leak, and traced it to supporters of Mehdi Hashemi, the director of the Global Islamic Movement whose headquarters was in Qom. Hashemi's position was a powerful one: his brother was married to a daughter of Ayatollah Montazeri, and ran the ayatollah's private office in Qom. The Global Islamic Movement was a liaison organization which controlled many, though not all, of the relations between the Islamic Republic and its sympathizers throughout the Middle East and beyond. It may have been involved with terrorist groups and hostage-takers as well, though this is less clear. Hashemi was a mullah, and a radical supporter of the Islamic Revolution, who may well have been scandalized at the notion of any relationship with the United States, even to obtain weapons. More leaflets were handed out in the streets of Tehran on 15 and 16 October, in spite of the warning from the Ministry of Intelligence, but they went largely unnoticed. Several days later the full story of the visit by Robert McFarlane and Colonel Oliver North to Tehran (see below, Chapter 8) was published in the Lebanese magazine *Ash Shiraa*, which was edited by Hassan Sabra. Sabra's contacts with Hezbollah, the fundamentalist Shi'ite movement in Lebanon which is an off-shoot of the main Hezbollah organization in Iran, were close; and Hashemi, through the Global Islamic Movement, was responsible for liaison with the Lebanese Hezbollah. He authorized the leaking of the story to Hassan Sabra, knowing that it would be picked up by the Western news agencies operating in Beirut.

When, in March 1987, he appeared on television to confess his crimes – a familiar method of Reyshahri's in dealing with political subversion – Hashemi said he had criticized the government by means of 'unfounded disclosures under various headings such as "The Vigilant *Ulema*"' (*ulema* means the clergy as a body). 'These disclosures,' Hashemi continued, 'ultimately created discord among public officials, and made people sceptical about the government.' Ayatollah Montazeri, greatly embarrassed, issued a statement denying that Hashemi had used his private office in Qom to further his campaign (though Hashemi confessed publicly that he had) and Montazeri's students were encouraged to sign a statement condemning Hashemi. Several leading figures declared their support for Montazeri, and the Imam Khomeini himself allowed it to be known that he still had full confidence in him. That ended the speculation that his position as Khomeini's successor was in doubt.

Hashemi himself stood trial in August 1987, the first mullah to do so since the Revolution, and evidence was produced to show that a large number of murderous gadgets, from booby-trapped pens, shoes and remote-controlled model airplanes to bottles of cyanide, had been discovered in his apartment. He confessed to having carried out murders, and to having worked for SAVAK during the Shah's time. Reyshahri's Intelligence Ministry appeared to have done its work well: Hashemi's opposition to the contacts with the United States had been successfully associated with treason, murder and thought-crime.

The immediate assumption was made in the West that the whole affair had been arranged by Rafsanjani, in order to damage Montazeri's chances of taking over on Khomeini's death. To add verisimilitude to this, Montazeri was described in various Western newspapers as a hardliner, deeply opposed to the United States. Montazeri's opinions about the United States have shown no obvious deviation from the official line, but it is difficult to think that they can be particularly extreme, given that he has criticized the Revolutionary Guards in public for over-reaching their authority, and has warned against imposing Islamic codes of behaviour too fiercely. There was clearly a strong element of political power-play in the Hashemi case, but it does not appear to have been between the leading figures of the régime; rather, it looks like the reaction of the establishment against its radical critics lower down the scale. The McFarlane-North visit was a very considerable embarrassment to Rafsanjani and other leaders, and they appear to have acted decisively to deal with anyone who tried to make capital out of it.

As a foot-note to the affair, Hassan Sabra, the editor of the magazine which published the original story of the visit, was driving with his eight-year-old daughter through the streets of Beirut in September 1987 when two gunmen drew up beside his white Mercedes and fired into it. Both he and his daughter were wounded. It had become known that Sabra was planning to publish the memoirs of Mehdi Hashemi – memoirs which, it seemed, would contradict the account of unmitigated political evil which Hashemi himself gave on television and at his trial. A few days before the shooting, Sabra had been visited by two emissaries from Tehran, one of them a Revolutionary Guard. They warned him not to publish Hashemi's memoirs; if he did, he was told, he would pay dearly for it.

With the destruction of the more liberal, Western-oriented politicians like Bani-Sadr, Bazargan and Qotbzadeh in the early years of the Islamic Republic, the fundamentalists came to power. For them, links with the West are dangerous and potentially damaging. None of the religious leaders have any experience of the non-Islamic world. Of the senior clerics who came to power in 1979 only one, Ayatollah Mohammad Beheshti, had spent time abroad (mostly in the German Democratic Republic) and had learned German and some English. His more open ways and greater understanding of the world outside Iran's borders might have made him a useful successor to Khomeini, but he was assassinated by the Mojaheddin in 1981. For the most part, since the study of the Koran was assumed to contain everything necessary for human life, no great attention was paid by those who ran the government and the Islamic Republican Party to the detail of the matters over which they presided.

The civil service was different. A large majority of the men and women who had been in senior positions in the Shah's administration had left the country after the Revolution. Many of those who stayed were imprisoned, and some were executed. The upper echelons of every ministry in Tehran were almost entirely empty when the revolutionaries formed their government. But men were available to fill the places. The universities of Europe and the United States were full of Iranian students in the last years of the Shah: many of them had taken refuge there in order to escape persecution at home. It was people like these who flocked to Neauphle-le-Château to link up with Khomeini's revolution, and who flew back to Iran to take part in it, or to join in the business of reconstruction when the Revolution was over. They were young, energetic and well-educated; and they quickly filled the upper ranks of the civil service.

A great many of them had been influenced by the writings of Dr Ali Shariati, who had in some ways trodden much the same path as they had a decade before. From 1960 to 1965 he had studied at the University of Paris and obtained his doctorate there, and had then returned to Iran. Already there was a good deal of unease among the clergy about the Shah's determination to westernize Iran, and when Shariati began lecturing on politics and religion he quickly made an important reputation for himself. Soon, cassettes of his lectures were being passed around among those younger generation who had an education and a social conscience. He appealed to many of them in a way that another teacher and philosopher, Al-e Ahmad, older and more insular than Shariati, did not. Al-e Ahmad greatly influenced some groups of far left-wing students, and his writings had a pervasive effect on most aspects of opposition to the Shah; but it was Shariati who fuelled their resentment of Iran's dependence on, and cultural subservience to, the West. He enunciated the sense of alienation which so many better-off, young, Western-educated Iranians instinctively felt. He pointed up the contrast between what they had been taught abroad and what they knew to be happening at home:

> Since World War II, many intellectuals in the Third World, whether religious or non-religious, have stressed that their societies must return to their roots and rediscover their history, their culture, and their popular language . . . Some of you may conclude that we Iranians must return to our racial roots. I categorically reject this conclusion. I oppose racism, fascism and reactionary returns. Moreover, Islamic civilization has worked like scissors and has cut us off completely from our pre-Islamic past . . . Consequently, for us a return to our roots means not a rediscovery of pre-Islamic Iran, but a return to our Islamic, and specifically our Shi'a, roots.

The Shah had harked back to a pre-Islamic Persia, to the period of the Achaemenians, as a way of giving Iranians a sense of their national identity; that it was a period of imperial greatness with an all-powerful Emperor was not, of course, a coincidence. But for young men and women who instinctively rejected all this as shabby and corrupt, Shariati touched their innermost feelings. He died at the age of 44 at Southampton, in England, having felt obliged to leave Iran. It was alleged that he had been murdered by SAVAK, but this was never established.

Under his influence the intellectual resistance to the Shah drew closer to the religious resistance; together, the two strands brought about the Revolution. The generation that was attracted by Shariati has provided the majority of government ministries in Iran with their senior civil servants: men whose loyalties are very strongly with the ayatollahs who run the government, but who come from a much wider and better educated background than any ayatollah.

I was sitting in the office of just such a man, listening as he told me about the nature and the essential goodness of the Islamic Revolution. It was a spartan room: a desk, two chairs, a sofa, a picture of the Imam, and the symbols of his education and awareness: several piles of books, a globe, a map of the world, and a powerful shortwave radio on which he could listen to foreign broadcasts. He was very much aware of the world outside. Honesty shone from his horn-rimmed spectacles; you could feel it in his very gestures, the way he ran his stubby fingers through his hair, and slapped the palm of one hand noisily with the back of the other to make a point. He insisted that it was perfectly safe to say the things he did, and he presumably knew where the boundaries of free speech lay in Iran. But it is one thing to say things in words that are carefully chosen, and another to have those words written down and printed in a context which might prove embarrassing. I would rather annoy my reader by leaving the man anonymous, than feel I had done something to damage him. Good men in government are rare enough, without endangering the species further.

And he was good. He was not corrupt, he lived his life according to the rules of the Koran, and he was a strong advocate of letting other people live their lives as they chose. He reminded me of a Mormon: decent, purposeful, clean-living, and inclined to back one into a corner for long periods of time in order to describe the attractions of his faith. For a man like this civil servant to be in charge of things in Iran is akin to the Church of the Latter-Day Saints staging a revolution in the United States.

He began by giving me his view of why the Shah fell:

'You have only to read the books by the American ambassador here, Sullivan, or your British ambassador, Parsons, to see how the Shah was under the control of foreign powers. His government was imposed on us. He himself was imposed on us, when the British overthrew his father in 1943. Everybody in the country knew that when he was in power Iran was simply based on foreign imperialism. It was rooted in the system.

'And then the religious leaders, the Imam himself, and Motahari and Beheshti and the others, started telling people they could solve their problems not through Western systems, or Marxism, but through Islam. And when people tried it, they found it was a gate that led them to freedom and independence.'

But what, I asked, did he say to the argument put forward by Sir Anthony Parsons, the former British ambassador whose book he himself had quoted, that the Shah had staged the real revolution by introducing land reform and bringing Iran into the twentieth century, and that Khomeini's had been a counter-revolution? He laughed, glad to be presented with an argument which was worth opposing. I felt as if I had just questioned the foundation of the state of Utah:

'What the Shah tried to introduce here wasn't a revolution:

104

whoever heard of a king starting a revolution? All it was, was a way of sustaining the interests of Britain and the United States here. In 1962 the Shah went to America for forty-two days, and came back with instructions to put American policy into operation here. They told him what to do. He implemented land reform, certainly – and he put one of the biggest feuda-lists in the country in charge of it. What sort of land reform is that? He took some of the best land in the country, in Khuzestan, and forced the peasants off it, in order to grow – what do you think? Asparagus! Nobody in Iran had ever seen asparagus before. It wasn't for us, it was for sale to the Americans. If Mr Parsons thinks that is a revolution, I don't.'

I asked him to tell me about his own past, and realized that his reluctance sprang from modesty: he was describing the ideal background for a successful political career in Iran, and he was worried that I would think he was boasting. He was 36, and came from a political family which had supported Mossadeq and the nationalizing of Iran's oil. His brother had been arrested in 1953 for protesting against the action, planned by Britain and carried out by the American CIA, to overthrow Mossadeq. His own formative political experience had been the riots of 1963 which led eventually to the exile of Ayatollah Khomeini. He was only twelve at the time, but he lost two of his close friends who were arrested and killed for taking part in pro-Khomeini demonst-rations. He wrote articles against the Shah's land reforms while he was in his early teens, and at the age of 17 was taken to SAVAK headquarters and warned about his activities. Then in 1970, when he was 19, he was arrested and tortured, and while he was in prison he made his first contacts with members of an under-ground group, MKO.

After his release and a period of national service, he was accepted for a course in economics at the University of Tehran. By then he was living the life of an urban guerrilla, learning how to use weapons and spending time in the working-class areas of South Tehran and recruiting people to the cause. But he soon gave up the violent side of revolutionary activity and concen-trated on its organization, working day and night at duplicating pamphlets and literature to prepare the way for Khomeini's return. In Iran, the Xerox machine was as important to the Revolution as the cassette recorders which relayed Khomeini's speeches to his supporters. After the Revolution, all this dedicat-ion was rewarded with a series of senior posts in the civil service. At 36 he was doing a job which most Western governments would reserve for someone in his late fifties.

Wasn't there a danger, I asked, in trying to *make* people good? He laughed again: he didn't often get the chance to answer difficult questions. Everyone had a choice, he said. If the government imposed the system without explaining it to people, and teaching them the reasons for the rules, that would be dangerous; but as long as they could choose between good and evil, and knew how to choose the good, it could not be dangerous. 'I believe the future belongs to those who seek justice, spirituality and divinity. I believe too that if you Europeans could understand us better, and understand what we are doing, then it would benefit both us and you.'

I asked him, brutally, if he felt free to talk to me when the country was run in effect by the thought-police. At this stage my 'minder' from the Ministry of Islamic Guidance intervened to say that it was generally known that this man had often made serious criticisms of the government, but had never suffered for it. He himself intervened: 'We aren't in Russia here, you know. We can talk freely. It should be natural to discuss government policy in the fullest way, and to criticize it where necessary. I have often done that when I have talked to the Revolutionary Guards, but I have never had any problems. I have even criticized the clergy, but I have never had any problems as a result. The police have never approached me, or anything like that. Honestly,' he said, his eyes shining behind the horn-rimmed glasses, 'I'm saying this with sincerity.'

Another office, another kind of civil servant. We are in a different part of Tehran, in an altogether different and less exalted branch of government. I have met this man by chance, and he has invited me in, partly in order to talk to someone from the West, and partly, it may be, to ask for my help in getting a visa to Britain. Ali – which is not, of course, his name – is no hero, revolutionary or otherwise. He took no part in the overthrow of the Shah, and he is very anxious to avoid being sent to the front to fight the Iraqis. If the senior civil servant I talked to was a kind of Don Quixote, this man is certainly Sancho Panza.

'I'm a nationalist, I suppose. I never liked the Shah, and I was glad when he went. But I'm certainly not a strict Muslim, like a lot of the guys here. One thing that really annoys me is the way they always talk about the enemies of the government: "the enemies of God", they call them. Why can't they say "Iran"

– "the enemies of Iran"?

'I'm really worried now. I signed my volunteer papers to go and fight, but I wrote on it 'I will only serve in Tehran.' It scared the shit out of me just to write the words down, I can tell you, because they give people the sack for that if you work in a government department. But they haven't said anything to me yet. It's unbelievable – you know, there are guys here who've been to the war-front, and now they're volunteering to go back. That's not for me, friend.'

He gives me a jokey nudge, but looks round to check that the door is closed. In his job, he has to deal with the general public, so explaining away my presence isn't too difficult. After studying in the United States for some years, he speaks good American English, colloquial and expressive. He feels utterly trapped, 'like a fly in a web', he says. He came back to Iran because his family needed him; they were elderly, religious and uneducated, and having their son around was important to them. Now they are dead, and he has done his duty, he's trying to get the money together to leave again.

His wife wants to get out too. She's a democrat, he says – that means she doesn't like wearing 'all this scarf bullshit'.

'We used to go into the mountains, but we've gotten sick of being stopped. "How do we know this is your wife? How can you prove it? Do you have your marriage certificate with you?" It happened four times on one trip, so we stopped. Who needs the hassle? I like soccer, but I can't take her there because it's not Islamic. They only like shooting bows and arrows, you know that?'

Grumbling for him is a way of life: and to have a Westerner to grumble to makes an extraordinary difference to him, even though he knows nothing about me and will never see me again after this chance, fleeting encounter.

'It'd be easy enough for me to get on here if I did the kind of things they like – conformed, you know. If I grew a beard and wore shirts with long sleeves, that kind of thing. But I figure to myself, why bother? I don't like them, and they don't like me, so we're quits. It's true they don't sack me, I suppose I ought to be grateful for that.

'They're not all bad, you can get along with them. It's just I don't really belong. It's not my country any more, you know

107

that? One of the other guys here, he was a big Muslim, you know – prayed all the time, grew a beard. Then he went to London. Came back a changed man, I'm telling you. No more praying for him. But they didn't get rid of him. They just didn't give him the kind of job he used to want. Him and me, we look at each other sometimes, and we know we got a lot in common now. But we don't say nothing about it.'

As he says, he doesn't belong. His time was the time of the Shah, when American things were popular, there was a lot of money around, and you could make plenty of cash on the side. Bribes is an unpleasant way of describing it, but in his job there were plenty of inducements offered. He says there are still people taking bribes, but not at his level; you have to be more senior to get real money. The country has changed around him. The free and easy ways are gone. And there are other, smaller changes which are just as annoying.

'When these guys came in, I'm telling you, they even smashed the johns in this building. UnIslamic, was what they said. Now you've got these steps and the hole, you know? You really gotta aim right. And no toilet paper, just a plastic jar and a hose. We used to have a real bath downstairs, with hot water. They smashed that too. What's unIslamic about being clean, I ask you? It just isn't my kind of place any more.'

Two men, with two views of the system: one looks up at the stars, the other looks at the smashed toilets. 'You must be able to choose,' the first man said to me. Sancho Panza has made his choice, and is just waiting to put it into effect. No doubt Don Quixote will be glad to see him go. You can't make a revolution to fit everyone, he would probably say.

Divorce, Crime & Islamic Punishment

Short, sharp, severe but not intentionally cruel save
when it is desired to awe the evil doer – such is Persian
justice.   Dr. C.J. Wills, *Persia As It Is*, 1887

IT WAS THE most informal court of law I had ever been in: an
upstairs room in a small modern building, with a desk, several
chairs, a window that opened out onto a verandah, and a picture
of Ayatollah Khomeini looking suitably severe. The divorce court
in the town of Rey, just south of Tehran, was in session.

When we arrived, there were only seven people in the room:
the judge, a mullah in his sixties with a long, ugly, intelligent face
and humorous eyes set above an aquiline nose; his clerk, an
ingratiating thirty-year-old, who scribbled notes on the case with
a ball-point pen on loose sheets of paper and pushed files and a
copy of the Koran towards the mullah when he needed them;
and the couple involved in the case, who had brought along their
three noisy children.

Conditioned by the solemnities of Western courts, I was
embarrassed that we should have arrived a minute or so late, and
that we made so much noise sitting down and getting settled.
Only the clerk took any notice of us, and since the mullah
seemed unconcerned he turned away. The mullah was just
posing his first question to the husband: 'Seven months ago, you
filed for a divorce from your wife here, and an appointment was
made for you both to appear in court again today to let us know
whether you wanted to carry on with the divorce. What is your
opinion now?'

The husband was a man in his late twenties. His humorous,
quick face with its frame of carefully-combed, curly hair gave him
the look of a jack-the-lad: the sort of person who might offer you
an attractive rate for a black market currency deal. As it turned

out, he was a taxi-driver. He presented an unlikely picture, with a ten-month-old baby on his lap, feeding it from a bottle. The baby's lips slurped from time to time and the rubber teat slipped from its mouth, but its father rarely noticed it immediately. He might well have offered to take the baby in order to impress the judge with his loving, attentive family ways; the awkwardness with which he was feeding it seemed to indicate that he was not familiar with the operation. 'Yes,' he replied. 'We've tried to get along together, but it doesn't work.'

The sharp features of the judge were turned towards the wife.

'I don't want a divorce, with these three children. I want to live with my husband.'

She was about ten years younger than he, wrapped in a *chador* but with black high-heels showing underneath it. Her young, unlined face bore a discontented expression which seemed to have become a fixture; she was like a piece of delicate fruit that had somehow grown corrupt. The two older children played around her, bored already, pulling at her *chador*. She pushed them away with unconscious irritation, as she sat out the rest of her case: 'The trouble is, he doesn't pay me a proper allowance. And he's married to someone else now, and I've got to live with my married sister.'

I leaned across to our 'minder' from the Ministry of Islamic Guidance in Tehran and asked him in a whisper how old the wife was. To my great embarrassment, he broke into the proceedings and asked the judge. For the first time, the judge acknowledged our presence, inclining his head with great courtesy, and asked the girl himself. Eighteen, was the reply.

'Would you like to put any questions to them about the case?' the mullah said to me. His expression was mildly ironic, but he seemed to mean it. I, however, found it as hard to join in the cross-examination here as I would have at the Old Bailey in London: long years of obedience to the rules of court had rendered me dumb. The duel continued.

Through the open window insects buzzed occasionally, and the noise of children playing in the streets outside filled the room whenever there was a moment of silence. The electric fan whirred away, keeping down the summer temperature and stirring the dove-grey robes which the judge was wearing over a white shirt with its collar buttoned like a surgeon's. His hands were together in the Christian attitude of prayer, as an aid to more concise thought. The sunlight glittered on his silver ring set with an engraved cornelian.

'I've gone back to her time and again, but it doesn't work. We

110

can't get along. And now I've got this other wife . . .'

The husband's voice trailed off in embarrassment; there was nothing against his taking a second wife in an Islamic society, but the judge was perfectly well aware that the marriage had occurred after the beginning of the present divorce case, and that it represented a form of escape for the taxi-driver. And since the seven-month wait was imposed on him by the judge in order to give the original marriage a chance, it was clear the husband had ignored the spirit of the ruling.

'The house needs looking after,' said the wife, pressing her advantage. 'But he doesn't do that, and he doesn't pay me an allowance to look after the children. She won't let him.'

'His other wife?'

'Of course. She tells him not to do the work, and not to give me the money.'

'I'll pay you when I get it. But things are difficult, nowadays. You can't find passengers easily, and it costs a lot to run the cab.' He looks at me, as though sensing a potential customer; there is a jauntiness about him, a resilience, which is his most endearing quality, and which might make him an amusing companion. It is unlikely to make him a good husband to either wife for long.

'It's your duty to look after her, and after your children. There is no need for you to divorce her just because you've married another woman,' said the judge.

He looked across at me. 'We have divorce laws here, but we prefer to keep families together if it's possible.' It was not quite what I expected; nor had I expected him to be quite so tough on the man in the case. But when he glanced back at the erring husband his eyes had a noticeable glitter in them.

'If you don't pay her the proper amount of maintenance, I'll make sure you do.'

But the wife was not prepared to leave it there, and interrupted the judge sharply.

'I don't accept that. He won't pay up. Even if he says he'll pay, he won't do it.'

The judge did not seem at all angry that she should have challenged his authority like this.

'Anything else you want to say?' he asked, ironically. She shook her head sourly, a shrew at eighteen.

The clerk interrupted his scribbling to push a piece of paper across to the judge with an obsequious inclination of the head. The judge studied it carefully, and jotted a few calculations in the margin.

'You'll have to pay her 30,000 *rials* a month to take care of her expenses and those of the children.'

The couple bickered between themselves about the amount, and the bickering soon turned into a row. The baby started crying, the bottle fell unnoticed to the ground. Meanwhile the mullah was listening to the proceedings abstractedly, playing with his cornelian ring or looking out of the window. No one rapped the desk with a gavel or cried 'Silence in court,' even when they started shouting at one another. Eventually it died away, as they realized they were getting nowhere.

It seemed to me that the judge had allowed the scene to continue for two reasons: partly in order to see what the state of the couple's relationship really was, and partly to edge the case on to its next stage. In the sudden silence, he gave his ruling:

'Come back together in a month's time, and we will see how you both feel about getting a divorce, now that we have discussed it here in court. In the meantime,' he turned to the husband, 'you must come here every ten days and pay 10,000 *rials* for her maintenance.'

Now that he was one stage closer to getting his divorce, the taxi-driver's old jauntiness had returned: 'You bring home your day's earnings to one wife, and before you know it you've got to pay half of it to the other one.'

But his all-men-of-the-world-together approach drew no sympathy from the judge, and his wife pulled her *chador* around her with irritable tightness, and took the baby from him sharply. It had no further use to him as a prop now. They all trooped out together: the tired, bored children, the straying father, the discontented spoiled wife. Her sharp voice could still be heard long after the door had closed behind them.

The laws of the Islamic Republic about divorce are predictably brief, and are mostly concerned with the dowry the wife brings to the marriage, and whether or not the wife is menstruating at the time of the divorce; if she is, it is usually invalid. The action of divorce itself is simple enough: it has to be witnessed by two just men, and the husband has to use the following simple formula: 'I make my wife free, upon remittance of her dowry.' What I had not expected was that there would be a real examination of the conduct of both parties, with no special bias towards the husband.

The wife can initiate a divorce only if her husband is impotent or does not provide for her. But that does not make her a disposable item of her husband's property. The mullah in Rey was not acting as an agent for the husband: he was trying in the first instance to keep the family together, and in the second to

112

establish a balance between the two of them which took the interests of the wife and the children into account. 'Irreconcilable differences' are the grounds of the great majority of divorces in Iran: though this is, of course, a country where adultery is a criminal offence, punishable by death; it is not grounds for divorce.

In the empty courtroom the judge explained these things in his thoughtful yet somehow mocking fashion, using the previous case as his example.

'You see the less attractive side of human nature in your court,' I suggested. He inclined his head in agreement.

'The next case,' he said, 'will show that.'

It did. The couple who came in were a generation older than the previous one, having lived together in a bitter, loveless marriage for eighteen years. The husband was a curiously farouche figure with a huge, crooked nose and a bad strabismus which meant that only one of his eyes was focussed at any time, the other being off at a disconcertingly wide angle. Most of the time, as a result, he looked at the floor, his eyes covering the expanse of it between them. His wife was a sharp-featured woman in her late thirties, who could have been at least fifty. They had each calculated their strategy with care: the husband, a builder by trade, had turned up in a ragged shirt and a pair of dirty jeans. 'I am a poor man,' his clothes proclaimed. Anticipating this, his wife had run a calculated risk by coming to court, not in a meek *chador*, but in a loose black over-garment which opened from time to time, showing an expensive white outfit underneath. The scarf she wore on her head was expensive, too. 'Don't let him fool you', her clothes replied.

Their divorce was well advanced; the process had begun a year before, and the point of dispute was the financial settlement.

'How much do you earn?' the judge asked.

'About 3,000 *rials* a day.' The answer was directed at the floor, and it irritated the judge.

'Those are the wages of a labourer. If you work so cheaply, come to my house and work for me.'

The wife smirked with pleasure that her husband's big act had failed. The first round had gone to her.

The clerk handed the mullah a sealed envelope: it contained the report of two assessors, chosen jointly by the couple from among their respective families to work out the details of the divorce settlement. The assessors' proposal was that, since the husband did not hold any property in his own name, he should settle an income of 7,000 *rials* a day upon his wife: seven times the maintenance figure established in the previous case. The size of the amount took the builder by surprise and threw him into a sudden rage.

'I've been betrayed by that fool of a cousin of mine. I should never have suggested his name as an assessor. This woman has got at him in some way. I demand a new assessment.' His voice was loud and harsh, filling the room, but he still glared ambiguously at the floor, his hands clenched between the legs of the dirty jeans which had failed to make the impression he had hoped.

The judge, however, saw a lever here which he could use to achieve a reasonable arbitration. He looked up at the ceiling, the palms of his hands together again, and quoted from the Koran:

By another sign He gave you wives from among yourselves, that you might live in joy with them, and planted love and kindness in your hearts. Surely there are signs in this for thinking men.

His gaze rested coolly on the builder again.

'Another assessment would be pointless; why should it produce an answer which would be any different? No. If you don't want a divorce on the terms your own cousin has agreed, then you must go back and live with your wife.'

The builder blustered, using the rhetoric of the Islamic Republic against one of its clerical supporters: 'During the Shah's time we were oppressed. There's no reason why we should be oppressed now.'

The mullah was taking no notice; he was busy jotting down figures again.

'You should pay her four million *rials* as a divorce settlement. Then you will not have to live with her again. But you must take pity on her, and on your three children. They have to live somehow.'

'No! I'd rather go to jail than pay. I'd rather be hanged. I can't live with that woman for another second – but I can't pay as much as that.'

The judge's quick ear must have detected a deal in the making; but before he could take advantage of it, the woman broke in. It was special pleading, but coming from her, ugly and prematurely old as she was, it had a certain force.

'I came to live with you eighteen years ago, when we only had one room which we had to rent. I bore you three children. Now we have a big house, but you don't want to live with me there.

114

Even when you left me, I still went on looking after your parents.'

The judge, taking advantage of the mood, joined in:

'You say you're ready to go to jail or be hanged, but you aren't prepared to live with the woman God has given you.'

The homilies had done their work: the builder's anger faded, and he saw the need to play for a little sympathy himself.

'Look,' he said, holding out his dark, gnarled hands with their broken nails. 'You can see my hands. You can see for yourself that I've worked hard all my life. This is my money, and I've earned it. I've had it up to here with this woman.'

'A wife is not like a labourer you hire. She's not just a house-keeper and a cook. She has the right to be supported by you; that's the Islamic interpretation of marriage. If she bears you children, and cooks and works in the house, that is something extra. When she came to you, she was a young woman – and now she's an old one, who's given her life to you. You must try to make up to her for your neglect, by paying her a reasonable amount of money for her upkeep. If you can't bear to live with her, as you say, then you must make arrangements for her to live somewhere else.'

The deal hung in the air, delicately outlined. For a while, nothing was said. The judge himself sat motionless. Then the husband spoke.

'I can't afford four million. I'll pay a million.'

'Perhaps we should appoint just one assessor, who would make a binding arbitration, after looking at all your assets.'

'Two million.'

Providentially, the telephone rang at this precise moment, and the judge seized the opportunity to increase the pressure. The caller was another colleague who was consulting him about some tricky legal point which had arisen in his own court, and the judge was careful not to give the impression he was in a hurry. At one point while he was still speaking the builder looked as though he was about to suggest to his wife that they should do a separate deal, away from the court, but she ignored him, brushing an imaginary piece of fluff from the expensive white outfit which had done nothing to make her look younger or more attractive.

At last the call was over, and the mullah pushed the telephone away. 'What were you saying?' he asked.

The delay had done its work: the builder's resistance was crumbling fast now. 'Let's finish this today,' he said.

'All right, but you must sign a statement first that you agree to the divorce.'

The obliging clerk provided the documents, and the builder

signed. His wife, nervous at this moment of formality, agreed eventually to press her forefinger onto an inkpad and make her mark with a finger-print.

'Now the settlement.' The mullah was inexorable, knowing the builder was in a weaker position now. 'You cannot give her less than three million.' He was silhouetted against the sunshine in his grey and white robes, monochrome and motionless. It was plain that the deal was about to be done; all that it required was a respectable figure from the builder. The gnarled hands gripped the knees of the jeans, the eyes shifted focus. In the silence, children shrieked as they played outside.

'Two-point-eight million.'

It was just enough. An old man, bent almost double, was allowed to bring in tea, and the judge, pleased with his *coup*, drank noisily through a sugar-cube in the approved Persian manner. The builder and his wife drank theirs, side by side, without looking at each other or speaking.

All that remained was to arrange the custody of the children. There were three of them: Mohammed, aged 17, Ali Reza, aged 10, and a 7-year-old daughter, Fatima. In the usual way under Islamic law, sons go to the father and daughters to the mother. In this case the judge seemed to waver. Then he made his final declaration: the builder was to have the sons. The wife said her grovelling thanks to the mullah and swept out triumphantly. The loss of her sons seemed to matter little in comparison with the vindication she had received. The builder said nothing, and if he looked at the mullah before leaving, his strabismus made it impossible to tell. The clerk busied himself with clearing up the papers.

The mullah sat where he was for a little, looking at me in his sceptical, ironic way.

'We try to do our best to expound justice according to God's will,' he said at length, as though he felt that something still required explanation. I replied that I had been impressed with his even-handedness, and had expected him to favour the men over the women.

'One thing I didn't understand, though. You seemed to have doubts about awarding custody of the sons to the father, and yet you did it anyway.'

'A divorced man with two children will always find it hard to re-marry. I didn't want him to get off too easily.'

He got up and walked round the table to shake hands with me. I realized then that he had the heavy, painful limp of a polio victim, and was far shorter than his long face and hands had

116

suggested. The surprise must have shown in my face; there was real mockery in his eyes now.

'Not everything we think beforehand is true,' he said.

Another court, darker and more crowded than the divorce court: there is no chance that individual cases will be sifted with care and thought here. This could be a magistrate's court in Britain, dispensing penalties for traffic violations: there is the same speed with which the proceedings are taken, there are the same formula judgements, the same resigned acceptance on the part of the offenders. But in this court the judge, who is also a mullah, does not bring his gavel down with a bang and say the equivalent of 'Fined £10 – next case.' Minor cases are heard in this court, certainly, but they are minor criminal cases; the punishment here is whipping.

The accused shuffles into the dock and, if he is sensible, pleads guilty. The evidence is given fast and in a monotone, the mullah pauses momentarily to consider the requisite punishment, and sentence is passed. Today, in the queue of prisoners, there is a well-known lawyer who was stopped by the police on the way home and found to have a bottle of illicit Iranian vodka in his car.

Being found in possession of alcohol is an offence, but not as bad as having drunk alcohol. The only question in this case, therefore, is whether the lawyer had drunk anything from the bottle. The question is put.

'No, I did not.' There is, perhaps, a tinge of relief in his voice: the police and the *Komitehs* do not invent the evidence in these cases, and the bottle was unopened. The arresting officer confirms that he had not been drinking.

The mullah looks down at the piece of paper in front of him, and then up at the accused again.

'Twenty-five lashes.'

The accused in the previous case had also been caught with a bottle of vodka, but he could not deny that he had been drinking from it. He received eighty lashes – a penalty which may, if he is unlucky, do him permanent injury. Twenty-five is unpleasant, but bearable. The lawyer has got off lightly, and he knows it.

He is taken down immediately to the basement of the court, and into the whipping room. The guard is not rough with him: all this is as much a routine as if he were writing out a cheque to pay his fine. Inside, two men are waiting on either side of a low table. There are straps for his wrists and ankles, and he has to lie down, still wearing his shirt and trousers, while they are fastened. The waiting is perhaps the worst part of it.

One of the men selects a whip, made of rigid leather. He takes a step forward, his right arm high over his head, his left hand holding the end of the whip until the moment of the stroke. The whip whistles in the air and comes down hard across the lawyer's shoulders, just below his neck. The pain is intense, but he is determined not to scream or make a fuss. The tightness of the bonds helps him to control his reactions.

'One,' intones the other man.

The next blow lands an inch or so below, on the upper shoulder-blades. His clothing provides no real protection whatever.

'Two.'

Each of the strokes is laid with care and skill, an inch or so lower than the previous one. The red and purple lines of bruising travel parallel to one another down his back, over his buttocks, and down his legs to the ankles.

'Thirteen.'

Painful though the previous strokes have been, the remaining twelve are much worse since they cover the same area, back to the top of the shoulders. It helps a little to control the pain, and his reaction to it, if he concentrates on every detail, examining it objectively as though it is happening to someone else: the clothes the two men are wearing, the sound of the whip in the air, the exact place it lands on his body, the precise physical reaction.

'Twenty-five.'

The straps are undone, and one of the men helps him off the table. His back is on fire with the pain.

'Thank you,' he murmurs, without thinking. The man says nothing. For him it is simply a transaction. The lawyer is free to leave: the penalty has been paid, a physical fine has been exacted. The entire process, from walking into court to limping slowly, painfully away from it, has lasted less than half-an-hour.

Islam is a religion of the Law. It does not differentiate between spiritual and temporal authority; there is no separation between Church and State. Therefore a crime against society is a crime against God, and must be punished with great severity; it is not for men to be lenient where offences against God are concerned. The Holy Koran specifies the punishment with exactitude:

The recompense of those who make war against Allah and His Messenger and spread corruption in the land is that they should be put to death or crucified, or that their hands and feet should be cut off on alternate sides, or that they should be banished from the country. (5:33).

Surgeons have been employed in some Islamic countries, though never in Iran itself, to sever the hands or feet of criminals, and public executions have been reasonably frequent. This has not impressed the régime in Iran, however, which believes that countries like Pakistan and Saudi Arabia regard such penalties as a little Muslim camouflage, to divert attention from the sell-out that is going on in such countries to Western ideas and Western corruption.

How harshly, then, does it punish crime? The best overall answer is probably, not quite as harshly as its reputation and its own laws would imply. The official position is that, while the Koranic penalties must be enforced in a truly Islamic society, the government cannot introduce them fully until every Iranian citizen has enough to eat and a roof over his head. Only after that will robbery and murder be wholly sacrilegious, since hunger and deprivation will no longer exist as a cause for wrong-doing. But in the haphazard conditions which exist in Iran, this more lenient approach is not necessarily followed in the farther reaches of the country, where so much depends on the interpret-ation of the Koran by individual ayatollahs. And what the West as well as many Westernized Iranians would regard as atrocities undoubtedly occur, even in the main cities.

In Shiraz in February 1986 four convicted thieves, each of whom had received lesser penalties for past convictions, had the four fingers of their right hands cut off on the same day. The following May another man found guilty of repeated theft suffered the same penalty in front of a big crowd in a park beside the main Tehran bus terminal. The head of the Tehran judicial police, whose men carry out amputations and executions, said that the sentence had been carried out there so that travellers would carry the word around the country.

The standards by which such things are judged in the West are so different from those which apply in Iran, that it is difficult to compare them. Officials who uphold a system which believes that justice should be seen to be done find it difficult to under-stand why Westerners should be particularly horrified by an electric guillotine (which may have been manufactured in a Western country) capable of amputating a hand in a tenth of a second. One such machine was used at Qasr prison in Tehran in 1985, and at Mashad the following year. An unknown number of executions take place each year, for drugs offences and for political crimes. The government makes a virtue of the fact that it puts people to death 'mercifully' – that is to say, they are shot or hanged instead of being subjected to some worse form of execution. Worse forms certainly exist, including crucifixion, though there is no evidence, published or anecdotal, that this has ever been carried out.

Amnesty International, the London-based human rights organization, says it heard of eight cases of stoning to death for adultery in 1986. The Islamic Penal Code of Iran specifies the size of the stones to be used:

In the punishment of stoning to death, the stones should not be too large, so that the person dies on being hit by one or two of them; nor should they be so small that they could not be defined as stones.

We could find no evidence, when we were in Iran, of any stonings that had taken place in the larger cities, but there was no shortage of anecdotal evidence, especially from country areas. In a village to the east of Tehran, for instance, there was a harrowing story of an adulterer who was buried up to his chest. His neighbours stood at the permitted distance and threw rocks of the prescribed size at him for half an hour or more, while he remained conscious and called out to them, begging them by name to spare his life. Finally one man, taking a larger rock, ran over and smashed his skull with it. Another story tells of an adulterer who also failed to succumb to his injuries, and was despatched by a shot fired by a Revolutionary Guard who happened to be back in the village on leave. The soldier was charged with manslaughter, and sent to prison.

The documents which Amnesty International sent to the Iranian government, detailing its condemnation of political executions and torture as well as of Islamic punishments like stoning, received an almost puzzled response from one deputy during a debate in the Majlis in June 1987:

Amnesty International's report describes execution, flogging and hand amputation as . . . inhuman and cruel. If amputating the limbs of a person with gangrene is inhuman and cruel, then so is corporal punishment, execution, flogging, and the severing of hands. But the fact is, these punishments are not inhuman and cruel, they are of positive benefit to society and are carried out for the good of mankind.

The punishments which are most unacceptable to Western opinion are in fact relatively rare. Thousands of men and women are convicted every year for theft, for adultery, and for murder, and the most usual punishments are prison, or the lash, often accompanied by a heavy fine. The victim or his family are allowed a say in the penalty, and sometimes a convicted criminal can choose between a range of punishments. The system is not intended to be society's revenge on wrong-doers, so much as to teach them the error of their ways and warn others who might be tempted to commit the same crimes.

Nowadays the courts are systematized. An ayatollah without full legal training can hear lesser cases – the theft of goods under a certain value, driving offences, drinking alcohol – and can impose sentences of up to seventy lashes or a fine of a million *rials*. More serious crimes are passed on to higher courts, where the judges are also ayatollahs but have specialized in the administration of justice.

In the early years of the Revolution no lawyers were allowed in a criminal court; the judge questioned the accused and the witnesses, and reached his own conclusions about the guilt or innocence of the person charged. The system was much the same as at the divorce court in Rey. But in the higher courts, secular lawyers, who spent the first four or five years after the Revolution without a function to perform and were mostly unemployed, are starting to be used once more. Accused men and women are now able to hire lawyers to give them advice, and to plead for them in court in cases which demand a technical interpretation of the law. There are also purely civil courts which deal with cases of commercial law.

A lawyer who no longer practises said that having the clergy as judges had speeded up the legal process immensely:

'The court I worked in was a civil one, and when the Revolution happened we had a backlog around four years long of cases – people suing each other, or trying to get compensation for injuries or wrongful dismissal. Then they put in an ayatollah. Believe me, he cleared that backlog in around three weeks. Just cut through it all. You see, before that the old judges would discuss the whole thing with the lawyers day after day, and then it would get put off once again, and everybody would really be waiting for the parties in the case to come to an agreement themselves, which the judges would rubber-stamp.

'The delaying was all part of a deliberate pressure, though of course no one ever admitted it. Now, you get a decision fast. And you don't question it much, believe me, because it's got God behind it. If you go to appeal, you can get double the sentence. It may not be what we were used to, or what you're used to in the West, but I would have to admit that if I had a case against someone myself, I'd rather it was sorted out quickly and cheaply than have it drag on for years, like it used to.'

Allamah Sheikh Mohammed Kashef Al-Ghita is a very different kind of lawyer: an academic who specializes in the three branches of Shi'a criminal law: *Hodud*, or Penalty; *Qesaas*, or Retaliation; and *Diyah*, or Compensation. Like so many Iranian jurists, he is a man who has spent the greater part of his life in the study of Islamic jurisprudence. He has no doubts whatever about the system, or about the truth and justice of what it propounds. And when he explains it, he certainly has no idea of the effect his words have on a liberal-minded, humanitarian Westerner; though even if he did, he is unlikely to worry about it:

'If an adult, sane man knowingly and deliberately has sexual intercourse with a woman who is forbidden to him, it is an obligation on the authorized judge to order him to be flogged with a hundred lashes; his head will be shaved and he will be forced to leave the city for a period of one year. But if he is in a position to satisfy his sexual urges in conformity with the law – that is, if he is married – he will be stoned to death as well. If the same applies to the woman, she too will be stoned to death; otherwise she will be given a hundred lashes.'

And yet he stresses that it is not at all easy to get a conviction for such 'crimes'. Adultery can only be proven in court if the accused person confesses four times, or if four just men, or three just men and two just women, have actually witnessed the act. The witnesses must be unanimous, and if there are fewer than the required number those who give evidence can be punished for slander; which carried its own unpleasant penalty: eighty lashes. In practice, if the only evidence against an offender is his own confession, and he disavows the confession or else repents of what he has done, he will not be stoned to death. The same rules apply to women. Anyone who is convicted three times for adultery will, however, be beheaded; and beheading is also the punishment for rape.

Shi'a law demands that there must be twenty-seven reasons

for a judge to order a thief's hand to be severed, and in practice there are never any more than half-a-dozen: that the criminal was acting out of greed rather than necessity, that he is an habitual criminal, that his victim was poor or sick, and so on. It seems likely that in the known cases of amputation the law was stretched in order to teach people a lesson.

Murder, Sheikh Al-Ghita accepts, is the most serious crime that can be committed. In practice, the penalty is usually a very long prison sentence accompanied by a large fine in compensation. But the principle of *Qesaas*, Retaliation, exists, and can be demanded by the family of the victim. It is rarer for murder than for physical assault which leads to mutilation; there, the principle of an eye for an eye and a tooth for a tooth has frequently been accepted since the Revolution. During 1986 a woman who had lost her left eye was permitted to gouge out the left eye of the woman who had attacked her, in a formal ceremony that was attended by the families of both of them. In the same year, members of a group which was found guilty of having planted bombs in Qom and other cities were sentenced to suffer 'retaliation' before they were executed: a fearful thought.

No one in Iran seems to doubt that since the Revolution, and the introduction of its fierce penalties, crime, and violent crime in particular, has dropped considerably; though that may owe as much to the vigilance of the *Komitehs* as to the punishments that are inflicted.

But there is one area where crime has risen fast: drug addiction and drug-dealing. Almost every month there are announcements that dealers, and less frequently addicts, have been executed, but the problem seems, if anything, to worsen. There is nothing particularly new about it: opium has always been smoked in Iran, and has never been hard to obtain. But heroin constitutes a greater problem. Relatively little of either drug is grown in Iran: it is imported in large quantities from Pakistan and Afghanistan, by two overlapping groups of people. In Afghanistan the anti-Soviet guerrillas have for some years controlled the areas where opium poppies are grown, and have used the profits to buy weapons and maintain their fierce guerrilla war against the Russian invaders. From there the raw material is taken to the refugee camps across the border in Pakistan, where it is processed into opium for smoking and into heroin; and although the best markets are in Western Europe and North America, some comes into Iran through Baluchistan, which is remote and difficult to control, and where the smuggling of goods and people has a long history.

The dislocation which followed the collapse of the Shah's régime, the upheavals created by the war with Iraq, the refugee problem, the growing unemployment: all of these have provided recruits for both the use of drugs and the peddling of them. Although the penalties for possessing drugs are fierce, the profits are correspondingly high; and most well-to-do young Iranians seem to know how to get hold of drugs if they want them.

One such place is the area off Ferdowsi Avenue, near the National Bank. Most of the men who are hanging around in the doorways of buildings, or sitting on the pavement with their backs to the walls of shops are money-changers: people who make their living in the grey area between honesty and outright crime, in a way that many Persians have done for centuries. Every time I walked along that stretch of Ferdowsi Avenue I was approached by half-a-dozen men offering to change whatever foreign money I had into *rials*, at a rate which was often nine or ten times the official one. These people are just about tolerated by the authorities; but among them, and taking their protective colouring from them, are the dealers in drugs and in anything else that turns an illegal profit. They are often the front men, whose job is to make the introduction between customer and supplier; few, no doubt, would be careless enough to carry drugs on them, when there is always the possibility that the black market currency dealers may themselves be raided by the *Komiteh*.

In theory, Khomeini's Iran represents a return, not simply to the ideals of Islam, but to the maximalist conception of it as a guide to the details, great and small, of everyday life. As it happens, Khomeini has published his own commentary on these matters. In the 1950s, at the Faizieh Theological School in Qom, his reputation as a teacher was growing and people would write to him from all over Iran to ask his opinion on questions of religion. These opinions were collated and turned into a book, which he published in 1960; after which he was entitled to refer to himself as an ayatollah.

The book, *Towzhih al-Masa'il*, or *Explication of Problems,* is a best-seller in Iran, an immense tome which contains more than three thousand rulings on the conduct of daily life and religious observances, from the laws on inheritance to matters of personal cleanliness and the right way to slaughter animals. There is

124

almost nothing so private – in Western eyes, at any rate – that Ayatollah Khomeini does not lay down the law about it; from the different varieties of bleeding in a woman's menstrual flow to the correct way to face when defecating, and the correct way to clean oneself afterwards. But he is most himself when discussing the various ways to rebuke sin in others:

'Enjoining right or forbidding wrong is approached in three successive steps.

1. *First by heartfelt expressions of disgust, so that the transgressor knows that one disapproves of his act.*
   a. This may be done by facial expression, cutting off communication or staying aloof.
   b. If this does not stop the behaviour, one should try step 2.
2. *Verbally express one's disapproval.*
   a. It is best to be firm, but polite and courteous if possible.
   b. If one must be harsh, one should never resort to lying or commit other sins (the exception is if the wrong is so serious that it must be stopped at all costs.)
   c. If this brings no result, go to step 3.
3. *One must act forcefully to prevent the wrong.*
   a. The method of action depends on the circumstances of the wrong. One should never take stronger action than is necessary.
   b. If taking action means killing or destroying someone, it should only be undertaken with the approval of a leading mujtahid (an expert in Islamic jurisprudence).
   c. . . . Killing must be the last resort.
   d. If one acts beyond the necessary limits, he himself will be guilty of a sin.'

The purpose is not merely to punish sinners, it is to reform them. Islam, as taught by Ayatollah Khomeini, is not a religion of reconciliation or forgiveness, but it is not totally concerned with the revenge of the holy on the unholy. And if it cannot reform them, as it cannot reform the drug-pushers or the people with Western ideas and Western ways of behaving, it certainly has the power, and the organization, to force them to obey the rules in their outward lives, whatever they do in private.

7

Imperial Echoes

When our company had approached to within five or
six steps of the King, the steward made a sign to
Monsieur Sherley, his brother and myself to dismount
in order to kiss His Majesty's feet, for it is thus that this
prince is accustomed to being saluted. He was five or
six steps ahead of a large squadron of cavalry, and
while he stretched out his leg he pretended the whole
time to look in another direction.

Abel Pinçon, *Relation of a Journey to Persia, 1598-99*

NIAVARAN IS A SMALL, completely unremarkable little village in
the foothills of the Elburz Mountains, with a few shops, a tea-
house, and fifty or so houses straggling up the hillside. Nowadays it is part of the municipality of Tehran, which has spread
northwards to encompass it; though the city centre, if you could
see it, lies ten miles away and a thousand feet below it to the
south. Nearby, a military camp has been set up in one of the
grand parks which decorate the northernmost suburbs of the
city; in this camp volunteers from throughout the Muslim world
are trained in the techniques of terrorism and suicide attacks. But
that is not visible from the centre of the village, and nothing, so
far as I could tell, had changed in Niavaran since the first time I
had been there eight years before: with one exception. Every
shop then had carried a more than usually large photograph of
the Shah, the Empress, and usually their eldest son for good
measure; for this, if anywhere, was the Shah's home village. He
had chosen the pleasant, dry, sparse air of the Elburz Mountains
for his summer palace, and he and the Empress came to like it so
much that they lived there during the other seasons as well,
spending more time at the Niavaran Palace than at any of their
other residences.

The display of imperial photographs by the villagers was not
simply intended to be ingratiating. The people who lived here,
untouched for the most part by the expanding city of Tehran

until the Palace was built, were bedrock royalists, peasants who had always revered their Shah regardless of the dynasty and its political weakness or strength. It was hardy, traditional mountain villages like this which provided the best recruits for the Shah's army, and in particular for his Imperial Guards, the Immortals. The reverence such people felt for their monarch was little short of religious. But although he might appear every night on the television screens of Iran, they rarely saw him in person. The numerous attempts on his life over the years meant that the Shah showed himself to his people as little as possible, and even the villagers at Niavaran were lucky to get more than two or three glimpses of him a year.

When he visited the Golestan Palace in the old centre of Tehran for some ceremonial occasion, or went to the airport to fly further afield in Iran or to another country, he would go by helicopter. It was partly symbolic: the monarch flying above the turmoil of things below. It was also prudent, and his security advisers and his own instincts (together with the appalling traffic of Tehran) dictated that he should avoid going anywhere by road if he could. It was not that the mass of his subjects was hostile – far from it. But there was a continuing threat to him throughout his reign. In February 1949, for instance, when he was 29 and had ruled for nearly eight years, there was an attempt on his life. A man posing as a photographer fired five shots at him from a range of six feet. One shot struck him in the face and another in the shoulder, but he was not badly hurt.

> The man then threw down his gun and tried to escape, and in their fury at this assassination attempt, some of my young officers unfortunately killed him. He must have been a curious character. We discovered that he had been friendly with various arch-conservative religious fanatics, yet in his flat we found literature of the Tudeh or Communist party. His mistress was the daughter of a gardener at the British Embassy in Tehran. (*Mission For My Country*, 1961)

The combination of motives suggested by links of that sort – Marxism, Islamic fundamentalism and the faintest hint of possible great power involvement – provided the Shah with suspicions which, during the immense upheavals which resulted thirty years later in the Revolution, became a certainty in his mind. His bloodstained uniform was placed on reverent display at the Iranian Officers' Club in Tehran, and remained there for thirty years almost to the very day. Then, in February 1979 the

127

Officers' Club was sacked and the uniform torn into tiny pieces by people who shared much the same mix of political and religious opinions as the man who, in February 1949, had tried to shoot him.

After the attempt on his life the Shah rarely went among his people again. This was not the impression the officially-controlled news media gave, however. On the main freeway out of Tehran to the west, miles from any centre of population, a curious dilapidated shed-like structure still stands by the side of the road, its corrugated iron roof rusting, its seats broken or plundered. It is the reviewing-stand from which, every year, the Shah would review his armed forces. His personal helicopter would land nearby, and he would be driven fifty yards or so through cheering crowds of soldiers dressed in civilian clothes. He would then take his seat in the reviewing stand while the hugely expensive military equipment on which he lavished the resources of the state were paraded in front of him. Then, when the review was over, he would drive back the fifty yards to his helicopter. That night's television pictures, carefully shot and edited, would give the impression that the Shah was moving freely among his people. For most of his reign he could have done so; but he and his advisers preferred to play it safe with soldiers in disguise.

For me, on my first visit to Iran, the sight of the Shah's helicopter, closely accompanied by another in order to confuse any attempt at mid-air assassination, was a paradigm of his rule: distant, abstracted, divided from his subjects by an advanced technology. Yet he always wanted the appearance of closeness. The way the Shah presented himself, and was presented, was a matter of obsessive interest to him. In the year before the Revolution the Shah hunted through articles about himself and the Iranian crisis in the British and American press, firing off orders to his ambassadors in Washington and London to protest in the strongest terms about references that were critical, regardless of their quality and significance.

His trusted ambassador in London, Parviz Radji, found it hard to distinguish the substantial from the ephemeral in British life in general, and in British journalism in particular. The diary which Radji published later showed an intense concern with what was being said about Iran. It was as though both he and the Shah felt that all would be well in Iran, if only things could be presented more favourably. This is a symptom of a court mentality, and the less subservient friends of the Shah in Britain and the United States noticed with some anxiety from the mid-

128

seventies onwards how difficult it was to penetrate the screen of anxious, flattering courtiers around him and his thoughtful, liberal-minded Empress – even to the extent of warning them about the screen of courtiers itself. Each time, the warning would be silently deflected by officials whose jobs depended on their ability to avoid upsetting the Shah. Radji's diary for 27 September 1976 contains an account of his conversation with the forthright Sir Denis Hamilton, an executive of Times Newspapers, the company which owned the London *Times* and *Sunday Times*. Sir Denis was a supporter of the Shah, Radji noted.

> But he thinks the Shah can no longer be spoken to. Every time a reference is made to some of the more contentious issues of his rule, there is a display of clout (sic) from the Court, threatening a unilateral break in economic and commercial links. 'I've seen,' he goes on, 'how his ministers treat him – all that bowing and hand-kissing . . .'
> I send a cable to Tehran, retaining most of Denis Hamilton's observations but omitting the reference to the Shah's treatment of his ministers.

Those on whose advice the Shah depended were usually too concerned with their own careers to risk the imperial anger by telling him the necessary home truths. The various generals whom he appointed to command SAVAK during the seventies were no less affected by the desire to please rather than to warn; and the sudden swings of policy, from toughness to liberalization and from concession to martial law, were ordered on the basis of intelligence which was, until the very end, filtered and pasteurized to render it acceptable to him.

On each of my visits to Iran I applied through the usual channels, and through whatever unusual ones seemed to offer a parallel chance of success, for an interview with the Shah. In August 1978 my first application seemed to be close to success: through the agency of a friend of mine I was able to give Amir Abbas Hoveyda, the Shah's court minister, an indication of the line of questioning I would follow. I chose my words with considerable care, not wanting to compromise on the tough line of questioning which it would be my duty to follow. Hoveyda seemed to me, on the basis of this fleeting connexion, to be a decent, frank and distinctly worried man; he assured me that my questions would be set before His Imperial Majesty for his consideration, and promised that I would hear from him within a few days.

The call never came. When I tried to contact Hoveyda again, ringing his private direct line, a blandly pleasant, youngish voice, very different from Hoveyda's, answered every time, blocking all my questions politely but decisively. He was, presumably, a junior official who had been given the task of fielding my calls. It is perfectly possible that Hoveyda, knowing the Shah's intense dislike for my organization, decided not to tell him of my application for an interview at all: if so the court filter, once again, had protected him from anything in the way of unpleasantness. In that case, though, Hoveyda's decision may have been the right one, not simply from his own point of view but from that of the Shah as well. It was becoming clear to those around him, if not to the Shah himself, that the interviews he gave were increasingly damaging to him and to his political interests.

In May 1978 he had made a poor impression during an interview with several Iranian newspaper and television correspondents. His answers to their ingratiating questions were haughty and dismissive; asked, for instance, about the continued existence of the Rastakhiz, the only legal political party in Iran which he had founded himself, the Shah asked them, 'Has multi-party democracy proved to be such a bed of roses in the West?' Nevertheless, he seemed uncertain of himself and indecisive about the course of action he would take to deal with the growing unrest. None of his questioners was daring enough to ask him directly about the repeated demonstrations which had, in the previous few days, forced the military to surround the bazaar in Tehran and fire live rounds into the air, while the Shah himself had cancelled an official visit to Bulgaria on the pretext that he was suffering from a cold. In Iran, journalists too were courtiers of a kind.

Television interviews with the Shah had always been common enough in the West, as part of his projection of himself as ruler of a Great Civilization in the making. But he had never been particularly concerned with giving interviews to his tame press and television at home; and when he did, they were watched with great care for the light they shed on his current mood and concerns. This time, his apparent lack of self-confidence made a deep impression in a country which had come to expect strong, often ruthless leadership from him. Furthermore, his control over any political opposition to his régime had been so intense since the disturbances of 1963 and 1964 that any sign of its weakening was certain to have a serious effect. Throughout the summer, convinced that the Shah's grip had started to relax, people took greater risks in opposing him. By July it was possible to see hostile graffiti on the walls of Tehran, and SAVAK's agents were not always fast enough in painting it out.

By the end of August the demonstrations were bigger and better organized than they had ever been; and each time people made their protest without being shot down or arrested, they were emboldened, and became further convinced that the Shah's hold on power was weakening. Iran had become a text-book example of the dangers that befall a repressive government which finds itself obliged to liberalize. During one large demonstration at the beginning of September, a few days before the Jaleh Square massacre, a middle-aged man wearing a suit and tie broke away from the main body of marchers and ran over to us as we were filming. He was waving something which turned out to be a hundred-*rial* note, and as he stood in front of us he over-dramatically inscribed a large X over the face of the Shah which appeared on the front of the note. A well-known writer on Iran, who was standing with me at the time, pointed out the implications of such an act of defiance:

'If a man like that doesn't care about being recognized, then it means he isn't afraid of SAVAK any longer. And if he isn't afraid of SAVAK, then the Shah's had it.'

Such momentary insights changed people's perceptions of the Shah's chances of survival, as much as the daily parade of trouble on the streets of Iran; and just as his interview on their domestic television service had convinced many Iranians, with their swift instincts, that the Shah was in serious trouble, so the interviews he gave to the Western media presented people in the outside world with clear indications that he was starting to lose his grip. In October, speaking to a correspondent from *Le Figaro*, he described the situation as 'discouraging' more than twenty times during the hour they were together.

A few days before, he had been interviewed for American television, and had apparently found it hard to concentrate either on the questions that were being asked, or on his answers to them. He rarely lifted his eyes from the magnificent carpet in the room in the Niavaran Palace where the interview took place. The pauses between the questions and the Shah's answers grew longer and longer, and the answers themselves more and more vague. It was deeply embarrassing to watch. The fact that the Shah was fighting a courageous battle against cancer, and was receiving a debilitating and painful course of treatment for it, was a carefully guarded secret; that may have accounted for his public performances. Someone who was close to him during those months says he was also suffering a good deal of pain in his feet, possibly from gout, which troubled him physically more than the cancer.

The Shah's mood was not always so negative: but even journalists who interviewed him at better, more confident moments found him strangely unaware of the true nature of the problems he faced. Time and again he would refer to Communist instigation of the rioting against him, and he seemed to know little about what was going on in the streets of his cities. But then he never saw the streets of his cities with his own eyes: he flew above them at a height of several hundred feet, and relied on his secret policemen and his courtiers to tell him what was going on.

Nowadays, of course, there are no photographs of the imperial family, nor of Reza Shah II, the Shah's son who succeeded to the title in exile, in the windows of the shops and cafés in Niavaran village, and there have been none since 1979. There are, however, few photographs of the new rulers either; a couple of Khomeini, one of Rafsanjani, and that is all. For those in the village who were genuine royalists, the fall of the Shah will have constituted a personal as well as a national catastrophe, but those days are now long past and things have settled down again. There are plenty of goods in the village shops, and up here, away from the big centres of population, the local *Komiteh* is relatively relaxed.

Tira and I arrived in Niavaran early, and decided to have lunch at one of the two cafés which were open. It was a hot August day, but up here in the mountains there was a good breeze. The workmen sitting in the café we selected were a little scandalized by our arrival, and there was a general feeling that we should eat our meal outside; not necessarily because we were not wanted, though they had probably never catered for a Western woman before, even one in *hejab*, but because the men who were eating inside, in the noise and the atmosphere of good fellowship, would feel too uncomfortable to have us in their midst. And so a special table was set for us, with white paper in lieu of a cloth, outside the café under the shadow of an elderly beech-tree, and the proprietor, a bandit-like figure with only one eye, smiled apologetically (but never glanced at Tira) and placed his hand over his heart at frequent intervals to show us how sorry he was that his place should be so unfit for us to eat in.

There was only one dish available: *abgusht*. We ordered it, though my attempts to make myself understood were otherwise mostly unsuccessful, and it was with some difficulty that I was able to ask for bread, tea and Coca-Cola. The roar of noise from inside broke through to us each time the bandit brought us the things we had ordered, and subsided as the door closed behind him. A hubble-bubble, *qalian* in Farsi, filled the window beside our table, and two others were in use inside the café. As I looked in from time to time, glimmering faces inside bowed their heads politely or smiled, and then everyone else would laugh at them. The *abgusht* arrived.

It was seven years since I had last had *abgusht*, and the complexities of eating it in the approved style had, alas, completely gone from me. The word itself means little more than thick soup with a meat base (literally,'meat water') though my London Library Persian language book gave the strong impression that it was a clear soup: which made it all the more difficult to cope with it when it arrived. That a performance of some kind was required was indicated by the fact that while the *abgusht* came in a large pot, we were provided with two small pots and a pestle with which to grind it up. What it is we had to grind, neither the resources of the London Library nor of my own memory were unfortunately sufficient to tell.

The bandit clearly felt he was not up to the task of explaining, and politely left us to get on with it. Later, under the careful tuition of Mahmoudi, our driver, we learned how to extract the meat, the chickpeas, the tomatoes and the potatoes from the soup, mash them up into a kind of paste by means of the mortar and pestle, and eat them separately with bread and with the soup that was left. But Mahmoudi was not driving us today, and we were on our own in every sense. Only the innate good manners of the workmen kept them from watching the outlandish way we dealt with their familiar dish. We found it delicious.

At the end, when I asked for *hesab*, the bill, the bandit looked at me questioningly, and assuming that it was simply my mispronunciation I made the international sign by scribbling something with an imaginary pen on an imaginary pad. No *hesab*, he said, laughing noisily and raising his eyes in a kind of mock apology; he could not write. He could, however, make the sign with his fingers for 900 *rials* and we paid, leaving the pleasant shade of his beech tree and his mixture of politeness and amusement. By now, we reasoned, the gates of the Niavaran Palace should be open.

The first time I came here, I was turned away from these gates for so much as asking my driver (again, not Mahmoudi) to stop while we got the camera out for some filming. Two of the Shah's

Immortals, his praetorian guard, marched over to us at once and ordered us off. The second time I came to the Palace was on the morning after the Revolution, when the Immortals were standing shivering in their underwear looking very mortal indeed, and their gaudy uniforms were piled up on the back of a truck, ready to be taken off for burning. Now, on this third time of returning, the Palace had been open for a week as a tourist attraction for the people who, notionally, had taken it for themselves.

There had been a certain amount of debate about the wisdom of such a move. Might it not, one member of the Majlis asked, act as a centre of attraction for those who privately sympathized still with the Pahlavi dynasty? What did it matter if they did? another countered; the Islamic Republic was firmly enough based now for people to be allowed to see for themselves the corrupt life-style of the blood-sucking Pahlavis. He and his supporters won the day; the decision was taken to refurbish the palace as it had been when the royal family fled, and to clean up the grounds and turn them into a public park.

It proved to be a little like visiting the Winter Palace in Petrograd in, say, 1924. At the gates of black, unornamented steel which the Immortals had once protected against visiting television crews, but not against the revolutionary crowds, there were banners declaring the invincibility of the Islamic Republic and an end to the corruption of the past. In the guardhouse, where a smart sergeant had once been posted, two watchmen in civilian clothes sat talking and laughing. They were in their mid-thirties, and seemed pleasant enough; and although one was tossing a handgun back and forth in his hands, it had a brass cloakroom tag pinned to the trigger-guard, which somehow reduced it to the everyday level of umbrellas and briefcases. I made a joking reference to the gun, and the man holding it explained that a senior member of the Revolutionary Guards was paying the palace a visit.

'The *former* palace,' I said, in mock-reproof. I had used the tactic a couple of times before, with street names of the Shah's time which had been rebaptised in suitably revolutionary fashion, and I had found that something about the style of the joke seemed to appeal to the Persian mind. Both watchmen rocked with laughter, and the handgun slipped between the knees of its guardian, the barrel pointing perilously inwards. For a brief moment I consider making another joke, but doubted if my rudimentary Farsi was up to it.

We were asked to leave our bags and were handed another

brass tag in their place, and a small, elderly, unshaven man with an extremely dirty shirt gave me the most perfunctory of searches: a pat on the chest and on each of the pockets of my trousers, and nothing more. Since it was still lunchtime, the gun-minding watchman explained, there were no women searchers, so Tira could go in unchecked. Why the searches anyway?

'Who knows what may happen? You have to be careful.'

But careful of whom? Royalists? Or hypocrites (that being the name by which the Islamic Republic refers to the Mojaheddin)? The watchman smiled and brandished the revolver, making the tag jingle against the butt, to indicate that they were ready for anything and anyone, even if he couldn't precisely say which direction the threat might come from. My own feeling was that the security, such as it was, had resulted from the Majlis debate on the wisdom of opening the palace to the public. Neither the arguments in favour nor those against had been specific in any way, and the security was unspecific too. I stopped asking difficult questions and bought two 100-*rial* tickets instead.

The grounds of the palace were kept remarkably well; it was hard to imagine that when the Shah and Empress were here, the standard of care could have been higher. The grass, coarser than the English variety, was manicured in the kind of parallel stripes which form the effect an English gardener strives for. Geraniums grew in star-shaped beds, whose earth was newly turned and free of weeds. In the shade of the tall maple trees which must have been planted at the time the original palace was built, sprinklers were at work, trailing clouds of water which glittered in the early afternoon sunshine. The sound was as refreshing as the effect. A little further away was the grass plot from which the Shah's helicopter took off on Tuesday 16 January 1979, when he left Iran for ever.

Seeing it all again, seven years afterwards, I found the memories remarkably fresh in my mind. Even the neatness of the grounds was familiar, because the imperial gardeners, in the absence of any instructions to the contrary, had gone on working even though the Shah had left. The iron gates had opened and the camera crew and I had been swept in on a flood-tide of demonstrators, singing and chanting rather than shouting slogans, and unarmed except for the occasional piece of wood. We swept past the shivering trouserless Immortals, unable for the time being to stop and film them because of the pressure of the crowd. But it was less like the storming of the Winter Palace than a scene from the French Revolution: the peasants and artisans breaking into the grounds of the count's château.

The crowd boiled along the pathways and lawns, past the old house built by Reza Shah and towards the new one his son built in 1957. The mood did not seem to be one of destruction, but more, almost, of a kind of militant curiosity; they wanted to see how he and the Empress had lived, not to burn the place to the ground. We raced along with them, Bill Handford holding the camera as steady as he could and filming as he ran, but a line of volunteers with armbands, the kind of men who later became Revolutionary Guards and *Komiteh* members, stopped us at the point where the pathway opened out into an open area in front of the main entrance to the palace.

One of the volunteers shouted out something to the crowd, and everyone halted in a mood of mass disappointment; the looting fever was undoubtedly on them, and if they had broken their way in the contents, and perhaps the building itself, would undoubtedly have been destroyed. But everybody was obedient, and I realized then that the great majority of them were probably not revolutionaries at all, but men and women from Niavaran village: simple people who had been royalists in their hearts until, perhaps, the Shah had left, and might well be royalists again, if the time were ever right to acknowledge it. They stood where they had been stopped, trying to peer in through the windows twenty yards away, but there was little to be seen: a desk with a few trinkets on it, some expensive curtains, a painting gleaming faintly in the quiet darkness inside.

The volunteers took a step forward, and the crowd moved instinctively, obediently, back. No one wanted trouble, and if their curiosity were not going to be satisfied by the men who were emerging already as their new masters, then they would not challenge their authority. They turned and walked away, herded by the volunteers, their sticks and pieces of wood trailing now, casting occasional regretful looks back at the palace they wanted to be able to say they had seen. None of them paid any attention to the Immortals, who had been given blankets to put round themselves by now and were looking a little less like condemned men. The volunteers rejected our requests to film through the windows of the palace, but they had no objection to our filming the grounds and of course the wretched Immortals and their heaped-up uniforms. We got our pictures of them and of the quiet, wondering crowd, and left. With the fall of the imperial palace, the Revolution could be said definitively to have been completed.

Seven years later, Tira and I walked across the place where this crowd-scene took place, noticing the kind of things I had not had time to notice then: the nineteenth-century French street lamps painted a civic dark green, and bought wholesale, no doubt, in Paris. On a line of shaded benches, which might or might not have been there before, a seated queue of quiet, polite citizens had formed, and moved up a couple of spaces to make room for us. We might be all waiting there to apply for something: residents' parking permits in an expensive part of London, perhaps. The women were wrapped anonymously in *chadors*, but their faces mostly had the look of education and money about them. There were two men, who also seemed to be middle-class. They tried not to stare at us, which was a measure of their politeness, while we waited for a guide to come over and take our tickets. Collectively, we constituted the first tour of the afternoon.

Looked at in isolation from its attractive setting, the palace was scarcely handsome. It suffered from the faults that buildings of the mid-fifties usually do suffer from: a lumpish shape, over-much concrete, and rooms which are never quite the size they should be. Even in 1957, when it was built, it must have looked as though its owner thought he was buying style, and was simply spending a great deal of money. It summoned up memories of Frank Sinatra, thin oblong bow-ties, and cars with too much chrome. The very rich are not often very tasteful: the money they have spent usually seems to get in the way.

The Niavaran Palace had its virtues, all the same. It was only two storeys high, and parts of it were attractively tiled in yellow and blue. It was not built to overawe the visitor, but to remind him that he was entering a family home; and for that reason perhaps the decision to open it to the public did not have quite the effect its advocates in the Majlis had intended. It certainly did not appal the visitor with its extravagance, nor did it symbolize the immense corruption of Iran in the Shah's later years; instead, it shrank the imperial family to normal, understandable terms. Given that the various Pahlavi family members are thought to have possessed no fewer than forty-five palaces and mansions between them in Tehran alone, it was the scale of their total spending, rather than the Shah's personal style of living, which deserved critical examination.

We walked in single file to the front door, over which a particularly disapproving portrait of Khomeini now hung, and took off our shoes obediently in the porch in order to protect the carpets inside. This enhanced the reverential feel of the place, as though it were Iran's equivalent of Lenin's Tomb we were entering, and not its Winter Palace at all. Inside, it was cool and surprisingly gloomy. We shuffled round while the guide told us, as guides will, the measurements of each room, the provenance of every major piece of furniture, the size of every one of the great carpets from Isfahan which covered every floor. The carpets were the only objects of serious artistic value in the house; the rest were mostly things the Shah and Empress had received as presents from the rich and famous like themselves. There was, for instance, a dreadful gold-plated bowl from Richard Nixon, with the presidential head, like the profile on a Roman coin, superimposed on that of the Shah. There was no question which of the two heads was in the place of honour: Nixon's was the one.

By this time the guide allowed us to wander round at our own pace, and had ceased altogether to bother about the six Iranians who were on the tour with us. Everything now was in English.

'When they are wanting coolness or sun, they press this button like I do, and see what follows.'

What followed was that a large panel in the roof opened slowly and silently over the central atrium of the house, allowing the sun's rays to cut downwards into the gloom and pick out the pattern on the largest and most remarkable of the carpets. The guide pressed the button to close the roof again, but could not resist playing with it once or twice, to show off its responsiveness. We resumed our exploration of a house which contrived neither to be grand nor intimate, and whose rooms, like those of Versailles, were all interlinked so that you had to pass through each one to reach another.

The furniture seemed to have been chosen at random, with nothing matching anything else; there was green, red, gold and white upholstery, often in the same room, and everything from Second Empire to 1950s in terms of style. But although the guide denied it vehemently, what may have happened is that some of the imperial furniture vanished from the Niavaran Palace before there was proper control over it, and has been replaced from the other Pahlavi family residences in Tehran. The smaller objects in the house, right down to the Empress's gilded Kleenex box, had been numbered carefully and labelled.

The Shah's bedroom was austere: a narrow single bed in an alcove, with a portrait of his father glowering on the wall. The Empress, by contrast, slept in a vast gilded four-poster. 'Society' portraits of her and her children, expensive but tasteless, hung on the walls. The guide, with something salacious in his voice, allowed us a glimpse of the Empress's clothes: glitzy robes of pink and blue and green, crammed together in her surprisingly small dressing-room, and a hundred or so pairs of shoes. By now, though, the burden of tastelessness has shifted. The imperial family was no more lacking in taste for choosing the furnishings and clothes they did, than we were for peering at their private possessions and passing judgment on them. The Shah's hubris may have been intolerable, and his régime cruel towards its opponents and corrupt in many of its dealings; but he himself paid the price for it all, when many of the men and women who had a more direct responsibility are living on the proceeds in the pleasanter cities of Western Europe and the United States. I felt a sudden revulsion, and we hurried out into the sunlight.

I may have communicated my feelings unconsciously to the guide, because directly we were outside and I wandered off on my own to examine the outside of the palace, he followed me and started questioning me in a hostile way.

I answered him curtly enough, but then his colleague, having watched me taking notes, leaned across and said something to him that I could not hear. 'My friend says that when you get back to *Engilistan*, never mind your notes, you will say bad things about Iran.'

I turned on him angrily. 'Tell your friend that he is insulting me, and that it's as though I were to ask him how much he steals from the palace.' I walked quickly away, not certain how to bring the incident to an end.

Tira, meanwhile, had been talking to the two women who were on the tour with us. Although they had realized we were Western journalists, they had no apparent fears about speaking to her of their dislike for the *chadors* they had to wear, and their efforts to get together the money to come to Western Europe for a holiday. It seemed as though they had came to the Niavaran Palace to catch a glimpse of the old days, when the Shah was in control. We walked out side by side with the women, and as we passed the entrance to the palace the two guides smiled and waved at me, as though we had become friends; probably they had not meant to be offensive.

For the rest of the day I found myself thinking about the Shah and his palace, and back at the British Institute where we were staying I flicked through his memoirs, newly aware of the vulnerability that underlay the bombast:

> In my early years as King, and especially during the Mossa-degh period, I went through acute anxieties; and it is perhaps no wonder that my hair is prematurely white. Without the ability to relax I would surely have disintegrated physically, emotionally, even mentally. (*Mission For My Country*, p. 319)

One of the few mistakes my father made was to rely upon a

narrowing circle of advisers. Fearing Reza Shah, they flattered him rather than telling him the truth; and I am sorry to say they were by no means always incorruptible. My system is entirely different. . . . (*Idem*, p. 322)

In 1971, the Shah was at the height of his powers. His rule was unchallenged, Ayatollah Khomeini was in exile in Iraq, the immense corruption that took root after he led the OPEC countries in tripling the price of oil still lay ahead. So did the diagnosis by two leading French specialists in 1974 that he had cancer. According to his calculations, 1971 marked the 2,500th anniversary of the founding of the Persian Empire, and he celebrated the occasion in a fashion which may never again be equalled for ceremony, colour and sheer excess of every kind. In the flat plain at Pasargardae, in front of the tomb of Cyrus, the Shah and the Empress Farah stood at a microphone, while the helicopters which had brought them there high above the heads of his subjects waited to take them back. Field guns fired an immense salute, and an old man with a watering can pushed his way through the impeccable guard of honour and started watering the cacti, unaware that the great occasion had started in earnest. As the boom of the guns died away, the Shah read an invocation that began 'O Cyrus, Great King, King of Kings' and ended 'O Cyrus, rest in peace, for we are awake'.

The Tent City at Persepolis covered 160 acres, and 43,000 yards of flame-proof cloth in beige and royal blue was used to make the tents, which were grouped around a central plaza in which fountains played day and night. Each tent had a sitting room, two bathrooms, two bedrooms, and a kitchen. The followers whom each of the main guests had brought with them were relegated to orange and white tents a little farther away. Maxim's of Paris provided the food, and the best champagne was available twenty-four hours a day. Monarchs and presidents or their representatives from 69 countries attended, among them President Podgorny of the Soviet Union, Vice-President Spiro Agnew of the United States, the Emperor Haile Selassie of Ethiopia (who brought a retinue of 72 and a chihuahua dog with a diamond collar), King Constantine of Greece, and Imelda Marcos, the wife of the Philippines President. All of them fell, were removed from office, or disgraced in the years that followed, with the exception of King Constantine who had been overthrown already. 6,200 soldiers dressed in the uniforms of every Persian epoch since Cyrus marched past the assembled guests, and there was the biggest fireworks display in history.

Today the Tent City is still in use, though the beige and royal blue tents, and the orange and white ones, are faded and bedraggled. The fountains have long since been dismantled, and the flat and watered ground where the soldiers marched in their false beards has been churned up by tyres and half-tracks. Latrine trenches have been dug along the perimeter of the area. The City is now used to house the volunteers from nearby Shiraz while they undergo basic training for the war with Iraq. In the evenings, the soldiers chant about marching to Kerbala and Jerusalem, and the mullahs sing about the martyrdom of Hussein to men whose foreheads are bound with the white and red scarves of martyrdom. By the Shah's reckoning, the imperial history of Persia lasted 2,507 years; now a new period has begun, and it is impossible to know how long it will last.

8

The Great Satan

I conceive that the transformation [for the worse in
our political position in Persia] . . . is a condition of
affairs for which our own policy, weak in its conception and calamitous in its results, has been mainly
responsible; and that to cry over spilt milk is as futile
an expedient in politics as it is in any other walk of life.

George Nathaniel Curzon, *Persia And The Persian
Question*, 1892

IT IS MARKED on the maps of Tehran nowadays as 'The previous
embassy of the USA'. It is not listed in the telephone book, unlike
even the embassy of Iraq, with which Iran has been at war since
1980. The Swiss, who have the uneasy task of looking after
whatever remains of American interests in Iran, do not draw
attention to the link in any way, and the embassy itself, in what
used to be Roosevelt Avenue and is now named after a clerical
associate of the Imam, is better avoided nowadays. Revolutionary Guards are posted every few yards along the walls of its
compound, and to take a photograph of it is an extremely risky
undertaking. The walls are covered with slogans, some dating
from the days of the hostage crisis: 'We will make America face a
severe defeat', 'US is angry with us and will die of the anger.' A
large black crow with a grey head sits on the top of one of the
sentry boxes and watches us as we pass. Behind its high wall,
painted the same shade of grey as the crow's head, the previous
embassy of the USA has become a desolate and forbidding place.

There is a certain amount of bustle on the other side of the wall.
People are walking in and out of the main door, or standing
talking on the steps. Almost all of them are young. Over the
gateway on the corner entrance to the compound a sign reads
'Center of publication for US espionage den of documents', but
that is out of date now. The former embassy has been turned into
a training school for Revolutionary Guards – training, according
to Tehran gossip, for terrorist acts abroad, though it seems a very

public place to assemble future secret agents. The publication of the documents which were seized from the embassy when it was stormed in 1979 is now done somewhere else.

There is, however, a little office in the corner by the gateway where the published documents can be bought. We banged on the window, seeing signs of habitation, and an old man shuffled towards us from some inner refuge and pushed the window open.

'*Bale?*' he asked, with an air of self-sacrifice. He was wearing pyjama trousers and slippers, for it was three in the afternoon and we had broken in on his siesta. We explained that we were journalists and wished to buy some of the books of American documents which were on sale. Most of the explaining was done in sign language. He sighed, and said something over his shoulder.

A much younger man in an unidentifiable brown uniform and with large cow-like eyes to match came out to see what the matter was. We were handed a type-written list of the volumes which were available, together with a well-produced brochure in execrable English which explained the nature of the documents more fully:

The books about the US espionage deb (sic), mentioned in the list show overal ploitical (sic), military and economic dominance of great satan on our country.

Which indeed they do: up to a point. The list then proceeds to itemize the various types of documents, starting with the documents in clear, rather than in cipher, which were captured on the first day of the take-over of the embassy, and widening out into the contacts between the embassy and Iranian politicians, both before and after the Revolution, the activities of the Soviet Union as revealed by the American documents, and United States involvement in other parts of the Middle East. In all, they amounted to fifty-five volumes, each the size of an ordinary paperback; reasonably well produced, with the documents clear enough and obviously genuine, and with a translation into Farsi at the back. None of the volumes cost more than 352 *rials*, and each carried the same words on the cover: 'Documents from the US Espionage Den' at the top, and 'Muslim Students Following the Line of the Imam' at the bottom.

'Are you one of the students following the line of the Imam?' I asked.

The brown eyes of the young man behind the glass were

143

clouded with suspicion.

'Why do you want to know?'

'No reason, really; I was just interested.'

The suspicion faded. 'I used to be,' he said, with a certain pride.

'You were there when everyone went over the wall, in 1979?'

'Yes.'

On the strength of that I elicited a few more fragments of information: that the business of publication was indeed continuing somewhere else now, that it took much longer to publish each volume now, that it wasn't so much fun to do it nowadays. He made us each out a rather splendid receipt (I was vaguely reminded of a storekeeper in a Victorian grocery) and the old man wrapped up our volumes in some magnificent wrapping paper, along the lines of something you might get at the Victoria and Albert Museum, or the Metropolitan. The paper is grey, with white lettering ('The Center for the Publication of . . .' etc.) and a photograph of the students attacking the embassy gates, and, set slantwise across the paper in the most dramatic way is a CIA document in vivid red which says 'SECRET. This is a Cover Sheet' and proceeds to explain the procedure for dealing with secret information. It was, I felt, much too good to be used as wrapping-paper, and I asked for and was given a sheet of it as a memento.

On 4 November 1979, as the future documents salesman and hundreds of other Students of the Imam's Line came pouring over the gates and walls of the embassy, the staff inside crammed hundreds of documents into shredding machines, one of which was an immense grinder the size of a cement mixer. This churned up paper into a kind of dry grey flour, with perhaps a single letter or sometimes a vertical line of letters on each piece. There may be as many as a million pieces; and those of the Students who still remain have the fearful task of reassembling the pieces to form coherent, readable documents.

The reward for all this painstaking labour was considerable, especially in the early days. The documents which were found untouched in the embassy, together with those which could be reconstituted, were powerful weapons with which to discredit moderate politicians of a liberal persuasion who were trying to keep their place in post-Revolutionary political life. The Students denounced anyone who was unfortunate enough to have been mentioned in the embassy documents in a favourable, or even sometimes a neutral, way.

Now that those days are past, the grey flour has lost much of its early political force. Those who genuinely were American agents, or could be made out to seem as though they were, have long since been arrested or left the country. But the work goes on. To a Western reader, the documents show United States policy towards Iran in a sorry rather than a criminal light: as having been poorly informed, influenced by dubious and unreliable figures in the Shah's hierarchy, and woefully lacking in a clear awareness of what constituted American interests.

But to the supporters of the Islamic Republic the documents show something altogether different; as the introduction to one selection of them demonstrates:

> America, Superdevil of the 20th century, has for so many years exerted intense effort to expand its hegemony and impose its policies worldwide. Pigheadedly, she continues her seditious campaigns to exploit, tyranize, intimidate, spy, assassinate . . .
>
> It is our sincere hope that [the publication of these documents] will help expose the true visage of this bastion of evil, at present hidden under a mask of sophistry, misleading propaganda and deceiving policies.

The earliest documents, those which the Students found in clear in the safe of the *chargé d'affaires*, Bruce Laingen, are plainly genuine, and are reproduced in their entirety. There is no real effort to distinguish those which are genuinely damaging from those which are purely administrative; for the Students, the very words 'secret' or 'confidential' seem to be enough to justify publication. So we have random letters, invitations, briefing papers and bureaucratic formulae of all kinds jumbled up with political assessments and the occasional item of intelligence. A study of the *Washington Post* and the *New York Times* during the period covered by the documents would probably yield more hard information about Iran and fewer unsubstantiated or mistaken opinions.

What is clear, however, is that the US embassy had very little idea of what was going on in the months that led up to the Revolution, and little more after it. Its sources of information within the Shah's régime were considerable, but swung backwards and forwards from hope to despair as 1978 went on; while there were no discernible sources at all among the supporters of Khomeini. In one of the documents published by the Students and written as late as 30 November 1978, a mere six weeks before the Shah left Iran for good, Ambassador William H. Sullivan reported to the Secretary of State, Cyrus Vance, as follows:

> While we realize distrust which most opposition leaders have in Shah's promises, we believe it is unrealistic for them to insist on Shah's abdication . . .
>
> We . . . believe [Khomeini] has implacable hatred for Shah and for the Pahlavi dynasty. His only program seems to be a negative one, designed to serve his personal revenge. His concept of an 'Islamic republic' is nebulous, and in the face of the power controlled by the armed forces, is unrealistic. Therefore, we believe politicians must make their choice based on prospects for retaining the integrity of the country and without reference to the probability that Khomeini would renounce it.
>
> . . . In any event, we doubt Khomeini personally commands all the power that is often attributed to him. We feel many groups, which are far from religious Moslems, accept Khomeini as a symbol and use his rhetoric because it serves their own purposes and coincides with their own aims. We doubt he would have much concept of how to organize the govt of a nation.
>
> . . . We consider time for beginning of realistic negotiations with Shah is now.

There is no doubt that this document, like most of the others printed by the Students, is entirely genuine: it contains most of the misunderstandings and miscalculations which marked US policy during this entire period. But by no means all the documents have the same stamp of authenticity. Some of those which have been assembled from hundreds or thousands of tiny bits of paper are much more questionable; for instance, these supposed instructions to a CIA agent:

Top Secret
To be mentioned in passport:

> According to the information given about your identity in your passport, you are a bachelor born on the 8th July 1934 at Anthorp [Antwerp?] in Belgium; eyes: blue; without any particular sign; height: 1.88; profession: Commercial representative. A Belgian can have Flemish as his mother tongue and live on [sic] the French territories [sic] of Belgium, in the region of G.T. for example. You can equally claim to have been born at Anthorp where you have worked for a society. And

that you have later been transferred to the central office of this society in Brasel [Brussels?]. Though Anthorp is only a 90 minutes ride from Brasel, you have decided to settle in the suburbs of the latter . . . Your address is as follows: 17th, G.T. road, Belgium.

That is self-evidently not genuine in its present form, though it may have been inaccurately reconstructed from genuine fragments. But most of the documents about clandestine activity as well as about policy matters are real enough, and the most convincing thing about them is the growing awareness within the embassy of the predicament in which US policy found itself: by the late 1970s Washington had no alternative but to back the Shah, even though the Shah might not survive in power.

This was not like the Philippines, seven years later, where the United States supported a favourable dictatorship until the point where it could no longer survive, and then switched gracefully to the opposition and ordered the old dictator to vacate his palace. In Iran the United States had helped to crush the opposition: and by the time that Washington realized that the Shah could not survive, it was much too late to appeal to the opposition for help.

The United States had come to put all its regional eggs in the single, ultimately fragile basket of the Pahlavi dynasty through a series of miscalculations which began in earnest in 1953. The Students who nowadays occupy their time in the patient piecing together of their interminable documents believe they are constructing a unique archive of evil; instead, they are merely adding to the evidence which demonstrates how a great power managed to misunderstand completely where its own real interests lay.

'I owe my throne to God, my people, my army – and to you!'

The man to whom the Shah owed his throne was Kermit Roosevelt, the Central Intelligence Agency representative in Tehran. Roosevelt quotes the remark in his book *Counter-Coup: The Struggle for the Control of Iran*, which was re-issued in 1979 at the height of the political turmoil in Iran, much against the wishes of the CIA itself. By the time of his fall the Shah was convinced that the CIA, together with the British, had engineered his problems; but although that is not true (the CIA's own documents, as published by the Students, show that clearly enough) it is certainly the case that the Shah owed his throne to the success of Operation Ajax on 19 August 1953, as planned and executed by Roosevelt.

Faced with a powerful constitutional threat from his prime minister and political enemy, Dr. Mohammed Mossadeq, the Shah had briefly lost his nerve and fled the country. But Mossadeq's policy of nationalizing Iran's oil had created considerable tensions within the country, and the oil boycott staged by Britain and other Western countries was starting to bring about real economic deterioration. Kermit Roosevelt used British SIS contacts in the police, the armed forces, and the Bazaar, and welded them together skilfully into a royalist coalition.

Bribing key officers in the police and army, and bringing out partisan crowds onto the streets, he led his counter-coup and persuaded the Shah to fly back to Tehran. Thousands of demonstrators cheered the Shah's journey through the streets, while some of Mossadeq's supporters were attacked and murdered. Their bodies were taken to the Elburz Mountains and buried secretly. The reinstatement of the Shah on his throne was smoothly planned and frugally conducted: it cost only $100,000 to bribe the crowd and the officers, and the remainder of the million dollars which had originally been set aside for the operation was not required.

And so the United States bought the post of chief protector to the Shah at a bargain rate. Britain, which had held the post for a hundred years, had handled the crisis over Mossadeq's nationalization of Iran's oil so maladroitly, and was anyway so weakened since the end of the Second World War, that it had no chance of its regaining its old position. For the Americans it was mostly new territory; they had had little to do with Iran in the past, and at first lacked the background knowledge to make their own assessment of United States interests there.

For that reason, just as Kermit Roosevelt accepted British advice over where to place his bribes, so the State Department and the newly elected President Eisenhower accepted the British analysis of the situation in Iran: that the Shah (whom the British had set on the throne in 1941 in place of his pro-Nazi father, Reza Shah) was the figure who would best preserve Western interests in a strategically important area. But while the British, as controllers of the Iranian oil industry, had good reason to back the Shah against the National Front government of Dr Mossadeq, with his nationalizing ambitions, it was not so clearly in American interests to do so.

Washington, however, shared the British assessment that Iran occupied an important square on the strategic chessboard. This was true, but scarcely a new idea; Curzon had adopted it in his book *Persia and the Persian Question* in 1893:

> Turkestan, Afghanistan, Transcaspia, Persia – to many these
> names breathe only a sense of utter remoteness or a memory
> of strange vicissitudes and of moribund romance. To me, I
> confess, they are the pieces of a chessboard upon which is
> being played out a game for the dominion of the world.

The Cold War gave new life to these earlier British ideas of a
Great Game being played out in central and southern Asia. By
1953 Soviet Russia was a more serious threat than Imperial
Russia had been, and it had been with great difficulty that the
Western allies had forced Stalin to withdraw his troops from Iran
after the end of the Second World War. The British belief that Iran
was under threat from the Russians was therefore easily
accepted in Washington; so was the much less accurate link
which the British made between the nationalism of Dr Mossadeq
and outright Communism. The fact that Mossadeq received
support from the Communist Tudeh Party reinforced the notion.

The powerful Time-Life empire of Henry Luce, in its newsreel
for March 1952, characterized what it called 'the ageing, neurotic
Mossedeq' as a possible precursor for the Russians:

> [A]ny new instability in Iran might pave the way for Russian
> infiltration. This in turn could outflank the Turkish bastion, a
> main strongpoint against communism in the Middle East, and
> open a Red road to the Mediterranean and to Suez, to the oil of
> Iraq and Arabia, to the coveted ports of the Persian Gulf, and
> even to Pakistan and India.

With the exception of Turkey, each of the areas named was a
particular concern of British, rather American, foreign policy at
the start of the 1950s. Britain might be in the process of losing its
position in Iran, but it had won the argument in the United
States. In future, Washington's Iranian policy would simply be a
continuation of Britain's.

And yet the dangerous, neurotic near-Communist of Anglo-
American imaginings was in reality an elderly liberal whose
thinking had developed along specifically Western European
lines. Dr Mossadeq had studied law at the Ecole des Sciences in
Paris and obtained his doctorate in Switzerland, where he was
called to the bar and practised for many years. What made him
unacceptable in the eyes of British foreign policy was that he
regarded Iran much as Western European countries regarded

themselves: as independent entities with a right to control their own resources.

For the British, who had long treated Iran as something of a colony, this was an unacceptable challenge: and the Americans, who in less sensitive parts of the world were starting to support nationalist leaders in British colonies against their colonial masters, chose to regard it as unacceptable also. After Kermit Roosevelt's successful operation in putting the Shah back on his throne, Washington was committed to keeping him there. By blocking liberal, secular nationalism in 1953, the Americans had unwittingly played an important part in ensuring the rise of fundamentalist Islamic nationalism a quarter of a century later.

Now throve the armourers. From 1950 to 1963 the United States provided the Shah with military assistance worth $829 million and weapons systems worth $1.3 billion. The Shah, who was fascinated all his life by advanced weaponry, continually asked the Eisenhower administration for more, with the vocal support of the vice-president, Richard Nixon, who had met the Shah and was impressed by him. Eisenhower, however, resisted on the grounds that better training, not more expensive weapons, were required to deal with any threat from across the Soviet border.

President Kennedy, elected in 1960, was less interested in the threat to Iran from outside, and more in the possibility of internal revolution. He made a loan of $35 million contingent on a programme of social reform, and urged the Shah to appoint Dr Ali Amini, the Iranian ambassador to Washington, as his prime minister. For a century and more, Iran's rulers had been told to run their country in the interests of outside powers; now the Shah was being ordered to run it in the interests of his own people – as defined by the theories of liberal economists such as Barbara Ward and W. W. Rostow.

The White Revolution which he launched in 1962 (as opposed to black revolution or the red revolution which he maintained were the alternatives) had land reform as its central feature. That, indeed, was a liberal measure which was to have a profound effect on the prosperity of the country; but it also brought Khomeini, who had recently become an ayatollah, to national prominence in Iran when he took a leading part in the resistance to the Shah's refusal to exempt religious endowments from the programme of compulsory land purchase, and to encourage the emancipation of women. Khomeini's arrest in June 1963 was accompanied by serious rioting in Tehran.

But however advantageous the White Revolution was to many

150

Iranians, it came complete with colonial trappings. There was an influx of thousands of American technicians, support staff, military men and their families; and they were accorded the principle of extraterritoriality in a bill which passed through the otherwise tame Majlis by a majority of only 74 to 61. One deputy asked why a foreign refrigerator repairman should have the same legal immunity that Iran's ambassadors had abroad. Ayatollah Khomeini characteristically couched it in terms that were stronger, more personal and more ominous:

> 'If the Shah should run over an American dog, he would be called to account. But if an American cook should run over the Shah, no one has any claim over him . . . If the men of religion had any influence, it would not be possible for the nation to be at one moment the prisoner of England, the next of America.'

The debate, and the rioting which accompanied it, went largely unnoticed in the United States. So did the exiling of Ayatollah Khomeini.

The presidential election of 1968 brought the Shah's friend Richard Nixon to power. When they had first met, in 1953, they had taken to each other and found that they shared the same anxieties about the Soviet Union. Now Iran was the dominant regional power, and President Nixon was in a position to give the Shah what he wanted. The number of uniformed American military advisers was greatly increased, and the Shah was given almost unlimited access to the non-nuclear military technology of the United States. When Nixon came to Tehran in May 1972 he looked across the negotiating table at the Shah and said simply, 'Protect me'. The meeting placed the Shah on a new level: no longer the leader of a client state but an equal, regarded by Nixon and his National Security Adviser Henry Kissinger as a fellow-strategist.

Only the Department of Defense, echoing Eisenhower's reservations, resisted the opening of the American arsenal to Iran and tried to introduce a note of caution. But Kissinger issued a memorandum in July 1972 that arms sales to the Shah were to be encouraged. In the four years that followed, Iran became the largest importer of US-produced arms in the world, at a cost of $4 billion. At that level, the United States was becoming as dependent upon Iran as Iran was on the United States.

After the resignation of Richard Nixon, James Schlesinger, as Secretary of Defense, asked President Ford in September 1975 for a review of US arms sales policy to Iran, doubting 'whether our policy of supporting an apparently open-ended Iranian military build-up will continue to serve our long-term interests.' But Kissinger was still in control of policy towards Iran and the review took years to produce. Two months afterwards, Schlesinger was replaced as Defense Secretary by Donald Rumsfeld.

By 1976 there were 24,000 Americans working in Iran; 1,270 of them were retired military men, hired by US manufacturers to work in Iran as arms salesmen. The US embassy and its military mission employed 2,000 Americans. Two years later, in the months that led up to the Revolution, the figure for US citizens living and working in Iran had almost certainly risen to more than 40,000. Resentments arose. Americans were paid much more than Iranians doing identical jobs for the same companies – even when those Iranians had received equivalent degrees from the same American universities. On oil projects in Abadan Iranian technicians were housed in quarters which were separate from and inferior to the American quarters; air conditioning, for instance, was standard only for the Americans.

In Isfahan, where Bell Helicopters employed 1,700 people on a forty-five acre site near the city, there were regular complaints about the behaviour of American workers, some of whom used to roar at speed around the city on motorbikes late at night. Street fights took place there between groups of Iranians and Americans. Anti-American feeling was high in both cities, and it was noticeable later that both played a significant part in the events leading up to the Revolution. In Abadan the Iranian oil workers went on strike in the autumn of 1978, and workers in the civil service throughout Iran began to follow their example. In Isfahan, the Islamic Republic was established in practice before the final act of the Revolution took place in Tehran.

The Americans, having adopted the British colonial pattern in Iran in 1953, found themselves facing a full-blown independence movement along colonial lines by 1978. And, a little like one of the less experienced colonial powers of Europe, the United States found itself with no favoured alternative to support in Iran, and no time in which to create one. Within six years of being asked to be the protector of United States interests in the region, Iran was turning into its worst enemy there.

The man who was to pay the price for Washington's years of unheeding dependence on the Shah was Jimmy Carter. The Shah himself was unenthusiastic about Carter's election to the presidency in 1976: under a Democratic administration there seemed to be less chance of obtaining what he wanted in the way of weaponry. The Shah had felt most comfortable with the Nixon-

Kissinger approach, whereby nothing was allowed to interfere with the strategic interests of the United States as they perceived them.

Carter, by contrast, had campaigned on a promise to link American arms sales to a country's record in human rights. Nevertheless his incoming administration was quick to exempt Iran from any prohibition on the grounds of its strategic importance; and when the Secretary of State, Cyrus Vance, visited Tehran in May 1977 he promised the Shah that the United States would honour all the arms contracts that had already been signed, and offered him the AWACS airborne early warning system and 160 F-16 fighters. The Shah's response was to ask for 140 extra F-16s.

Carter was also prepared to sell Iran the technology for generating nuclear energy, and approved a $1.1 billion package of military equipment. But the AWACS deal ran into trouble with the House International Relations Committee, on the grounds, later fully justified, that 'the security of advanced electronic devices could not be assured in Iran'. The subject was debated for three months, in a manner that the Shah found deeply humiliating.

The subject of Iran's internal policies was less of a problem. The Shah, remembering no doubt the measures he had taken under President Kennedy in 1963, had introduced some modest reforms and had done something about the use of torture by SAVAK. Carter accepted the changes the Shah was trying to make:

> My intelligence briefings revealed that despite the Iranian standard of living from the distribution of oil revenues, the Shah's single-minded pursuit of his own goals had engendered opposition from the intelligentsia and others who desired more participation in the political processes of Iran. SAVAK was notorious for its ruthless suppression of any dissent and I was informed that there were 2500 (the Shah said 'below 2500') political prisoners in Iranian jails. The Shah was convinced that immediate suppression was the best response to opposition, and he was somewhat scornful of western leaders (including me) who did not emulate his tactics.

In November 1977 the Shah visited Washington DC. The meetings with Carter were to go well; but 60,000 Iranian students had gathered in Washington to demonstrate against him, some of them carrying pictures of Khomeini. A counter-demonstration had been rather ineptly organized by the Iranian embassy, using military cadets, and while the President and Mrs Carter greeted the Shah and his Empress on the White House lawn the two groups clashed. The tear-gas which the Washington DC police had been using to damp the fighting down drifted across the lawn and affected the eyes of the visitors and their hosts as they stood to attention for the two national anthems.

It seemed trivial enough; but in Iran, where the new mood of mild liberalization enabled the pictures of the tear gas incident to be shown on television, it demonstrated to people what they had not previously been allowed to know: the degree of hostility which existed outside the country to the Shah. And with the Persian's ready ability to detect hidden messages, many of the people who watched their televisions that night assumed that the entire incident could have been allowed to happen only with President Carter's agreement: in other words the television pictures were a sign that Carter had implicitly withdrawn his support from the Shah. It was a significant success for the opposition, at a time when the Shah himself believed his position had never been stronger.

Seven weeks later, the Carters were in Tehran themselves, spending New Year's Eve with the Shah. It was to be the last full year, by the Western calendar, that the Shah would spend in his country; but as Jimmy Carter raised his glass to welcome 1978 it was entirely without irony that he toasted 'an island of stability in one of the more troubled areas of the world'. Less than a week later, secure in this sense of stability, the Shah, or perhaps his information minister, Daryoush Homayoun, authorized the sending of a scurrilous letter signed with the pseudonym 'Ahmad Rashidi-Motlaq' to the newspaper *Ettelaat*, accusing Ayatollah Khomeini of homosexuality and of being a British agent. The letter was published on 7 January 1978, and the angry demonstrations and loss of life at the hands of the police which followed proved to be the overturned candle which started the fire and burned down the house.

In the aftermath of the fall of the Shah, almost exactly a year later, every government with an embassy in Tehran examined its reporting during the difficult months of 1978 to see whether the Revolution had been predictable; and the general verdict was that no one had predicted it with any accuracy. The Israeli *chargé d'affaires* won a good deal of kudos for a report in which he came close to suggesting something of the sort, but neither the Israelis, the French, the British, the Russians nor the Americans – the embassies with the best connexions in Iran – forecast with any real accuracy what would happen. As late as August 1978 the CIA, in its National Intelligence Estimate, reported that Iran could not be considered to be in a 'pre-revolutionary' position, because

> . . . those who are in opposition, both violent and non-violent, do not have the capacity to be more than troublesome.... There is dissatisfaction with the Shah's tight control of the political process, but this does not threaten the government.

The CIA, by this stage, was working extremely closely with SAVAK, and was influenced by SAVAK's own, moderately optimistic view of events. The US embassy, which did not share that particular set of blinkers, was however equipped with others.

Part of the price that the United States paid for its close relationship with the Shah was that it was obliged to bow to the imperial wishes and avoid any links with opposition groups or with individual political dissidents. Before 1978 there were none. After the disturbances in January that year a group of National Front people made contact; but that was all. Few political officers in the embassy could speak Farsi, and although relations with the military and with security organizations were extremely good there was virtually no contact with the Bazaar and none at all with the clergy. As for locally employed staff, the majority were Armenians or Bahá'ís; there were very few Shi'ite Muslims. The ambassador himself came to rely heavily on the gossip provided by his Armenian driver. Apart from him, the only Iranians whom William Sullivan spoke to at any length were probably army officers, the Shah's ministers, and the Shah himself.

American journalists, like British and French ones, were provided with a far more accurate picture of what was going on, since they were often in daily touch with demonstrators and the leading ayatollahs. By the autumn, having witnessed the strength of feeling on the streets, and watched the draftees in the army wavering in their loyalty, a number of American and British journalists were openly questioning the Shah's chances of political survival; but on 28 October Ambassador Sullivan was still reporting:

> . . . the Shah is the unique element which can, on the one hand, restrain the military, and, on the other hand, lead a controlled transition . . . I would oppose any overture to Khomeini.

But Sullivan, like President Carter himself, had inherited a bureaucratic machine which was capable only of viewing the situation from one direction. His embassy had become an office for selling equipment and weapons systems, and its political reporting rôle had been heavily reduced long before he was posted to Iran. He faced hostility from Zbigniew Brzezinski's National Security Council, which tried to undermine his influence and that of the State Department. Brzezinski, indeed, seemed convinced that the Russians were behind the trouble in Iran: not a mistake which Sullivan made. Above all, Sullivan was reporting to an administration which for much of 1978 had been concentrating on the Camp David negotiations with the prime minister of Israel and the president of Egypt to the exclusion of almost everything else.

On 9 November, without any prior warning, Sullivan switched. His telegram, entitled 'Thinking the Unthinkable', suggested that the Shah, far from being the unique restraining element, might actually leave the country and Khomeini might return to Iran and take up a Gandhi-like position, choosing a leader who would be suitable to the Iranian military. The embarrassing expression 'Gandhi-like' is omitted from Sullivan's account of the telegram in his memoirs, and it is hard not to sympathize with him for leaving it out. As late as February 1979 a writer in the *New York Times* was suggesting that Khomeini might provide the Third World with a model of humane governance, and in the same month I suggested in a broadcast that although justice in the Islamic Republic might turn out to be rough, it seemed unlikely to be savage. But then journalists are used to making public mistakes and having to live with them. Ambassadors also have to live with their mistakes, but they are usually made in private.

It is doubtful whether it would have made any difference to the situation at all for Sullivan to have recognized the dangers to the Shah before he did. Afterwards his reporting to Washington was often more accurate than that of other observers: he forecast both the weakness of Bakhtiar and the intransigence of Khomeini. But it made no difference whatever to US policy, which was rudderless now that the Shah had left. US policy was the Shah; and from January 1979 to the present day there has been no settled policy to replace it.

One evening in 1986 an announcer on Iranian television warned viewers that they should watch an important programme later that night, but gave no indication of the subject. When the programme began, it proved to be about the take-over of the American embassy, seven years previously, which had been the beginning of the hostage crisis. There had been programmes on the subject before, but this one differed in that the pictures which were shown had not been taken by people in the crowd outside; they were recorded by the fixed security cameras which the Americans themselves had installed on the main buildings of the embassy.

Soundlessly, in black and white, the waves of attackers came swarming over the walls and gates and charged towards the embassy entrance. The pictures showed a few of the Marine guards trying to stand in the crowd's path, but they disappeared under the sheer weight of the attack. The pictures lasted for a matter of minutes only, but they were an extraordinary record of an incident which led to the humiliation of the United States and the ending of the political career of its president.

The great majority of the hostages who were taken in the embassy that day were to remain prisoners for 444 days. But Marine Sgt. William Quarles, who had been out jogging when the attack took place, was released early. He was black, and the Students of the Imam's Line who were in control of the embassy decided to free him, together with thirteen other blacks and women prisoners, as a gesture to people whom they believed to be oppressed by white American society. A photograph taken by one of the Students immediately after the storming of the embassy shows Quarles, who stands head and shoulders above the other Marines as well as their captors, resisting while a blindfold is being tied around the eyes of one of his comrades. He had been in his apartment on the other side of the street from the embassy, and had heard the security officer give the order over the walkie-talkies they all carried: 'Don't fire your weapons. When they come for you, give up.'

Quarles was an intelligent man, who had joined the Marine Corps because he wanted to see the world. Like one or two of the other Marines, he had learned a little Farsi. He also spent his free time outside the confines of the embassy, and had Iranian girl-friends who were politically aware and well informed, and warned him some days beforehand that there was going to be an attack on the embassy. Quarles seems to have reported this to his commanding officer, but no extra precautions were taken. There had been similar reports before, and nothing had come of them.

Nothing could have been done to keep the Students out, but better security inside the embassy would have prevented some of the more serious effects of the attack. The previous February, while Ambassador Sullivan was still there, there had been a brief attempt to take over the compound. Because it had been anticipated, the numbers of staff had been thinned down, most of the classified documents had been shipped back to Washington, and the remaining files had been collected in the code room. When the attack took place, all the documents were destroyed, together with the cryptographic material. Nine months later, staff numbers had risen again and many of the documents had been shipped back; and on the day the second attack occurred some of the most sensitive documents were stored, not in the code room with the shredder, but in the office of Bruce Laingen, the *chargé d'affaires*. At the time, Laingen was at the Ministry of Foreign Affairs, asking for greater protection for the embassy. The Marines failed to knock down his door and get to the documents before the crowd of students arrived.

The disaster was complete, and there was worse to come: in particular the botched attempt to rescue the hostages. When the 444 days were over, it was President Carter who received the entire blame for everything: and in particular for the original cause of the attack: the decision to allow the Shah to come to the United States for medical attention, a few days before. The Shah's strongest supporters in Washington, Henry Kissinger, David Rockefeller and Zbigniew Brzezinski, had urged Carter for months to let him go to New York for treatment of the cancer from which he was suffering. Since equivalent medical facilities were available in Mexico City, their purpose seemed less to do with the treatment than with a signal to America's friends that it would not desert them, whatever happened. Carter reluctantly agreed.

When the hostages were eventually released, one of them, Moorhead Kennedy, who had been an economic officer in the embassy was scathing about the lack of thought behind American policy:

'[W]hat happened in Tehran was the diplomatic equivalent of Pearl Harbor. It was bad. We totally missed the significance of the Revolution. We supported the Shah much too long. We couldn't cut loose from him. We felt we owed him a debt of honour, and we sacrificed an embassy so he could have an operation. It was laziness, sheer intellectual laziness.

'When I was facing execution, one of the things that occurred to me was that I and a group of us had reported honestly, the embassy had done a very good job. But our

158

warnings were not given the attention they should have been in Washington. The same people [who had supported the Shah] blindly thought everything would be onward and upward in our relations with Khomeini. Of course it wasn't.'

The reactions of other hostages, interviewed in the US military hospital in Wiesbaden where they were being treated before leaving for home, were less thoughtful.

Donald Hohman, of the US Army, said, 'All I want to see is a scorched-earth policy in Iran. I want to make it clear to them they don't have the right to treat people the way they treated us.'

Malcolm Kalb, economics officer, who had spent 373 days in solitary confinement after trying to escape: 'I'd give them eight billion dollars' worth of bombs.'

Bruce German, from the budget and management section: 'I'd only want to go back in a B-52.'

Marine Sgt. William Quarles, who had spoken a little Farsi and had been released early because he was black, had a different perspective.

'I hear people say "Send in the Marines", or "Let's nuke the hell out of them, so that the United States can look good in the eyes of the world." But I don't think Americans really understand . . . [The Iranians] began showing me official US classified documents that proved my government had been interfering with their culture. I began to realize that the US has been doing things there that these people didn't like. It makes you realize that there are two sides to every story, and seeing what I have since I have been home, the media doesn't tell Americans all the things that are going on, all the things this country has participated in over there.'

But Quarles' insights were not shared by ordinary Americans, who, interviewed on television, expressed the wish to 'turn Iran into a parking lot'. Businessmen and students who had come to the United States to find sanctuary from Khomeini's Revolution were attacked and beaten up in the streets in California and elsewhere, simply because they were Iranian. An Iranian student who was involved in a serious car crash which was the fault of another driver was advised by his lawyer not to sue for damages. 'In this climate,' the lawyer said, 'no court will give you a sympathetic hearing.' In this climate, too, any attempt to reach a *modus vivendi* with Iran – still the most important power in the region – was impossible.

Robert McFarlane and Oliver North landed at Mehrabad Airport shortly after eight o'clock on the morning of Sunday 25 May 1986. It would have been difficult to select a worse time to come. It was Ramadan, when nothing very much gets done in Iran, and when the attention-span and temper of government officials is noticeably short. Worse, a serious battle was going on between several of the leading figures in the Iranian hierarchy over policy in the war and the economy, and it was going to prove extremely difficult to find anyone to negotiate with. The faulty timing was only one of a series of mistakes and misunderstandings which had gone into the planning of the venture.

The Boeing 707 jet, painted black, was the most conspicuous object on the apron at Mehrabad Airport, but it was nearly an hour and a half before anyone came to greet them. Apart from the crew, there were six of them: McFarlane, the former National Security Adviser to President Reagan; North, a senior member of the National Security Council staff; Howard R. Teicher, another NSC staffer; George Cave, a retired CIA official who served as a full-time consultant to the Agency and spoke fluent Farsi; a CIA communications technician, whose task it was to keep in contact with Admiral Poindexter, the current National Security Adviser, in Washington; and Amiram Nir from the office of the Israeli prime minister. It was Israel which had supplied the aircraft, and the kosher chocolate cake in the shape of a key which they had brought with them as a goodwill present. The cake somehow came to symbolize the whole absurd endeavour; later, it was eaten by the Revolutionary Guards at the airport. Lt.-Colonel North, at the suggestion of the CIA Director, William Casey, had also equipped himself with a poison capsule, in case the Iranians decided to kidnap him.

In fact the Iranians took very little notice of him or the others. They were eventually taken to the Esteqlal Hotel, which had formerly been the Hilton and was now owned by the government. They were installed in several suites on the top floor, each of which was thoroughly equipped with listening devices. That night the first high-level meeting between American and Iranian officials for five years took place. It was not, however, nearly as high-level as McFarlane had been led to expect. He and North later described the man who came to the hotel to see them as a deputy prime minister, but he was in fact an assistant to the prime minister, and not a very senior one at that.

McFarlane started off well enough, with a declaration that Iran was a sovereign power and that the United States should deal with it on the basis of mutual respect rather than intimidation.

The Iranian official replied with a speech which was partly intended to explain the nature of the Islamic Republic – that it depended totally on God and possessed a unique ideology – and partly to cover the fact that there was nothing serious for him to say. McFarlane and the others had come in the expectation that a deal could be agreed fast: the United States would supply Iran with the weapons it needed for its war with Iraq, and Iran would hand over the American hostages in Lebanon.

But it was clear right away that the groundwork which the American side had thought was done had scarcely been started; and the Iranians, expecting that the Boeing 707 had brought half the weapons which had been agreed as part of the overall deal, were taken aback to find that only a quarter of that amount had been brought. McFarlane started to get angry, and sent a message back to Poindexter in Washington, trying to explain his frustration at the lack of high-level contact:

'It may be best for us to try to picture what it would be like if after a nuclear attack a surviving Tartar became Vice-President, a recent grad student became Secretary of State, and a bookie became the interlocutor for all discourse with foreign countries.'

But the real problem seemed to lie with the interlocutor whom McFarlane, on North's urgings, had chosen to make contact for them with Iran: Manucher Ghorbanifar, an Iranian businessman living in France who had connexions with the arms trade. The CIA, who had used him in the past, had dropped him in 1980 because it had always found it 'difficult to filter out the bravado and exaggeration from what actually happened'. Lt.-Col. North had however been impressed by him; and when he told the Iranian side at the Esteqlal Hotel that McFarlane had been promised a meeting with Rafsanjani, President Khamene'i, and the prime minister, Moussavi, and the Iranians asked him who had promised that, North replied 'Ghorbanifar'.

The next night a more senior figure, an adviser from the Ministry of Foreign Affairs, came to see them at the Esteqlal. This man quoted an old Persian saying: 'Patience will bring you victory.' North, however, made a hard and fast offer: ten hours after the release of the American hostages, an aircraft would land in Tehran with the spare parts Iran needed for the HAWK anti-aircraft missiles it had already received from the United States, together with two sophisticated radar systems. The Iranian foreign affairs adviser countered with a list of the weapons Iran would want, including TOW anti-tank missiles complete with technicians. McFarlane had already sent a message to Poindexter which warned that the negotiations would be painfully slow, and adding 'At bottom they really are rug-merchants'.

It became clear to McFarlane as the meeting wore on that 'the basic difference was that they [the Iranians] expected all deliveries to occur before any release took place'. At one point the official said they had been in touch with the Hezbollah leaders in Lebanon, who were assumed to be holding the American hostages, and that they would agree to release them if Israel withdrew from the Golan Heights and Southern Lebanon, and Muslim fundamentalists held in prison in Kuwait were freed. This scarcely held out the prospect of serious negotiations. At 9.30 that evening the Americans handed over a draft agreement, and told the Iranian side that they had until 4 a.m. the following morning to free the hostages. At 2 a.m. the Iranians asked for a delay until 6 a.m., but the official did not return until 7.50. When he did, he said he thought they could get two hostages out. McFarlane's patience snapped.

'It's too late,' he said, 'we're leaving.'

The black 707 took off an hour and five minutes later.

It had been a ludicrous episode. The Iranians were probably never in a position to give an outright order to the kidnappers of the American hostages, and it was naïve of McFarlane to believe they could. Nor were they enthusiastic about the weapons deliveries that had already taken place during 1985 and 1986: 508 TOW missiles from Israel, 18 HAWK missiles from a CIA front company and a further 1,000 TOWs from the United States. There had been mistakes, and suspicions that the Americans had grossly overcharged them for what they had received.

In the months that followed more HAWK spares and TOW missiles were sent to Iran, and two hostages, Father Lawrence Jenco and David Jacobsen, were released in Beirut; Jacobsen was freed the day before the magazine *Ash Shiraa* broke the news of the deal. Jenco and Jacobsen were presumably the two whose release had been offered during the final meeting in Tehran. Presumably, too, the Anglican negotiator Terry Waite was kidnapped early in 1987 because of his involvement with Lt.-Col. North in arranging the release of Jenco and Jacobsen. During a long conversation with a senior Iranian figure a year later I asked about the North-McFarlane visit and was told that it had been sanctioned from the top – presumably by Khomeini himself – but that it was never taken seriously and that every one of the contacts whom the Americans met during their time in Tehran was working for the Ministry of Intelligence. He also confirmed that everything the Americans had said during their time at the Esteqlal Hotel had been recorded, and that the transcripts would be made public if and when it suited the Iranians to do so. I felt, however, that I detected a certain underlying unease about his responses. Perhaps Hojat-ol-Eslam Rafsanjani had indeed had Khomeini's permission to open negotiations with the Americans; it would have been uncharacteristically thoughtless of him if he had not. But the judgment shown by the Iranian side had been poor as well, and nothing of value was achieved.

As for the hostages, the senior Iranian I spoke to insisted that although his government was in regular contact with the kidnappers of some of them, Iran was not able to give direct orders to set them free; it had to be a matter for negotiation. That may well have been true of some of the hostages, though if they were in the hands of Hezbollah itself, the links between Hezbollah's leadership in Lebanon and the parent organization in Iran were so close that an order would have been enough for them to be freed quickly. No doubt the entire matter is a good deal more complicated than it seems; which is why the McFarlane-North initiative came to nothing.

In October 1986, in what proved to be the last in the brief series of contacts between the two countries, North and others met with go-betweens in Frankfurt and gave them a Bible signed by President Reagan two days before. North told the Iranians:

'We inside our government had an enormous debate . . . over whether or not my President should authorize me to say "We accept the Islamic Revolution [sic] of Iran as a fact." He went off one whole weekend and prayed about what the answer should be, and he came back almost a year ago with that passage I gave you that he wrote in the front of the Bible I gave you. And he said to me, "This is a promise that God gave to Abraham. Who am I to say that we should not do this?"'

It was not true; North himself had proposed the whole idea, Bible, signature, quotation and all, in a memorandum to Poindexter three days before. There was, it seemed, no one to say he should not do this.

The Tower Commission, which examined the whole affair, was scathing about its 'unprofessional' quality, and about the contrast between the Reagan Administration's public condemnation of negotiating with terrorists for the release of hostages, and of those countries and companies which sold arms to Iran, while in private the Administration was doing both itself. Soon, however, the issue became subsumed in the more general question of how much the President had known about the payment to the Contras in Nicaragua of the money which Iran had spent to buy American missiles: 'a neat idea', North had described it.

The specifically Iranian element quickly became forgotten, and in the United States Iran ceased to be a country with which the Americans could do business, and resumed the rôle it had occupied ever since the overthrow of the Shah: that of America's enemy. So much so, that when an Iraqi aircraft made an unprovoked attack on the USS *Stark* in the Gulf, killing 37 Americans, President Reagan threatened Iran with reprisals if there were any further attacks.

The curious fact is that the Islamic Republic of Iran has fulfilled some at least of the functions which the United States, following the British line, had originally trusted the Shah to carry out. The revolutionary authorities have been no less anti-Soviet than the Shah; they have suppressed the Communist Tudeh Party more brutally than the Shah did. They broadcast anti-Soviet propaganda daily to the Muslim Soviet republics on their borders. The square which Iran occupies on the strategic chessboard is no less secure from Soviet encroachment now than it was before the Revolution.

The US State Department, appreciating the significance of Iran in the region, would clearly like to establish some form of relationship with its leaders, but recognizes that the basic anger which exists among ordinary Americans against a country which has damaged and humiliated two of their Presidents is too great for anything very constructive to be done. Thirty years' worth of faulty judgments about the true nature of American interests in Iran cannot be set aside that easily.

164

Street scene, with ayatollah. No woman would dare go out in public without wearing some form of Islamic dress, and in this case even her little daughter is wearing *hejab*. Large-scale street art featuring Ayatollah Khomeini is much less common in Tehran than in Qom and some other cities.

Margaret Thatcher and Uncle Sam, as depicted in larger-than-life-sized paintings on the wall of the British embassy compound in Tehran. Mrs Thatcher, most unIslamically dressed, is running out of Northern Ireland – an area of the globe with which the Iranian revolutionaries feel an unreciprocated affinity. Uncle Sam is being marched off Iranian territory by a large Islamic Republican fountain pen.

The Faw peninsula, February 1986. Iraqi bombers are attacking within seconds of our arrival. The Western journalists are taking cover, but some of our Iranian minders have decided to stay upright and see as much of the action as possible.

A few hours later, dressed in a highly inadequate chemical warfare suit, I am questioning an elderly *basiji*, impressively equipped, about his reasons for volunteering for the front.

The mother of a dead volunteer walks along a line of graves at Behesht-e-Zahra, the vast and ever-growing cemetery in South Tehran.

The court-house in Rey. The judge, a mullah, is questioning a middle-aged woman who is contesting an action for divorce by her husband, a wealthy builder. He is half-hidden behind her. Sitting beside him is a cousin who has acted as an assessor in the case. The man on the left is the clerk of the court.

Above, left Hojat-ol-Eslam Ali Akbar Hashemi-Rafsanjani, the subtle-minded and witty speaker of the Majlis (parliament), and second most powerful politician in Iran and *right* Martin Charlesworth, lynchpin of the tiny Western community in Tehran, who runs the British Institute for Persian Studies. *Below* The former U.S. embassy in Tehran. Below the sign is the shuttered window where, during office hours, printed collections of the documents seized in the embassy can be bought. The notice-board contains advertisements for them. (It was possible to take this picture because the watch-tower was empty.)

Tira in full *hejab* at Qom. She found her *chador* difficult to manage, but useful as a means of covering up not just the Western clothes she is wearing underneath but also a sizeable haversack.

Women attending Friday Prayers in Tehran. Those wearing white are the wives or mothers of men who have been killed in the war. During the Prayers men and women are strictly segregated.

Mahmoudi, our excellent driver, demonstrates how to mash up the meat and vegetables of a Persian *abgusht*.

A stallholder in Qom offers everything for the conscientious worshipper. In front of him are the tablets which are placed on the ground for the forehead to rest on during prayer, while behind him are burial shrouds which are covered with religious texts and carefully folded in polythene wrappers. A shroud bought in Qom is regarded as having especially holy qualities.

Lunching with the mullah. My host is Hojat-ol-Eslam Sayyed Zade
Tehrani, a courteous and hospitable but mildly disapproving man
who never lost an opportunity to show devotion to his leader: even
to the extent of allowing his portrait to dominate the sitting-room.

A section of the beautiful Khajou bridge in Isfahan, built in 1650. The river runs through the bridge's 23 lower arches. This is Friday, and holiday-makers have gathered to meet their friends or do their washing in the waters of the river.

An Armenian caretaker prepares to let us into his seventeenth-century church in Julfa, the Christian quarter of Isfahan.

A quiet section of the main Tehran bazaar. The stalls, though often apparently insignificant and selling little of value, are usually sophisticated, profitable agencies which lend and change money and deal in a wide range of commodities.

A hardware shop in the bazaar sells – apart from abacuses, kettles and cooking implements – flails (a bunch is hanging just below and to the left of the picture of Ayatollah Khomeini). Enthusiastic believers buy them in order to flog their shoulders and backs in the approved fashion on Ashura, the day of mourning for the death of Hosayn, the Prophet's grandson, at the battle of Kerbala.

9

The Pebble on the Ground

I took notes of these matters, and promised to bring
them to the notice of some of my friends in the English
Embassy if I got the chance; and we then conversed
for a time, while I smoked a *kalyan* which they brought
me. They questioned me closely as to the objects of
my journey, and refused to credit my assertion that I
was travelling for my own instruction and amusement, declaring that I must be an agent of the English
Government.

'Why don't you take Persia?' said one of them at
length: 'you could easily if you liked.'

Edward Granville Browne, *A Year Amongst
The Persians*, 1893

THE AUDIENCE SHIFTS expectantly in its seats, the lights go down,
and a wiry, energetic figure in his thirties stands on the stage,
illuminated only by the glare from the slide-projector, and begins
a lecture entitled 'Greeks and Persians', the burden of which is to
explain how much of the culture, politics and architecture of
ancient Greece was heavily influenced by the powerful civilization of Persia, further to the East. The auditorium is almost full;
only about ten of the hundred chairs which have been painstak-
ingly arranged all afternoon in the auditiorium are empty, and
most of those are in the front row. A huge slide showing a detail
from one of the buildings at Persepolis lights up the room and the
face of the lecturer, a second or two after he taps the floor with his
wooden pointer as a signal to the tardy and forgetful person who
is working the projector. An almost tangible sense of relaxation
fills the hall. You don't have to follow the full complexity of
Martin Charlesworth's argument, or even understand the
peppering of jokes, to feel that however much things outside the

lecture hall have changed since the Revolution, some things are immutable: the annual course of lectures at the British Institute for Persian Studies in Tehran, for instance.

Looking round me at the audience, I find that it divides naturally into three categories: diplomats, either British or those who are part of the Anglophone social grouping to which the British belong – Australians, New Zealanders, Portuguese, Norwegians; young Iranian archaeological students, who have only begun to come to the British Institute in recent years; and there are older Anglophile Iranians, with British and academic ties. They take up two entire rows, elderly men and women who fan themselves from time to time in the evening heat of the room and rustle a little as they shift in their seats. For them, these lectures and the party at the British embassy every year on the Queen's birthday are all that is left of a long-gone imperial connexion.

Gatherings such as the one tonight give them the feeling that not every link has been severed with the past, while they act as a reminder to the students of the wider world outside Iran. Here in the Institute, European rules apply; and as the lecture gathers speed one young woman quietly takes off her headscarf to reveal a head of distinctly foreign blonde hair. I am still watching her when the wooden pointer knocks warningly on the stage floor again, and I recall my duty; I press the projector button to show a new slide: as it might be, a close-up of the stone-work at Pasargadae.

'To the north of the city,' wrote Edward Granville Browne in 1887, 'are numerous gardens . . . some in the villages of Shimran, like Kulahak and Tajrish, which serve as summer retreats to the Europeans and rich Persians, distant five or six miles from the town . . .' This is the area where the British Institute for Persian Studies established itself at the end of the 1970s. As you drive up the Shemiran Road towards the Elburz mountains, what were once isolated villages have now coalesced to form a single continuous wealthy suburb; and in the area which Browne, with his careful orthography, called Kulahak and is more commonly spelt Gulhak in Roman letters, the Institute, unmarked, announces itself with a battered blue-painted metal gate. It is set in a wall which is covered with graffiti of a general political nature, but nothing specifically hostile or insulting to the island of Western scholarship within; most, indeed, are exhortations to vote for particular candidates in the presidential election of 1980, which no one has bothered to clean off.

Inside the gates stands a small guardhouse, unoccupied now

that there is no longer the money for a guard, and filled with the metal bedsteads which archaeological students once used to sleep on in the Institute's heyday; and beyond that are Martin Charlesworth's house, and the main building which contains the lecture-hall and the empty dormitories. The Institute is designed a little along the lines of something Martin Charlesworth might excavate: a flat building in mud-coloured brick, set in a pleasant garden planted with overhanging trees and rose-bushes. Our driver Mahmoudi, never having been out of Iran in his life, suggested that it was just like England, and it seemed too difficult to explain the differences.

Tira and I are the only guests at the Institute. Where once every one of the seven bedrooms and two large apartments were occupied by archaeology students who had gathered for the season's dig somewhere in the vastness of Iran, and even the lecture-hall had to be turned into a large dormitory, now bedrooms and lecture-hall alike are empty. People stopped coming to Iran from Britain when visas were introduced, and became almost impossible to get, in 1980. We have a suite of rooms to ourselves, where we come back to relax and read after the heat and activity of our days in Tehran or wider afield, and the noise and jollity of the time when there would be fifty or more people here are long gone.

The name of the British Institute of Persian Studies has a faintly Victorian ring to it, but it was in fact founded in 1961 and comes under the aegis of the British Academy. It is now in limbo, neither fully operational nor quite done away with. At its peak in 1978 it had a director, an assistant director, an administrative officer, a secretary, and two or three Fellows. A librarian was in charge of the Institute's 12,000 books. Now all those jobs are done by Martin Charlesworth, who achieved the cliff-hanging title of temporary acting assistant director in 1980, and was then promoted to acting director since he was the only one left. For some occult reason it is not possible for the Institute to possess a full director while full diplomatic relations have not been restored between Britain and Iran. There is constant pressure on Martin Charlesworth to cut down on the little he spends, and the British Academy may eventually decide to divert that little to its other Schools of Archaeology and Institutes for Studies in places where students are allowed in as a matter of course, and visas are easier to obtain.

Outside, water from a hose plays on the dry grey earth to revive the roses, and the water in the swimming-pool laps invitingly against the blue tiles. The Institute has, altogether, the pleasant air of a Persian retreat; even the noise of traffic on the Shemiran Road seems muted. It is a little enclave, not only on Iranian territory, but on the territory which belongs to the British embassy; a wire fence now divides it from the delightful grounds of the compound where many of the embassy staff lived, until the crisis between Britain and Iran in 1987 brought about the eventual withdrawal of every British diplomat from Tehran, and the sound of English children playing and the signature-tune of the hourly news on the BBC World Service would float across to the Institute.

Not much else did, however: the gate in the fence was kept firmly padlocked on the embassy side, and there was no link between the Institute's electrical system and the generator in the embassy compound, so that during the nightly power-cuts the bright lights in the diplomatic houses shed a faint glimmer in the darkened rooms of the Institute. Sometimes, when there was work to be done and no light to do it by, the separation could be annoying; but Martin Charlesworth and his wife were merely philosophical about it.

The Institute may have little to do with the embassy in practical or administrative terms, but it is, in its way, just as strong an upholder of the continuing British influence in Iran. The Iranian authorities must have watched the enclave in Gulhak with some care, and have come to the conclusion that it is neither a nest of spies nor a tool of imperial interests, but exactly what it seems: a small and under-funded organization with a useful part to play in preserving Iran's archaeological sites. In the driveway two ancient Land Rovers, much scratched and dented, hint at the continuing possibility of expeditions. Parts for them are difficult to get and extremely expensive, and there is no money for full-scale expeditions of the old type, though there has always been just enough for Martin Charlesworth, exercising the parsimony which has had to become second nature to him, to travel alone to the farther reaches of Iran, checking on the condition of archaeological sites, logging them, and demonstrating to the authorities that the Institute is still in business.

Not long before we arrived, he had been on an expedition which took him down to Khuzestan, the predominantly Arabic-speaking region where much of the war with Iraq is being fought out. As journalists, Tira and I were obliged to sign an under-taking when we arrived in Tehran that we would not go there, on the grounds that too much that is secret is to be seen in the area; but Martin Charlesworth had been allowed to travel around Khuzestan as he chose, photographing and sketching archaeological sites. Some of them, the mounds which covered cities or palaces for instance, had often been used as strong-points and fortifications by both the Iraqis and the Iranians; and as he worked the occasional jet screamed overhead, and he could hear the distant sound of gun-fire.

Charlesworth's success in proving to the revolutionary authorities that he is genuine has been considerable. Britain and the British have a long and unenviable past as far as Iranians are concerned. As with so many other countries which were touched by the British imperial presence, the past is remembered there, long after the time when the British themselves have forgotten all about it. There is a Persian proverb to the effect that if you trip over a pebble on the ground as you walk along, be sure that an Englishman has put it there. A quarter of a century after British forces withdrew from the Persian Gulf, and thirty-five years after the last detectable intervention by Britain in Iranian affairs, the reputation lingers.

This is not something restricted to the ignorant and ill-informed: the best-educated, most sophisticated Persians frequently believe that the British are still working behind the scenes in Iran, and the more intelligent they are, the more subtle are their theories. At the time of the Revolution, Khomeini's aides Ibrahim Yazdi and Sadeq Qotbzadeh both spoke to me of the machinations of the British government and its faithful agent the BBC in supporting the Shah; the Shah, by contrast, was obsessed by the notion that Britain was supporting Khomeini in order to weaken him. 'Lift up the Ayatollah's beard,' he is quoted as saying, 'and you will find "Made in Britain" underneath it.' Large numbers of Royalists, now in exile in the pleasanter parts of the developed world, still believe that the BBC, on the British government's instructions, set out to destabilize the Shah's régime by broadcasting everything Khomeini said and calling people out into the streets to demonstrate.

For a hundred and fifty years, until its decline into a predominantly European power, Britain had indeed involved itself in Persian affairs and intervened on a number of different levels. For most of that time, Britain was the super-power in whose sphere of influence the Persians found themselves; it inculcated a kind of expectancy in them, and their quick minds and their weakness for conspiracy theories did the rest. A long, complicated and blasphemous joke, current among the less religious in Iran, ends with the punchline, 'And God said to Khomeini, "You think I don't know you're British?"'

Another, which is less involved, features various national

types and the things they want most in the world. The American wants all the wheat he can get hold of, the Russian wants the biggest Xerox machine so he can copy everything, the Persian (who usually appears in his own national jokes quite uncharacteristically as a simple-minded clown) wants the biggest stomach; while the Englishman asks for the biggest hat. The reference is to the Persian expression 'putting a hat on someone's head', which means deceiving them, conning them, using them.

There is no shortage of examples of the way in which Britain put its imperial hat on Persia. Situated as it was between the British sphere of interest in the Middle East and its Indian Empire, Persia was subject to British pressure throughout the nineteenth century; and as the Qajar dynasty's hold on power became progressively weaker, the demands of Britain and the other imperial power with interests in Persia, Tsarist Russia, became more peremptory. In August 1907 an Anglo-Russian convention was signed in St Petersburg, dividing Persia up into zones of interest, with the northern part abutting the Russian border regarded as being in the Tsar's zone and the southern part, with its oil-fields and its Gulf ports, as being in Britain's. Neither government saw fit to notify the Persians.

In October 1910 Britain sent an ultimatum to the Qajar Shah, demanding that officers of the British Army in India should be placed in charge of policing the roads of southern Persia, at Persian expense; and in the same month, when the minister of foreign affairs in Tehran proposed to stop the pension of a former Shah, who had been a supporter of Britain and Russia, the ambassadors of the two countries ordered their uniformed servants to follow the minister through the streets of Tehran and wait outside his house until the pension was paid.

During the First World War, Britain and Tsarist Russia sent their troops into Persia and divided it between them It was always believed that Britain had played a part in encouraging the coup of Reza Khan – later to become Reza Shah – in 1921. Twenty years later, in the Second World War, British and Soviet troops moved into Iran to overthrow him, on the grounds that he was over-sympathetic to the Axis powers. The BBC Persian section was founded at the same time, partly in order to prepare public opinion for his abdication. He was replaced by his son, Mohammed Reza, whose suspicions of Britain and the BBC during the Revolution of 1978-9 were not, therefore, without a certain historical perspective, even if they failed to take into account the way Britain had changed.

In 1953, when the Shah briefly fled the country during his

struggle with the Nationalist leader, Dr Mossadeq, it was the British who came up with the plan for large-scale demonstrations in the streets to undermine the Mossadeq government; and, for good measure, the British played off the leading cleric, Ayatollah Kashani, against Mossadeq in order to weaken the latter's hold on power. It is scarcely surprising, in the circumstances, that during the last months of 1978 the Shah should have asked the British ambassador if he thought the Americans were stirring up the crowds in the streets, and the American ambassador if he thought the British were encouraging Ayatollah Khomeini. To the day of his death he believed he had been the victim of a conspiracy originated by the British.

In Gulhak, the British played the part of a local imperial power for almost a century. In 1835, after the mission had taken to camping there during the summer months to escape the heat of the plain, Muhammed Shah gave the British minister extensive rights in the village. The inhabitants were excused military service, they paid their taxes to the British minister, and were protected from any interference by Persian officials. It is tempting to see in these extraordinary rights, which were not given up until 1928, some of the grounds for the contempt the British government and its servants came to feel for the weakening Persian state, which in later years led to the Anglo-Russian Convention of 1907 and the subsequent intrusions into domestic Persian politics until the 1950s.

The symbol of British imperial influence was, however, the Legation building on its magnificent fifteen-acre site in what is now the very heart of Tehran, but which was, in the mid-nineteenth century, an area of desert just outside the city walls to the north. Within the magnificent gateway, which seems from photographs of the 1870s to have been designed in a style halfway between an Indian fortress and a British public school, 1,500 plane trees were planted. Many of them still survive, and the compound has the delightful air of a park, with embassy buildings and the private houses of some of the embassy officers situated here and there in its cool spaces. The Shah of the day allowed the British minister to keep peacocks, but nowadays the branches of the plane-trees and their descendants are usually occupied by green parakeets which have made their home in the embassy grounds and fly from tree to tree in imitation alarm, uttering high-pitched squawks.

It was here, in July 1906, that one of the great occasions of modern Iranian history took place: a peaceful equivalent of revolution, known as the great *bast* – *bast* meaning sanctuary. Nowadays it might be called a sit-in, though on an immense scale. A crowd of sixteen thousand, exhorted by the *ulema* and the mullahs, took over the Legation compound, arranged their own food and sanitation, and by staying there without threatening anyone compelled the Shah of the day, Muzaffaru'd-Din Shah Qajar, to dismiss his hated chief minister and grant a constitution and the establishment of an elected parliament. These Gandhian tactics were only partially successful, and a month afterwards another *bast* took place in order to get the Shah to agree to elections. This, too, he had to accept, much to the dislike of the Russians and the British. It is curious to look at photographs of the great *bast:* thousands of men standing quietly, mullahs in their black or white turbans at the front and their followers behind, stretching for as far as one can see, silently exerting their will on the Shah and on the Great Powers who supported him.

Nowadays the arched gateway of the nineteenth century has been replaced by a more prosaic affair, topped by an Office of Works lion and unicorn, one on each pillar. Guards recruited in Bangladesh man the gates, and the brass plate declares that this is the British Interests Section of the Royal Swedish Embassy, since diplomatic relations between Britain and Iran have not run smoothly since the Revolution. No one, however, has any doubt who the compound belongs to.

'The building with the animals, Mr John?' said Mahmoudi, the first time I asked him to drive there; his reference was to the lion and unicorn. We headed down through the noise and intense heat of Ferdowsi Avenue, and eventually, after standing around in the hot sun for some time, Tira and I talked our way through the gates and into the Chancery building; British embassies the world over have the knack of making visiting citizens feel as though they have come on an unsuitable day. Since the Revolution, double locks and armoured glass have protected the embassy's inhabitants from outsiders, and all mechanical objects had to be surrendered at the demand of the cool young woman behind the layers of glass, in case, presumably, we went on the rampage, photographing and tape-recording everything we came across.

I remembered how it had all looked on the day in November 1978 when the mob broke in and set fire to the Chancery building: the heaps of sodden rubbish everywhere, the charred handrail of the staircase, the smell of burned papers and burned

172

cloth. I counted myself fortunate at the time to have been there when the attack took place, since it was a news story of some importance and I might easily have missed it, given the amount of violence going on everywhere: my colleagues were busy elsewhere on that day of fires, and I had joined up with an American crew from NBC to film the burning embassy. It was the second attack by a crowd on a British embassy I had seen in seven years. No one took any notice of us. The activists were too busy forcing the gates with the lion and unicorn above them, despite the gallant efforts of a junior diplomat to keep them out single-handed. Unfortunately we were not able to film him from where we were standing: it would have made him a national hero in Britain if we had.

This was no peaceful *bast*; the crowd had come prepared to set things alight, and they swarmed over the fence, sweeping everything before them. A good deal of damage was done, but no one was hurt. The British ambassador of the day has since suggested that, far from being a revolutionary mob, the arsonists may have been set on by the Shah's secret police, SAVAK, in order to get British support for the tougher measures which the Shah was just about to introduce. One of the generals the ambassador telephoned for help told him that Britain's policy had brought trouble on its own embassy, by arguing against martial law. Nothing at that extraordinary time can be ruled out on the grounds of its unlikelihood, and it is true that the forces of law and order stood by and watched as it happened. But both at the time and afterwards, it seemed to me to be just another part of a day of violence and destruction, and by no means – given the history of British support for the Shah – an unlikely target for the crowd's anger. The American embassy was not attacked, it is true, but it was heavily defended.

The ambassador in question was the admirable Sir Anthony Parsons, who cheerfully showed us round his wrecked Chancery the next day and proved to be both kind and helpful over the succeeding weeks, in spite of the heavy pressure on him. His book, *The Pride And The Fall*, is a scrupulously honest account of the Revolution, in which he examines why he did not recognize until too late the inevitability of the Shah's overthrow. His approach contrasts nowadays, as it did at the time, with that of many Western diplomats and businessmen in Tehran. Then, most of the Westerners one met were certain that the trouble would pass, and often seemed to feel that it was blown up out of all proportion by the foreign journalists who swarmed over Iran during those final months. Nowadays, people who were in Iran at that time usually maintain that they saw the Revolution coming long before; by which, presumably, they mean that they had occasional nervous twinges at the behaviour of the Imperial court and the resentment it often aroused among ordinary people. It is not insights like these that Sir Anthony Parsons criticizes himself for lacking.

There were people in the British Embassy who had a wide circle of Persian friends and realized the likelihood that the Shah would fall, but they were not at the more senior levels. For the most part, working in the cool atmosphere of the embassy compound, with the parakeets screeching in the plane trees, or living above the smoke of the city in the peace of Gulhak, and rarely escaping from a British or a Western atmosphere, it must have been as difficult for the majority of British diplomats as it was for American ones to think the unthinkable. Only the most fully aware of them will have realized that out on the streets the military power which was the Shah's ultimate guarantee was starting to crumble.

At the end of Martin Charlesworth's lecture on Greeks and Persians, as everyone stood up and greeted their friends, or fanned themselves in the heat, a tall figure who had been sitting over to the side of the lecture hall came across and shook hands. I had met Edward Chaplin, the first secretary at the British embassy, during my visit to Iran the previous February, when I and two other British correspondents had been flown down briefly to the Faw Peninsula and shown Iran's latest success in the war against Iraq. Back in Tehran, we had been invited to the Chaplins' house, in the middle of the British embassy compound, for what turned out to be an extremely pleasant lunch.

Over the roast lamb, Iran's major import from New Zealand, the conversation turned to the question of the pleasures and difficulties of a posting to Tehran; and Edward Chaplin and his wife Nicola were equally enthusiastic about being there, and about the advantages of living in a country with so much that was interesting and attractive about it. Mrs Chaplin's only complaint was that living as they did in the embassy compound in the centre of Tehran they were a little isolated from the other families, who lived up in Gulhak beside the British Institute.

During the months that followed, the Chaplins decided to move to Gulhak themselves, and joined the convoy that travelled northwards each afternoon, taking the diplomats from the

174

embassy and whichever members of their families might have been down in the centre of Tehran for the day. These arrangements were so normal and run-of-the-mill, given the circumstances, that it can never have occurred to anyone that they might one day be of interest to anyone outside the small embassy group; let alone form part of a diplomatic incident.

On the afternoon of 28 May 1987, Edward Chaplin was driving his wife and their two children home to Gulhak in their distinctive Range-Rover. They had set off with the minibus carrying the others from the embassy, but became separated from it in the traffic. They were going along the Modaress Expressway and approaching the turn-off to the Shemiran Road, where the Gulhak compound is situated, when they passed a Nissan Patrol jeep, of the kind supplied to the Revolutionary Guards and the local *Komitehs*. Iranian citizens might drive a little more carefully on seeing a jeep of that kind, but foreigners, and particularly diplomats, rarely worry; the Revolutionary Guards are under orders not to meddle with them. But in this case the Nissan Patrol trailed them for a short way, and then speeded up. It overtook Chaplin's Range-Rover, and then cut in front of it, forcing it off the road. Chaplin got out, angry at the jeep's driver, and at the same time the doors of the jeep opened, and several men in the grey-green uniform of the Revolutionary Guards got down and started walking towards him

Almost certainly, Edward Chaplin knew nothing of an equally obscure event that had happened in England, nearly three weeks before. In the unexotic setting of the C & A store at the Arndale Shopping Centre in Manchester, a little before five o'clock on 9 May, the Iranian vice-consul in the city, Ahmad Qassemi, had been stopped by a woman store detective as he was leaving the shop, and asked to go into the manager's office. In his shopping bag which he was asked to empty out onto the desk, were five pairs of socks and a purse; they had come from three different shops in the centre, and Qassemi did not have the sales slips to show that he had paid for them. The sales slips he did produce were for different amounts, and bore a different date. The total value of the goods he was accused of stealing was £7.55 ($12.08).

The police were called, and Qassemi was taken in a police van to Bootle Street police station, where he was questioned, and accused of shoplifting. He told the police he had diplomatic immunity, and half an hour later the Iranian consul-general in Manchester confirmed his identity. He was held for another five hours – a delay which was not explained – and then released on condition that he presented himself at the police station in seventeen days' time.

On 26 May he did not, however, appear. Neither British law, nor the strict definition that Britain, like most Western countries, applies to diplomatic privilege, seem to have been fully understood in the Manchester consulate or in the Iranian embassy in London; and unwisely Qassemi seems to have been told by his superiors that he was not required to go to the police station after all. Shortly before eight o'clock on 28 May, as two plainclothes policemen were sitting outside Mr Qassemi's house in the Manchester suburb of East Didsbury in an unmarked car, he came out of his house, got into his car and drove off. The police account gave the impression that he had seen them, recognized them as police officers, and was trying to escape. This is not, however, certain.

At 9.20 Qassemi was stopped and taken to Bootle Street police station for questioning. He was held there for nearly nine hours, during which time he says he was assaulted by two policemen. The report of a medical examination on him, carried out on 1 June, showed that he had weals on both wrists, and a left scrotal mass two inches by one inch which was fluctant and tender, and was probably a blood clot. In the opinion of another doctor, this was consistent with having been kicked hard in the testicles. There were no signs of other bruising, and no broken bones.

That evening, Qassemi was charged with shoplifting, driving recklessly, and causing £20 of damages to the wristwatch of a police officer. No evidence was later produced of how such damage might have been produced. He was allowed bail. By now, the way the police had treated Qassemi had overtaken the issue of the shoplifting as the main subject of attention. Iranian consular officials in London complained to the Foreign Office that his injuries had been so severe that they almost caused his death; this seems hard to credit. Tehran Radio warned some days later:

'The barbaric treatment of the attaché of the Islamic Republic in Manchester by the English police will be followed by the anger of world Muslims . . . [The results] would be similar to what the anger of Muslims did to some Western nations hostile to the Islamic Republic of Iran, making them change their attitudes. The British government should therefore foresee the consequences of its policy.'

The reference appeared to be to the kidnapping of American, French and British citizens in Lebanon.

Given the time difference, the injury which Qassemi suffered in the Manchester police station on Thursday 28 May can have happened only about three hours before the Nissan Patrol jeep stopped in front of Edward Chaplin and its occupants started walking towards him. They grabbed hold of him, and started pulling him towards their jeep; but Chaplin, who was tall and well-built, resisted as best he could and struggled to get back to his car. At that point they set about him, punching him in the face and body. His nose started bleeding, and his lips were cut. As it happened, the West German ambassador drove up the road a minute or two later, and saw what was happening. He had a couple of Iranian bodyguards with him, supplied by the Tehran authorities, and he asked them to go to Edward Chaplin's assistance. They however, refused, on the grounds that they were there simply to protect him, not someone else.

Another of the men from the jeep had meanwhile climbed into the Range-Rover and, ignoring Nicola Chaplin's shouts of alarm and the crying of the two children, he drove them off at high speed towards Gulhak, intending presumably to leave them and the car there. But a little farther along the road the car was stopped for a second time. An unmarked car, which may have been driven by men from the Security Ministry, pulled across in front of them and three armed men got out of it, pointing their guns at the driver. They demanded to know what he was doing, and it took him a little time to explain to them. The assumption was that other groups had received the same orders as the men in the Nissan Patrol jeep: to look out for the Range-Rover with British diplomatic number-plates and arrest the driver. Neither group apparently knew that the other was also involved in the hunt.

Edward Chaplin was by now lying down on the back seat of the Nissan jeep, with a hood pulled over his head. He was occasionally pushed about and hit by the men in the seat in front of him to make sure he stayed lying down, but he was not punched again. He was taken, hooded and bound, to a house somewhere in North Tehran. Once there, he was better treated: he was allowed to wash the blood off his nose and lips, and was given fresh clothes to replace the ones which were bloodstained. The guards became noticeably friendlier, and – a touch which only those who know their Persians can appreciate fully – one of them asked him for help in getting a visa to go to Britain. Chaplin's answer is not recorded.

As darkness fell and the Ramadan fast was over for the night, he was given something to eat and drink. Around midnight he was taken to another place where he was questioned about black market offences he was supposed to have committed. He received no indication that he might have been arrested in retaliation for the arrest of anyone in Britain. As the night wore on, a new group of guards came on duty, and asked him why he had been picked up. They seemed to have no more idea than he did, but his efforts to persuade them to let him go were not successful.

Chaplin slept fitfully, sitting in a chair, his hands still bound. People came to see him from time to time during the day, mostly in order to argue with him over the terms of a statement they wanted him to sign. At last, when he had made them water down some of the wording and add a section about the circumstances of the arrest and the fact that he had not known who they were or why they had stopped him, he signed. It was three o'clock in the afternoon. The hood was placed over his head again and he was taken out to a car. After driving around for some time the car stopped and he was pushed out. He pulled the hood off his head and looked around: he was in the Shemiran Road, a short way from the British compound at Gulhak.

The news that Edward Chaplin had been freed went some way towards easing the tension that had built up at the Foreign Office in London. Nevertheless there were still two worrying aspects to the situation. The first was that the Iranians, having retaliated almost blow for blow for the injuries suffered by Qassemi, were now threatening to charge Chaplin with serious crimes as a reprisal for the fact that Qassemi had been charged with shop-lifting. The second was that if things went wrong it was perfectly possible that the Iranians might stage a demonstration outside the embassy in Ferdowsi Avenue and storm the building, perhaps taking the people inside hostage. But the prime minister, Mrs Thatcher, who was in the last two weeks of her election campaign, was in no mood to back down over the affair, and continually urged her foreign secretary, Sir Geoffrey Howe, to act toughly.

The Iranians were adamant that Qassemi would not answer bail for the shoplifting offence, since they still insisted he had diplomatic immunity. However, one problem was solved when the Crown Prosecution Service reversed a magistrates' ruling that Qassemi's passport should be surrendered as a condition of bail. There were immediate suspicions that the Foreign Office had put pressure on the CPS, but the Foreign Office denied it hotly. The Iranians, not understanding the finer points of law in the magistrates' court, interpreted the decision as a sign that

Britain was prepared to do a deal.

But what kind of deal was still in doubt. The Iranian *chargé d'affaires* was called into the Foreign Office almost every day, but the way he reacted to the various British statements suggested that a good many of the finer points of phrasing in them had passed him by. On 4 June the attempt was made to end the matter at a stroke: the consulate in Manchester, which was important to the Iranians as a centre for the surveillance of the relatively large number of Iranian students at universities and colleges in the north-west of England, was to be shut down. The staff of five, including Qassemi, were told to leave the country. There would be no trial for shoplifting after all. Arrangements were made to withdraw as many people as possible from the British embassy in Iran, to avoid giving the régime in Tehran too much leverage.

Two days later the Iranians, anxious not to be outfaced, ordered five British diplomats including Edward Chaplin to leave. That too dealt with the individual problem, but left the diplomatic battle unresolved. By this stage, however, the Foreign Office had worked out the profit and loss position, and had come to the conclusion that Iran would have more to lose from a complete break in relations than Britain would. There were various reasons why Iran would want to continue to be represented in Britain, chief of which was that London is the centre of the international arms trade, and a full diplomatic breach with Tehran would be followed by the closure of the Iranian arms-buying commission in the offices of the National Iranian Oil Company, a few hundred yards from the Houses of Parliament.

Nevertheless, during the days that followed there were more expulsions. Britain set a ceiling on each side's representation of sixteen diplomats each; Iran expelled four more British diplomats. By 17 June Britain responded by withdrawing all but two of its own diplomats, and the following day effectively expelled fifteen Iranians. It had been a close-run thing, but in the end Iran decided to accept the position and not to break off relations. Each side was left with a single diplomat each. As always, there were plenty of volunteers from among the large Iranian student population to help with the daily tasks of running their country's embassy in London, but in Tehran the enormous compounds in Ferdowsi Avenue and Gulhak would from now on be occupied only by the Bangladeshi staff and by one solitary junior diplomat whose main job was to keep an eye on the property.

Everyone hoped that later, quietly, it would be possible for the diplomats who had been withdrawn to be sent back to Tehran, or others sent in their place; but it was an indication of the much reduced importance of Iran in British eyes, both as a market and as a regional power, that cutting the embassy staff to one should have been regarded as a triumph for skilful diplomacy. A decade earlier, when the Shah was in power, and British government ministers travelled to Tehran at the rate of one or two a month in the hope of winning contracts which often turned out to be distinctly questionable in value, such a result would have been regarded as little short of a national disaster.

The library at the British Institute for Persian Studies is the heart of Martin Charlesworth's kingdom. It has the smell of leather and paper, and of the peculiar dust which books generate, and there is an air of bare, white neatness, like the atmosphere in a college library in Cambridge. Sitting there in its mosquito-free coolness, with the shelves creaking under the weight of a million words, it is easy to understand why Charles V gave up his Empire and Montaigne his hopes of political advancement in order to study. There are a few rarities here: an early edition of Sir Richard Burton's *Pilgrimage to Al-Medina and Mecca*, a first edition of Howard Carter's *Tomb of Tutankhamun*. But it is the books on Persia which are unrivalled outside the great collections: from a splendid volume called *Merv, and the Man-Stealing Turcomans*, which has the figure of a man-stealing Turcoman charging across the spine in gilt, to *Aramaic Ritual Texts from Persepolis* and *Les Schismes dans l'Islam*, and a full bound set of the Journal of the Royal Asiatic Society from 1877 to the present day.

Martin Charlesworth's time at the Institute has not always been quiet since the Revolution. The Revolutionary Guards used to search the place from time to time, and in 1982 a group of Mojaheddin supporters were caught in the house that abuts on to the Institute's grounds. The fighting went on for several hours, but at the end the Charlesworths, taking refuge in their house, heard everything go silent, and then the war-cry of the Revolutionary Guards: *Allahu Akbar!* But the authorities, after the first eighteen months of the Islamic Republic during which all foreigners were harassed and investigated repeatedly, eventually decided to accept the Institute on its own terms.

Not many Iranians come to the Institute, even now: most people see no reason to run their heads into what might turn out to be a noose. But a few students and academics, the bolder and more enterprising ones, occasionally ask to visit the library. Sometimes Charlesworth might get a call from Iranian television, which broadcasts programmes about Islamic art and pottery, or from some official organization which is putting together a handbook or an encyclopaedia and needs to consult him. Recently some governmental ayatollah asked if he would write a book about his experiences as a foreigner during the Revolution, which would be published by the official publishing house. Whatever happens to the Institute, Martin Charlesworth won't be leaving Iran. His wife is Persian, an archaeologist herself, and their children are being brought up as much in the Persian manner as the English one. The house is full of cousins and brothers and sisters, and on the first evening we were there a sheep was slaughtered in the approved manner for some family celebration. And yet Charlesworth is also the lynchpin of the tiny British community and its allies. He not only keeps it educated with his lectures, he entertains it at Christmas with the pantomimes he helps to write and stage and direct.

No doubt one day, if the Institute survives, it will be easier for students and scholars from Britain to visit it again. There will always be British enthusiasts for Persian literature and the Persian language: the tradition that goes back beyond Edward Granville Browne, Edward FitzGerald and James Morier to the first English visitors to Persia will certainly not die out. But Britain will never, surely, play an important political part in Iranian affairs again. The enormous embassy compound will continue to be much too large for the reduced pretensions of British foreign policy. In a way, the mullahs who organized the great *bast* in the embassy grounds in 1906 have completed their work; their successors, by overthrowing the Shah, also rid the country of the final vestiges of serious British influence in Iran.

The last Englishman to play something of the old proconsular rôle was Sir Anthony Parsons, who throughout his five years as ambassador saw the Shah on a regular basis to hear his views and give him advice about the course of action he should take; the Shah could not rid himself of the habit of seeing Britain as one of the arbiters of Middle Eastern and Gulf politics, with a particular stake in Iran and a particular ability to influence events there. The illusion persists under the Islamic Republic: a slogan photographed in Tehran carries the words 'USA is worse than USSR/ USSR is worse than USA/Britain is worse than both'. But those days have finally gone, even if Iranians do not entirely realize it yet. There will be plenty of pebbles lying on the ground for them to trip over, but they will no longer have been left there by Englishmen.

181

10

Godly Pastimes

... the quick, versatile, subtle mind of the Persian,
stored, as it usually is, with anecdotes, historical,
literary, and incidental...

Edward Granville Browne, *A Year Amongst
The Persians*, 1893

'IN THE NAME of God the Compassionate, the Mighty . . .'

It is 4.45 in the afternoon, and the television news in English is
beginning. Given that there may well be fewer than a thousand
native speakers of the language in the whole of Iran, it is a mildly
quixotic gesture by the television authority to maintain a department to translate and broadcast the news in English on a daily
basis. Perhaps it is nothing more than a survival from the days of
the Shah, when the English-language television service had a
large audience of expatriate Americans and British people. The
atmosphere then was so free and easy that an Englishman who
applied for the relatively lowly job of studio director was told that
the post had been filled, but that they were looking for an overall
editor for their news service, and the job was his if he wanted it.

Nothing is as relaxed and careless as that in the Islamic
Republic, and every aspect of the English news is distinctly
forbidding: the set, the choice of news, and above all the person
reading it. A young woman in hood and dark red tunic sits at a
desk with an old-fashioned colour separation overlay screen
behind her, on which maps and occasional still photographs
appear as signposts to the news items she is reading out: the war,
the latest statements of the Imam Khomeini and senior members
of the government, world crises and problems. The depersona-
lizing nature of her Islamic clothes makes it difficult to gain any
real indication of her age, or even of her country of birth. But
there is no mistaking her strong mid-western accent.

Tira, herself born in Chicago, is certain that the newsreader
must be an American by birth and upbringing, and each afternoon that we are able to watch the English news we study her

182

appearance and delivery for clues. The phrasing of the news reports is often more British than American, but that would imply only that the person writing it was educated in Britain. We ask the officials at the television station and the Ministry of Islamic Guidance to arrange an interview with her for us, but the answer, while never an outright refusal, is always vague and unsatisfactory. The woman in question is clearly reluctant to speak to us, and the officials have no desire to put pressure on her to do so.

All they will do is to give us a few details about her. She is indeed a native of the United States, brought up somewhere in the mid-west, who met and married an Iranian who was studying at an American university. By the time his studies ended and they came to live in Iran, she had converted to the Muslim faith; and the television authorities, searching for someone to read the news for them, approached her. In any other country it would scarcely merit attention; but Iran, with its closed society and its deep hostility to the United States government, is different. Obviously, the decisive factor was her conversion to Islam; that, in the eyes of the authorities, makes her fully acceptable, and is a guarantee of her reliability.

The news she reads is mildly partisan, but that is all. The latest reports from the war front are presented entirely from the Iranian angle – what else? – but there are no sweeping or unlikely claims, and no bombast about the aims or likely outcome of the fighting. The only item which smacks of propaganda is one which tells of the shooting, on the Iraqi President's orders, of a government minister who has fallen out of favour. Later, back in the West, I can find no reference to this, and it may be that the political goings-on in Baghdad are considered to be a reasonable field for a little inspired fiction by the compilers of Iranian television news. But when there is something closer to home – a claim about the shooting down of an Iraqi fighter-bomber, we are shown video-tape of the wreckage which looks genuine enough, and there is a dispassionate account of the damage its bombs did before it was destroyed.

Reports of the day's events in the Middle East are presented in straight enough form, even when they relate to Israel:

'A demonstration in the Palestinian city of Nablus was dispersed this afternoon by Israeli soldiers. Five people were injured, none of them seriously.'

A Sinn Fein demonstration in Belfast, another subject of regular

183

political interest in Iran, is also reported without comment. Even the term 'Northern Ireland' appears, although it is not in use among the IRA's supporters, with whom the Iranian government officially sympathizes. The source of this particular news item is given as the London *Sunday Times*.

The pattern is a familiar one in Third World countries: senior journalists in television and newspapers, who have often been educated in the West, are usually allowed to exercise an objectivity in foreign news reports which they are strictly denied in dealing with domestic news. The difference in Iran is that the religious base of the state amounts to an ideology which has very pronounced opinions on subjects such as Israel and even Northern Ireland: and yet there is apparently no compulsion to slant the coverage of news events in either place.

The news in Farsi is much longer – an hour, instead of fifteen minutes – and is presented by two newsreaders, usually men, one of whom gives the Iranian news, which comes first, and the other the world news. The pattern is the same on most nights: first, the day's communiqué from the war; secondly, the Imam Khomeini's message for the day, given to whichever group of people he has received in audience; thirdly, the doings that day of Khomeini's designated successor, Ayatollah Montazeri; and then the rest of the news.

There is, however, little or no serious reporting of political and economic affairs within Iran itself. The newspapers are allowed a little more latitude than television is, but essentially the viewers and readers of Iran have to obtain their knowledge about their own country in the way they have always obtained it: by word of mouth, by rumour, and by direct observation. The authorities are wary nowadays of giving too much away; when, in 1985, they announced that a water shortage would be dealt with by turning off the supply in certain areas of Tehran, which the newsreader proceeded to name, they found that the water shortage became much more acute: the people in those areas immediately filled every available receptacle before the supply was cut.

As for politics, the rule is clear: it is permissible for journalists to speculate about changes in the government, even at the topmost ranks, as long as they do so in a way which does not bring discredit on the system. What is not permissible is any suggestion that the Islamic Republic does not enjoy the support of its citizens. Anyone, for instance, who wrote an article about hostility among women to the wearing of *hejab* would lose his or her job instantly, and might well be arrested. Here again, television is more tightly controlled than the newspapers; and the

184

journalists who work on it, even if they want to bend the rules, have less opportunity to do so in the confines of a brief broadcast news report.

And yet it is not, curiously, illegal to listen to foreign radio broadcasts: not even to Radio Baghdad or Radio Israel. Perhaps the authorities, remembering the huge audiences for the BBC and other Persian-language services from abroad during the Shah's last months in power, realize that it would be futile to attempt such a thing. One estimate has put the number of radio receivers in Iran at 25 million, and people still listen to foreign stations in very large numbers. It can be important to do so: when the Iraqis were bombing Iranian cities, for instance, they would regularly announce beforehand over Radio Baghdad which targets they were planning to attack that night, and people would move out accordingly.

A regular feature broadcast on Radio Baghdad is the announcement of the names of Iranian soldiers and airmen who have been captured in the war, and anyone with a relative at the front makes a point of trying to listen. When the cousin of a man who worked for a member of the foreign community in Tehran became a prisoner of war, the family received calls from relatives and friends all over Iran to make sure they had heard that Radio Baghdad had broadcast his name. But with habitual Persian scepticism, no one believes the claims the Iraqis put out about the war, any more than they accept unquestioningly their own government's claims. All the information, from whatever source, is taken in and passed on to others, and it forms a gradual overall picture which varies depending on the personality and expectation of the individual.

Ayatollahs, government ministers and their supporters in the Majlis all complain from time to time about Iranian television programmes, on the grounds that they are too 'liberal'. Usually the complaints refer to the way women are portrayed in films or series, and on at least two occasions senior officials of the television service, Islamic Republic of Iran Broadcasting, have been demoted or sacked because of the programmes the IRIB has shown. None of these programmes has, however, been made in Iran; and the trouble has always arisen over the judgments made by individual television executives on whether a particular sequence was or was not acceptable to the stringent limitations imposed by the Islamic authorities.

As a result, programming tends to be extremely safe and deeply predictable. The film *The Messenger* is usually shown on the birthday of the Prophet Mohammed, and features and series from Yugoslavia and West – as well as East – Germany are often shown, dubbed amateurishly into Farsi. Wildlife programmes from the BBC, and in particular David Attenborough's *Life on Earth* series, are very popular and have been shown several times. The IRIB makes its own programmes on Persian history, avoiding contentious subjects and emphasizing the influence of religious leaders rather than that of the shahs. Twice a week the Revolutionary Guards, the *Pasdaran*, put out a television programme, which concentrates on their activities in the war; the Guards have their own camera crews, and some of the best films which have been made about the war on the Iranian side – *The Bridge to Freedom*, about the recapture of the city of Khorramshahr, for instance – have relied heavily on their footage. Advertisements are a distinct rarity, but they do occasionally appear; when they do, they are mostly for cars and electrical appliances.

A typical day's television programming is as follows:

CHANNEL 1
16.30 Sign On
16.35 Verses of the Holy Koran
16.45 English News
17.00 Programme for Children
18.00 Sports News
18.10 Provincial News
18.30 Sports Report (handball match between West Germany and Yugoslavia)
19.10 Call to Prayer
19.30 Desert Architecture
20.30 Iranian and World News
21.30 Economics Programme
23.00 Programme in Arabic

CHANNEL 2
10.00 Sign On
10.05 Verses of the Holy Koran
10.10 Children's Programme
11.05 Family Programme (lessons in sewing, classical comedy, child care)
—
18.45 Sign On
18.50 Verses of the Holy Koran
19.00 Cultural, Art and Economic News
19.10 Call to Prayer
19.20 Lessons in Arabic

19.40 Selection of Students by the Universities (special programme)
21.20 Miscellaneous (cartoons, etc.)
21.50 The Shrines of Iran
22.30 Iranian and World News.

It is a serious-minded schedule, and justifies the IRIB's North Tehran nickname of 'Mullahvision'; though, whether deliberately or not, it is usually possible by switching channels to sit through an entire evening's television without watching the religious programmes, with the exception of the readings from the Koran and the Call to Prayer, neither of which lasts long.

There is, just occasionally, a lighter programme or two, despite the Imam's declared disapproval of fun. One is called *Hidden Camera*, and is an Iranian version of the old television standby, *Candid Camera*. A survival from the days of the Shah's television service, it is extremely popular, and the day after it has been shown people recount the ludicrous incidents in it at great length to each other. Like its Western original, it goes in a great deal for machinery which breaks down in various spectacular ways. One show, for instance, was entirely given over to a Paykan car which was sold to unsuspecting buyers, and which fell apart, bit by bit, directly they drove it out of the show-room. The salesman in each case crowed 'Hidden Camera!' in the approved manner, and the dupe was duly chastened, annoyed or amused, as the case might be. There have often been complaints in the Majlis after an episode like that, and perhaps an expression of displeasure from some senior ayatollah.

The man in overall charge of television broadcasting is Mohammed Hashemi-Rafsanjani, the brother of the most powerful politician in the country, the Speaker of the Majlis, Ali-Akbar Hashemi-Rafsanjani. Mohammed Rafsanjani has a seat on the war defence council. His deputy, Mohammed Zoragh, is a pleasant-looking little man with thick glasses who dresses casually and says 'Hi!' when people pass him in the corridor. Nobody is willing to talk to a Westerner about the conditions in the television service, but although there is a relatively relaxed atmosphere in most of the offices, Mohammed Zoragh, for all his apparent pleasantness, is not a man whom the members of his staff want to cross. The pay may not be particularly good at the IRIB, but the work is congenial, and now that times are hard no one wants to run the risk of being sacked. The result is even safer programmes, and even fewer showings of *Hidden Camera*.

There is tight physical control at the main television head-

187

quarters, at Jam-e-Jam, set in an attractive park in North Tehran. Soldiers stop and search every visitor, and even with an official pass it is a difficult place to get into. Returning there has particular memories for me: two days after the Revolution in February 1979, when I was inside the main television building trying to satellite to London a report which included the material we had filmed at the capture of the Niavaran Palace, one of the dozens of volunteers who were manning the main gate a couple of hundred yards away fired his revolver by mistake. Another group of volunteers who were guarding the television building assumed they were being fired at by counter-revolutionaries, and opened fire themselves in the direction of the main gate. The men down there immediately assumed that counter-revolutionaries had infiltrated the television building. The battle that began in error lasted a good two hours, and mortars and heavy machine-guns were brought up by the men at the gate to subdue us, while we, the 'loyalists' in this absurd war-game, broadcast appeals to the people of Tehran to bring more weapons and come to our aid.

A great deal of ammunition was expended, and a certain amount of blood. At one stage a man came running into the control room, where we were still trying to feed our material up to the satellite in spite of it all, and shouted to us that the counter-revolutionaries were about to break through and kill everybody. We made for cover as best we could, but all I found was an upright locker. I stayed there for an uncomfortable fifteen minutes, listening to the incoming bullets smacking against the walls, until someone came around in a more collected state of mind and explained that the whole thing had been a mistake. At least three men were killed and twenty or more wounded that evening. Those of us who were working for British or American television emerged nervously from the building at about one in the morning, to find the walls blasted by heavy rounds, the streets littered with thousands of empty cartridge cases, and no taxis running in the entire city. We were picked up eventually by a passing ambulance, and, crammed together on the blood-soaked stretchers, were driven at appalling speed through a number of road-blocks to the InterContinental Hotel. It had been a kind of *Hidden Camera* in real life.

It is one of the curiosities of watching television in this most consciously Muslim and anti-Western of countries, that during the intervals between the programmes the IRIB plays Western classical music: a Vivaldi horn concerto, a Mozart symphony, a Schubert overture. When the new television authority was set up under Sadeq Qotbzadeh in the first week after the return of the Ayatollah, there was a great deal of confusion about what constituted decent Islamic programming. The staff of the television service was itself in complete disarray: some had fled, and there was no clear programme-making structure. As the system gradually settled down, and the interminable live debates about the nature of an Islamic Republic gave way to shorter, more organized items, it became clear that something would be required to fill in the awkward gaps between the programmes.

Under the Shah it had been easy enough: in obedience to the general rule that Persian, non-Islamic culture should be stressed, there were short recitals of music for the *tar* and other classical instruments. These, it was realized, would have to go, having become ideologically unacceptable; the Islamic tradition was now to be emphasized at the expense of the Persian one. But it was not felt suitable to play recordings of Koranic chanting, as though the only value of religion were to act as a buffer between secular affairs; and there was no other strictly Muslim music available.

At about this time, during one of his regular press conferences, Khomeini was asked what he thought about Western pop music. It was, he predictably replied, totally decadent and unworthy of being introduced into an Islamic Republic.

'And what about Western classical music?' the questioner persisted.

'If it is good, then it is acceptable.'

The television authority's problem was solved; Vivaldi, Mozart, Schubert and Beethoven were all pressed into the service of Islamic entertainment, though nothing more modern than Tchaikovsky is heard. As for the gentle, exploratory, intelligent music of the *tar*, with which Western stringed instruments like the guitar are cognate, it is almost entirely banned from the national airwaves.

There is no shortage of other anomalies in the Islamic Republic. If, for instance, you want to take up chess in Iran, and need a set to play with, it is necessary to go through much the same undercover procedure as it would be to buy hard drugs. Indeed, I was shown one place where I could buy a chess set, off Ferdowsi Avenue in the centre of Tehran: an upstairs room, occupied by two or three men who seemed to be there all day, doing deals in various illegal commodities which in all probability included drugs. I could, I was told, also buy a pack of playing-cards or a backgammon set there. And so, in the country where chess has been played for two thousand years and where the term 'checkmate' probably originated, it is now difficult to play it at all. 'Chess,' said one ayatollah soon after the Revolution, 'ruins the brain.'

The reasons why the authorities are opposed to playing-cards and backgammon are a little clearer, since both can be used for gambling, and are to some extent games of chance and therefore unIslamic. It is perhaps understandable that the men and women who took over the American embassy in 1979 should have confiscated a 'Monopoly' set which the hostages were playing with, because the revolutionary government was opposed to international capital as well as to games of chance; and there was logic too in taking away the dice from a backgammon set which was sent to them during their imprisonment by a well-wisher. But chess is not a game of chance, and yields little opportunity for gambling; it does, however, have strong links with the Persian past, and none with Iran's Islamic tradition, and it was presumably that which has ensured its illegality.

The Prophet himself approved of riding as a sport, and therefore a limited amount of horse-racing is permitted in the Islamic Republic, even though it is a good deal reduced from the days of the Shah. It never entirely died out, even after the Revolution; in the Turkoman country, in the steppes of north-eastern Iran close to the border with the Soviet Union, it continued at a number of different race-courses. The Turkomans are difficult people to force into political or religious harness. They have roamed free for millennia, and their passion for horses was something they were not prepared to give up.

The authorities bowed to it, only insisting that there should be no form of betting; and in the spring of 1986 a race-course was opened in Tehran itself, in the outlying area of Nowruzabad. But it was badly planned. The company that opened it used a motorcycle track as its model, so that it is too short to ensure a good race, and the stand side of the course is on a higher level than the farther side. The resulting slope endangers the horses' legs, and no one with an animal of any value will consider entering it at Nowruzabad.

Having taken the difficult step of opening the Nowruzabad course, the authorities now intend to support their investment by encouraging more owners from the Turkoman country, where the best horses in Iran are bred, to race there. Consequently two of the courses in the Turkoman steppes have been closed down, in this battle of wills between a government which disapproves of too much spectator-enjoyment, and owners whose lives are bound up with their horses. Outwardly, the government's one restriction on racing – that there should be no gambling – is obeyed; but no one has any doubt that a great deal of betting goes on in private. The owners are certainly not racing their horses for the prize-money alone, since that is small. It is, at all events, a curious country which forbids its citizens to play chess, but goes to some lengths to encourage them to race horses.

The problem of applying specific religious rules to the complexities of everyday life has proved to be considerable, particularly in the area of sport. Soccer, athletics, handball, hockey, even motor-racing were all regarded as being acceptable, though not for women. Weight-lifting received specific approval from the government, until a number of Iranian champions defected publicly to the Mojaheddin in 1986; after that the television sports programmes featured it a great deal less frequently. Soon after the Revolution a controversy grew up about the status of boxing: was it, or was it not, *haram* – forbidden? It was not, certainly, mentioned by the Prophet with approval; but all he appeared to say on the subject of sports was 'Train your children in swimming and archery'. Under the Shahs, boxing thrived in Iran, and its opponents regarded this in itself as grounds for its official banning.

There was an appeal to Ayatollah Montazeri, the nominated successor to the Imam Khomeini, for his judgement on this delicate matter of law. After giving the matter due consideration, he told the Iranian Boxing Federation that boxing was not, after all, *haram* provided that no one who took part in it was hurt. Since the object of boxing might be described in simple terms as being to hurt one's opponent, the ruling was not without its difficulties. The Federation, however, decided not to concern itself with such thoughts, grateful that it had been given the official seal of approval.

In the year 1363 of the Muslim calendar, 1983-4 in the West, the government's statistics show that more than 47,000 book titles were registered as having been published; that puts Iran in roughly in the same category as Western Europe and the United States in terms of book production, despite the shortages of paper created by the war with Iraq. Prices of books are low – between 1,000 and 1,500 *rials* on average – and even the well produced dictionary and encyclopaedia, *Mo'in,* costs only 2,000 *rials* for each of its six volumes. A wide, but sometimes curious variety of Western books is available in translation. George Orwell, for instance, who never envisaged anything remotely like an Islamic Republic, is on sale in the larger bookshops in Tehran.

'*1984* is very popular,' a polite, elderly salesman told me, looking at me very carefully as though to show he had no intention of being ironic. '*Animal Farm* is less so. A book about pigs does not altogether appeal to us.' This time, I decided, the irony was inescapable.

The basis of Iranian censorship has changed considerably. Under the Shah, it was primarily political. Anything remotely critical of his régime was confiscated and sometimes destroyed on the spot at airports. Professor Anne Lambton's book *Persian Land Reform 1962-5*, which criticized the basis on which the Shah's main reformist policy was carried out, was never allowed into Iran during his reign. Neither, on a rather different level, was *The Crash Of '79*, a thriller about the world economy which, written some years before the Revolution, forecast serious economic and political problems in which Iran, and the Shah, would play an important part; though not by any means the part they did eventually play. It became fashionable for people to smuggle the book into the country.

Nowadays, however, the Islamic authorities are less concerned with trying to keep out critical views of themselves (*The Reign of the Ayatollahs* by Shaul Bakhash, which is not a particularly favourable account of the Revolution and its aftermath, is available in Tehran, at least in English) than with preventing the importation of immorality. And so, while articles in magazines like *The Economist, Time* and *Le Nouvel Observateur* which criticize the Islamic régime are allowed in, advertisements for gin and whiskey, and revealing pictures of women are cut out or obliterated. An issue of *Time* which contained an article about economic changes in Hungary, for instance, seemed an unlikely subject for the censor's attentions, and yet several of the main photographs illustrating it had been blocked out with a black marker pen. The pictures in question showed women modelling bathing-costumes.

Similarly, books for academic use are not interfered with. The British Institute for Persian Studies, for instance, has imported works on Kurdish nationalism and books published by the Hebrew University of Jerusalem, without any difficulties. But if a Westerner leaving Tehran wanted to sell his collection of paperbacks, the shop he sold them to would have to submit the entire collection to the Ministry of Islamic Guidance for approval, and each individual book would require a code number to show that it had been passed for general consumption.

Strangest of all are the judgements in the case of individual Western authors. Iran must be the only country in the world where Agatha Christie's name appears on the list of banned writers. No detective novels are permitted, perhaps on the grounds that they glorify, or at any rate draw their existence from, the committing of crimes. Nevertheless the customs men and women at airports do not confiscate the lurid paperbacks of Western visitors, in the way that political books were once confiscated under the Shah; the prohibition on Agatha Christie, Raymond Chandler and the others applies only to books sold in Iran itself. As for other writers, Jane Austen is acceptable, because she is regarded as a classical writer, and for the most part the Islamic authorities approve of the classics; Barbara Cartland, however, is forbidden. Many people in the West, of course, would approve of a society which published Jane Austen and refused to accept Barbara Cartland, but the decision is not taken on literary grounds; it is the heaving bosoms and lingering kisses of romantic novels which the censors of the Ministry of Islamic Guidance find indecent and objectionable.

The Iranian cinema, which was praised in the West before the Revolution, despite the political censorship it had to endure, now operates under very difficult conditions because of the change in emphasis of the censors. At least two films have been withdrawn from exhibition after being completed because they showed men and women holding hands. In the case of one of them, which was anyway mildly daring in that it dealt with a post-Revolutionary family in Tehran, the hand-holding was not an act of love: one of the male characters reached out to help a woman up a steep slope. That, however, was too much for the board of film censors, all of them mullahs: they refused it a certificate, and the director's plea that the scene alone should be cut was rejected.

In that particular case it is likely that the subject-matter of the film, and its treatment of life after the Revolution, was the real cause of its being withdrawn, and that the fact that a man touched a woman in it was merely an excuse. But the possibility that a producer and director can go to all the expense of shooting and editing a film, only to find at the end of the process that it cannot be exhibited, is enough to ensure that no films which are in any way questionable will be made; which is presumably the prime aim of the board of censors. As a result, there are fewer and safer films made in Iran, and many more imports; though the difficulties of finding foreign films in which all the characters behave decently are quite considerable, and the foreign exchange with which they have to be bought is in short supply. The business of showing films is therefore in almost as poor a state as the business of making them.

Several Iranian film-makers have managed to continue by making films for children, some of them remarkably good, or by concentrating on politically acceptable costume dramas, in which women appear in full *hejab*. And because there is far less censorship of violence than of relationships between the sexes, and usually none at all, action films involving the destruction of gangs of robbers or of evil land-owners, though crude and bloodthirsty, are common. Japanese costume dramas also appear regularly in the cinemas of Tehran and elsewhere, and there are even a few elderly Western films from time to time.

Two which were on show in Tehran in the summer of 1986, having proved acceptable to the Ministry of Islamic Guidance, were British films of the seventies: *The Wrong Box* with Michael Caine, which was an adaptation of a black comedy by Robert Louis Stevenson about a mislaid coffin (again, the respect for a classic author may have helped it to be accepted) and *The Sea Wolves*, a lacklustre naval epic with Gregory Peck, Roger Moore, David Niven and Trevor Howard in which British seamen took on German ones, and defeated them. The audience applauded them cheerfully. Curiously though, as we have seen, the holy city of Qom, the bastion of Muslim values, had secured the much more up-to-date and therefore more violent *Escape To Victory*, starring Sylvester Stallone, whose ultra-American ethos had clearly been acceptable to the censors. None of these films, it can be assumed, caused any anxieties on the grounds of immorality; indeed, only *The Wrong Box* provides parts for actresses, and they are minor. The moral foundations of the Islamic Republic will not have been undermined by the screening of any of them, not even *Escape To Victory*.

The poor variety in the cinema has led those who can afford it to look to videos for their entertainment. The gradual easing up in Iranian life means that people no longer hide their video cassettes; rather the contrary, since they have become something of a status symbol among the better off. Pornographic tapes, the most risky of all, are rare in Iran, but there are large numbers of copies of Western thrillers and comedies, most of which have been smuggled into the country. Bahrain, as the video-copying capital of the world, is the most common source of tapes in Iran, as it is for the whole of the Middle East. And so the pressures of the godly state have obliged people to look increasingly to the home for their entertainment, because there is so little outside. The most important connexion in Persian society has always been the family, protecting and providing for its extended members; now the Islamic Republic has guaranteed the family's place as the main source of entertainment as well.

11

Cruelties

For my part, wondering why he [Shah Abbas I] thus
ill-treats his subjects, the only reason I can find is that
it is necessary to keep a tight rein on their innate bad
instincts . . .

Abel Pinçon, *The Relation of a Journey Taken to
Persia in the Years 1598-1599*.

THE BOMB WENT off at 8.22 in the morning, without warning. It
had been contained in a car parked in Ferdowsi Square, and a bus
was passing close to it at the instant it exploded. The passengers
sitting on that side of the bus took the full force of the blast, and
most of them died. Several pedestrians and motor-cyclists were
killed as well, and there were dozens of injuries, many of them
serious.

Mahmoudi brought the news when he came to pick up Tira
and me in Gulhak, half an hour later; he had heard about it
within minutes on the taxi drivers' grape-vine, even though he
had been in another part of the city altogether. He was philosophical about such things; for him, they were just another aspect
of everyday life. I asked him to drive to Ferdowsi Square to see
the place where the explosion had happened.

'Like in old days, Mr John,' he grinned; the old days being
those in which he had driven his correspondents at breakneck
speed around Tehran in search of demonstrations and
massacres.

We could see the statue of the poet Ferdowsi in the centre of
the square from some way off, above the level of the cars and
buses, but the traffic jam was immense. A blue jeep had broken
down in the middle of the road, adding to the confusion, and the
summer heat, beating down on so many stationary, fuming cars,
put others in danger of breaking down as well. A hundred and
fifty yards away, we came across the first signs of the explosion:
shop windows were shattered, and shards of glass protruded
dangerously around the edges. Tira and I decided we would get

196

out and walk the rest of the way to the square, leaving Mahmoudi to follow us and find us as best he could.

Several Revolutionary Guards were standing around holding walkie-talkies and trying to move the crowds along. The biggest numbers were around the entrance to an office building, staring at the places where people had been hit, and sometimes killed, by flying glass. There was still a great deal of glass all over the street and the pavements, in spite of the efforts of a single-minded man with a broom to sweep it away. Behind shattered windows a carpet-dealer was looking in despair at his stock, which had been shredded by the blast. He stooped, and picked up a long sliver from the middle of a grey and blue carpet, and laid it absently over his arm.

I had seen dozens of such scenes before, in Northern Ireland, in Southern Africa, in Lebanon: the tension wound so high that it could break into savagery at any moment, the apprehension that people might start looking for scape-goats and seize on any outsiders who might be present. A physical heat emanated from the crowds, adding to the tension; and there was no disguising who we were, or where we came from. Tira, even in her *chador*, was as recognizably Western as I was. Old habits returned: I found myself deliberately relaxing and slowing down my reactions, in order to avoid any unconsidered word or action; I pitched my gaze away from the faces of others; I did my best to avoid the appearance of nervousness, and did not lick my dry lips.

People pushed by us, not caring how they elbowed us or anyone else aside, carried away by the fascination of the place where the massacre had taken place. They pulled at each other in their desperation to get a look at the burned skeleton of the car which had contained the bomb. They crowded excitedly around the pools of blood, now dry in the heat, which marked the places where passers-by had been hit by shrapnel or splinters of glass, travelling outwards from the heart of the explosion at speeds of fifteen hundred miles an hour. The desire to find someone to blame, to make others suffer for the suffering and fear which the bomb had caused, was growing by the minute.

The police knew the crowd's mood could become violent very fast. They pushed into the crowds, trying to break them up and get them moving. The senior officer stood on the running-board of his jeep, bellowing out instructions by loud-hailer:

'The man with the white trousers and grey shirt over there – get moving! Don't stand about any more! And you, the kid with the red bicycle – move along! Stop cluttering up the pavement!'

197

By now, people were beginning to stare at us hard. You are safe enough in a crowd if people respond to you in an individual way; but when they start to respond as a group you have to be careful. I piloted Tira out into the stalled traffic in the roadway around the impervious statue of Ferdowsi, walking slowly so as not to appear guilty or panic-stricken; better, I felt, to endure the blast of the fumes and risk the occasional fast-moving motorcycle than to stay on the pavements while we searched for Mahmoudi in this monumental traffic jam. And as the workmen arrived and started attacking what remained of the plate-glass in windows and doors with hammers, we found him. Once we had taken shelter inside the familiar discomfort of the white Paykan we were insulated from the impersonal resentments of the crowd.

At the time, everybody I spoke to about it assumed that the bomb had been planted by the Mojaheddin. The truth was never clearly established: Mojaheddin officials in London denied it instantly and with anger, and there was an organized telephone campaign to complain about the mere suggestion that their movement might have been responsible. The anger was no doubt explained by an unwillingness to be associated with the killing of ordinary civilians; though the Mojaheddin lay regular claim to a sizeable number of bomb attacks and ambushes against government officials and Revolutionary Guards in various parts of Iran. After this particular case, various suspects were rounded up and the Minister of Security, Mohammed Reyshahri, told an Iranian television correspondent in an interview that the bomb attacks had been carried out by small groups of Mojaheddin or Royalists ('. . . just about every counter-revolutionary band is involved in these bombings . . .') with the assistance of the Iraqis. Almost certainly, the suspects will have been tortured in order to obtain a confession, tried summarily and executed.

A campaign of assassination and bombing can have a savage effect on an unstable society. In Argentina, a sustained attack by left-wing guerrillas in the early 1970s on the lives of military men, policemen and their families induced a form of paranoia in the armed forces. It led directly to the military *coup* of 1976 and to the campaign of terror, planned and co-ordinated by leading figures in the government, in which up to eleven thousand people, the *desaparecidos* or disappeared, were kidnapped and murdered. The bombings and assassinations carried out by the Mojaheddin in the early 1980s had much the same effect on the authorities in Iran. 'Those who are against killing,' declared 'Ayatollah' Khalkhali, the infamous judge, 'have no place in Islam. If the survival

198

of the Faith requires the shedding of blood, we are there to perform our duty.' The survival of the Islamic Republic, as constituted under the Imam Khomeini, was now believed to require the shedding of the blood of supporters of the Mojaheddin.

The Mojaheddin-e-Khalq, or People's Fighters, began political life as a secret breakaway from the constitutional opposition grouping, the National Front, after the protest movement (of which Ayatollah Khomeini was the leading figure) was suppressed in 1963. The Mojaheddin's aim, like that of another and parallel breakaway, the Fedayeen-e-Khalq, was the violent overthrow of the Shah's régime. At that time, both were small underground movements regarded as belonging to the far left, and the reputation of the Mojaheddin was lower than that of the Fedayeen. The Mojaheddin wanted an end to Iran's defence agreements with Washington, a widespread process of nationalization, and the expropriation of the holdings of foreign multinationals in Iran. During the Revolution itself the Mojaheddin provided some of the best and most active fighters, but Khomeini disapproved strongly of their left-wing politics and ensured afterwards that they stayed outside the system of government.

The Mojaheddin were strong supporters of the take-over in 1979 of the American embassy and the capture of the hostages, calling for a final break between Iran and the United States and demanding the nationalization of all American-owned businesses. Within months of the Revolution their party had changed its character; it was no longer a tiny splinter-group, but a large and growing political movement which attracted thousands of educated young men and women who regarded it as a more attractive alternative to the clergy-oriented Islamic Republican Party which was the Imam Khomeini's chosen political instrument.

Khomeini's tactics from the first had been to divide the groups which supported him but did not form part of his own political structure, and to turn them where possible against each other. He had succeeded early on in breaking the liberals of the National Front, led by Mehdi Bazargan, the prime minister he himself had appointed. The Mojaheddin and other left-wing groups joined in the attack on the liberals with enthusiasm. Then it was their own turn. There is no doubt that they formed a serious challenge to the conservative clerics of the Islamic Republican Party: the Mojaheddin were too popular, and too well-organized, for Khomeini to be able to ignore them. What distinguished them from the other left-wing groups and greatly increased the support they received, was that they too were a strongly Islamic party. But their religious attachment was of a radical kind, unlike the traditionalist approach of the Imam and his political supporters.

Khomeini began to authorize the use of a powerful term of criticism against them: the Mojaheddin became known to Islamic Republican loyalists as *monafegin*, an expression inherited from the time of the Prophet meaning 'splitters' or 'hypocrites' – people who pretended to be supporters of the Faith but who in reality divided the faithful. The Communist *Tudeh* Party joined in the attack on them, just as the Mojaheddin had joined in the attack on the National Front, unaware that it would be their turn next.

The coalition of religious fundamentalists and political radicals had finally broken down, and the position of Abol-Hassan Bani-Sadr, the active and energetic President who had been elected in 1980 with the strong support of the radicals, was becoming increasingly weaker; while the Mojaheddin, with whom he had informal links, slipped farther and farther into outright confrontation with Khomeini's régime. Soon Khomeini was giving public support to Ayatollah Beheshti, who had been Bani-Sadr's bitter political rival since the presidential election. Shortly before he was deposed as President, Bani-Sadr concluded an alliance with the Mojaheddin and its leader, Massoud Rajavi; and on 29 July 1981 the two men fled the country together, setting up their joint headquarters in the village of Auvers-sur-Oise to the north of Paris. It was Bani-Sadr who had established Khomeini at Neauphle-le-Château, east of the city, three years earlier; he and Rajavi both thought they would quickly be returning to Iran.

During the four weeks before the two men left Iran, the Mojaheddin began their campaign to overthrow Khomeini's régime. On 28 June sixty pounds of dynamite exploded at the headquarters of the Islamic Republican Party in east Tehran during a secret meeting of the party leadership. Among the dead were Bani-Sadr's rival, Ayatollah Beheshti, who was the party's secretary-general, plus four cabinet ministers, six under-secretaries in charge of government ministries, twenty-seven members of the Majlis, and several officials. A total of seventy-four people lost their lives.

During the first week of August there were thirty attacks of different kinds; in them, fifty people were assassinated, and fifty more died in bomb explosions. In the weeks and months that followed, the Mojaheddin came close to destroying the structure of Khomeini's régime. Their bombs killed the new president,

Mohammed-Ali Raja'i; the new prime minister, Mohammed-Javad Bahonar; the chief of the national police force; the heads of military intelligence, civilian intelligence, and counter-intelligence; the prosecutor-general; the Friday Prayer leaders in Kermanshah, Kerman, Tabriz, Yazd, Shiraz, and a number of lesser towns and cities; the governor of Evin gaol; the leading political theorist of the Islamic Republican Party; the governor-general of Gilan province; and a number of judges, Majlis members, officers in the Revolutionary Guards, and civil servants. Altogether, over two thousand officials and religious leaders are thought to have died in the Mojaheddin's campaign of bombing and assassination.

The Mojaheddin's strategists believed that the moment had come for a final push against the régime; and they began staging sudden armed marches through the streets of Tehran and other cities, which resulted in pitched battles with the Revolutionary Guards. The intention was to stretch Khomeini's forces beyond the point where they would be able to cope: a tactic which had worked well during the Revolution. But whereas the Shah's army had lacked experience in street fighting, had been unsettled in its loyalties, and was subject to conflicting orders about shooting to kill, the Revolutionary Guards operated under no such difficulties. On 27 September 1981 several hundred Mojaheddin fighters staged an all-out battle with the Guards close to Tehran University, and suffered heavy losses. At least fifty-seven people were killed or wounded, and 153 of the Mojaheddin fighters who were taken prisoner were executed.

As the Mojaheddin's challenge faded, the results were seen to be threefold. First, any prospect, no matter how faint, that open political opposition within Iran to the Khomeini régime might be acceptable was now at an end. Second, the powers and position of the Revolutionary Guards were greatly enhanced. Third and most important, an officially-inspired paranoia settled on the country.

A leading Iranian writer, now in exile, has divided the political repression which followed the Revolution into three distinct phases. Suitably, he has given each phase the name of a different prison. The first, which began with the take-over of power and lasted little more than a few weeks, he calls the Alawi phase, after Khomeini's headquarters in the former girls' school in the Bazaar area of Tehran. Dozens, perhaps hundreds, of leading figures from the Shah's time were held there, and many were executed on the flat roofs of the buildings which formed part of the complex. This was not quite the grand tribunal which the writer and others had hoped for, a sort of Islamic Nuremburg Trial to cleanse the country of the corruption of the previous régime; but for the most part the executions were carried out quickly, and there was no excessive cruelty involved. Most revolutions go through a similar stage, and the blood-letting can have a cathartic effect, however unjust it may be.

He himself was caught up in the second phase, which he calls the Qasr period after the prison in which he was held. Although he had played a part in the Revolution and his credentials were impeccable, he was openly critical of the wording of the proposition which the new régime was putting forward in its promised referendum, since he felt that it was unfairly loaded. A group of revolutionary activists arrived one morning while he was out at a meeting to search his office. When he went back he was arrested and taken to prison in the Alawi complex. It was only a month after the Revolution; people were still talking about 'the springtime of freedom', and many of the guards were genuine revolutionaries. Once a senior figure came and talked to the writer about the hunger strike he was staging, and told him that he was worried about the conditions of prisoners.

'I went to the Agha,' he said – 'Agha', or lord, being the honorific people used for Ayatollah Khomeini – 'and told him that the prison here was becoming too crowded. I asked him about reopening Qasr.'

Qasr, thus opened as a humanitarian gesture, was later to become a centre for torture and execution; but at first, according to the writer, the brutality there was not systematic. In April Khomeini sent a representative to examine the state of the prison. Some of the prisoners showed him the marks of the whippings on their backs, and he was told about others who had been severely beaten in the testicles. He seemed genuinely disturbed by what he heard, but the beatings went on. One is reminded of Maxim Gorki's visit to a labour camp soon after the Russian Revolution; he too was disturbed by what he saw, but later put his name to a report that conditions in the camps were satisfactory.

After three months, in the early summer of 1979, the writer was released from Qasr, even though, because of some bureaucratic muddle, there were also plans to execute him. The phase which began not long after he was released was by far the worst of the three, and he gives it the name of the most fearsome of all the prisons in Iran, Evin. The earlier atmosphere of casual brutality, created more by individual guards than by the system, had given way to a settled policy of repression and extermination. At first the victims were Kurds and Turkomans and members of other ethnic groups which wanted to break away from the centralized control of Tehran. Then the Mojaheddin started their campaign of assassination and bombing, and the Evin period began in earnest.

The various means the Shah had used in his efforts to prevent the Revolution from occurring were thoroughly surpassed by his successors in their determination to ensure that the Revolution survived in its existing form; and in particular three men with a background in internal security, Assadollah Lajevardi, a former shop-keeper who was now Prosecutor-General of Tehran, and two mullahs, Mohammed Mohammadi-Gilani and Hosayn Mussavi-Tabrizi, were appointed by Khomeini to deal with the threat from the Mojaheddin. They were told to use whatever methods the situation required: a clear indication from the highest level that a policy of torture and murder, judicial or otherwise, was permissible. On Friday 18 September 1981, Mussavi-Tabrizi gave an interview to Tehran Radio in which he described what would happen to members of a violent opposition group who were captured:

'[T]hey will not be allowed to go to jail, to be fed and rest for several months, thus wasting the treasury's funds. They will be tried in the streets. They have taken up Molotov cocktails and stood up against the Islamic Republic system. In such cases they will be tried on the spot . . .

'All it needs is two [Revolutionary] Guards, functionaries or ordinary people as witnesses. Once the two witnesses testify that these people have been involved in clashes, be it armed or as supporters, against the Islamic Republic order, it would be sufficient to have them sentenced to death the same evening and executed.'

Two days later, on Sunday 20 September, Lajevardi is reported as saying:

'Even if a twelve-year-old is found participating in an armed demonstration, he will be shot. The age doesn't matter.'

In the days that separated those statements, more than three hundred people were executed.

Even now, the precise scale of executions in Iran is difficult to establish. The Mojaheddin's own organization publishes a regularly updated list of names, complete with personal details where possible, of victims of execution under the Islamic Republic. The 1986 list contains 12,028 names. The Mojaheddin have a vested political interest in emphasizing the brutality of the Khomeini régime; much of the support they have obtained in the West is primarily a humanitarian revulsion from that brutality, and the worse Iran's record appears, the more support they are likely to obtain. Nevertheless their total may well be accurate.

Amnesty International, the respected human rights organization based in London, does not use the Mojaheddin's figures, though it has used other information supplied by them. From official statements in Iran, and from its own sources, Amnesty recorded 2,444 executions in the last six months of 1981, adding the rider that the actual number was believed to be considerably higher. In 1985 it recorded 470 executions, and in 1986 115. In each case it repeated the rider. Whatever the exact figure, the pattern of a gradual slowing down in executions seems clear, though in the years in question this owed more to the Islamic authorities' belief that they had smashed the Mojaheddin as an effective threat within Iran than to any growing sense of humanitarianism.

Amnesty quotes a Mojaheddin member who was held in prison in Tabriz between 1981 and 1983 as follows:

'With time I got to know my fellow-prisoners and love them... Each time they would take prisoners away to be executed, and then new prisoners came to my cell, and I got to know them in the same way, and the same thing happened so many times.

'In the end it was so emotionally painful that I found myself hoping I'd be the next to be executed... [A]part from the physical torture, the emotional and psychological torture was terrible... [W]hen there were executions, we had to load the bodies onto a lorry, with maybe a hand or a limb missing from them. I had to do it three times, putting the corpses into bags and loading them onto a lorry.'

A woman student described how she had been held in a cell containing 120 women:

'One night a young girl called Tahereh was brought straight from the courtroom to our cell. She had just been sentenced to death, and was confused and agitated. She didn't seem to know why she was there. She settled down to sleep next to me, but at intervals she woke up with a start, terrified, and grasped me, asking if it were true that she really would be executed. I put my arms around her and tried to comfort her, and reassure her that it wouldn't happen, but at about 4 a.m. they came for her and she was taken away to be executed. She was 16 years old.'

All the indications are that trials in political cases are brief and usually perfunctory, and that the scale of sentence has already been decided on the basis of a prisoner's interrogation and the nature of the evidence against him or her. Two of the many accounts of trials support this:

'I had no lawyer. In the courtroom were a judge, a guard holding a machine gun, and two others. The judge accused me of participating in meetings of the People's Mojaheddin Organization and the People's Fedayeen Organization, and of supporting both organizations, of writing letters and spreading political ideals, and applying to foreign embassies for visas. I was not informed about the verdict or the sentence, but my family told me later I received a suspended sentence of five years' imprisonment.'

'. . . There was a mullah behind a desk who must have been in his early twenties. There were four chairs on one side of the room and I sat down with three other women. None of us had anything in common politically, each of us had been arrested for different reasons.
'We gave our names one by one and were each asked which organization we had been arrested in connexion with and what our political activities were. I said that I had been arrested because they couldn't find my husband, and another woman said she had been at a party and had no political affiliations at all.
'The court convened for no more than five minutes. There was no one else in the room, but there were interruptions the whole time. After five minutes we were told to leave the room and there were no further questions.'

Torture is routine in the gaols and detention centres of Iran, as it has been throughout Persian history, and the methods most commonly reported are those which have traditionally been used in Persian prisons: beating by whips or cables on all parts of the body, but particularly on the soles of the feet, the genitals, and the back. A medical doctor who examined a released prisoner for Amnesty reported as follows:

'I was able to count eighteen distinct marks on his back, consistent with whipping. These marks ran in several directions and appear to have been made with one type of 'whip' which produced lesions like tramlines with parallel outer pigmented tracks 3-5 mm. across with a pale central channel. The lesions were up to 30 cm. in length.

'[T]he whip lesions were impalpable and clearly of several months' age. Three small lesions were present on the left side of the chest . . . [T]hese could well have been caused by the tip of whatever whip was used.'

The man who bore these scars was a teacher who had criticized Iran's educational policies but had never, he maintained, belonged to any political movement. He said that being whipped had felt as though his back were being cut by a huge knife.

Other frequent forms of torture include 'football', where a blind-folded detainee is pushed from one prison guard to another, and punched, beaten and kicked. The disorientation which this causes helps to break down resistance to interrogation. Other prisoners have been hung up for hours at a time, sometimes with one arm stretched behind the back and tied to the opposite ankle. Psychological torture, such as submitting prisoners to mock executions, is common; so is the sexual abuse of men and women prisoners. A voluntary social worker, who insisted that she had not belonged to any political movement, said she was held in isolation at a *Komiteh* building in Tehran for five weeks and questioned. On one occasion she was forced to undress and submit to various forms of sexual intercourse. She was a virgin.

'I had never been close to a man before. I didn't understand what was happening to me. I was terrified. I'd heard that if women were raped in prison they would never be released. When it was over I kept vomiting, and couldn't stop crying.'

She felt unable to speak about what had happened to her until she left Iran, over a year later. Now, she said, she was afraid of everyone and had lost all confidence in herself: so much so that she could not bring herself to go out in the street on her own. She found any physical contact with men, including her own male relatives, unbearable.

Under the Shah, the same kind of people – young, educated, and often with leftish tendencies – received much the same treatment at the hands of his secret police, SAVAK. Founded in 1957 with the active and continuing help of the American CIA, and with links which were often close to the British Secret Intelligence Service, the French SDECE and the Israeli Mossad, the *Sazman-e Amniyat Va Ettelaat-e Keshvar*, or Organization of National Security and Intelligence, employed 4,000 full-time agents by the time of the Revolution, and probably tens of thousands of part-time informers. It was greatly feared, and with good reason. It spied on Iranian dissidents abroad, and maintained hundreds of prisons, 'safe houses' and clandestine interrogation centres throughout Iran. SAVAK's treatment of its prisoners was one of the major causes of moral disapproval of the Shah's régime in Western countries.

On the evening of 12 February 1979, the day which followed the final success of the Revolution, we were driving back to the InterContinental after long hours of filming the rejoicing which everyone appeared to feel at the overthrow of the *ancien régime* when we saw a large crowd of people marching down the street, singing and chanting fiercely. We jumped out of the taxi and started filming them; and immediately – such was the mood on the streets then – we were greeted as friends and pushed and pulled along to see what the crowd was rejoicing about.

It was, we found, the take-over of two buildings close to one another: an Israeli consular office, whose employees had wisely moved out before the Revolution, and what appeared to be an ordinary private house. At the first we filmed while an Israeli flag was enthusiastically ripped to shreds in front of us and people shouted slogans about marching on Jerusalem; but it was the second that the crowd really wanted to show us. The ordinary private house had been a SAVAK interrogation centre, in the middle of the city. Now, however, it was almost in ruins; the crowd had spent several hours going through it and ripping out everything: not simply the furniture and the pictures and the rings for securing prisoners to the walls, but the very frames of the doors and windows.

Nothing remained except the structure itself, so great had been the fury of the crowd's attack. The cellar was lit for me by innumerable cigarette lighters, and I was shown the marks of blood on the walls, and scratchings which might, or might not,

207

have been made by prisoners' fingernails: the crowd, in its heightened state, certainly believed they had. It was a terrible place, and only the constant declaration by everyone there that things would never be like that again in Iran made it bearable.

After the Revolution many of the functions which SAVAK had performed were taken over by the *Komitehs*. They and the Revolutionary Guards now kept watch on the population. No doubt they also maintain a system of informers, as SAVAK once did, but people do not seem to be so aware of it as they were with SAVAK. Under the Shah visitors were regularly warned about the spies who were believed to be everywhere; that is not the case now. The *Komiteh* system, which is a borrowing, conscious or not, from Soviet practice, is a far more efficient way of controlling the population of a country than the more traditional method of using spies and informers.

SAVAK ceased to exist as a coherent organization from the moment the Shah left Iran in January 1979, and its officers fled the country if they could, or faced the prospect of imprisonment or death if they could not. But within days of Khomeini's triumphant return a new organization had been set up to take its place: SAVAMA. And, in the traditional manner, a senior figure from the intelligence community of the old régime was appointed to head the replacement. General Hosayn Fardoost had been the head of the Imperial Inspectorate, one of the competing intelligence services which the Shah had maintained. Although he was nine years older than the Shah, they had been personal friends since the latter's boyhood, and Fardoost was rewarded accordingly; but at some point during 1978 he became convinced that the Shah would be overthrown.

He made secret contact with Khomeini during the final stages of the Imam's exile in Iraq. He also appears to have been in touch with the Ayatollah's secret committee in Iran itself. There were rumours later that he had passed information to the Russians, in case the Shah was replaced by a Marxist government. It is safe to assume, too, that he would have had close links with the Americans and the British, in order to maintain his lines of retreat.

Under his control, SAVAMA was not an exact replica of SAVAK and seems to have had relatively little to do with internal security, except in the field of counter-espionage. It appeared to deal primarily with foreign intelligence-gathering. It did not come under the Ministry of Internal Security, but reported directly to the innermost circle of government. In its early stages

it contained a number of figures from the old Imperial Inspectorate and several from SAVAK, each of whom had received
Fardoost's protection. They, in turn, brought with them their
contacts with foreign intelligence services and their files. But it is
safe to assume that under Fardoost SAVAMA was never fully
trusted by the new régime, and it was not long before he himself
came under active suspicion. He was arrested and held in Evin
Prison for several years, apparently forgotten.

In 1982, Israel invaded Lebanon, and the fragile unity of the
country was finally destroyed. New forces came to the fore:
among them, the Shi'ite population, who were large in number
but had always had a reputation for being docile and backward.
But the Iranian Revolution had charged Shi'ites everywhere with
a sudden new energy, and the régime in Tehran was anxious to
capitalize on the new position of influence it was being offered in
Lebanon. Since the Amal organization of Nabi Berri, the acknowledged head of the Shi'ite community, proved itself to be too
moderate and too reluctant to do what Iran wanted, Khomeini's
representatives in Lebanon worked through the Lebanese
branch of Hezbollah, the militant Shi'ite movement which the
Imam had himself founded in its present form on his return to
Iran in 1979.

From 1982, therefore, General Fardoost's brand of intelligence
work – foreign espionage and the trading of information with the
agencies of other countries – became much less important to the
Islamic Republic than the newer business of maintaining Iran's
influence and contact with guerrilla groups and fundamentalist
Muslim movements in Lebanon, the rest of the Middle East, and
farther afield. The more traditional intelligence rôles, such as
spying on the activities of Iranian dissidents in Western Europe
and the United States, and ensuring the flow of weaponry to
sustain the Iranian forces in the interminable war against Iraq,
still needed to be done. But the new demands required a new
structure.

As we have seen, this new structure, the Ministry of Intelligence and Internal Security (*Vezarat-e Ettelaat Va Amniyat-e
Kishvar*) is headed by Ayatollah Mohammed Mohammadi-Rey-
shahri, who has emerged as a serious rival to the position of Hojat-
ol-Eslam Rafsanjani, the Speaker of the Majlis. The organization
he heads has an annual budget of £120 million ($210 million),
according to a defector who told his story to an Italian magazine,
and it uses the Bank Markazi Iran to channel funds to its
operatives and informants in Europe, the Middle East and Africa.
It maintains Iran's links with revolutionary and fundamentalist

groups in Egypt, Sudan, Morocco, Pakistan, Afghanistan and Turkey, while in Lebanon, it is responsible for liaison with Hezbollah.

Elsewhere, the Security Ministry has placed its men into foreign embassies and consulates, from which it can keep watch on communities of Iranian exiles. The Iranian consulates in Hamburg, Cologne, and Manchester (the last was closed down during the diplomatic dispute with Britain in 1987) were regarded as being of particular importance in this respect. The Iranian mission to the United Nations in Geneva, which is housed in a building close to the InterContinental Hotel, has been identified as the headquarters of the organization's European operations.

The Security Ministry is also believed to have controlled the Iranian arms procurement agency, based in the National Iranian Oil Company's offices in Victoria Street, London. The agency, which was closed down by the British government in 1987, was the clearing-house for all the orders for weapons, missiles and ammunition which Iran buys throughout the world.

The political changes which accompanied the take-over of these functions by the Security Ministry under Reyshahri appear to have penetrated even to the prison cell of General Fardoost. He and his control over SAVAMA, the rival organization to the Security Ministry, were targeted for public exposure. In April 1987 Iranian television broadcast an interview with him, in which he confessed to having been a British spy. At the end of the broadcast an announcer promised that Fardoost would give further details later. But he seems to have resisted making the remainder of his confession along the lines his interrogators wanted; after a month, Tehran Radio said in a news item that Fardoost, who was 76, had died of a heart attack under 'intensive interrogation'. It sounded like a euphemism for torture.

You can see Evin Prison, where Fardoost died, and where the two contrasting régimes he served tortured so many others, quite clearly from the public road. Evin village is a pleasant, outer suburban area of expensive houses and well-kept gardens, on the north-west edge of Tehran. An expensive modern hotel looks across a valley at the prison, which is protected by a long concrete wall along the low hill-tops, undulating like the Great Wall of China. On the corners where the wall turns there are grey watch-towers, and behind them some of the blocks which constitute the prison are visible. Tira and I wanted to walk down towards the prison, which was about two miles away, but we found our way barred by a Revolutionary Guard with a sub-machine gun. He was perfectly pleasant, but there was no point in arguing with him: he had his orders. The authorities like to keep a *cordon sanitaire* around Evin.

We looked at it as best we could from two miles away. Evin contained, among its hundreds of other prisoners, a British journalist and businessman whom I had met briefly in 1978, Roger Cooper. Cooper was arrested at the end of 1985, apparently for having committed a currency offence, but once he was in prison *post hoc* justifications for his detention began to come into play: because he had been arrested on suspicion, the suspicion had to be substantiated. And since there was no evidence against him on the lesser charge, he was accused of one that was much greater, and altogether more vague: espionage.

He had been in prison for fourteen months, when with almost no prior warning he appeared on television, in a broadcast interview along the lines of those with Fardoost and the leader of the Tudeh Party, Nur al-Din Kianouri. But whereas Fardoost and Kianouri were abject in the confessions they made, Roger Cooper appeared to be in full command of himself and did not seem to have been broken by his interrogators. His friends remembered him as an amusing extrovert with a good deal of personal charm, but there was little sign of that in the thin grey figure who appeared on the television screen, looking much older than his fifty-one years. Nevertheless he made an impression during the interview of a kind that the prison authorities cannot have anticipated.

The interview, it later emerged, had been filmed several months before it was transmitted; why there had been so long a delay was never explained. Cooper continually glanced down as he spoke, either because he was reading a prepared statement or because he wanted to indicate to his audience that he was saying something which was not spontaneous. His words were spoken mechanically and seemed to have been well-rehearsed.

The broadcast, which appeared on the daily English-language news bulletin, was introduced by the usual presenter:

'We now draw your attention to an interview with the British spy, Roger Cooper, who was recently arrested on charges of espionage for the British Intelligence Service.'

Cooper was then shown sitting on a chair in the centre of what appeared to be a television studio. His questioner was off camera throughout the interview.

211

'My name is Roger Cooper, and I first came to Iran in 1958. And from then until the Revolution I lived in Tehran: in other words, about twenty years. And after the Revolution I came back several times on short visits. I originally came to Iran to study Persian, and after getting my BA in Persian literature, I enrolled in an MA course at Tehran University. I might add that in addition to Persian, I studied several other languages at the university level, including French, Spanish, German, Russian and Arabic. I've also studied Islamic history and the history of Iran.'

'. . . [Y]ou co-operated with many government organizations and ministries in Iran, and therefore had very interesting and sensitive information at your disposal. Please tell us if you used this information in your country's interest.'

'Well, yes. With all this work I was doing for the [Shah's] government, I soon became an expert on Iranian affairs. And it was natural for me at the time to use this expertise to promote my country's interest, especially in political and economic fields . . .'

There followed a long disquisition on the failure of the Shah's economic policy, the all-pervading nature of British influence in Iran under the Shah, and the importance of Tehran before the Revolution as a centre for espionage.

'According to your own statements, Britain used an intelligence system in order to control Iran. What rôle did you play in this connexion?'

'Well, I must say that I had links with the BIS – the British Intelligence Service – and co-operated with it in supplying and carrying out analyses of political and other problems. From my earliest days in Iran, I was friendly with British Intelligence agents, both in the embassy and outside it, and helped them in several ways. As I mentioned, it was easy for me to gather information, because my friends in many organizations were like a private intelligence network. Apart from this form of co-operation, I also did my best to promote British interests in other ways. If, for example, I met people who I felt could be useful to Britain, I introduced them to the embassy or the BIS.

'There is no doubt that your services were very valuable to your own intelligence agency. How do you evaluate these services?'

'Well, I believe my co-operation with the BIS was somewhat unusual. Apart from the reports which the British embassy sent to London, the authorities there also received my reports and analyses of current problems. So you might say that my co-operation wasn't ordinary espionage, but perhaps was on a higher plane.'

A careful reading of his words shows that Roger Cooper never admits having been a spy *per se*; he had links with British intelligence, he co-operated with it, his friends were like a private intelligence network – but his co-operation wasn't ordinary espionage. Above all, choosing his words with care, Cooper gives the name of the organization for which he supposedly worked as 'the BIS – the British intelligence Service'. There are various branches of what might be called British intelligence, but none of them is known as 'the BIS'; the most familiar is the Secret Intelligence Service, which is usually known by its initials, SIS, or by its alternative (though no longer accurate) name, MI6. Roger Cooper, as an experienced journalist, must have known this. As it happens, however, there is something called the BIS: the British *Information* Service, which has nothing whatever to do with espionage, but provides information abroad about British life and industry.

It had been widely expected that the broadcast would be the prelude to Cooper's release, or else at the worst that he would be charged with espionage. Neither happened. Perhaps a disagreement about his case within the régime prevented his release; or perhaps the authorities were angered by the realization that he had turned his carefully-worded confession into a message that he was not, after all, confessing to anything. At the time of writing Roger Cooper remains in Evin Prison, awaiting the decision of a judicial system which seems to have found him an embarrassment.

In 1982, when he was in Britain, Roger Cooper wrote an influential pamphlet for the Minority Rights Group, a London-based human rights organization, about the persecution of members of the Bahá'í Faith in Iran. He had been, he wrote, initially sceptical that the publication of his report might help the Bahá'ís; but he was persuaded eventually that it would. His authorship of the pamphlet, which received wide attention, may well have added to his difficulties once he was arrested. He wrote of it as follows:

Although, whether in English or Persian, it is almost certain to be banned in Iran, where mere possession of anything that could be considered 'Bahá'í propaganda' is a dangerous offence, it may be of use to those who meet or have dealings with Iranians abroad . . . . Official and unofficial Iranian attitudes towards Bahá'ís are largely (but not exclusively) based on misconceptions, so any attempt to correct these, and thereby perhaps moderate attitudes, is surely worthwhile.

It is always difficult for Westerners to understand the reasons for the depth of feeling that exists in Iran against the Bahá'í Faith. It is a religion of peace and tolerance, it has never advocated violence in Iran or anywhere else, it avoids any form of political involvement, and the Bahá'ís, who are under instructions to obey the laws of the country in which they live, have maintained their beliefs with great courage in the face of torture and death. And yet several thousand followers of the Faith in its earlier form were killed in Persia in the nineteenth century, while since the 1979 Revolution nearly two hundred Bahá'ís have been executed, and about eight hundred have been imprisoned.

Part of the reason lies in the origins of their religion. It began in the southern Persian city of Shiraz in the 1840s as a development of Shi'a Islam, just acceptable within the boundaries of its teachings, and preaching the imminent coming of the Hidden Imam. But it was very soon accused of heresy, and its central figure, Sayyed Ali Mohammed, who was styled the 'Báb' or Gate (that is, the gateway to communication with the Hidden Imam) was sentenced to death as a heretic in 1848. His execution took place in Tabriz in 1850, and Edward Granville Browne, who was fascinated by the Bábís and their Faith, relates the story, accepted by many Bahá'ís, that the Báb vanished unhurt after the first volley from the firing-squad, though he was later found and killed at the second attempt.

In 1863 Mirza Hosayn Ali Nuri announced that he himself was Baha'ullah, the Universal Manifestation of God foretold by the Báb. He was exiled to Acre, which was then part of the Turkish province of Syria, and laid the foundations of the modern Bahá'í Faith in his writings there. Its Shi'ite origins had long since ceased to be recognizable, and although the Bahá'ís teach that all revealed religions are true, they maintain that theirs is the one most suited to the modern age. That in itself is total heresy in Islam, which believes that Mohammed is the 'Seal of the Prophets' and that Islam is the final revelation: to suggest that it can be improved upon is the worst form of spiritual error.

The Bahá'ís, however, pressed on with their Faith, stressing the need to improve society through universal education, world peace, and the equality of the sexes, and through living pure and loving lives. They have no priesthood, and no public ritual. Anyone can become a Bahá'í without ceremony, and the choice is a free one; but once made, it is adhered to. There are few if any cases in Iran of Bahá'ís giving up their religion, even under torture. Their courage in the face of persecution has always brought them new converts; nowadays there are believed to be between 150,000 and 300,000 of them in Iran. But they are greatly disliked by most Iranians, who refuse to accept that their Faith constitutes a real religion, and who believe – in the face of all the evidence – that the Bahá'ís were especially favoured by the Shah and were linked with the corruption under his régime; that their religion was instigated and encouraged by the British, as a means of undermining the authority of the Islamic clergy in Iran; and that they are today under the control of Israel.

The Shah certainly allowed the Bahá'ís a measure of protection, and some members of the Faith grew rich under his rule. His long-serving prime minister, Amir Abbas Hoveyda, who was executed after the Revolution, was always regarded as a Bahá'í because his father had been one; but each individual Bahá'í is required to affirm his membership of the Faith, and Hoveyda did not, regarding himself instead as a Muslim. When the Shah turned Iran into a one-party state in 1975, the Bahá'ís, being forbidden to associate with political groups, were often penalized for their refusal to join his Rastakhiz Party.

The supposed links with the British are fictitious. Various British scholars, Edward Granville Browne among them, found their religion interesting and attractive, and devoted study to it. Abdul-Baha, the son of Baha'ullah, was given a British knighthood in 1920 for having supported the British cause in Palestine against the Turks during the 1914-18 War. But the Bahá'í Faith owed nothing to British help or British involvement. It arose as an independent entity and has become one of the world's fastest growing religions.

The choice of site for the Bahá'ís international headquarters in what is now Israel was an historical accident; when Baha'ullah was obliged by the Turks to settle in Acre in 1868, the foundation of the Israeli State still lay eighty years in the future. It is true that before the Revolution Iranian Bahá'ís, as well as being expected to travel to Israel to visit their World Centre in Haifa, were required to send donations to it; but the funds have never been used for political purposes in Israel.

Given the Persian's weakness for conspiracy theories, however, it is not difficult to see how even those who have no love for the Islamic Republic are prepared to regard the Bahá'ís as a subversive force. Before the Revolution, in the atmosphere of nationalism which the Shah fostered, the Bahá'ís were unpopular for the international nature of their doctrines; since the Revolution, they have paid the penalty for being heterodox at a time of fierce religious orthodoxy. Bahá'ís, under Muslim law, are *mahdur al-damm:* those whose blood can be shed with impunity. The official media vilify the Bahá'ís as corrupt and treacherous, and as agents of Zionism; but the Imam Khomeini himself, though bitterly opposed to the Bahá'í Faith, has never attacked it as he has the Kurds or the Mojaheddin. As with so many other things in Iran the persecution is neither officially sponsored nor officially condemned; the initiative is left with the more violent of the mullahs and the local *Komitehs*, and nothing is done to curb their excesses.

The National Spiritual Assembly which constitutes the leadership of the Bahá'í Faith in Iran, and the Local Spiritual Assemblies from which it is elected, have been an especial target. In August 1980 all nine members of the National Spiritual Assembly, together with two officials, disappeared. A little over a year later the nine who replaced them were arrested and executed. In 1981 two members of the Local Spiritual Assembly of Shiraz were executed, and in January 1982 six members of the Local Spiritual Assembly of Tehran and the woman in whose house they were meeting were shot. In June 1983 seventeen Bahá'ís, including seven women and three teenage girls, were arrested in Shiraz. Several of them, both men and women, were tortured in an attempt to get them to renounce their faith or to provide video-taped confessions that they had been spies and that the Bahá'í Faith in general was involved in espionage for Israel. They refused. All seventeen were hanged.

The régime as such may not have instituted this pogrom against the Bahá'ís, but it has taken administrative measures against them which amount to full-scale persecution. As a community, they pay great attention to the education of their children, which helps to explain why the Bahá'ís have been so successful in Iranian life. For some years schools have been instructed to demand evidence that children belong to one of the formally recognized religions (Islam, Zoroastrianism, Judaism and Christianity) before they can be enrolled. Bahá'í wedding services are not accepted as lawful by the Islamic Republic, so that individual members must either deny their Faith and marry according the rites of a recognized religion, or they must live in what the State regards as sin: an offence which theoretically renders them liable to whipping, or even stoning to death.

By July 1982 the government had dismissed all the Bahá'ís it employed in the civil service, and no longer paid the retirement pensions of Bahá'ís. In 1985 it went even further by announcing that civil servants who were Bahá'ís would be required to repay the full amount of the salaries they had received during their entire working lives; many, unable to pay, have been imprisoned. But these administrative measures, cruel as they are, seem gradually to be taking the place of the more brutal persecution of the Bahá'ís; as with other aspects of life, the fire has diminished somewhat during the latter part of the 1980s. Nevertheless hatred of the Bahá'ís is not something which was introduced by the Islamic Republic, and it will not fade altogether.

'Being a Bahá'í must be like being a black in America.' The feeling of being discriminated against, of being despised, of being perpetually in danger of random attack, was real enough, though the analogy would have been more exact if he had likened himself and his family to Jews in a mediaeval city. All his life he had been treated by ordinary Muslims as an outcast: as someone to be avoided where possible, and a convenient scapegoat at moments of social and political tension.

'I remember one time when we were in a village. I was seven or eight. We had a driver, and we gave him some ice to take home to his family because it was a very hot day. I went with the driver when he took the car home and gave the ice to his wife. I saw her throw the ice out and shout out something about Bahá'ís.

'Sometimes my father would come home and say he had met so-and-so, and after they had shaken hands he would see him go off to wash his hands. It was a ritual washing, like when a dog passes a Muslim in the street before prayers. Other times when you went to someone's house you knew that after you left they would wash out the chair you had sat on, and the cup you had used. It was always worse in smaller places where there was more ignorance and the mullahs had more power. Some people used to tell their kids not to play with us. I remember that.'

He is a young man, serious and well-educated in the way Bahá'ís usually are. His family is *haute bourgeoisie*, but the money has been heavily depleted by the exactions and losses incurred through years of public and private pressure. These are not the first troubled times the family has been through, and the young man's parents both knew poverty when they were young. But, again in the way of the Bahá'ís, they started again, and his father obtained a government job in which, as a result of hard work and intelligence, he did well. But he was continually passed over for promotion; the discrimination may not have been so savage under the Shah, but it was certainly there. In the end the father decided to give up and become a farmer.

'The first day in 1968 all you could see was stones and desert. The mountains were up there and the village was down there. But my father made a success of it. He was one of the few people who did make a success of farming there.

'But by 1978 all you could see round about was other people's property. The boom had come, and people had made a lot of money in building. So they wanted to turn my father's farm into a residential area, because it was more profitable for the developers. They didn't like us being there anyway. We weren't welcome in the village, and sometimes they'd turn all the loudspeakers from the mosque in our direction.

'Then the Revolution came, and the company that supplied us with our animals couldn't send them to us any more, because they'd all died. After that we had to try to import our animals, and that meant we needed permits. But the permits took a long time coming. That meant we weren't earning much money, and the bank wanted its loans back.

'In the end they took the farm away from us, and all our furniture got stolen. All my father's clothes went, and all the things from my childhood: you know, toys and books. And that was how we lost our heritage.'

The father's problems grew. He used to be stopped all the time in his car, and the Revolutionary Guards came to arrest him several times. He was unable to obtain a ration-book since they were distributed by the mullahs, and the family had to buy all its food at top prices on the black market. They moved to their house in Tehran; and in 1982 they decided they would have to leave the country altogether, since the farm had gone and they had no money except what they could get from selling their furniture and jewellery.

'The time when they just confiscated things or you could just pay money to keep out of gaol was over. Now they wanted people. Father went into hiding for two months, and he didn't contact my mother the whole of that time – it was too dangerous. The plan was for her to get out to Pakistan, and then he would join her a week later.

'Well, she made it. You could get out quite easily then to Pakistan through Baluchistan, if you pay money. They don't like Bahá'ís much in Pakistan now, because they're pretty strong Muslims too; but she got out all the same. It wasn't until she was safe that she found out my father had been arrested. There'd been a raid on the house, and they took him away. She wanted to go back, of course, but it would have been suicide. They'd have executed her for sure.'

The father was charged with helping his wife to escape, with sending money out of the country, and with Zionism. The case dragged on for several years, and there was never any result. Now it has fallen into abeyance; but at any moment, if the authorities chose, he could be arrested again and brought to trial. He has no money of his own to live on, and for them to send him money from abroad would be too dangerous. Instead, he has to exist on the generosity of relatives. His wife and son talk to him occasionally on the telephone, they in their new life and he in the old. During those difficult, strained calls they never mention the case against him; and the only way they have of judging whether he is in any trouble is from his tone of voice.

There are many Bahá'ís in worse conditions: their pensions stopped, obliged to pay back enormous sums to the government, imprisoned, perhaps tortured. Those who have survived best are the people who work for themselves – taxi-drivers, small businessmen, craftsmen. The richer Bahá'ís help the poorer ones. They are not like the early Christians, rejoicing in martyrdom; but since they only have to make a simple statement to cease being Bahá'ís, and thereby cut their links with the most important part of their lives, the simple statement remains unmade.

'It's difficult to understand, maybe, if you aren't a Bahá'í. It's a system of living. For us, working in a spirit of service isn't any different from praying. Being a Bahá'í is a progressive thing – kind of like going to school, except it never ends. It doesn't matter how many Bahá'ís are in gaol, or even killed, it'll carry on. And we certainly don't want to convert anybody. We just want to make them understand.'

12

On The Road

But when he [the Persian muleteer] is fairly started he becomes a different man. With the dust of the city he shakes off the exasperating manner which has hitherto made him so objectionable. He sniffs the pure exhilarating air of the desert, he strides forward manfully on the broad interminable road (which is, indeed, for the most part but the track worn by countless generations of travellers), he beguiles the tediousness of the march with songs and stories, interrupted by occasional shouts of encouragement or warning to his animals. His life is a hard one, and he has to put up with many disagreeables; so that he might be pardoned even if he lost his temper oftener than he usually does.

Edward Granville Browne, A Year Amongst
The Persians, 1893

WE HAD SKIRTED round the southern edge of Qom, and had left behind us the well-constructed freeway which links the holy city with Tehran and enables the civil servants to consult the ayatollahs, and the ayatollahs to make the journey to the capital to check that their instructions are being carried out. South of Qom the road had reverted to its pre-Revolutionary self: a narrow ribbon of black tarmac, two lines wide, across the dry yellow landscape. We were driving too fast, but that was something I had long grown used to; my first extensive experience of long-distance driving in Iran had been on this road in February 1979, a week or so before the Revolution took place, and Mahmoudi, then as now, was the driver.

He settled now behind a grey Paykan which contained at least seven human beings, and maybe more: two of the women on board may have had small children on their laps. In front of them was a line of four other cars. We were perhaps five yards behind the grey Paykan. I tried nervously to read Mahmoudi's speedometer, but it seemed to function irregularly, dropping back or surging forwards sharply at times when our speed remained constant. Mahmoudi glanced into the mirror and saw me peering at it, and grinned. I did not give him advice about how to drive, even at the times when I felt it was most needed; but if any of the six cars that were bunched together within a gap of maybe forty yards had lost a tyre, or even braked, we would all have been dead.

From time to time one or other of the cars in our group would edge out into the oncoming lane, only to dart in again like fish in a coral reef at the sight of some equally dangerous convoy coming towards us from the other direction. It was nerve-racking and exhilarating in roughly equal proportions, though it would have been comforting if Mahmoudi had shown signs of experiencing a similar balance of sensations. He did not. His exhilaration was unalloyed, and he rubbed his hand over his short grey hair and bared his teeth in pleasure at the speed. The car rattled on the uneven road surface; the dust flew by us in billows, but never enough to hide the rear of the gray Paykan just ahead of us; Mahmoudi's reversible speedometer dropped by a few more kilometres per hour.

Past us, in the opposite direction, hurtled enormous trucks, decked out in fantastic ways. There is a kind of truck art in Iran, using as its materials electric light-bulbs in a variety of colours (though the red, green and white of the Iranian national flag predominate), and plastic stickers which often cover the whole of the upper part of the windscreen with ogive arches, imparting to the truck something of the look of a monstrous metal mosque. The faces of ayatollahs, stencilled or painted onto the doors of the truck, stare out grimly at the passing traffic. Giant eyes, sometimes accompanied by a tear-drop, appear on the mudguards at the back, to keep watch on the traffic behind. Some religious enthusiasts have replaced their red brake-lights with green ones, which flare out confusingly at moments of stress.

Other drivers cover the rear of their trucks with quantities of reading-matter: hints on overtaking, advice on speed, the number-plates of the different countries they operate in, helpful religious slogans, warnings of danger, requests to Allah. The cabins of their trucks are decorated with small Christmas tree lights, again in red, green and white, and artificial yellow fur and green tassels seem to be *de rigueur*. The best and most enthusiastic drivers travel under a motto of some kind, expressing their philosophy or their piety. Some, emblazoned on the front and back of their trucks, say nothing more then 'Mohammed', in very large letters. Others proclaim 'Mash'Allah' (God is wonderful) or, more disturbingly, 'Insh'Allah' (if God wills).

'If God wills what, Mahmoudi?' I asked. 'Wills if we all arrive safely?'

Mahmoudi's face looked puzzled in the rear-view mirror, as though I had posed some complex philosophical question.

'Might it not,' I pursued, 'be easier for the drivers to leave the words off and go ten miles an hour slower?'

He laughed loudly at the hint, throwing his head back and taking his eye off the car in front. I determined not to make him laugh again.

'I was fastest truck driver from Tehran to Isfahan, Mr John.' His spectacles glinted in the sunshine at the memory. 'Driving Mack, Deutz, Leyland. Fourteen hours, sixteen hours every day.'

'Did you ever fall asleep, Mahmoudi?' I tried to calculate how long we would be driving today.

'Never, Mr John. Sometimes taking small sleeps, though.'

'At the wheel?'

He laughed again, and I cursed my lack of resolve.

'Always,' he said, adjusting to my sense of humour.

As a long-distance truck driver Mahmoudi had worked first out of Isfahan and then, in the mid-seventies, settling in Tehran where the work was better paid. He had married there, and now had three sons and a daughter. His wife, who was also from an Isfahan family which had settled in the capital, was proud of his prowess at driving trucks, but had nevertheless persuaded him to give it up in favour of taxi-driving.

'Why was that?'

'Wanting me to be home at nighttime, Mr John,' he said, craning his neck to take an apologetic glance at Tira in the mirror.

He hadn't enjoyed the change at first, clearly: the independence of being on the road, the companionship of other men as tough and resourceful himself, the knowledge of being responsible for a large cargo – all that had been replaced by the tame life of a Tehran taxi-driver, whose only concerns had to be to keep in with his despatcher and with the police.

And then had come the political turmoil of 1978 and 1979.

'Plenty money doing the reportage, plenty interest, plenty fun.' I remembered the immense amounts of money the American television networks showered on their drivers, sometimes without realizing it, and the problems which those who worked for the more parsimonious European companies had in competing with them.

'And now?'

222

'Working at Hotel Laleh, waiting for passengers.'

'Not many of them, I suppose.'

'Driving you, Mr John.'

It used to be said, rightly or wrongly, that every taxi driver who worked at the InterContinental and the other big hotels in Tehran was working for SAVAK. Perhaps that was true; though even at the time I felt it was more likely that SAVAK would question the drivers about the places they had taken their passengers, rather than have them on its payroll. Perhaps that was naïve of me; but the results were the same, and I always took the necessary precautions when I visited someone who might not want the authorities to know. It was best to assume that a certain amount of informing was going on, and that everyone, no matter how decent and trustworthy, was expected to give their modicum of information to the authorities.

Under the Shah, and no doubt under the ayatollahs, that would be the price of a relatively privileged job like working as a taxi-driver at a major hotel. I never asked Mahmoudi about it, either before the Revolution or when I came back, on the grounds that to do so would have been both offensive and pointless. I remembered, however, a Russian woman who worked for a Western family in Moscow saying privately that she had to fill in a form once a week about the people whose housekeeper she was. She could not refuse to do so, because she would have lost her job if she had; but she always made sure there was nothing damaging to them on the weekly form. It was the only honourable way out of a dishonourable and distasteful situation.

Mahmoudi was the most trustworthy of drivers. If we asked him to pick us up at seven in the morning at the British Institute, he would be there at six-thirty, and while he waited he would polish the aged Paykan or dive into the engine to repair some questionable part of it. Often it would emerge in the course of conversation that he had spent two or three hours beforehand, searching the city for petrol, but it was never said in such a way as to make us feel that he was looking for extra cash, or even for sympathy. Often, indeed, it was presented as a fierce achievement, something he was proud of. We drove nearly two thousand miles with him during our stay in Iran, and never ran out of fuel, had a breakdown, or were delayed because his car wouldn't start. What was a far greater and less likely accomplishment, we neither hit, nor were hit by, anyone else the entire time.

We often came close, however; and I remembered an appalling occasion in 1979 when Mahmoudi was bringing three of us back from Isfahan to Qom. The road was much worse then, and it was getting dark. As we headed towards the brow of a long hill, the road turned sharply to our right, so that it was impossible to see who was coming in the opposite direction. It was, like many Iranian roads, quite wide: five private cars could probably drive abreast along it. About thirty yards from the point where the road turned, a truck had broken down in the inside lane. Another truck was slowly wheezing past it up the hill. The car ahead of us pulled out to overtake the truck; and just as we were all exclaiming about the madness of Iranian drivers who overtook just a few yards short of a blind corner, Mahmoudi picked up speed and pulled out to overtake the car. If anything had been heading in the other direction we would have all spun into infinity over the steep hillside which dropped away on our left. Mahmoudi only laughed when my colleagues complained. I stayed quiet; something about his armour-plated assurance made complaints nugatory. But it was to me that he spoke:

'Always knowing what is coming, Mr John.'

He seemed to be at his best and happiest on the open road, jockeying in and out among the highly painted trucks in the full knowledge that other trucks, momentarily hidden from us, might well be coming towards us at equal speeds. Iran is a country of fast reactions, and when we found ourselves involved in some potential confrontation, Mahmoudi and the other driver were usually able to hoot and gesture before swerving aside to miss each other by a well-judged narrow margin. Even at the moments of greatest tension he would drive with one hand resting lightly on the steering-wheel and the other ready to change gear with a curious flourish which I had noticed right from the start, and which he might have learned when he drove his Macks and his Leylands to and from Isfahan.

He had a habit, too, of allowing his speed to drop away as he overtook a large truck, so that we would be out in the oncoming lane, and would find ourselves staying parallel with the emblazoned truck while Mahmoudi peered as best he could into the driver's cabin above us. What he was looking for was never clear: from that angle it was never possible to see the driver, so he cannot have been trying to spot his friends. Perhaps he was merely inspecting the decoration inside. He would never give any indication whether he had found what he was looking for, or was pleased or irritated by the trucks we passed; he invariably gave a slight shake of the head and a sniff, as though he had sampled them and made his judgment; that was all.

'What do you think of that one, Mahmoudi?'

'Just carrying vegetables, Mr John.'

It was as though he were saying that trucks, and his judgment of them, were his private business, and I learned not to question him about them any more.

He had plenty of things to say about the roads we travelled on, but it was not always clear how literally we were supposed to take them. On the back road from Qom, for instance, a short cut that took us through small, backward villages and some very rough country, he turned sinister.

'At night here men kill if find you drive.'

'Who are they, Mahmoudi?'

'Can't say, Mr John. But very dangerous.' To emphasize the point, he drew his finger across his throat, and then pointed to the burned-out skeletons of a couple of cars which happened to lie beside the road at that point. It was certainly wild country – but bandits so close to the best-defended city in Iran? It scarcely seemed likely, but he would not be drawn. No one I checked with afterwards had heard of any such incidents, but it gave the journey an added interest, at a time when we had come to imagine that its greatest dangers lay in the way Mahmoudi and everyone else was driving.

'Around City Way To Isfahan', said a battered sign in the town of Delijan, a third of the way along the road from Qom. Mahmoudi followed it. It seemed no loss to have missed the centre of Delijan, whose mosque looked from a distance like a poor imitation of Qom, and whose only claim to fame was that the road to Khomein branches off here, and the Imam himself would, it is said, make Delijan his first stop when he returned to Qom after visiting his home town. It was a rare occurence: Khomeini was invited back to Khomein by his fellow-citizens soon after his return to Iran in 1979 but refused to go. To Mahmoudi, however, this was familiar territory. The main road south from Tehran through Isfahan and Shiraz to Bushire in one direction and Bandarabbas in the other is the most important trade-route in Iran; more important even than that to Tabriz and the Turkish border. Mahmoudi must have been this way many times in his truck driving days.

The landscape between Delijan and the smaller town of Meymeh, the next place on the Isfahan road, is remarkable for its cosmic untidiness. The rock levels rear up as the result of some immense disturbance, and the red sandstone base, curiously streaked with green, is overlaid by a crumbling layer of some sedimentary rock. This has eroded and fallen over the sandstone, covering it with careless, unmatching boulders and rocks and smaller stones, all of which lies like dandruff on the shoulders of the hills. Beyond that the plain stretches away towards the Dasht-e-Kavir, the vast desert which covers half of Iran. It was exhilarating, daunting, and extremely hot; and Mahmoudi, knowing the stages of the road well, pulled into the forecourt of what would once have been a caravanserai and was now the forecourt of a petrol-station and a roadside café. The name of the place was Hastijan.

A bus was parked outside, together with seven or eight long-distance trucks. Mahmoudi walked slowly past them, assessing them. One, loaded with three enormous blocks of white gypsum, had a magnificent painting on a wooden panel, fixed to the side of the truck, of a green landscape, a river and a range of mountains, with fluffy clouds in a dark blue sky. At the time this was something I had not seen before, and I took it at first to be a representation of Paradise: the Paradise of a country where the land is habitually brown and stony, and the rivers, as in Qom, are beds of dry stones for half the year.

But it became clear when I saw more of these paintings later in our stay that they represented, not a religious but an earthly ideal: a landscape of the mind which was attainable but rare and distant, and which might be reached only by a truck driver who was prepared to travel hundreds of miles from the hot central plain of Iran. Some of these icons, indeed, contained a portrait of the truck they were decorating, together with a tiny representation of its driver, a blob of paint peering through a painted windscreen. *Et in Arcadia ego*, they seemed to say: I, too, have seen earthly perfection – and I drove there in my Deutz.

The café was large and cool inside, with fans slowly turning high above the tables. Mahmoudi, who was either known there or behaved as though he ought to be, was treated with some deference, while we, as Europeans, were watched and quietly commented on by everyone who was already seated. Mahmoudi's evident status and our rarity value, together with the innate politeness of the proprietor, obtained for us a table separated from the rest of the customers; and when the young boy who was called on to present us each with a glass of *Abeali* – the brand-name for a kind of yoghurt mixed with soda water – accidentally spilled mine over me, his father pulled him out into the kitchen and shouted at him angrily. It scarcely mattered to me, and I tried to explain that, but it was too late; the boy remained in disgrace for the entire time we were there.

As we grew more accustomed to the place, something else became clear: the bus passengers were restricted to one end of the café, and seemed to be given an inferior menu, while the truck drivers sat close to us and had the best to choose from. Tira and I stuck to *chelo kebab:* chicken legs on a bed of rice in which a lump of butter has been melted. The flavour was good, and in my case made up for the *Abeali,* which (when a second complimentary glass was brought to me) I found difficult to swallow, though Tira, used to the far more extreme drinks of Tibet, liked it: thereby earning Mahmoudi's approval.

The decoration was pleasantly eclectic and non-sectarian: large pictures of Ayatollahs Khomeini and Taleghani shared the walls with one of the Prophet, who was holding the Holy Koran in the light of a sunbeam, while beside them the Virgin Mary sat demurely with the child Jesus by her feet and various lambs beside her. Elsewhere, away from the central group, there were pictures of water melons; the Alps; a forest of fir trees; the proprietor of the café (photographed at a quiet moment in the war with Iraq), wearing his soldier's uniform and clasping an elderly rifle; another picture of Khomeini showing him with flames around his head and a thoughtful expression; and Charlie Chaplin and Jackie Coogan in a scene from *The Kid.*

The point came which all travellers in such places dread, and I had to find the lavatory. It was not a pleasant place in the summer heat, and it was necessary to fight the flies in order to get in, and one's nausea in order to stay there. A prurient interest made me look at the drawings on the walls: drawings which mostly seemed to be concerned with the female anatomy, but which were highly exaggerated in almost every way. Though I would not want to be an expert on such things, I noticed a considerable difference between the Persian kind and those I had seen in the ruins of the Museum in Beirut during the Israeli siege of the city in 1982. The Museum had been occupied for some weeks by the Syrians, who had looted it of its treasures and left, in exchange, their excrement in every corner and their graffiti on every wall. But unlike this particular example in Iran, the Syrian drawings were prudish: the women in them had enormous breasts, but all wore little bikini pants, carefully drawn in by the graffitist.

The owner of the café at Hastijan was a pleasant, short, bluff man in his early forties who seemed to have come through his war service with no obvious damage. He lived on the premises with his wife, who cooked the *chelo kebabs* and his three or four children who either waited at the tables, as I had experienced, or would do when they were old enough. The couple's bedroom was beside the washroom, and the door had been left open. Peering guiltily into it, I found its simplicity rather touching: it contained nothing but an ancient bed and a wooden chest, which presumably held their clothes, and photographs of their family which dated back fifty or more years. It was a building, and a life, which gave the couple little privacy. The washroom was blessedly clean, and I ran the tap over my hands as I rubbed them with the flat, thin, gritty blue soap of working-class Iran, which has no smell and seems almost completely dry. The proprietor himself was standing in the corridor when I emerged, and shook my damp hand with enthusiasm.

Outside, under the canopy of vine leaves which were growing over the terrace, it was hot and the flies were more a nuisance than ever, especially now that I knew where some of them spent their time. Mahmoudi was off filling up his tank and checking out his engine. Tira and I sat and watched the passengers filing reluctantly back on board the hot, crowded bus, and the truck drivers coming and going, or like Mahmoudi looking at the oil and the spark plugs. The driver of the truck with the picture of the idyllic landscape came out of the café and called to his wife, who had obviously been travelling with him and was playing with their child in the shade at the side. She was a handsome, strong-featured woman with a minimal headscarf, and she bounced the baby energetically on her knee a couple of times before hoisting it up and climbing on board the truck. The driver hooted the chromium-plated horn and the truck pulled out in the direction of the road, leaving an immense cloud of yellow dust behind it. Mahmoudi watched it go, approvingly.

'Scania,' he said. 'Very good.'

Under the Shah, Iran became a freeway society; not just for the wealthy but for the sizeable lower middle-class as well. It was the one enduring social benefit of the tripling of the price of oil in 1973, which the Shah was instrumental in planning, and which so undermined the basis of Iranian society that it brought about the Revolution. Between 1970 and 1978 the ownership of private cars quadrupled, and the length of 'A'-class roads doubled. An elaborate system of expressways was planned, and although relatively little had been achieved by the time the Shah fell, the Islamic Republic which succeeded him kept to his plans and has managed to continue the road-building programme in spite of the rival demands on money and manpower of the war with Iraq. Road-building and rural electrification are two of the genuinely important achievements of the new régime, and in spite of the shortages and restrictions Iran has remained dependent on the motor-car.

It is only fitting. Persians are independent-minded people who regard the ability to travel long distances for their own purposes as a fundamental necessity of life. When I saw the French anti-conservationist sticker '*Ma Voiture Est Ma Liberté*', my car is my freedom, on the back of a Japanese Mazda in the centre of Tehran, it felt entirely suitable. The car enables a people with strong regional feelings and a powerful sense of family to travel regularly to and from their home towns and villages; it makes it possible for a nation of traders to cover the length and breadth of the country to carry out deals and commissions of all kinds, whether legal or not; and a large population of moderately well-to-do people who have never lost the habit of enjoying themselves have the opportunity of travelling to the ski resorts and beaches which are within reach of Tehran. In this sense, all the comparisons are with Western Europeans or Americans, or perhaps with nearly-developed countries like Argentina and Brazil. The enduring legacy of the Shah's years has been to lift Iran permanently out of the category of poor and backward states, and the motor-car is the best expression of its altered condition.

And so no matter how difficult the conditions for buying and maintaining a car may be, large numbers of Iranians are prepared to cope with them. The price of importing a new foreign car is extremely high, and even a Paykan is increasingly expensive. In the winter of 1986-7 petrol was rationed, and it seemed as though it would remain that way; but in the spring of 1987 it was freed from rationing though it was very dear. None of this has, it seems, affected the level of traffic in Tehran, or on the roads to the skiing resorts, or on the major routes that cover the country. It is often necessary to make important sacrifices to run a car, but most people are prepared to make them. If they don't, they lose contact with their family, their home town, their business, their pleasures: the most important elements in the lives of a vast number of Persians.

Driving with Martin Charlesworth was a very different proposition from driving with Mahmoudi. It was, for a start, about thirty miles an hour slower, since the elderly grey Land-Rover of the British Institute was a great deal heavier than the white Paykan, and Martin had not contracted the Iranian desire to live danger-ously on the road. It was also a good many decibels noisier, since the Paykan at least belonged to the same family as a limousine, while the Land-Rover is still in essence an adaptation of the American military jeep. Everything makes a noise in an elderly Land-Rover, even when it is driving at 40 miles per hour along an Iranian freeway.

We were heading north-westwards in the direction of Qazvin, along the road which would eventually lead to Rasht, near the Caspian Sea, and on towards the USSR and Soviet Azerbaijan. Tira and I sat alongside Martin on the bench-seat of the Land-Rover, with its primitively effective cooling system adding to the noise. Martin was, as always, a fountain of information about everything from the Elamites and Kassites of the second millennium BC to the ownership of the estates we passed; and the difficulty, again as always, was keeping track of it all.

We were accompanying him on what was in his terms a tame and relatively local expedition, and one that was somewhat outside his area of specialization: an investigation of the state of repair of the Assassins' castles, in the westerly reaches of the Elburz Mountains between Qazvin and the Caspian. This is the territory explored by Freya Stark and described by her in *The Valleys of the Assassins*, which she published in 1936, and there could scarcely be a greater contrast between her rough and perilous journey on horseback up into the mountains from Qazvin, and ours. But hardship, though unquestionably romantic, is not the only source of interest in life, and given the relatively small number of Westerners who had been able to travel to Iran since the Revolution, even the freeway we drove along had the attraction of (relatively) untrodden ground.

There was no shortage of objects of interest: for instance the immense housing estate of Shahrak-e-Apadana on the westernmost edge of Tehran, whose site marches almost with that of the main airport at Mehrabad. The estate is composed of more than forty great blocks of flats, most of them uncompleted and likely to remain so. The sunlight shines through the glassless windows and shows up the rust on the metal fixtures which have been left naked. The land surrounding the unfinished blocks is rough and overgrown, and children from the completed blocks play among the concrete and the abandoned paving-blocks, while mothers jut their heads out of the windows of the inhabited flats to check their children's whereabouts. It must be a strange and lonely place to live, like a half-deserted city. But why should it be half-deserted, when there is a housing shortage in Tehran?

The answer is presumably that it was built by a private consortium, and the men behind the scheme vanished at the time of the Revolution, before it could be completed. . But to the subtle mind of the Persian, such an explanation is naïve; and an attractive conspiracy theory has been created to provide a more satisfying solution. The estate, it is said, was going to be laid out in the form of the words 'Javid Shah' – long live the Shah – in Arabic letters, designed to be seen from the aircraft taking off at Mehrabad nearby. The revolutionary authorities, according to the legend, naturally wanted to change this to 'Javid Khomeini', but the cost of building all those extra blocks in order to make up the extra letters proved too great. As a result they ordered that work on the estate should be halted, in order that the now-forbidden phrase should not be completed.

As an explanation it has a pleasant, childlike quality to its complexity. Everyone I spoke to about it in Tehran seemed to know it, and one or two accepted it completely. When examined on the map, of course, the buildings spell nothing; they are just laid out in a mildly random fashion. But no one, of course, can be entirely certain; and that narrow margin of doubt gives the conspiracy theory just sufficient ground in which to take root. Of course there's nothing to be seen on the map, the believers can say: that's because the estate was ordered to be abandoned.

The expressway heads on towards an enormous belt of trees – part of the government programme of afforestation – and the place where the Shah, carefully isolated from the populace, would review his troops, and the main factory where the Paykan is built, and the old studios which the Iranian film industry used to hire for its features. From the road the sets look real enough, with a mosque and a village, though the village is of the Potemkin sort, façades held up by wooden props. On the highest mountain-top to our right a highly sophisticated radar installation, bought by the Shah and operated by the Islamic Republic, is visible for miles.

A broad expanse of plain between mountain-ranges thirty or forty miles apart, a smooth expressway, even the white radar golf-balls above us: we could have been in Utah or Colorado here, and the overhead clatter of a police helicopter, keeping watch on the build-up of traffic this summer afternoon before the Muslim weekend, simply made the illusion more complete. Freya Stark may have travelled this way to discover the oriental strangeness of Persia, but for us, sixty years later, the discovery was the hidden progress of it all, largely unknown outside Iran itself because of the deliberate secrecy of its régime. The strangeness and the sameness had merged together, and it was like looking at something half-remembered through an unbreakable pane of glass.

Three o'clock on a Thursday afternoon in August was the time when the rush to the beaches of the Caspian started to build up, and from time to time we passed ambulances posted by the side of the road, waiting for a message on their radios that an accident had occurred somewhere. Our own radio blared out traffic news: 'There are jams on the main road to Nowshahr and Sari, and the police report a four-mile tailback at Gachsar, in the Elburz Mountains. A family of five was killed early this afternoon near Tajrish when their car was hit by a truck loaded with building materials . . .'

The familiarity of it all was uncanny, but a closer look showed the unfamiliarity as well. In the flood of cars that poured out of Tehran with us almost every one contained women in *chadors*, and the bedding and carpets stacked high on the roofs dispelled any memories of the tidy West. There were notionally five lanes on our side of this divided highway, but cars swooped in and out, ignoring the occasional lane markings, as though we were involved in a race to lay claim to virgin territory: an undisciplined, enthusiastic, and sometimes disastrous rush to win a little advantage. Beside the road a truck had halted, a motorbike impaled on its offside. There was no sign of its driver or passenger, but a piece of black cloth which might have been a *chador* hung pathetically from the wreckage. Fragments of shredded tyres and pieces of chrome-plated metal lay in the roadway as mementos of other miserable incidents.

Stranded groups of people stood glumly by broken-down cars, watching as some stalwart struggled with the wheel or dived into the engine. A little before we passed Karaj, which is a good thirty miles from Tehran but is being turned by the convenience of the motorway and the relative cheapness of land into a dormitory suburb for the capital, we ourselves fell victim to clutch-failure. But Martin sorted it out in a matter of minutes, and had topped up the leak with the requisite fluid which he always carried.

In Karaj itself we stopped to buy fruit: small, hard pears, heavy peaches, grapes, and a handsome melon with good whitish-yellow flesh. We washed it all down with a hose that was provided for the purpose outside the shop, and the shopkeeper, a spry young man who would have been in the army if Iran had introduced conscription at that stage added up the cost on a pocket calculator.

'It's no good writing it down in Arabic,' said his assistant. 'These guys won't be able to read it – they're farangi.'

'Of course I can understand it, you clown,' said Martin, and the entire shop, assistant, customers, shopkeeper and all, collapsed with laughter.

A few miles farther along the motorway we came to a line of toll-booths with red and green lights over them to guide us in the right direction and a fifty-*rial* fee to pay. In front of it, in the dead ground between two booths, a man sat under a coloured umbrella and chanted into a megaphone about the needs of the men at the front and the duty of every good Muslim to support them. A plastic bag in front of him bulged with currency. He was selling war-bonds, and the buyer was given a small piece of paper, like a lottery ticket. I thought at first it would entitle him to win something, forgetting that games of chance are forbidden in Iran. Martin Charlesworth explained that it was simply a receipt, so that the donor could, if he wanted, check that his cash had not been misappropriated. Martin, who inclines to a favourable view of the Islamic Republic, said the administration of the war-bonds has been mostly very good.

Highway policemen lounged beside their cars in the afternoon heat. Mostly their job was to check on speeds and deal with accidents, but they occasionally stopped private cars and checked them as a security measure. What they didn't do was to check for un*chador*ed women or unIslamic rock-and-roll tapes: that was a matter for the Revolutionary Guards, and the ordinary police showed no signs of wanting to go into that line of business at all. With their black-and-white cars and their dark uniforms they could have been a Highway Patrol somewhere in the United States.

The outskirts of Qazvin declared themselves in various ways: by an unmanned tollbooth, by an obligatory fountain in the middle of a roundabout, and by signposts about the war in which flowers grew out of hand-grenades and flags and rifles were prominent. We also passed three transporters carrying Chinese-made field guns, parked by the side of the road. The town has a reputation, no doubt centuries old and malicious in origin, of being a centre for homosexuality. Freya Stark, not surprisingly, says nothing of that. Granville Browne finds the Qazvinis 'more pleasing in countenance, more gentle in manners, and rather darker in complexion' than the Azerbaijanis, whose territory he has just emerged from. Robert Byron, who in *The Road to Oxiana* wrote one of the best books on travel in the English language, found another advantage in the town:

Stopping at Kazvin on the way back, I discovered the local white wine and bought the whole stock of the hotel.

If there is white wine in Qazvin nowadays, it will be very carefully hidden, and will have to await a new and very different dispensation in Tehran before it is brought out again. All we saw were the local grapes, thick and deep yellow in colour, which were sold for eating rather than treading. There were other things which were worth buying – proof that once you get out of Tehran food is in good supply.

'There's no butter to be had anywhere,' someone from the British embassy back in Tehran bleated, in the way people do when they think you have not fully appreciated the full extent of the privations they endure; but there was plenty of butter in Qazvin, an hour or so's drive away. The store we stopped at had a great golden dome of it, two feet across, made in a village nearby according to the shopkeeper, who seemed justly proud of this miniature mosque he had created.

There were jars of American mayonnaise, candles, Japanese tuna, and the Iranian razor-blades which are called, inauspiciously, 'Shark', and have a ravenous picture of a shark with open jaws to advertize them. More blood has been shed by them, the joke goes, than by all the sharks in the Persian Gulf. There were also boxes of the marvellous Isfahani confection *ghaz*, and great open trays of nuts, seeds, and raisins. We each drank a sober bottle of grape juice, marketed under the name 'Jar'eh', and headed off. We wanted to be in the Valley of the Assassins by nightfall, and the sun was shining redly in our eyes.

A town the size of Qazvin has three or four petrol stations, one at the point where each main road enters it. A bored policeman stood in the heat, limply directing the lines of fifteen or more cars towards the single row of pumps. A litre of normal-grade petrol costs 30 *rials*, which is a good deal less than it costs in Britain and is roughly the equivalent to the price in the United States. The pumps were mostly self-service, though Martin maintained that one particularly villainous-looking attendant would have come forward to help any woman who drove up. He seemed unlikely material for a cavalier.

By the time we had taken the road marked 'To Alamut' and had climbed into the mountains above Qazvin it was half-an-hour after sunset, and the great central plain of Iran, which with a little imagination could be said to begin there, lay below us in the fading, rose-coloured light. It was at this point that imagination began to play a bigger part in other ways: in the growing gloom a large canine of sorts bounded across the rocks, and gave rise to discussion about wolves, and where they go in the summer-time. It was, almost certainly, the dog of some hillside shepherd, though there were no sheep and indeed no people around. Wolves certainly flourish this close to Tehran: a week or so later we came across a building which a woman was having constructed to protect her horses from them during the coming winter; but we regarded the sighting as unsubstantiated.

We were to meet up with some friends who would already have arrived and set up camp: one of those 'you won't be able to miss it' arrangements. But as darkness came on, and we rattled our way from hilltop to hilltop, shattering the silence with the noise of our engine, it became clear to me that it was all a great deal more complicated than I had imagined. For a start, although I had thought in terms of a single Valley of the Assassins, I should have noted that Freya Stark was careful to put the title of her book into the plural. The valleys extend for twenty-five miles of rough country, and there are at least eight castles there; and the reason the Assassins had built them was the inaccessibility of the region. Even with four-wheel drive, we could confirm that the Assassins had chosen well.

We followed light after light, tracking them down to isolated farms or will o' the wisp cars which seemed to be flashing signals but were simply going up and down the same kind of hills we were. Sometimes we got out and shouted, and waited for some answering sound that was not the echo of our own voices. And eventually, in the one area which we had decided was impossible, or where we thought we had looked before, we found them: a small and civilized party on a hilltop, with food cooking on an open fire, good things to drink, and a wide area in which to settle down once the food was eaten and the talking had died away.

We three late-comers could not be bothered to put up tents, and slept, incautiously as it turned out, on blankets laid out on the soft stubble. It was incautious because a species of low-flying mosquito inhabited the area up to a foot or so from the ground, and benefitted from our visit immensely. Having found the grandeur of the night sky too magnificent to allow me to sleep, I discovered the mosquitoes and their flying habits early on, and pulled out of the Land-Rover a folding bedstead which Martin had brought with him. Tira and Martin were both sleeping too deeply to be told about the insect-life, but the bed seemed to keep me above the general operational area of the mosquitoes, and I lay in selfish, guilty freedom for the rest of the night.

The wheeling constellations and the occasional shooting stars (the Earth was making its annual entrance into the Asteroid Belt) were magnificent, and in the clear, thin, warmish night air of the mountains I felt almost drunk with the sight. In the darkness I strove for quotations: 'For I will consider thy heavens, even the works of thy fingers: the moon and the stars which thou has ordained. What is man, that thou art mindful of him: and the son of man, that thou visitest him?' I believed that I scarcely slept, and yet I must have: the Great Wain had disappeared by the end of the night without my realizing it, even though I felt I had watched its slow passage across the sky the entire time. The night was so silent it beat in my ears.

The next morning was less enjoyable. Martin counted forty-four bites on his right forearm, and Tira had a line of them across her forehead, as though the mosquitoes had been drilling test-wells. I was not free of bites, but was less affected. As I folded up my blanket the small yellow-green scorpion I must have shared it with ran up towards my hand, holding out its sting like a street-fighter holds a knife. I caught the scorpion in a glass and showed it off to the others, as they were eating breakfast. We watched with a mixture of interest and revulsion (and, in my case, a certain proprietorial pride) as it clambered around irritably, trying to get out and pay me back. At first I felt I should kill it, but the mood of the previous night had not entirely left me; so I went to the edge of the hill on which we had camped and flicked it out of its glass, high up in the air, and it fell harmlessly on the rocks below me and scuttled away into shelter.

The morning landscape was splendid: the hills we had toiled up and down the previous night were now revealed as gentle undulations of limestone, covered with thorn-bushes which gave them a variegated khaki effect, like Iranian army camouflage. White gravel roads crossed the hills here and there, and where the valleys were deep enough and the Shahrud river ran there would be startling patches of bright green, where the villagers grew their rice. Crickets with blue or scarlet underwings burst suddenly out of the dried bushes that looked like the bleached skeletons of small animals, and down closer to the Shahrud black dragonflies flashed about like military helicopters. Of the Assassins' castles, which my imagination the previous night had placed on every available hilltop, there was no sign whatever.

We loaded ourselves and the handsome alsatian dog belonging to some of our companions into Land-Rovers and jeeps, and moved off, leaving a servant (since roughing it had its limits) to take care of the camp and prepare something against our return. It took us more than an hour's driving, over roads which became mere tracks, and through occasional villages of sun-dried brick which seemed scarcely inhabited. Our objective was Alamut, the most important of the castles in historical terms.

The legend of the Old Man of the Mountains, the leader of the Ismaili sect, who drugged his devoted followers on hashish (whence the name 'Assassins') and sent them out to murder his political and religious enemies, has been a part of the European imagination since at least 1192, when Conrad of Montferrat, king of the Latin kingdom of Jerusalem, was murdered by them. Westerners have always been fascinated and repelled in roughly equal proportions by the concept of blind devotion to an incomprehensible religious cause: that, indeed, is part of the interest and horror which Khomeini's Iran has aroused in the West. An easily-grasped name has helped; within a century and a half of Conrad's death *'assassino'* was in common use in Italy to mean any murderer, and it spread quickly to France and from there, a little more slowly, to England.

As always, of course, the legend lacks accuracy: it is as though we drew our picture of modern Iran solely from the *Sun* or the *New York World*. For a start, the name 'Assassin' seems to have arisen, not because the Ismailis necessarily used hashish, but because their enemies attributed their fanatical behaviour to drug-taking, and what began as a term of contempt stuck; for a parallel example in Europe one could point to the Quakers. Secondly, the Persian Ismailis were never called 'Assassins', since that was a term which applied solely to the Syrian branch of the sect which was established later. But the core of the legend is the existence of a body of revolutionaries so dedicated that they could be ordered to undertake often suicidal attacks on the lives of their political enemies; and that is certainly true. The Ismailis are now an ultra-respectable group whose leader is the Aga Khan, but their origins, as a minority party which broke away from Shi'a Islam, were more violent; and the Assassins' aim was the revolutionary overthrow of the religious system represented by Sunni Islam which they regarded as evil and corrupt, and its replacement with a just society based squarely on the Koran. Comparisons with Khomeini's Iran are inaccurate in both religious and political terms, but it is sometimes hard for Westerners not to see some resonance there.

The founder of the Assassins was Hasan-i Sabbah, who was born in the middle of the eleventh century in the holy city of Qom. He was a convert to the Ismaili sect and by instinct a revolutionary, and he selected the mountain valleys near Qazvin as his base of operations. In particular, he chose the castle of Alamut, built on an inaccessible ridge of rock six thousand feet above sea level, and instead of capturing it by force he infiltrated it in 1090 and offered its owner an immense price in gold for it. The owner, having presumably no alternative, accepted and left.

The first of the Assassins' murders took place two years later, in 1092. Hasan-i Sabbah, calling his sixty or so devotees to him, asked which of them was prepared to rid the state of Nizam al-Mulk, the all-powerful vizier who represented Seljuk power in Iran. A man called Bu Tahir Arrani laid his hand on his heart as a sign that he was prepared to volunteer for the task, and at a place called Sahna, when the vizier was being carried by litter to the tent of his wives, Arrani approached him, disguised as a Sufi, and stabbed him with a knife. 'The killing of this devil,' said Hasan-i Sabbah when the news was brought to him in his castle at Alamut, 'is the beginning of bliss.'

For the remaining thirty-three years of his life Hasan-i Sabbah never left the rock; he remained there, studying in his immense library, adminstering his province, ordering the murder of his enemies, and leading an otherwise pious and abstemious life. Marco Polo, who travelled through Persia in 1273, knew a good story when he heard one:

> The Old Man . . . caused a certain valley between two mountains to be enclosed, and had turned it into a garden, the largest and most beautiful that was ever seen, filled with every variety of fruit. In it were erected pavilions and palaces, the most elegant that can be imagined, all covered with gilding and exquisite painting. And there were runnels too, flowing freely with wine and milk and honey and water; and numbers of ladies and of the most beautiful damsels in the world, who could play on all manner of instruments . . .'

We arrived at the village of Qasir Khan, at the foot of Alamut Rock, in the middle of the morning, and managed to make out the outlines of what is left of the castle on the long ridge of rock from our position several hundred feet below it. The Mongols who invested it in 1256 had done an efficient job of destroying it after it was surrendered to them; so good that a British traveller, Colonel Monteith, who reached the Alamut Valley in 1833, failed to recognize the castle. As for Marco Polo's tabloid newspaper account of life there, it is impossible, sadly, to believe that the valley, whose sides slope violently down to a single stream far below, can ever have been turned into anything; let alone a garden.

We had parked on the farther side of Qasir Khan, at the start of the path that led to the Rock. We could not hope, however, to avoid the attentions of the children of the village, and they gathered at a respectful distance, in a group of a dozen or so, to inspect us. The distance was respectful because of our accompanying alsatian, which seemed to develop deep anti-Persian and anti-boy feelings, and made little forays at the group. The group, for its part, fell back with shouts and cries of fear and enjoyment and then regrouped to throw stones and perform a goading kind of dance. Martin Charlesworth gathered together the measuring and surveying equipment he had brought from Tehran, and everyone else loaded up with walking-sticks, water-bottles, cameras, and other exploratory gear. The shouts of the village children, derisory more than hostile, faded behind us as we struck out for the Rock.

It was extremely steep and, for someone like me with no head for heights and shoes which slipped on all the rocks, it was an alarming experience. It was made all the worse by the chamois-like speed with which everyone else, regardless of age, sex or danger, moved up the slippery scree-slope and along the path which shrank to a few inches' width in several places and often disappeared altogether. In my case, pure embarrassment kept me going at first After that, one had to continue upwards, since going back was clearly going to be an even worse experience. I was, however, the last by a long way of all those who attempted the climb.

As I hauled myself up the final slope I came across a cave, and in it, sheltering from the heat, three Iranians in their early twenties. I stopped and talked to them, in order to rest and to cover my sense of shame at having covered the last hundred yards or so virtually on my hands and knees. The shame was merited: later I watched as the three ran down a slope which was as close to being vertical as anything I want to climb again, and which dropped uninterrupted for four or five hundred feet.

They had come out for the day from Qazvin, and were slightly annoyed that their vantage-point on the top of the Rock should have been invaded by non-believers.

'*Engilisi?*' one of them asked. He looked like the eldest, and wore a woolly hat.

I acknowledged that I was.

'*Marg bar Thatcher,*' Death to Thatcher, the woolly-hatted one said, quite conversationally, as though it was the kind of thing he always said to passing Englishmen perched above a precipice in the Valley of the Assassins.

'Don't be so bloody offensive,' I shouted, waving my arms and nearly slipping back down the mountainside.

'*Shoma biadab,*' I added, fortuitously remembering something from my trusty *Colloquial Persian*. It was uncolloquial Persian for 'You are being rude,' and I was proud of it. It was also effective. The man in the woolly hat was clearly very surprised, which further convinced me that threatening the life of the British prime minister was meant as a friendly kind of gesture, since it was plain to him that no Englishman who came to Iran could possibly think well of Margaret Thatcher. Embarrassed by his social gaffe, he placed his hand over his heart, rather as Bu Tahir Arrani had done on this same rock nine hundred years before, and made what seemed to be a bow. I was anyway so gratified by having remembered the word *biadab* that my irritation had passed. We all smiled, and exchanged polite words of farewell, and then the three of them ran off suicidally down the precipice while I struggled on to find Martin and the others.

The view was wonderful, and I think I shall never forget it; it was like being taken up on a pinnacle of the Temple and being shown all the kingdoms of the world. The mountains and rivers and the bright green of paddy fields and the slicks of near-desert reached off into oblivion. Everyone else, having long become accustomed to the view, was watching while Martin, complete with measuring-rods, was being lowered by rope together with two of the younger members of the party into a slit in the rock which contained a water-cistern, as used by the Assassins. The three Persians who were doing the lowering were, it turned out, visitors themselves and not guides, and they refused all offers of money for their help or the use of their ropes.

Of the castle itself, there seemed to be very little indeed: a few low walls of bricks and mortar, a few steps cut in the rock, a few pathways. The site of the marvellous library of Hasan-i Sabbah had been destroyed utterly, but not necessarily the books themselves, since the pusillanimous defenders of the place were allowed by the Mongols to leave Alamut with all their belongings when they surrendered. Looking out across the plain of Iran from his library, it cannot have been hard for Hasan-i Sabbah to decide he never wanted to leave the place again. Or perhaps, like me, he was simply reluctant to face the appalling journey down the precipice.

When we returned to the Land-Rovers, the children of the village were hiding; they had smashed one of the windows and poured water from a nearby stream into the inside, in retaliation for the scare the alsatian had given them. As we bathed our feet in the stream and ate water-melon, the children emerged and picked up stones again, to throw at the dog rather than at us;

when we shouted they dropped them and ran. We drove out of Qasir Khan with an escort of running children, all joking and laughing and trying to jump on the back of the Land-Rovers. I produced my camera, and started taking pictures of them: at which about half of them covered their faces and ran off, howling with fear, while the others, more resolutely, stood in the road and watched. Then the Land-Rover picked up speed and the clouds of dust hid the children, and the village, and the Rock of Alamut from us, and we became small objects moving across the marvellous plain we had seen from six hundred feet up, in the unchanged view the Old Man of the Mountains saw every day from his library.

13

Half the Body of Society

Consulted in all matters, the Persian wife is her husband's trusted confidante and counsellor, as most good English wives are. 'But she is veiled, the poor thing, closely veiled!' exclaims the pitying Englishwoman. Yes, she is veiled. And loth would she be to part with what she looks on as a distinction and a privilege. To her the veil is the badge of modesty and the token of respectability.

Dr. C. J. Wills, *Persia As It Is*, 1887

THE FIRST SIGHT of the Caspian Sea can be one of the most impressive experiences on earth. After the long journey through the Elburz Mountains, and the humid sub-tropical forests called jangali, or jungle, the road suddenly drops away and the Caspian lies in front of you, an ocean rather than a lake, stretching off to the horizon. All the way along the Iranian shore, little villages which were once fishing ports have been converted to resorts for holiday-makers from Tehran. Nowadays most of the villages are quiet during the summer, and the people who live there have been obliged to go back to fishing for their livelihoods, since large numbers of the well-to-do people who used to come to the Caspian for the weekend, or indeed for the whole summer, are now in exile and spend their summers in the South of France or on the beaches of Southern California.

But the main resorts, Nowshahr, Ramsar and others, have managed to keep most of their customers. The people who go there are not, by and large, from the wealthiest bracket, and it was usually the wealthiest who left Iran after the Revolution. The inhibiting factor is nowadays the availability of petrol for the trip: a hundred miles there and a hundred miles back, with traffic that can often be heavy on roads that are not of the best. A government which does not approve of fun ('An Islamic régime must be serious in every aspect of life,' the Imam Khomeini said in a broadcast on Iran Radio six months after the Revolution. 'There is no fun in Islam. There can be no fun or enjoyment in whatever is serious') is not likely to waste valuable resources on improving the road to the beaches of the Caspian.

Those beaches are often magnificent. But even from a distance there seems to be something curious about the swimmers. A large black stain on the water, as though someone had spilt ink there. You have to get a little closer to realize that the stain is the swimmers' *hejab*, floating around them on the surface of the water. This beach is restricted to women and young children, and although the Islamic Republic disapproves, on the whole, of beach holidays (elsewhere in the same Iran Radio broadcast of August 1979 Khomeini said, 'Islam does not approve of swimming in the sea') it is permissible if the sexes are strictly segregated and if the women wear Islamic dress, even in the water. The *chador* billows up unpleasantly around the swimmer, hampering the movement of her arms and legs.

Not surprisingly, there are few women in the water; most prefer to walk up and down on the sand, or sit with their children and friends, protected from the sun and the prying looks of men by their long grey, blue or black robes. The greatest concession they are allowed to make to the fact of being by the sea is that they can go barefoot on the sands. That, at any rate, does not seem to be frowned upon by the women *Komiteh* members who keep watch on the beach. Further out, male *Komiteh* men patrol the waters in speed-boats, to ensure that no one swims round from the men's beaches to spy on the women or sails round on one of the brightly coloured wind-surfers that cluster a few hundred yards offshore in order to join up with them illicitly.

I have seen less strictly segregated beaches in South Africa. It may well be, as many middle class Iranians maintain, that they are suffering because of their social background and the kind of lives they choose to lead: the authorities of the Islamic Republic know that the well-to-do middle-class are their greatest critics, even though the criticism is almost invariably silent. But there is a deeper consideration as well. The authorities feel they have to safeguard women from the worst aspects of their own natures and those of men. There is a deep pessimism in Shi'a Islam about the immoral propensities of human nature, which parallels the pessimism of Protestant non-conformism in Northern Europe and the United States. Women, it is felt, are weak and inclined by their emotional natures to be sinful, and therefore to be the cause

243

of sinfulness in men. As a result they must dress so that only their unadorned faces and hands are visible in public, and when they relax and enjoy themselves the greatest care is required to ensure that they are invisible to men.

One woman, her shoes in hand and her bare toes digging into the yellow sand of the beach looks out across the water to where the wind-surfers are turning and tacking. Women are not allowed to go wind-surfing. The waves lap round her feet but she pays no attention. Finally, she turns and settles down on the beach alone, digging her hands into the warm sand and allowing it to trickle through her fingers. Perhaps, as the supporters of the Islamic Republic maintain, she is glad not to have to run the risk of being regarded as a male's sexual plaything, and feels more secure because of the protective hejab she is wearing, despite the 90-degree heat and the humidity of the beach. There are, without doubt, large numbers of Iranian women who do feel that way: particularly peasants and working-class women. This particular middle class woman does not give that impression at all. It is as though she can still hear the echoes of the shouting and laughing that once filled this beach and all the others along the coast, in the days before people were obliged to behave modestly for their own good.

In the eyes of its supporters, one of the most important tasks of the Revolution of 1979 was to undo a process begun by Reza Shah forty-four years earlier: the forcible unveiling of women. In 1935 he ordered that teachers and schoolchildren should no longer wear *hejab*, and army officers – the chief supporters of his régime – were forbidden to appear in public with women who were veiled. On 8 January 1936 he went further: he attended a diploma ceremony at a training college for women teachers accompanied by his wife and two of his daughters, all of whom wore European dress. It was the first time any Persian woman had appeared unveiled on a public occasion. In the following years, Khomeini was to refer to Reza Shah's campaign for the emancipation of women as 'one of the darkest moments in the history of Islam', and said that it gave women the choice of becoming prostitutes or staying at home. His own wife stayed at home.

Under Reza Shah's son, Mohammed Reza Shah, women were given the vote, and government programmes ensured that they were better educated, and trained to take a much greater part in the economic and political life of the country. The Shah's twin sister, Princess Ashraf, who was one of the royal group who appeared without a veil on that January day in 1936, was a powerful supporter of the emancipation of women, and she used her considerable influence over her brother to encourage him to introduce a Family Protection Bill, which gave women the right, under certain circumstances, to sue for divorce, and obliged men who wanted to take a second wife to obtain the consent of the first one. Measures like these undermined the whole basis of Islamic law, and threatened to turn Iran into a secular society along the lines, if not of Western Europe as the Shah intended, then certainly of Turkey or Nasserite Egypt.

The Shah himself had married a young, well-educated and liberated woman, Farah Diba, in 1959. In his artless and revealing book *Mission For My Country*, published two years later, he wrote:

> I think my matrimonial experiences and my general observa-tion have taught me a little about women and their ways, and about how our wonderful Persian women can best realize themselves. My country has seen many startling social chan-ges in the thirty-five years since my father assumed the throne, but seasoned observers declare that the most sweeping advances of all concern the emergence of our women. Now it seems to me the time is opportune for Iran's women to reappraise their needs and potentialities if they are most fully to enrich their own lives and those of their husbands, their children and their fellow-countrymen.'

Impatience, hubris, and an absence of his father's ruthlessness are all apparent in that passage, and those three qualities were to lead to the downfall of his hopes of turning Iran into a secular, Westernized society in which women would play an equal part with men. Nevertheless in the years before the Revolution an unprecedented number of young women were being educated at universities in Western Europe and the United States, and were coming back with advanced ideas about the way they should dress and behave in public, and the jobs they were qualified to do. But from 1978 onwards, a reaction set in among precisely these educated young women; and so, while those who were slightly older were endeavouring to follow the Shah's line of emancipation, many of the more recent graduates were willingly putting on *hejab* and taking part in demonstrations.

The reasons for the change were complex, and had a good deal to do with the growing revulsion for the waste and corruption which the immense rise in oil prices of 1973 had caused in Iran. Opposition to the Shah took the form among women of a return to the older Islamic certainties. The fact that Reza Shah had founded Tehran University and ordered that women as well as men should be taught there, and that his son should have extended the education and advancement of women was no longer counted in their favour by those women who had bene-fitted greatly from the process. As the opposition to the Shah swelled and erupted onto the streets of Iran's cities, the *chador* which the Pahlavi dynasty had banned became the uniform of those who wanted to bring the Pahlavi dynasty to an end.

In August 1978, during my first visit to Iran, these changes were still taking form. The Ministry for Women's Affairs remained active, but was getting increasingly nervous about continuing to play the rôle the Shah had given it in helping to encourage the emancipation of women. Princess Ashraf was no less determined to ensure that her brother did not back away from his commitment; but the women who were trying to carry out the ministry's policies were finding that their task was becoming more difficult, and even sometimes more dangerous.

I telephoned the ministry one morning from my room in the InterContinental, and managed eventually to speak to someone who appeared to have the authority to arrange the things I was looking for.

'Things are a little difficult at the moment,' said the voice at the other end, in the accents of an expensive British girls' school. I asked her about the ministry's work, and it seemed as though there was nothing which we would be able to film. I found out later that this was because virtually all the current projects had been allowed to lapse while the political unrest continued; the ministry and its workers had been particular targets for the demonstrators, particularly in provincial towns and cities.

I managed after long and polite argument to get myself an invitation to visit the ministry that afternoon. There I realized the strength and success of the opposition to the Shah's régime. The officials at the Ministry of Women's Affairs were on the leading edge of the changes the Shah was endeavouring to impose in Iran, and it was clear, six months before the Revolution, that the policy of reform and modernization had been all but abandoned. The women I spoke to, well-educated and expensively dressed, did nothing to disguise their depression.

The woman I was eventually allowed to see – a friend of Princess Ashraf, judging by the affectionate message scrawled in French across a photograph in a silver frame on her desk – listened to my request for something to film and called in one of her coolly-dressed, elegant assistants. The ministry had been

246

working on a project in a small village on the edge of the desert to the east of Tehran, and we were to be allowed to film it.

It was a good choice. The village was not a Muslim one at all, but Zoroastrian: one of the few which had kept to the ancient fire-worship of Persia after the Arab invasion and the conversion to Islam. Accordingly, the women of the village were not obliged to wear *hejab*. We received a remarkably friendly welcome, and were able to film everything we needed to do with the project. The only problems arose during our journey to and from the village. Our guide, the elegant assistant from the ministry, was not prepared to compromise her principles, or those of the ministry, by wearing *hejab*. But with great embarrassment and a certain amount of nervousness she told us, as we headed towards the poorer suburbs where the strongest supporters of Ayatollah Khomeini were to be found, that she thought she had better put on a headscarf.

Some weeks later, wandering past the bookshops of the Charing Cross Road in the West End of London, I turned into Collett's, the specialists in left-wing literature. The Iranian shelf was full of books and pamphlets, and I looked through them to see if there was anything of real interest. There was – to me at least. One booklet, printed in English, bore the title *Iranian Woman: An Answer to Mr John Simpson*.

It turned out to be a closely reasoned critique of my documentary by an Iranian Marxist academic, who proved conclusively that women's rights were being destroyed under the Shah, and that the wearing of *hejab* and the barring of women from certain professions, so far from limiting their scope in a revolutionary Iran, would enhance it and prevent their becoming the sexual playthings of men. I had come across religious fundamentalism in Iran among the peasants and the working-class, and could understand that; but, like a large number of Western journalists and diplomats, I found it a great deal harder to understand why intellectuals on the left should be so enthusiastic about what looked, at a distance, like black reaction.

This alliance, so little understood by many of us who watched it taking shape before us, between the educated left and the religious conservatives, brought about the downfall of the Shah. The fierce political in-fighting which took place in the years that followed have tended to break the alliance down, so that many of the intellectuals who lived in exile in Paris, London or Los Angeles before the Revolution, writing their angry pamphlets against the Shah, are exiles once again. The shelves marked 'Iran' in left-wing bookshops bear pamphlets and books condemning the Khomeini régime in terms not always very different from those in which they once condemned the Shah. And once again it is the treatment of women which forms one of the major causes for anger. One such book, *Women of Iran* by Farah Azari, speaks of Khomeini's fear of women's sexuality, and accuses the Islamic tradition of regarding women purely as breeding machines to be used for satisfying male lusts. A few years before, the accusation, if not by Ms Azari herself then by other feminists, was that the system headed by the Shah was permitting and encouraging much the same kind of sexual exploitation.

Mrs Barzin Maknoun does a job which is in its way the Islamic Republic's parallel to the one which the elegantly dressed figures at the Ministry of Women's Affairs were trying to do, six months before the Revolution. Mrs Maknoun is in her forties, a professor at Tehran University, and her task is to promote literacy among Iranian women, as part of a UNESCO programme. She is a forbidding figure as she sits on a sofa in a corner of a room on the seventh floor of an office block at Palestine Corner, Revolution Avenue: her *chador* is wrapped tightly around her, and she wears heavy glasses with thick frames which depersonalize her face. You could pass her in the street half-an-hour after meeting her, and not recognize her among all the other earnest, frowning women in *chadors* and heavy glasses.

Mrs Maknoun speaks the American-accented English which she perfected when she did her master's and her PhD at the University of Illinois in Champaigne-Urbana. She finds it difficult to be personally friendly, even to Tira who is also wearing *hejab* for the occasion, and she makes it clear that she expects her views to be misunderstood and distorted. She is that kind of person. She does, however, have some grounds for her hostility, at least in her own eyes; her husband, who had studied in the United States with her, was murdered outside their house in Tehran not long after the Revolution by men she says were American agents. She does not elaborate. In 1980, at the time of the hostage crisis, she was involved in a lecture tour in the United States connected with her academic work. She insisted on wearing her *chador*, and received a good deal of hostility and personal abuse. She maintains that she bears no ill will to Americans as such, though she could be forgiven if she did.

It is, as always, hard for a non-Muslim Westerner to find a common intellectual meeting ground with a true believer like Mrs Maknoun. For her, life is a matter of clear certainties: the

248

Holy Koran contains everything that is needful for this world and the next, and any argument will end with an appeal to its teachings.

'The things that concern women in Iran are often misunder-stood, purposely so, in the rest of the world. It is our task here to show what Islam says about these things, and about what the real Islamic woman should be. You have to study the Holy Koran, which shows that only Islam gives true rights to women – and more rights to women than to men. But women are not fit to have every kind of responsibility. A woman cannot become what Imam Khomeini is, for instance.'

'You mean that women aren't the intellectual equals of men?'

'No, I don't mean that at all. What we believe is that men and women are actually equal, but that they're made differ-ently. Men are stronger in some things and women are stronger in others. A woman can get as close to Allah as a man can, but in a different way. A man can use his intellect to get there, and a woman will use her emotions. But they are both equal in the sight of God. You see, there are big differences physically between men and women, and these differences make it difficult for them to do the same things. A woman can be a mother and care for a child, because of her high emotions. A man cannot do that. His duties are to support his wife and his family, because he's made that way.'

'So do you believe that the way women are regarded in the West is the cause of a lot of our social upheavals?'

'We think women should have different goals from men. The problems have come up because women in the West are trying to be the same as men. They're doing the same jobs as men, and that's why social problems arise. Women work outside the home, but they also have to take care of their children, because by nature she's the one who bears the child. The whole burden rests on women now, because they're trying to be equal with men. But Islam says no to all this. Islam says the best thing for a woman is to be a wife and mother. That doesn't stop a woman having a job or a profession – she can do that if her husband agrees with it, but her first job is to take care of the children. And it's the job of the man to take care of her.'

None of this is, perhaps, very different from the advice a Catholic priest in, say, the West of Ireland might give to one of his female parishioners who was thinking of going to work in a big city; but it is curious to hear it from the lips of a successful professional woman in her forties, with a string of degrees.

The difficulties of debating an issue with someone who can take refuge behind the certainties of a revealed religion are considerable. 'Women's movements in an Islamic society,' Mrs Maknoun has written in a paper for a UNESCO conference on the status of women, 'are all directed towards a single objective: an achievement of the social justice which has been defined by the system of Divine Laws.' And elsewhere in the same paper she says:

'In a western industrialized country the motive for women's social movements is usually to achieve a higher ratio in the share of social material rewards such as earning more salary, and being promoted to higher ranks in social management in order to further enjoy the utility of power. But none of these motives can be considered as being Islamic . . . The studies of women's problems from an Islamic point of view are basically different from those of other schools of thought in all aspects such as social and political movements, and the social status of women.'

The problem is, of course, that if the Islamic Republic is based squarely on the Holy Koran and the teachings of the Prophet, there can be nothing about it which requires fundamental change. The women's movement in Iran cannot permit itself to be compared with those in Western countries which want to improve social systems which are imperfect. For her to entertain criticism of the structure of society in the Islamic Republic would mean calling into question the doctrinal theories on which it is based. Here the comparison is less with Catholic priests in the West of Ireland than with Communist Party officials in the early, enthusiastic days of the Soviet Union. Intelligent, active-minded, thoughtful, sympathetic, such officials could nevertheless accept no hint of criticism of the system itself. Discussion founders.

Mrs Maknoun turned to the question of the compulsory wearing of *hejab*; something which most Westerners find extremely hard to accept. But, Mrs Maknoun said, that was because they naturally identify with middle class Iranians who are the most likely to be affected by the laws on dress:

'If you consider that the full population of women in Iran is probably more than 17 million, maybe only a hundred thousand or so are still dressing in a Western way: that's less than one per cent. But the way they talk about it abroad, you get the feeling that every woman in Iran is against wearing *hejab*. If you go to Friday prayers in Tehran you can see hundreds of thousands of women wearing *chadors*, and it's no problem at all for them. They wear them because it's natural. Women like that are in the majority – maybe ninety-nine per cent. Western journalists come here and ask us why we are making the other one per cent unhappy. But when any revolution happens, there's always some group of people which is unhappy. It's just inevitable.'

In the squalid slums of South Tehran at the time of the Revolution I found that every woman I spoke to preferred wearing *hejab* to Western clothes. The precise reasons varied, but they could all be subsumed under two headings: convenience and tradition.

'It's just a lot more decent. I come from a village to the south' – she named it, but I was never able to find it on a map – 'and everyone wears the *chador* there. So when I came to Tehran I didn't want to change my habits completely. You feel as though you're a proper woman when you wear it.'

That was a woman in her early thirties, with three children of different ages around her. We had taken up our position beside the communal water-stand at the end of a dirt track. Behind us, too close for hygiene, was the rubbish-dump, around which flies buzzed noisily while dogs rooted for edible scraps. The women usually took a certain amount of persuasion to talk, but the presence of a woman translator helped. No one younger than their middle twenties would speak to us. Another woman, slightly younger than the first, was more practical:

'It's easier to wear *hejab* if you don't have much money. Clothes are expensive in Tehran, and I don't have much time to make my own, with the children needing to be looked after. I have never worn my indoor clothes in the street. I wouldn't want to. It would be completely wrong.'

I did not find anyone who said that the *chador* protected her from the attentions of men; perhaps that would be too difficult to say to a Western man anyway. Nor did I find anyone who gave a

251

specifically religious reason for wearing *hejab* – that it was ordained by the Koran, for instance. But there is no doubt that the efforts by the Shah and his father to do away with the veil had disturbed people at a deep level of consciousness, especially the poorer sections of the community; and the posters advertising Western films in Tehran gave the impression that licence and exaggerated sexuality were rife in Iran. Many poorer men would make the journey from South Tehran to the city centre in order to look at the posters, and at the Westernized women who wore short skirts and revealing dresses in the streets; and the reports which went back to the poorer areas of Tehran, and out to the other towns and cities of Iran, lost nothing in the telling.

Persian women have always played an important part in society. They have never been restricted to the home, as women in the Arab world have been. They run offices, they own property, they control businesses. Women played an important part in the Revolution, and since then their part in the opposition to Khomeini has been an important one too: of the 12,000 people who the People's Mojaheddin resistance group details as having been executed for political offences under the Islamic Republic, approximately one in seven was a woman.

The leading civil servants who run the country and have often been educated in the West do not seem to object to the position women have in Iranian society as much as the older clergy frequently do. It is the tradition of the *ulema* to look to Arabic models rather than Persian ones in social matters, partly because Arabic is the language of Islam, and partly because Persians have traditionally been less rigid in their religion than Arabs, and have always accomodated other faiths in their society. But even the clergy are obliged to retreat a little. There are women who are members of the Majlis, even though they speak more rarely, proportionately to their numbers, than men do.

At one Friday prayers in 1985 the speaker of the Majlis, Hojat-ol-Eslam Hashemi-Rafsanjani, said that only three areas of public life were closed to women: the law, religion, and the army. Already that line is in the process of being breached, as much from necessity as from social pressure. Women have started training as soldiers, in combat units as well as support ones. Only the law and the *ulema* are left, unalterably, as a male preserve.

The vast majority of Iranian women will never, of course, be involved in any of these areas. But the improvements which the Ministry of Women's Affairs under the Shah fought to obtain have in many cases been maintained and extended under the Islamic Republic. Because women had played a distinguished part in the Revolution, they were able to command a certain number of jobs as civil servants in the new dispensation, and as the war created a shortage of manpower, women, as always in wartime, were called upon to fill the gap. Partly as a result of that, there are more women in the civil service now than there were under the Shah, and they have been able to introduce for themselves some extremely favourable conditions. Most ministries and all universities, for instance, have kindergartens which take the children of women civil servants from the age of two. Iran has one of the world's best maternity laws: a woman in full-time employment can take three months' paid leave when she has a baby, and until her child is two she can work half-time for half the salary. 'I don't particularly like wearing all this,' one obviously pregnant middle class woman with a job as a civil servant said, gesturing at her tunic and hood, 'but if it's the price I have to pay for getting the kind of benefits they're giving me, then I suppose it's worth it.'

Another price that has to be paid is the tameness, the drabness, the lack of inspiration in the official presentation of the rôle of women in Iranian life. Only one women's magazine is permitted to be published in Iran, and yet its circulation is small. *Zan-e-Ruz*, or *Today's Woman*, comes out monthly with a print-run of 55,000. It is wholesome in a specifically Islamic way, uncontentious, and unexcitingly presented. Its editorial policy, according to the staff, is to show women how to live a better and more religious life.

Zan-e-Ruz is not a new magazine; it has been published for the past thirty years, and has always been a little stodgy and middle-of-the-road. It has also always had a mildly Islamic flavour: Ayatollah Morteza Motahari, who is the Islamic Republican Party's chief thinker on matters that relate to women, was invited to submit articles during the 1970s about the position of women in Islam – a piece of intelligent pre-vision which ensured its survival after the Revolution, when all the other women's magazines, which concentrated mostly on fashion, were closed down. It did not, however, help the editorial staff, most of whom were men. After the Revolution all of them were dismissed.

The *Zan-e-Ruz* offices are in the building of the Kayhan publishing company, which produces one of Iran's major daily newspapers, as well as a number of specialized magazines. The main lobby of the building is decorated with the portraits of Kayhan staff who have died in the war with Iraq, but the busy reporters, executives and messengers who pass through the lobby never give them a glance. Any journalist walking in there would find it a familiar environment: there is an air of bustling activity which large news organizations always generate.

Zan-e-Ruz is run by an editorial board of three women, and has a staff of four reporters. All seven have degrees from Iranian universities, and a couple from Western ones as well. About thirty others, some of them men, work on the production and administrative side. The editorial people occupy about a quarter of a vast modern open-plan office, divided off into small sections by glass partitions four or five feet high, and the women who work there all wore a version of the Islamic office uniform which is a little closer to a full-scale *chador* than the more relaxed tunic and hood. If there were a feminist movement on the Western model in Iran, these women would belong to it; they count it as one of their main successes that the editorial staff is now entirely female.

'Things are so much easier for us now,' one of the editorial team says, glancing at the occasional man who wanders past from one of the other magazines on the same floor. 'Nowadays when I talk with one of my male colleagues I feel that I can talk to him freely, without having to worry about any . . . attraction.' She is in her late twenties, a serious-faced, pale woman with heavy glasses. 'When we're covered like this it means we can talk to each other just as human beings, not as man and woman.'

The magazine is itself dully presented, on paper which is sometimes expensively coated and sometimes simply recycled, depending on what is available and how much foreign currency it costs. Within its limitations, it tries to cover as wide an area as possible: the cover of one issue has a picture of a line of women soldiers, booted and veiled, marching towards the camera gripping rifles through the material of the *chador* so that their hands do not show, and biting hard on the edges of it so that only their eyes and noses appear: not a very efficient way of preparing for battle, perhaps.

Inside, after an editorial about the way the Revolution's aims are being put into practice, a woman who does show her hands and mouth is interviewed about medical research, under an approving quotation from the Koran. There are cartoons, on the mocking, satirical model of the Soviet magazine *Krokodil*: rich Westerners lord it over poor Third World beggars, the United Nations is presented as a pompous façade which ignores the real problems of the world (such as, presumably, Iraq's invasion of Iran), and a firing squad of the developed world's media prepares to shoot down an Iranian prisoner with the weapons of television, books and film. But there are one or two gentler touches: a reader's photograph of two boys clinging on to the rear end of a Tehran bus and talking to each other. *'Jaigah vijeh!'* says the caption: 'Special stand-point'. It is not particularly funny, but it has the comfortable, cute tone of women's magazines the world over.

Other articles give advice about teaching children to read, while warning them not to clash with what they are being taught at school, how to pray with greater sincerity, how President Daniel Ortega of Nicaragua is confronting the Great Satan and winning – with the help of women. A short story entitled 'New Season' is about a young woman's uncertainty, not exactly about a man (although one makes a fleeting and unexplained appearance) but about what she should do with her life; it ends in the approved manner with hints from the Koran and a decision to devote herself to the national good, and the good of her as yet unborn family. There are two pages of poetry about nature – one is reminded of Dr Wills' observation that middle-class Persian women read and write poetry – and hints about caring for roses and cooking with garlic.

A feature of many editions of *Zan-e-Ruz* is a pull-out section on making clothes. Since these are invariably indoor clothes, with knee-length hems and short sleeves, they present the magazine's graphic designers with an ethical problem; it is solved by showing a photograph of the clothes in question, but cutting out the face, legs and arms of the model and replacing them with sketches; even in the sketches, however, the figure wears a headscarf. Letters deal with problems of house-keeping, and nothing more personal than ways of getting stains off clothes is allowed to intrude.

A know-your-rights column, 'The Limits of the Law', gives advice on the legal position of householders, and of women considering a divorce; divorce being possible for a woman only if her husband is impotent, or if he refuses, as we saw in the courtroom at Rey, to pay for his wife's upkeep. There is also news of the war, an extremely complex full-page crossword puzzle, and several pages of advertisements for home goods and services of different kinds: a new type of electric samovar, hi-fi systems, florists and cake-shops. Photographs on the back cover tend to be of a spiritually uplifting nature: the shrine of Fatima at Qom, for instance, or the Caspian Sea at sunset. The magazine is intended to soothe the Woman of Today rather than to stimulate her, and there is no question of raising difficult questions.

There is no shortage of ideas and material coming in to the *Zan-*

e-Ruz office: the shelves hold a number of British and American magazines, from *Better Homes and Gardens* and *Your Health* to, interestingly enough, *DAV* – the publication for disabled US veterans. The editorial staff use some of the story ideas, and take photographs out of the pages of these magazines, which explains the often fuzzy quality of the reproduction. But they rigorously play it safe in terms of editorial content. Why, then, does *Zan-e-Ruz* keep its circulation? No doubt many of the 55,000 subscribers want to be soothed; life is hard enough without subjecting yourself to difficult reading. Others continue taking it because they always have. 'I can't say I like it,' one well-to-do woman said, as she flicked through the pages. 'It's certainly not very interesting. But one day, you know, it'll be interesting again, like it used to be. I suppose I'm always waiting for that.'

In the lobby of the InterContinental Hotel a waiter comes up to Tira and me in a state of some embarrassment. I assume he is going to tell us that the kitchen is out of tea or English cake, but instead he says he cannot serve Tira in the main lobby: a restaurant is set aside for men and women who want to eat together. But we ate here this morning, I tell him. He spreads his hands apologetically, and murmurs 'The rules . . .' It reminds me strongly of sitting with a black friend of mine in the Carlton Hotel in Johannesburg, in the days before blacks were regarded as honorary whites if they had the money to enter an expensive hotel. There too a waiter came up smiling his apologies and murmuring about the rules. There too it was possible to find somewhere where the rules did permit us to eat together.

So are women the victims of a sexual apartheid in Iran? A Western woman would say they were. When, for instance, Tira wanted to use the lavatory at the house of a mullah we visited, she was not allowed to use the one in the room next to the main living-room, as I was; instead, one of the children was told to conduct her to the women's lavatory, which was outside in the garden. She found the unwillingness of strict Muslims to shake her hand understandable enough, but their refusal to look her in the eyes was much more annoying; it made her feel as though she did not exist. Other men seemed disinclined to talk business while she was with me.

Many middle class Iranian women, too, have the feeling that they are discriminated against. One, who had lived in England and the United States, described herself as a democrat, who hated the whole concept of *hejab*. She and her husband used to go out at the weekends for long walks in the Elburz Mountains, but finally gave it up because they were stopped so many times by the Revolutionary Guards and the *Komitehs*.

'It was always the same thing: "Who are you? How do we know you're married? Where's your marriage certificate? Where's your birth certificate?" It used to make me very angry, but I knew I had to keep quiet, because if a woman gets mad at them they go crazy. Once they stopped us four different times on one trip. So we don't go to the mountains now, because it isn't worth the hassle. Who wants to have to carry their marriage certificate round with them everywhere they go?

'There are other things we've had to give up too. I used to go to soccer games with my husband, not because I liked it that much but because he liked it and we wanted to be together. They stopped that. No women allowed at soccer grounds, because it was non-Islamic and they didn't want us looking at men wearing shorts. I ask you. Crazy. If we go skiing, I have to go down different ski runs from the men, and they're not such good ones. There are different ski-lifts for us, and different restaurants as well. I even have to wear a tunic over my down jacket: can you imagine that? And a hood over my anorak hood?

'What's worst of all is if you give a party and the *Komiteh* come round. We gave one once and we were all taken down to the headquarters for examination and questioning. They wanted to check our nails to see they weren't too long and didn't have polish on them, they checked us for eye make-up, lipstick, everything. They let us all go at the end – after all, we'd been in a private house – but once they have done that to you and maybe pushed you about or beaten you up, you don't want to go through it all again. So when we give parties nowadays, the women all come without make-up.'

The more absolutist elements in the Islamic Republican Party are unquestionably on the retreat now. At first there was a debate about whether unmarried women should be allowed to ride in cars with men, but when it was pointed out that regulations could never be drawn up in such a way as to allow taxis, for instance, to take women, the proposal collapsed. There was also an attempt to stop women riding horses astride, but this too was abandoned – though in theory there are only certain hours of the day during which women are allowed to ride.

257

But these things were the products of the kind of extremism which revolutions always stimulate; a more sober view of the position of women in society was produced by the Islamic Republic's leading authority on the subject, Ayatollah Morteza Motahari. Motahari, who was assassinated by the Forqan terrorist group in May 1979, was a moderating force in the Revolutionary Council, and his book, *The Rights of Women In Islam*, was compiled from a series of articles he wrote for the old, pre-Revolutionary *Zan-e-Ruz* magazine in 1966-7. It demonstrates his familiarity with the writings of Western philosophers and authors, and is notable for its sympathetic approach to the question of women's rights. He is deeply critical of the Christian doctrines that woman was created secondary to man, and that woman first brought sin into the world by Eve's temptation of Adam, and he dismisses the view that celibacy is superior to marriage as a superstition: 'The root cause of sexual abstention and celibacy is a feeling of aversion against the female sex.' The burden of his argument is that men and women possess equal, but not necessarily identical, rights:

'Man and woman are equal in their being human, but they are two kinds of human being with two kinds of characteristics and two kinds of psychology. . . . Islam has not considered there to be identicalness or exact similarity of rights between men and women, but it has never believed in preference and discrimination in favour of men as opposed to women. Islam has also observed the principle of equality between men and women. Islam is not against the equality of men and women, but it does not agree with the identicalness of their rights.'

It is an intelligent, humane and literate thesis, backed up by wide reading in the works of Western philosophers from Spencer to Bertrand Russell; but it boils down to the concept of woman primarily as the passive, home-based partner of her husband, whose rights he cannot, as a matter of practical and religious duty, ignore. In practice, it means there is an obligation on the male members of a family – the uncles, brothers and nephews if no husband or father is alive – to support the women of the family if they choose not to work; and if there are no male relatives at all, then the state is required to support them.

The position of women in Iranian society since the Revolution is approached on a number of different levels: there is this philosophical level, as established by Ayatollah Motahari, in which the equality of the sexes is enshrined. There is the level of the law-makers, influenced by the far less egalitarian approach of Arab Muslims, who for social more than religious reasons have usually tended to regard women as being on a lower plane than men. There is the level of the law-enforcers, who frequently treat well-to-do middle class women as potential enemies of the Islamic Republic, with social habits that undermine the religious basis of the state. And there is, finally, the level of everyday society, which is as much influenced by Persian custom as by Shi'ite dogma. Persian women have never been the meek inhabitants of the inner rooms; they have traditionally played an equal part in family life and often a dominant one. Traditionally, too, they have been well educated, and that tradition continues under the rule of the ayatollahs, even though women can only be taught now by other women, and cannot themselves teach male children. A woman who marries keeps her own money and her own property, and can take it with her if the marriage ends in divorce.

When the Revolution took place many of what Westerners would regard as the improvements which the Shah had introduced in the legal treatment of women, were swept away. Polygamy is legal again, and men may have as many as four wives if they can show that they have the money to keep them. Like the Islamic punishment of criminals, many people have heard of examples where men have taken a number of wives, but it is very difficult indeed to find a precise name or location. No doubt it happens, just as the stoning of adulterers and the severing of thieves' hands happens, but it is not at all common. The custom of taking temporary wives, or *sigheh* has been permitted once again: a form of legalized prostitution, since the temporary marriages can last as little as a night. The age at which a girl can be married has now been reduced to nine. None of these are things which Western society finds acceptable, though that is of little consequence to the rulers of modern Iran.

'Women are at least well-treated in Iran,' said the editorial assistant at *Zan-e-Ruz*, the magazine which once printed Ayatollah Motahari's articles about the nature of women in an Islamic state, and nowadays, in its worthy way, does its best to inform and entertain the women who are governed by the rules as Motahari sketched them out. 'We don't have the kind of rapes and attacks on women that you have in the West. I can walk in the streets of Tehran at night without fear, and Western women cannot go out in their cities at night-time. There is great respect for women in an Islamic society.'

'I feel trapped in all this,' said the woman who had given up going for walks in the mountains with her husband, gesturing irritatedly at her *hejab* as it lay on a chair where she had thrown it. 'But, you know, we are Persians. All these mullahs – there's nothing they can do about that. Things will get better, you'll see.'

14

City of God

As might be expected from so holy a place, the population contains a large number of *seyids* – fanatics
inured to long impunity of conduct – and is much
addicted to bigotry and superstition. No Jews or Parsis
live here; and English ladies, resident in the Telegraph
offices, have usually found it prudent to veil in public.
These superstitions are now dying fast throughout
the East; but Kum is one of the places where an
accidental spark might still be fanned into a disagree-
able flame.

George Nathaniel Curzon, *Persia And The Persian Question*, 1892.

THE HOLY CITY of Qom is famous for many things: its shrine, its
domes, its carpets, its blue pottery, its curious sweetmeat *sohan*,
its piety and its unpleasant salty drinking-water. It has never
been a popular place among Persians who are not religious: a
much-quoted proverb says that a dog of Kashan is better than the
nobles of Qom.

Mahmoudi put it less epigrammatically as his Paykan rattled
along the desert highway from Tehran.

'No good sleeping tonight in Qom, Mr John.'

'Why is that, Mahmoudi?' I always enjoyed his judgements on
people and places.

'Getting their water from here, Mr John.'

He laughed wolfishly and jerked his thumb at the extraordinary lake of salt which lay on our left: a white inland sea with the
shadows of clouds travelling over its surface and the brilliance of
the sunshine on its poisoned waters. The beach around it is
crusted with salty residues, and nothing grows within a quarter
of a mile. The only greenery is in the rocks: geological layers of
some greenish stone, running through the hills for a mile or
more. It is not, of course, true that Qom gets its water from this

261

great inland sea, the *Daryache-ye-Namak* or Salt Lake; but every water source in the entire area is tainted with saltness.

Qom itself begins among low hills and the clustering of power-lines across the open desert, and its outskirts are signalled by an enormous steel sculpture of the 'Allah' symbol which has been adopted by the Islamic Republic: a kind of sword in brackets which suits the ethos of the state which has committed itself to cutting off the hands of foreign agents. The sculpture is so designed that it can be read from every angle, and it stands prosaically in the middle of a traffic roundabout. A bus with the legend 'My God' on a strip of clear green plastic on the winds-creen wobbled past us at speed and the driver waved and smiled a gappy yellow smile in answer to our shouts of anger and alarm. 'Kerbala 1,125 km.' said a sign-post optimistically, Kerbala being the holy place in Iraq which Iran most wants to capture. A mullah sat under the sign, guarding a mound of suitcases, cardboard boxes and plastic bags which seemed to have been dumped off by some passing bus. Perhaps he was on his way to Kerbala. A little farther off an anti-aircraft gun glinted in the sunshine: Qom has been bombed again and again by the Iraqis, in an attempt to strike at the force of feeling which has been at the heart of Iran's resistance in the Gulf War.

No one could call it attractive. It is flat and dun-coloured and dusty. But at least it presents much the same aspect as it did when Curzon and Granville Browne and the English ladies who lived at the telegraph office were here. Apart from a large modern hotel block, built to accommodate the tens of thousands of pilgrims who come to visit Fatima's shrine, and the metal skeleton of a vast new mosque which is under construction on the edge of the city, the skyline looks much as it always has, the golden, green and blue domes rising from the mud-brick buildings.

A river, itself called the Qom, runs through the heart of the city. It rises, suitably enough, outside the town of Khomein, the birthplace of the Imam. But in the summer the waters dry up altogether, and the river ceases to exist. Its bed is as broad as the Thames at Richmond or the Seine at the Pont Neuf, and instead of water there are only stones. Bridges cross it, piers jut out into it, gulleys and drains open into it – but in August it is a river of colourless shingle, heaped up into banks or hollowed out into channels by the action of water that disappeared months ago and has left only its dry bones, like the skeleton of an animal in a desert.

Qom is devoid of the pleasures which make other cities

attractive to westernized Persians. There are no fashionable clothes stores, no video rental shops, no fast-food restaurants. Qom is one of the few places in Iran where women appear in the street entirely veiled, a black covering over their faces as well as the *chador* which covers their heads and bodies. During the entire reign of Reza Shah, from the 1920s to the 1940s, many women never left their houses for fear of being attacked by the soldiers and police who were under orders to enforce the Shah's laws forbidding the wearing of traditional, religious dress. Women were obliged by these laws to go unveiled, and men had to wear suits and a curious peaked cap designed by Reza Shah himself; and Qom was the city where the laws were fiercest in their operation. Nowadays another set of laws on clothing applies, and is enforced with the same determination as sixty years ago. Where the Pahlavi dynasty of Reza Shah and his son tried to make Persians modern, the Islamic Republic of Ayatollah Khomeini is trying to make them pure.

We had come to Qom to do some filming, accompanied by a rather impressive Iranian cameraman whom we had hired. The best cameramen dress and behave like insurance salesmen or librarians, and Ali Torabi could have been either. His only complaint was that his superiors at Iranian television had kept him too long in Tehran, working for foreigners like us, when he wanted to get down to film the war: not because he wanted to be martyred, but because that was where the best pictures were to be obtained.

At the war front, too, he would be free from the attentions of on-lookers: the greatest plague that afflicts the cameraman in the Third World. Ali Torabi had scarcely set up his tripod in Qom before fifty or so young boys had gathered in front of him to watch. They were neither hostile nor noisy; they were, indeed, perfectly friendly. But they would not accept the basic proposition that they could watch us just as well from beside or behind the camera as they could from in front of it. Neither reason nor aggression in English or Farsi had any effect on them; they stood there just as silently and respectfully, sometimes moving a pace or two in obedience to our furious demands, but never clearing the shot.

A policeman came and ordered them to leave, and they dispersed, only to re-form again directly he had swaggered off. A *Komiteh* man turned up, his walkie-talkie wrapped in a copy of the Qom newspaper like a piece of fish; he talked into it for effect (there seemed to be no answering voice from inside the news-paper) and cleared the on-lookers rather less effectively than the policeman had. This time they did not wait for him to go away before clustering round us again, in numbers which had grown by now to more than a hundred. We were the biggest attraction in Qom, when all we wanted to do was to film people walking naturally in and out of the mosque that overlooked the river of dry stones. After we had enlisted the help of a middle-aged man in khaki pyjamas (both words originating in Farsi, incidentally, and exported first to India and thence to Britain) a man in an Adidas sweatshirt with long, Qom-length sleeves, and an old character with five days' stubble who looked like any bazaari hanger-on and said in good American English, 'Who are you shooting for? NBC? CBS?', we managed to get a few shots that were reasonable; but not many. We had to get away from the crowd, so we called up Mahmoudi, who looked as though he had more radical and physical suggestions for dispersing the crowd, and drove off faster than they could follow us.

The inhabitants of Qom are descended mostly from Arab settlers who fled from what is now Iraq to escape from the victorious enemies of the Prophet's grandson, Hosayn, killed at the battle of Kerbala. At that stage Iran was mostly Zoroastrian in religion, and the Arab refugees converted the Persian inhabitants to Shi'a Islam, while becoming converted themselves to the use of the Persian language. A little over a century later Fatima, the great-great-great-granddaughter of Hosayn, died in Qom, and her tomb became one of the holiest shrines in Iran.

The square in front of the great mosque is a magnificent place, open and clean. Afghan refugees lay their brightly coloured blankets along the wall of the shrine, and their women annoy the faithful by wearing their red and blue tribal clothes and not being too particular about *hejab*. Although the religious stalls set up close to the great entrance sell beautifully woven linen shrouds for the pious to take into the shrine for blessing, as well as the more usual prayer-objects, any number of hucksters were at work in the square as well. In the photographers' booths you can have your picture taken by putting your head through a hole in a screen, on which has been painted a figure in full religious garb. The result is to make you look like an old-fashioned ayatollah, even though you are wearing only a shirt and trousers. Women, too, can have their photographs taken there, though the photographers seem to prefer it if they keep their *chadors* on. Other stalls sell crudely printed T-shirts, plastic knick-knacks, and the *sohan* which is one of Qom's claims to fame. Packed in a round, flat metal can about the size of a can of film, *sohan* is a flat disc of caramel with squashed pistachio nuts baked into it. The shops in the city pile the cans one on top of the other till they reach the ceiling, and look like a veritable library of film; and if you go in, as I did, with someone the shopkeeper knows, he will go to great pains to pull down a can for you from the top, where they are fresh. Mere passing pilgrims are given cans of less recent vintage.

Beside the great gate of the mosque a notice in Farsi sand English reads: '1. Photography is strictly forbidden. 2. Nobody except Muslim is allowed into the shrine.' A few Westerners have managed to penetrate its mysteries: Fraser in 1821, Bicknell in 1869, Arnold in 1875 (though he lost his nerve after entering the outer court). Each was disguised as a Muslim. I would dearly have loved to see and smell the vast frame of sandalwood that covers the tomb, and watch as visitors kissed the doorposts of the tomb chamber, and inspect the extraordinary silver and crystal furnishings of the outer chamber, now adorned with a large photograph of the Imam Khomeini. Instead, Tira and I had to wait outside in the bright sunlight while Ali, the cameraman, and his fat, unhandy sound-recordist went in on their own.

There was a brief tussle when the mosque guards, seeing the camera rushed over to stop them entering; but Ali pushed his way past them with a couple of well-aimed punches, and Tira and I were left in the doorway, standing on the gravestones let into the ground, which gleamed like alabaster in the sunlight. The square was noisy with the laughter of the Afghan refugees and the shouts of the hucksters selling their consecrated shrouds and their T-shirts, or offering to photograph passers-by in their specially designed sets, while low-ranking *rowzeh-khani*, or preachers, offered to recite improving tales. This was Persia, as Edward Granville Browne and Thomas Herbert and the Sherley brothers, and the intrusive trio of Fraser, Bicknell and Arnold, had known it. We sat in the hot sun and waited, as birds perched heraldically on the tops of the minarets, and mullahs in white and grey moved majestically through the crowds like so many pigeons.

One particular mullah strides into view, an elegant, clean, imposing figure in the midday heat and the noise of the square. The people he passes defer to him and move aside to give him greater room. He is a figure of consequence among them, and they treat him as such. He does not, however, lord it over them; indeed, he scarcely seems to notice them or the respect they accord him. Watching him, I find myself reminded of a Biblical pharisee: with his crisp robes and his head at a grand but not necessarily boastful angle, he could be walking to a meeting of the Sanhedrin. In the Iranian theocracy, he is a man of secular as well as religious power – if, of course, the Iranian theocracy recognized any distinction between the two.

The mullah's spotless white turban presents, no doubt, an imposing frontage; but the coil of white linen, brilliant in the sun, encircles the place where his hair is thinning on the crown of his head: the pate gleams through the carefully-combed brown covering like earth through worn grass. He is, perhaps, forty, and his beard has a faintly reddish tinge which does not appear in his hair: what I can see of it. He is not, I should judge, above adding a little dye to enhance its natural attractions; a dandy, then, as well as a figure of significance. His gown, which reaches almost to his ankles, is black like that of some fastidious Oxford or Cambridge don, thin enough for the light to shine through the fabric and fine enough for the slight breeze to catch in it and billow its folds about him, so he has to catch them with his white, ringed hands (the engraved cornelian catching the sunlight) and rearrange the lie of the gown on his shoulders. There is a kind of political artistry in the way he walks, his hips swinging, his shoulders moving masterfully. He is a man who knows with exactitude where he belongs in the scheme of things, and what duty is owed to him by others.

Not far away, her back against a wall, sits a blind woman, a little bundle of bones and rags and *hejab*. She could be any age from fifty to ninety, and has probably never seen in her life. There are no eyeballs behind the lids, and her face is skull-like, the sharp unfleshed bones catching the sunlight, which makes the sockets where her eyes should have been darker and emptier than ever. A crude wooden bowl is set out in front of her, with a couple of small-denomination coins lying in it as an inducement to passers-by to add others to them. She swivels her head around as he approaches, her heightened hearing able to detect a soft footfall in the surrounding noise, and perhaps even assess the amount of alms it could represent.

The mullah, however, passes her by, his head still held at an angle that makes the insignificant things of life invisible. Her claw of a hand, the colour of earth, follows the faint wind of his passing, and remains outstretched towards him as he walks on; perhaps she smells the faint aroma of soap and saintliness in his passing. She says and does nothing, but the claw knows his exact position still.

He is eight or ten paces beyond her before he stops: maybe he was so deep in thought that he needed time to register her presence. He checks, and the white turban turns towards her, and I am reminded more than ever of a pharisaical quality as he reminds himself of the duty he owes to others, and fishes in the depth of his robe for a coin. He pulls out a twenty-*rial* piece with the name and superscription of Allah on it – Caesar's head disappeared from the coinage with the Revolution – and walks back grandly to place it in the outstretched claw. Words are exchanged, but are inaudible in the noise of the traffic, and the mullah turns and walks on. The claw turns the coin over experimentally, and since it is worth guarding it is secreted in a purse somewhere inside the rags, rather than in the wooden bowl with the two five-*rial* pieces in it. The old woman's lips move a little, but whether in gratitude or in expectation of something to eat it is impossible to be certain. Then the claw goes out again, searching for more coins from more such mullahs.

The use of the term 'mullah' is first recorded in the English language in 1613. It was picked up by Sir Anthony Sherley during his Persian travels and used by him in the book he published that year. It is in use in Farsi, Turkish and Urdu – the languages spoken in Iran and the countries bordering it – and was originally a corrupt Persian pronunciation of the Arabic word *maula*, meaning 'master'. To the ear of a Persian, it still retains a slightly racy tone, much as the word 'boss' might have to the ear of an English-speaking person. It represents, however, something rather vaguer than the generic word 'priest', for instance, does in the Christian tradition. The Christian priest is ordained by the laying on of hands: the bishop who performs the ceremony was ordained in the same way, so that the original laying on of hands in the founding of Christianity is perpetuated.

But Islam is, as we have seen, a religion of the Law: it is passed on to each new generation by teaching. It does not possess a hierarchy in the same sense as the Roman Catholic or Anglican Churches do. An ayatollah does not stand in the same relationship to a mullah as a bishop does to a priest; and a *hojat-ol-Eslam*, as a kind of halfway stage, is not the equivalent of a dean. The gradations of the Shi'ite clergy relate to study and teaching, rather than to promotion within a spiritual career structure.

The meaning of the titles indicates as much: *hojat-ol-Eslam* means 'proof of Islam': that is, a mullah who has given evidence of his learning but has not yet achieved the status of an ayatollah. Ayatollah itself means 'sign of God', and denotes the two hundred or so mullahs who have reached the stage of learning at which they can teach others and interpret Islamic law. There are, indeed, five Grand Ayatollahs, who are the leaders of the Shi'a faith, and of whom the Revolution has made Ruhollah Khomeini the foremost. But even they are not to be compared with, say, a college of cardinals; they have almost as much in common with, say, the Supreme Court of a country, or even with the heads of its main universities.

As for the mullahs of Iran, there is no easy Western comparison whatever. Collectively they form the *ulema* – an Arabic word which means 'men of religious learning'. To find a parallel for the extraordinary range of their involvement and activity it is necessary to look at other near-theocracies – mediaeval Europe, say, or Cromwellian England, – or at countries where politics have assumed the status of a religious faith, like the Soviet Union or China. Mullahs in Iran can be found in the Majlis, in the universities as teachers, in the courts as advisers and as judges, in government ministries as political directors, in the welfare offices attached to their mosques as supervisors of the rationing system, and at the war front in a rôle not wholly different from that of Stalin's political commissars, who had the job of maintaining morale and were supposed to lead the men they worked with by example rather than precept.

This does not mean that they are necessarily loved; and those who are not religious, and often suffer for it, are often deeply opposed to the *ulema* and its involvement in everyday life. But the undoubted bravery of many mullahs in the war has won for them a grudging respect even from those who tend to resent them. They are not regarded as being hypocritical, for instance, like the clergy in Europe in the late Middle Ages, perhaps because they do not set themselves exaggerated moral standards and then fail to live up to them.

There are, however, stories of corrupt mullahs – 'Ayatollah' Khalkhali, who could not account for millions of dollars' worth of confiscated goods, seems to have been one – and although some are admired for their way of life, others are resented or despised. People follow individual ayatollahs as they would political leaders in a Western democracy, and it is always a clear guide to someone's political line in Iran to see whose picture they display alongside that of the Imam. There is no such thing as a single clerical party: the clergy are as differentiated in their approach to government as any other group of individuals; but if the cycle turns in Iran and those who are associated with the present régime are swept away, many others will be swept away with them.

'The Imam Khomeini said recently that you always exaggerate everything, and make it worse than it really is. Why do you do this?'

We were sitting in the back of our car, with Mahmoudi at the steering-wheel and a handsome, prematurely grey-haired man of 38 in the robes of a mullah sitting in the seat beside him. The mullah's face was turned towards me with a soulful expression on it, as though he would have liked to understand the perversity of the world but found it impossible.

The Imam Khomeini did not, needless to say, mean me as an individual; the 'you' was plural, and meant the organization for which I work.

'In hot weather and on bad roads,' I replied, 'I think these subjects are difficult to discuss.'

The pleasant face with its wide-set grey eyes over a badly broken nose continued to look at me soulfully. With his colouring and that nose he looked less like a Persian mullah than a Welshman: possibly a Methodist clergyman who had played a good deal of rugby in his time. Only the black turban which proclaimed that he was a *seyyed*, a descendant of the Prophet, placed him squarely in his his real context. I did not like him very much at that moment. Tira, dressed modestly from head to foot in a *chador* which she had had made specifically for this trip, nudged me warningly. As for the mullah, he swivelled round in his seat and looked enigmatically out of the car window at the mean streets and mud-brick buildings which surrounded us.

We drove in near-silence until we reached his house: a desolate development in a flat khaki landscape, draped with electricity cables. But like all Persians who can afford it, his house had a small, high-walled garden where a few tendrils of plants struggled with the natural disadvantages of their environment. I found it touching, and praised the efforts at a garden as highly as I could. A new mildness entered the atmosphere, as though a small fountain had suddenly sprung up in the dry earth in front of his door. The mutual friend who had introduced us ('He is a man you will like. You can ask him anything about being a mullah, and he will answer you') was relieved, and shook the mullah warmly by the hand and gripped his shoulder as we went into the house: Tira first, followed by me.

His house was unfinished: he had moved in about three months before. The stairs to the main living room had an incomplete look to them, and the plastering of the walls was sketchy, so that here and there the grey blocks from which the house had been constructed showed through. The living room itself was large and spacious and light, and furnished with little more than the big cushions (*nazbalesh*) which Persians rightly prefer to chairs, and thick, factory-woven carpets on the floor, overlapping one another. The mullah – who was not really a mullah nowadays, but a *hojat-ol-Eslam* by the name of Seyyed Zade Teherani – was clearly not a poor man, but he preferred his carpets bright and new. A pleasant, stuffy odour of new wool and hessian arose from them, and mingled with the faint smell of fruit and rose-water which seems to permeate most Persian houses.

He left us there to look at the large photograph of Ayatollah Khomeini in a recess in the wall, and the pictures of a man in uniform who was sufficiently like the mullah to be his brother. The man wore an open-necked shirt and, with his grizzled beard, could have been an ageing rock-and-roll star.

Birds sang fitfully outside, and the heat seeped in. Flies buzzed around us, settling annoyingly on our hands, our necks, our lips. From the kitchen on the dark floor below us there came the encouraging sounds of cooking, but we had seen, and were to see, nothing of the woman who was doing it.

After ten minutes, Seyyed Zade Teherani came back, padding across the thick new carpets in his socks. The mullah's robes were gone, and he was wearing a grey shirt and grey trousers. Without the garments that set him apart from the rest of the world, Teherani seemed quiet and self-contained and rather defensive. His little daughter, a girl of about seven, came in carrying a bowl of bright red and yellow apples that was almost too big for her, and set it down in the exact centre of the carpet, in the circle of white and maroon where the pattern came together. The apples were sweet but much attacked by worms. She stood beside her father with her arms round his neck as he sat with his back resting against the big red *nazbalesh*, presenting her hands so that she, and we, could admire the chipped red varnish on her finger-nails. It was a pleasing domestic picture: The Mullah At Home.

'As a nation,' he said, 'we enjoy explosions. Please ask me any questions you like, and I will answer them as truthfully as I can.'

For my part, I saw no need for explosions. I simply wanted to know why a man chose to be a mullah, and how he went about it, and what the consequences were in his life. It was not always easy to draw the basic information from him, because he remained defensive, and seemed certain that I was out to extract something which I might regard as damaging to him, or to Iran, or to Islam itself. If it had not been for the presence of the friend

270

who had introduced us, I doubt if he would have continued; but he did, and like all of us he warmed to his theme because it concerned himself.

In 1964, when he was 16, he had decided that he wanted to join the clergy. He was a good deal older than most boys who take that decision, and his reasons were not set out with any great clarity of personal insight: it was as though he were talking purely for the record. When I pressed him about this, though, he insisted that his motives were precisely what he stated them to be:

'My reason was simply that I wanted to guide people, to help them live their lives correctly, as the Holy Koran dictates. You should remember that this was a time of great upheaval in Iran: the Imam Khomeini had been sent into exile, and the Americans and British gave the Shah his orders, and told him what policies to follow. Everything was so materialistic then, and the people were being diverted into corruption and they were oppressed.

'No members of my family had ever joined the clergy before. I don't think they really approved of my decision: they didn't give me that impression at the time. But they never tried to stop me, and now they are very proud of me. They come and listen to me, and bring their friends to hear me, and they know that my decision, taken when I was so young, was the right one.'

It was Zade Teherani's preaching that had reconciled his family to his choice of career. If he had had ambitions to become an ayatollah, he would have had to study for upwards of forty years in Qom or Mashad or one of the other centres of Shi'ite learning. But as a *rowzeh-khan* he was able to bring himself to public attention relatively early. *Rowzeh* in Persian means 'garden', and in the sixteenth century, under the Safavid dynasty, when graphic and bloody depictions of the sufferings of Hosayn and the other martyrs of the Shi'a faith were common, a book entitled *The Garden of the Martyrs* was published. It became extremely popular almost at once, and preachers began using it for their texts, thus becoming *rowzeh-khani* – 'readers of the Garden'. It is not always a very elevated profession; in Qom, in particular, *rowzeh-khani* wander around the city, competing with one another in the violence of their emotions and hiring themselves out to work on the feelings of the faithful.

Zade Teherani was however a good deal more dignified than

271

that. He was well-educated and restrained, and his handsome face and quiet, confident bearing had attracted patrons who were wealthy and had good taste. He would preach in private houses, or in schools, or at the headquarters of big organizations, as well as in mosques. He could, no doubt, work on people's feelings with the best of them, but for the most part his sermons were about the duty a Muslim owes to his faith, his family and his country.

'You have to have the talent to speak in public, and the ability to learn your material well; that takes a good deal of research. And you have to have the will to do it well. No one can teach you that, and you cannot read about it in a book. It has to come from inside you. I never read my sermons from notes, because that makes you slow and lifeless. I know what I am going to say in advance, but I do not always know how I will say it; that comes from the inspiration of the moment. Before I give a sermon I find out about the people who are hiring me, and what kind of subject they are interested in. Sometimes, if I can, I go to see the hall where I will be speaking. Mostly, I find, they prefer to hear about the way to become a better Muslim, and how politics and religion go together. The war, too, is an important subject: I often preach about the war, and the duty of Muslims to fight in it and to support it. I find that people like that.'

'To the extent that you persuade them to volunteer?'

'Sometimes. Going to the front is our religious duty. I tell them that, but it is up to them whether they take any notice. I am a preacher; I cannot order them to do anything.'

'Is your work well paid?'

'I have enough. The money is not important to me, anyway. It is Islam that is important.'

'But this house is an expensive one. Did you pay for it from your fees for preaching?'

'Allah is generous.'

'Are the authorities in Qom generous too? By which I mean, do they pay you a stipend?'

'No. The only money that the authorities in Qom pay out is for study. I do not study nowadays, I preach. And for that I am paid by the people who hire my services.'

The seminal period of his preaching had been the year that preceded the Revolution. 'We followed the Imam's guidance from the start,' he said, his wide-set grey eyes straying now to the forbidding picture of Khomeini in its recess on his wall, an inscription of Koranic praise at the foot of it, and the Ayatollah's own eyes fixed questioningly on a point just over the photographer's right shoulder, one eyebrow raised, as though someone had walked in unannounced at the moment the picture was being taken. Zade Teherani had endured a certain amount of danger in following the cause of the Ayatollah. On several occasions when he was preaching he received notes warning him that SAVAK agents were waiting outside to arrest him. On all but one occasion he managed to slip out with the crowd of worshippers, hiding his distinctive, prematurely grey hair under a hat. The one time he was captured, he was held in a cellar overnight, and threatened with death by SAVAK if he continued to preach. He took no notice.

'Later, I was arrested in August 1978 with several other members of the clergy. We were told to take off our clerical robes, but we refused. We said to them that only those who had given us our clothes, at the theological school, could take them away from us. They tried to make us sign a paper saying that we would never preach again. And they asked us questions continually, just as you are doing. But they let us go in the end. It was nothing more than intimidation. They wouldn't have dared to do anything serious to us. Things were so tense in Iran then that it would have caused a real upheaval.'

I asked him about the man in the photograph who looked like a rock-and-roll singer. It was indeed his brother, who had been in the Revolutionary Guards, and was missing in action. He had last been seen after a battle in 1981, shortly after being seriously wounded, but Teherani thought he might have recovered and be still alive as a prisoner. Even if his brother were dead, Teherani said, he would not be unhappy: the Revolution needed martyrs, and it was an honour to be one.

It made him sound smug and self-satisfied, and as he lay against his cushion sipping the tea his daughter had brought in, my irritation flared up again: wrongly, as it turned out. I had seen him as an elegant, plump despatcher of others to the front-line, remaining behind himself because his duty of preparing more would-be martyrs was more important than fighting. It was not like that at all.

'I had hoped to be a martyr myself,' he said, with great matter-of-factness, as though he were talking about a transfer to another

273

parish; which was, presumably, rather as he would regard it.

'I never had the chance, though. I was a major in what we called then a People's Unit. It was before the *Basij* – the Volunteers – were organized. This was at the start of the war, when nothing much was organized and we were fighting for our lives. I was the operational commander, and most of the time I wore military uniform. The only time I put on my clerical robes was at the time of prayer – if I got the chance. But we were very hard pressed a lot of the time: so hard pressed we didn't always have time to pray, which caused us a great deal of concern and anxiety. I was at Abadan and Khorram-shahr for more than three years, and we were fighting for a lot of the time.'

Was he never injured? I asked, knowing the high rate of casualties. For the first and only time in our meeting he laughed, and it was the laughter of self-amusement. He had, he said, been invalided out of the army. He had dived into a fox-hole when his position came under fire from a machine-gun in the Iraqi trenches opposite. Only his feet had been sticking out, and he received a bullet in the ankle. Later I noticed that he still had a slight limp.

We sat for a while looking at his album of war photographs: Teherani with his friends, many of whom were dead; Teherani at the controls of his anti-aircraft gun, Teherani holding a large piece of shrapnel which had nearly made a martyr of him after all, Teherani preaching in the open air with hundreds of volunteers hanging on his every word, Teherani lying in his hospital bed with his leg in plaster, managing a brave smile. The odour of sanctity permeated the photographs.

'We find it amusing that you in the West should accuse us of forcing young boys into the mine-fields. When I think of the problems we used to have, stopping them from volunteering, that makes me angry. It's wrong to let people expose themselves needlessly to danger; that's completely against Islam. No, I'm not saying that young boys never went out. They did, and we lost quite a lot of them. But I always tried to stop them. It's a good thing to give your life for Islam, but suicide is something altogether different.'

A white cloth had been spread over the carpet, and Teherani's three children had all appeared now, bringing in the dishes for lunch. The efforts by Teherani's wife, whom we heard but never saw, had resulted in a marvellous *morgh pulao* – a dish with chicken and saffron rice, spiced with *zereshk*, little redcurrants with a sharp taste, which added colour as well as flavour to it. Even the little daughter sat with us, eating and being fed from her father's plate: she was regarded as being young enough not to need protecting from adult male eyes. But the woman who had prepared the meal had to eat her share of it with the servants in the kitchen; and although Teherani was extremely hospitable to everyone, including Tira, and answered her questions as readily as he answered mine, he seemed uncomfortable that she was there.

The meal, however, helped to mellow all of us, and as we ate our apples and sipped our tea at the end of it, we were able to turn back with less hostility than before to the question of how Iran appeared to Western eyes.

'If people in the West were told the truth about Iran, they would realize that it was much more favourable than they think,' he said. I did not find it impossible to agree with that, but tried unsuccessfully to make him understand that the barriers were erected by his own government, rather than by people like me; I, after all, had tried for months to come to Iran, and had found it extremely difficult. We argued for a long time, hampered on either side by the host-guest relationship, which made it difficult to be blunt about the way we felt. Several times I saw a hurt look in his grey eyes at the things I was saying, and I felt constrained, having just eaten his *morgh pulao,* to throw away my best points. At last the cameras came out, his as well as ours, and he took photographs of Tira and me without apparent qualms, and allowed Tira to take some of him and me together. At the end, as we were starting to make the kind of motions that indicated a preparation to leave, he darted away and came back carrying an extraordinary object.

'People say the clergy have no taste,' he said, and added proudly, 'Let no one say that of *us.*'

The object he had brought over was a stuffed seagull. He stood it on a piece of wood and moved back to get a better look at it. I was afraid for a moment that he was going to present it to us.

I had not been in Qom since 1979, a few days before the Revolution. Then, too, I was accompanied by a camera crew, and our endeavours were largely frustrated by crowds of silent, interested people. We penetrated the mean side-streets ('the maze of intricate streets and alleys of which the greater part of the city . . . is composed', Curzon called them) in order to find the house of one of the foremost religious figures of Iran, the Grand Ayatollah Mohammed-Kazem Shariatmadari. Our directions were not particularly clear, and we were soon lost. Outside a *madrasseh*, or religious school, we came across a group of a dozen or so mullahs. One of them was a most striking figure, taller than any of the others and with a fine head of red hair with which his turban could not fully compete. Red hair is not unknown in the Middle East – it can be found quite frequently among the Shi'ites of Lebanon, for instance, who have a good deal of European blood in their veins as a result of the Crusades; but in Iran it is extremely rare.

I tried my halting and primitive Persian on this man, drawn to him by his exotic appearance, and he answered me in English, in the accents of the London outer suburbs. He was a convert to Shi'ia Islam, and was training to be a mullah at that particular *madrasseh*. We were unable to talk for more than a few minutes, and he clearly found our sudden arrival a little embarrassing. But he confirmed what was already being assumed outside Qom: that Ayatollah Shariatmadari was no supporter of Ayatollah Khomeini, and that there was strong rivalry between their *talabehs* or students.

Shariatmadari had the reputation of being a cautious man, who had no desire to challenge the authority of the Shah, but was nevertheless critical of the policy the Shah had been following. Some months before, in January 1978, a group of *talabehs* had taken refuge in Shariatmadari's house, but were pursued by a detachment of soldiers who had attacked the house and killed one of the students in it. On several occasions in the past, Shariatmadari had supported Khomeini, and even pleaded with the Shah on his behalf after Khomeini's arrest in 1963. But he never trusted him, and never got along with him. The red-haired student explained a little of this to me, whispering in order not to seem too obvious to his fellow-*talabehs*. Finally he pointed out the complex route we had to follow to get to the Ayatollah's house.

We did not have an appointment, but given the Persian tradition of hospitality it did not appear to matter. From the hallway we could hear Shariatmadari's reedy voice telling the porter to allow us in. He had given one famous interview to the BBC Persian service, a year or so before, condemning the shooting of a number of demonstrators on the streets of Qom by the army. Perhaps he liked the attentions of Western journalists and the respect they accorded him. We were ushered into the room

276

where he was giving audiences, and found him in bed, wrapped in a synthetic furry blanket and resting on two enormous red cushions covered with white lace. He was, however, fully dressed, in black turban, a grey tunic, and black cloak.

I asked, as respectfully as I knew how, if he would allow us to film him. Having experienced only the forbidding style of the Imam, I was a little uncertain how to treat this smiling, quizzical old gentleman who received people in his bedroom.

'*Bale*,' he assented, with a glance of amusement at the beard of Bill Handford, the cameraman.

At this stage, Khomeini's supremacy was still not finally established. His had been the uncorrupted voice outside the country, and Shariatmadari had been tainted by remaining inside it, and co-operating with the Shah's régime; but Shariatmadari remained the more senior ayatollah. Not long before, he had indicated in a famous lapidary sentence the sharpness of the distinction between his political position in Qom and Khomeini's in Neauphle-le-Château: 'Things are different if one man sits under an apple tree and another sits under a tank.' Nevertheless, as the red-haired Londoner had said to me, 'The Islamic Republic isn't something you can have differing views on,' and Shariat-madari's line, as he developed it to us, was very little different from Khomeini's, now that the Shah had left and the government of Shahpour Bakhtiar was clearly about to crumble. Such differences as there were, were those of tone and intensity; Shariatmadari was a poor politician, as events were to show, but he was a gentler and more forgiving man than Khomeini.

It was a long audience that he gave us, and not without tedium. His voice with its Turkish accent – he came from Tabriz, not far from the border with Turkey – droned on and on, detailing the exact approach he took to the Islamic Republic, its effects on the religious and political rights of Iranians, the steps that would be necessary to introduce it, and the stance it would take in the world at large. It was as though he were saying, If you come to see me you must listen to everything I wish to tell you. It was difficult to detect any points on which he disagreed with Khomeini's line, though he did say at one point, 'The Islamic Republic will not be dictatorial, or government by one person,' which may have been intended as an oblique criticism of Khomeini's pre-eminence. All the while, as he talked, his sharp amused eyes glinted through old-fashioned spectacles at us, and the elderly *hojat-ol-Eslams* who were sitting round the bed kept up a discussion between themselves, the discussion of deaf men unaware of the loudness of their voices.

'There will,' said Shariatmadari, 'be more clashes between the supporters of the Islamic Republic and the army, but if all sides think calmly about their position, I hope the matter can be settled with little bloodshed.' He stopped talking, and tea was brought. A few minutes later, with great courtesy, he wished us a good journey to Tehran. The amused look was still there as we closed the bedroom door behind us.

Shariatmadari was the archetypal moderate: his opinions and reactions were far gentler than those of Khomeini, his instincts much more tolerant, but he lacked both power and determination to use his popularity in Azerbaijan and in the country at large to press his own claims to supremacy. At the crucial moment he was always liable to lose his nerve, as his subsequent career showed. The political party which his supporters founded, the Islamic People's Republican Party, could call on a great deal of public support, especially from middle-class people who felt that it, like Shariatmadari himself, was moderate and would shield them from extremism; but Khomeini declared it illegal, and Shariatmadari, recoiling from the risk of violence, accepted the destruction of his political power meekly.

In 1982 he was implicated, perhaps wrongly, in the *coup* attempt planned by Sadeq Qotbzadeh, the former foreign minister who had flown from Paris to Tehran with Khomeini in 1979. After Qotbzadeh's execution Shariatmadari was lucky to escape with his life, but he suffered a penalty never before inflicted on a grand ayatollah of the Shi'a faith: he was unfrocked, and although he was not forced to shave off his beard he was forbidden to wear his *seyyed's* black turban. The humiliation was total, but even so Shariatmadari would not call on his supporters to protect him from it. He remained in his house in Qom, seeing his former *talabehs* but not teaching, preaching or issuing statements: a 'model' whose supporters were forbidden to follow his religious example.

Returning to Qom seven years later, I was struck by the extent to which it had become a political as well as a religious centre. Enormous portraits of Khomeini and those grand ayatollahs who supported him glowered down from the walls and hoardings, much as pictures of Lenin do in Moscow. Portraits on such a scale are rarer elsewhere in Iran. Khomeini seemed to want to impose himself on Qom in a way that was not regarded as necessary elsewhere: not even in the capital. When we interviewed a leading ayatollah for television, I had an argument with him and his officials lasting half-an-hour about whether a large portrait of the Imam should hang on the wall behind him. My argument

278

was that it was absurdly big, and would look as though Khomeini was peering over his shoulder the whole time; and I soon realized that this was precisely the case, metaphorically speaking. The ayatollah wanted to demonstrate his loyalty by answering my questions in the shadow of his political as well as religious leader. Anything else might be regarded as dangerously individualistic and unauthorized.

We argued on and on, trapped in a small overheated room with the television lights blazing in our faces, and the cameraman, Ali Torabi, looking extremely bored about it all. It reminded me of the kind of problem one might have had with a Russian official under Stalin, or a Chinese one under Mao Tse Tung. In the end, of course, we compromised: a small framed picture of Khomeini was brought in and set on the table in front of our interviewee. Honour was satisfied; and the cameraman who was tired of this kind of work and wanted to get down to the war front understood entirely when I asked him to zoom in on the ayatollah's face as quickly as he decently could, and lose the intrusive picture of his leader. Politics, it seemed, were for the clergy; everyone else with a job to do should get on with it as best they could.

15

The War of Attrition

> And in truth the Persian is no fine-weather soldier;
> nor is he a mere fighting machine. Hardy and of a
> powerful physique, he is at the same time very intelli-
> gent, amenable to discipline, sober, and ready to
> follow his officers if he can only trust them.
>
> Dr C. J. Wills, *Persia As It Is*, 1887

'Land is land – it doesn't matter. It's just earth and rock. We can give it back to the Iraqis after the war. What matters is the victory of Allah. This isn't a war for territory, it's a war for Allah.'

The speaker is a short, intense young man in a ragged uniform, who was educated in the gentle city of Norwich, in England: about as far from this barren shell-blasted waste as it is possible to imagine. Around him crowd twenty or thirty of his fellow-volunteers, anxious, whether they understand the questions and answers or not, to make sure the point is not lost on the questioner. *'Allahu Akbar!'* they chant, having picked the one word 'Allah' out of what their comrade was saying. It is impossible for a foreign journalist to visit the war-front, or to come across troops who are leaving for the front, without hearing this sort of thing; and no one I spoke to who had heard it ever doubted that it was genuine.

It goes a little against the grain for post-industrial, Western man to accept it all at face value. Who is ordering them to say this kind of thing? What personal advantages do they obtain as a result? How can they, after the enormous losses of so many years of fighting, still maintain any form of enthusiasm for it? The natural comparison for Europeans to make is with the First World War: the mud, the shelling, the trench-fighting, the use of gas, the huge offensives bogging down and achieving a few hundred yards' advantage – all have a dreadfully familiar ring for us. But the First World War lasted for four years, and by the last eighteen months of it the morale of each of the main armies was stretched almost to breaking-point: the Iran-Iraq war which began in September 1980 has continued for far longer than that. There have been no reports of serious mutinies on the Iranian side, no evidence that men are turning on their officers or surrendering voluntarily, or displaying any of the other symptoms of war-weariness.

We were driving one afternoon down the curiously-named Hejab Avenue, which used to be called Los Angeles Avenue, when Mahmoudi jerked involuntarily at the steering-wheel and pointed out something ahead of us.

'*Basiji*,' he said. The *Basiji* are the volunteers for the front, and before every major offensive they gather in their hundreds at centres throughout Tehran and every other town and city to pick up their uniforms and be transported to the training bases behind the front line. Several buses were parked by the side of the road, and the *Basiji*, who varied in age from teenagers of fifteen to men in their late forties or early fifties, were streaming across the road to climb aboard. They were waving the red or white scarves they had been given to tie round their heads in a rather piratical manner, and were chanting the usual responses about capturing Kerbala, the Shi'ite shrine in Iraq. Like the great majority of volunteers I had seen before and was to see later, they seemed mostly to be of working-class or peasant origin; and indeed the name of their organization, *Basij-e-Mustazafin*, means 'Mobilization of the Deprived.' Educated, middle-class *Basiji* certainly appear at the front – the man from Norwich was presumably one of them – but in far fewer numbers than the proportion of Iranian society they represent.

Not long before, a foreign television team had filmed just such an occasion as this, a detachment of *Basijis* leaving Tehran for the front, and had come across a young boy of about thirteen weeping bitterly. It was a natural assumption for Westerners that the boy was crying at being sent to fight in the war, and this was how the incident was represented in the broadcast report. The Ministry of Islamic Guidance in Tehran was angry at what it maintained was a deliberate distortion of the facts. According to the Ministry, the boy had been told that he was too young to fight, and this was why he was crying. The recording of the boy's words showed that this was indeed the case. But the Ministry was equally wrong to assume the television station had deliberately falsified the position for reasons of anti-Iranian propaganda. It simply cannot have occurred to anyone involved that young boys might weep at being forbidden to die for their country.

There was little exaggeration, earlier in the war, in the stories about young boys and men running ahead of the main body of troops in order to detonate any mines that might have been planted in the way of their attack. The newspapers, and radio and television, carried frequent accounts of deaths of this kind. What was wrong, again, was to assume that the only way anyone could be made to do such a thing would be to force them out at gun-point. But I have talked to dozens of *Basijis*, whom I chose to question carefully ignoring those who seemed to be in command, or who acted as spokesmen, and they confirmed not only that this kind of behaviour had been completely voluntary – and indeed was discouraged by some commanders – but that they themselves, if necessary, would do such a thing.

One Friday evening, in a cemetery in the city of Qom, I came across a group of *Basiji* who had gathered to honour their dead comrades. Several of them had been injured: one, for instance, had lost his foot. But even he was trying to obtain some kind of dispensation which would allow him to return to the front. Men from Kitchener's Army would have recognized the impulse, and so would young Germans in 1945; it is simply that in countries where the circumstance does not arise, the leap of imagination which is required to understand such an impulse is hard to make.

But for seven years the working-class and peasantry of Iran have been taught by every means at the Islamic Republic's disposal that martyrdom is the ultimate achievement for a human being. Given the poverty and rootlessness of large numbers of these *Basijis* – these Deprived – it is not perhaps surprising that so many have opted for precisely that honour. This does not mean, however, that the majority of the population, or even the majority of the young men of Iran, necessarily want to fight, or to join the armed foces. But Iran's population explosion has been on such a scale that there is no shortage of manpower for the front. The Islamic Republic can fight its war with Iraq by relying for the most part on volunteers.

To explain it all away in purely social terms – the rootless poor are prepared to sacrifice their lives, the middle class are not – is however a shallow response. There is a great deal more to this extraordinary phenomenon than social structures, or the lack of them, can explain. In Qom I consulted a leading ayatollah, Dr Mohammad Mespah, who has a senior position in the Information Department, and asked him to explain to me the – to a Western mind – incredible willingness of so many people to fight.

'Any individual Muslim should participate in a war against the enemies of his religion, because that is a means of obtaining God's blessing, just as practising religious duties is. And so the way one views a holy war is inseparably related to the way one views Islam itself.

'But the motivation which makes people fight in a holy war is that death does not represent the end of life for a human being. On the contrary, immortal life begins after death, and the kind of salvation that a man has in the next world is dependent on the kind of life he lives in this world. And taking part in a holy war is a way of assuring oneself that one's immortal salvation in the next world is guaranteed. It's only natural therefore, that anyone would wish to be killed seventy times, and still come back to life in order to be killed all over again. It is this kind of perception which creates the desire for martyrdom among Muslims.'

Even this is not, however, an explanation; it is a rationale. For people to be prepared to sacrifice themselves over so long a period of time there has to be what one might call a culture of sacrifice. Iraq, for instance, is a deeply Muslim country with an impressive military tradition and an army with a strong sense of discipline and a ruthlessness in maintaining it. This, combined with reliance on greatly superior weaponry, has enabled the country to continue fighting for so long. But there is no comparable willingness among Iraqi soldiers to throw their lives away for the cause. Indeed, the number of prisoners of war held by the Iranians has usually been, on average, seven or eight times the number in Iraqi hands. Iranians, in other words, do not surrender nearly so readily as Iraqis. But one estimate of the casualties in the war indicates a six-to-one ratio in the Iraqis' favour; Iranians, in other words, are a great deal more ready to be killed.

The Shi'a faith is itself a culture of sacrifice, founded as it was by the followers of 'Ali, the Prophet's son-in-law, and Hosayn, the grandson of the Prophet; 'Ali was murdered in 661, while Hosayn was killed at the battle of Kerbala some twenty years later, when his two hundred men, completely outnumbered, refused to surrender. Hosayn's head was cut off and later buried with his body at Kerbala. The great Shi'ite celebration of the tenth of the month Muharram marks the death of Hosayn with harrowing scenes of ritualized weeping and self-flagellation. Suffering and martyrdom, and the sense of a great historic wrong committed against them on Iraqi soil by Sunni Muslims, are the conditioning which every religious Iranian Shi'ite receives from earliest childhood.

In Hejab Avenue in Tehran the last *Basijis* are finally loaded onto their buses, and the sweating drivers check that the doors are properly shut. With a great hooting of horns, the convoy slowly heads out into the middle of the road, the cars and trucks keeping at a respectful distance. The *Basijis* lean at dangerous angles out of the windows of the buses in order to wave their scarves at us and chant about Kerbala and Saddam Hussein, and – because they could never quite understand that we were British and not American – about 'Amrika' as well. Different men, in different circumstances, might have sung about Tipperary and what they were planning to do when they met the Kaiser, but these men are off, in their own estimation, to do something a great deal more transcendent than merely march on Berlin. Their task is to capture Kerbala, and then perhaps move on to Qods – Jerusalem – itself. We stand and watch them sweep slowly down the hill, the chanting growing fainter, the scarves becoming scarcely identifiable, until the heat haze and the exhaust-laden atmosphere of the Tehran streets hide them from us altogether.

In February 1986, when the war had been going on for more than five years, Iran showed that, even if it could not bring the war to a speedy conclusion, it was capable of taking the initiative and keeping it. The Iraqis might have the equipment, but they would not be able to win the war, and the Iranians would not, therefore, lose it; though on what terms it might be brought to an end was as unclear then as it remains at the time of writing, a year and a half later. This key moment came when the men of the Revolutionary Guard crossed the Shatt-al-Arab waterway under cover of darkness and launched an amphibious attack against Iraqi positions in the Faw Peninsula which had hitherto seemed impregnable. It was a remarkable feat of military planning and execution.

The Iraqi defenders escaped as best they could, leaving large amounts of equipment behind them, and the Iranians found themselves for the first time in possession of a sizeable amount of Iraqi territory. From now on, the war would be fought at least in part on Iraqi soil: a pleasing thought to a country which had been unable to dislodge the invaders for so long. Anxious that the world should see the progress they had made, the Iranians sent out a general invitation to the world's television, press and radio to come to Faw to inspect it for themselves. It was this invitation which was brought to my notice by the Iranian embassy in London at the very moment when I had despaired of ever getting to Iran again.

The world's television, press and radio were not, for the most part, particularly enthusiastic in their reply. Such invitations had been issued time and again by both Iran and Iraq, and huge amounts of money and considerable lengths of time would be invested in sending in correspondents or camera teams, who would spend most of their time at expensive hotels in the capital, waiting for the opportunity to travel to the front. When they arrived there (and there were occasions when they did not) they would find that they were kept some miles back from the front line, with little to see except unburied bodies and a few trenches. Sometimes an explosion on the horizon would show where the fighting was now taking place. Most news organizations had decided that there were better ways to spend their money.

The reluctance to take the visiting journalists to the front line arose from the fear that some of them would be killed; if that happened, the reasoning went, it would be taken everywhere as evidence that the victory was not as decisive as the victors had maintained: the enemy would still be very obviously in the field. The Iranians did not impose these restrictions on their own people: week after week Iranian television shows remarkable coverage of the war and its tank battles, its infantry charges and its bombardments. Thirty-six cameramen, sound-recordists and reporters have been killed on the Iranian side in battle: a higher figure than in either the Second World War or in Vietnam.

But for me, the invitation seemed a useful way of returning to Iran, though it was made clear early on that Tira, as my television producer, would not be allowed in. 'No women at the war-front' was the principle on which the Ministry of Islamic Guidance operated, much to Tira's fury. In my case, I went not particularly because I wanted to see the war, but because I had the impression that it might be possible for me to stay on in Iran for a week or two afterwards. Most of the other Westerners on the trip – only a dozen or so of them – had come on the same principle. Few of us expected to be shown anything particularly interesting at the front itself.

We assembled at the military air base in Tehran: two other British correspondents, my colleague Nick Nugent from the BBC External Service, and James Allen from the *Daily Telegraph*, who had seen a good deal more of events in Iran than almost any other Western journalist; the NBC correspondent Henry Champ, who had been a friend of mine ever since he arrived in London, and his British camera crew, a CBS crew, who were also very pleasant and friendly, and an assortment of others from Western Europe and the United States. It was, in other words, precisely the kind of turn-out one would expect, and the only member of the party who did not look as though he were used to doing this kind of thing was a short, rather stout German in a tan suit and a tie. I had noticed him the moment he walked into our hotel in Tehran: he had looked so ill at ease, and was so laden down with luggage, that I took him for a Swiss or German businessman who did little travelling. As it turned out, he was the Middle East office manager for one of the big West German magazines, and the local Iranian embassy, misunderstanding his rôle, had invited him to go on the Faw trip, and had refused to change the invitation even when the mistake became clear. He was a pleasant man, very nervous, and full of forebodings about what was going to happen.

'Don't worry,' said a Frenchman, 'nothing ever happens on these trips. They always make sure of that.'

The German did not look altogether convinced. He was sweating heavily in the heat.

We flew down to the city of Ahwaz in a Fokker Friendship airliner which was to become famous within a matter of thirty-six hours, and arrived in the early evening. Ahwaz is an ugly, mud-coloured place under leaden skies, lying along the sluggish Karun River in Khuzestan, the Arab province of Iran. The heavy yellow alluvium of the Karun delta gives the city its tone and clogs its streets, so that the soles of your shoes are heavy with mud after twenty yards of walking. What was extraordinary, however, was that although the war was being fought a matter of thirty miles away, and Ahwaz had often been attacked by the Iraqi air force, all the lights in the city were blazing and the shops were open for the evening trade as we wandered out in small groups to look around. Goldsmiths were sitting drinking strong Arab coffee from small cups and looking hopefully at this sudden influx of potential customers, but none of us, I think, bought anything, on the whispered advice of one of our guides: the gold, he said, was much better quality in Tehran.

The best hotel in Ahwaz, none too good, had put itself out for us as well as it could. In the past, Western oilmen had stayed here and, no doubt, grumbled about the standard of its comfort. Nowadays arriving guests had to walk over the Stars and Stripes, the Union Jack and the Hammer and Sickle, painted side by side on the marble step in front of the main door, in order to get into the place, while a notice on the door itself required them to respect the rules governing Islamic dress. Outside was a large sign which showed an Iranian soldier under an apparent shower of blood and bore the words 'We are all warriors and never fear from war'. We made the best of the hotel, though we were two or three to each of its small, bleakly appointed rooms. After a brief and disturbed night's sleep we were roused early for a military briefing on the situation at Faw.

The arrangements for the briefing were of some political and military interest in themselves. The men who had captured Faw belonged to the Pasdaran, the Revolutionary Guards: the highly committed, highly trained force which the Islamic Republic had created in order to defend itself from external and internal attack. For most of the war the Revolutionary Guards had done the most difficult fighting, and had been sent to the most dangerous areas; and by and large they and the *Basiji* had acquitted themselves well. The regular army, by contrast, had been little more than bystanders at some of the most significant points in the war. They had not fought with great distinction in the early stages of the Iraqi invasion, and there were always doubts in the upper levels of government about the loyalty of a force whose officers, in particular, had been recruited and had received their training under the Shah. The ayatollahs tended to follow the Soviet example: they created their own parallel army, which owed its very existence to the Revolution, and the army was obliged, grumblingly, to accept its demotion.

'In the Name of God,' someone began: a tall, serious young man in his early twenties with bad posture and an inadequate tuft of beard under his chin. He stood in front of a large yellow map and made sketchy, nervous movements at it. He seemed to be a very junior figure indeed; and it was only as the briefing went on that it became clear that he had, in fact, played an important part in the planning and command of the attack on Faw.

'The enemy were superior in every way,' he said, seeming to gain a little confidence from being in front of his familiar map. I wondered if he had ever addressed a group of foreigners in his life before. 'They never thought that a military force would be able to cross the river here.' He pointed with his stick to the wide wound of the Shatt-al-Arab, cutting its way through the marshes on either bank.

'Our aim was to cut off Iraq's access to the Persian Gulf, and in order to do that we had to fool the enemy by staging another operation, further to the north.' He gestured at some point close to the ceiling, well off the top of his yellow map. 'As a result of our attack we captured 800 square kilometres of enemy territory and an Iraqi army headquarters. Altogether the Iraqi losses were 15,000 dead and 22,000 captured – mostly men of the special Presidential Guards.' Even allowing for a certain amount of enthusiasm in the reckoning, it was an important victory.

Another man took his place before the map: a thirty-year-old, this time, who was operations director of the Revolutionary Guards. Neither he nor his colleague appeared to have any military rank, which is one of the peculiarities of the Guards; their officers, someone said later, simply emerge. This man lectured us about the strategic objectives: how they planned to establish a base in Faw for the capture of Iraq's second city, Basra, while closing the waterways and air corridor to Iraq. He had read his military history:

'There were worse tides for this attack than for the D-Day landings in Normandy. Napoleon himself rarely managed to get his own military plans accomplished, because of tactical problems on the ground. We achieved great success in that.'

He paused, as though there was something else he was supposed to say, and it had temporarily gone out of his mind. Then he remembered.

'Our military brothers helped us by providing helicopters and so on. After the initial attack had succeeded.'

I looked round at the representative of their military brothers: a tough, self-reliant colonel of roughly colonel's age, smart in his light green uniform with a camouflage cravat at the throat. He looked straight ahead, not reacting in any way. It may have taken a little effort.

At the airport we were issued with blue overalls, which were intended to protect us against gas attacks; but they were poor quality, and all the same size; and for someone of six feet, two inches like myself they were absurd: the sleeves came half-way up my arms and the trousers half-way up my calves, like ludicrous plus-fours. A square box with a strap attached to it contained a gas mask, of roughly Second World War efficiency. We pulled on our overalls and investigated our gas masks with the usual nervous joking, and it seemed to me that some dealer in defence products had made a killing from the Iranian government, if our equipment was typical of the consignment. When we had tied ourselves up like so many blue parcels, we were led out to the helicopters which were waiting for us.

The helicopters, elderly American Hueys from the time of the Shah, were painted the predominant colour of Ahwaz: the yellow mud-colour which would camouflage them as they flew low over the Karun flats. I disobeyed instructions in order to keep close to the NBC crew, who had agreed to film for me as well as for themselves, and we crammed into the first helicopter together. Another five people joined us, making probably only double the number of passengers the Huey was supposed to take, and after an interminable time we lifted off. We hovered for a little, waiting for the two other Hueys that were going with, and then headed south-westwards, towards Faw. But the trip did not last long. I saw the pilot shake his head as a signal to his colleague, and point back to Ahwaz. There was, it seemed, too much early morning fog to make the trip in safety.

It is always difficult to know exactly what one feels in such a situation: disappointment and relief clamber over one another inextricably in the mind. For two hours or more we sat in the waiting-room at the airport, our anti-gas suits heating up and getting slippery with sweat on the inside, and drank too much sweet Iranian tea. It was after eleven o'clock when the sudden announcement came that we were to make the trip again. I noticed the face of the reluctant German falling; his brief sortie in the helicopter before must have aroused all his worst fears about the trip.

There were even more of us in the lead Huey this time: so many that the pilot, a big, unshaven, impressive-looking man in his late thirties who knew exactly what he was doing and spoke good American English, had an argument with his co-pilot about whether it was safe to take us. The problem, apparently, was that more Iranians had to be taken to Faw as well as ourselves. In the end the pilot shrugged and accepted. We were so tightly crammed in behind him, sitting on the floor of the Huey with our chins on our knees, that shifting position was an operation that required two or three people if it was to be successful. We swooped along in convoy, the three Hueys strung out over two-thirds of a mile. The yellow mud-flats below us were beginning to green with palm-trees, and when I could turn my head I could see the flat oblong buildings on the ground and the Karun curving its way two hundred feet below us. It was turning into a beautiful clear day: too clear to be flying into a war zone.

And then we were within sight of Faw and dropped down to seventy or eighty feet, and things became very tense. The co-pilot was pointing to something above the horizon, and then white and grey clouds suddenly erupted out of the ground in neat lines across my field of vision, eight miles or so away. The pilot turned and grinned. The Iraqis were bombing at a distance, not over Faw itself but along the front line occupied by the

Iranians. There were impassioned radio conversations between the pilot and the ground, and the decision was taken: we had to go in to Faw, because it was now too dangerous to go back.

We flew in very low indeed, just above the level of the palm trees, and the discomfort of sitting hunched up for forty minutes or so faded suddenly in the anxiety of the moment. This was not just another neatly organized press facility, with all the danger neatly edited out: the pilots were worried, and wanted to put us down fast and get their valuable machines away as fast as they could. A little ahead of us was the landing strip, with a few small gesticulating figures visible on it: a great gold-coloured square, bulldozed out of the surrounding mud and marshland. Our helicopter sank down onto it jarringly, and the co-pilot started yelling, 'Out! Out! Out!' the instant we were settled.

For perhaps half a minute we ran out of the range of the rotors and the fierce hail of dust and mud they were throwing in our eyes and faces, and started to disentangle ourselves and our belongings. Our pilot was already in the air again, heading off to the south-west as the second Huey came in from the north-east, filling the air with the racket of its rotor-blades. The third stood off, waiting for its turn; and before it had properly settled the bombing began.

The Iraqis had known we were coming. They had followed the progress of our Fokker F-27 the previous day, and they had tracked our helicopters on their radar that morning. Their bombers, two miles above us in the clear blue sky, had plenty of time to scramble and catch us while the Hueys were setting us down. The sudden columns of earth and smoke heaving up into the air around us were the witnesses to that. But they were less frightening than the heart-stopping noise of the Iranian anti-aircraft guns around the landing-zone as they opened up in an effort to defend us. It was appallingly disorienting, as we tried to get our bearings and understand where we were meant to go.

'Get down! Get down!' people were screaming at us, and I threw myself, elbows first, into some dead bushes beside the edge of the zone hoping they would break my fall. They did, and I rolled over and managed to get my stills camera out of my shoulder-bag – the one that didn't contain my gas mask. Taking photographs, I had always found, was a kind of therapy under fire: it gave me something to do and stopped me worrying. As the columns of earth and smoke continued to rise around us, and I snapped away, the therapy started to work.

The third Huey was only now disgorging its tightly-packed occupants, and the shock and disorientation must have been twenty times worse for them than it was for us. The bombs seemed to be landing all round us, and the deafening explosions from the anti-aircraft guns were terrifyingly close: it took time to realize that those were the only explosions which were not harmful to us, and the latest arrivals by helicopter didn't have that much time.

Now a new order was being shouted: 'Get onto the trucks! Get onto the trucks!' The trucks were a good fifty yards away, on the edge of the landing zone, and the drivers, in their agitation, began revving up and starting to move. Obliged as I was to stay with the NBC correspondent and crew, I had to wait while the cameraman, Nick Reed, coolly finished filming the chaos around us and collected his gear. The television cameramen had behaved in exemplary fashion, standing out in the open to film the explosions, while everyone else was trying to dig themselves into the ground to escape them.

I didn't notice the reluctant German: too much was happening around us for that. But the heat, the fear, the dreadful noise of the artillery and the bombing, and the fifty-yard run for the trucks in the constricting overalls we were wearing, proved fatal for him. He reached the trucks, almost the last to get there, and was hauled on board as it was pulling out at speed; and as he lay on the floor of the trucks, with the crash of the guns still going on around us, his heart gave way under the strain of it all. He was dead before anyone had realized it; and although the doctors at the field hospital had orders to leave the Iranians who had been wounded in the bombing and look after him, two hours and more of effort failed to resuscitate him. I admired him for agreeing to come on the trip at all. Many bureau managers would have found a way of refusing.

Away from the landing zone, things were easier for the rest of us. We bucketed along the pot-holed roads, through the shattered remnants of the town of Faw, whose mosque tower was the only building any size to have escaped damage. Now the green flag of Islamic revolution flew above it, and everywhere we went the flag was visible, a symbol of the most important battle that Iranian soldiers had won in centuries. Everywhere, too, we were cheered on by soldiers in makeshift uniforms, units of the rear who occupied each crossroads and lived in whatever undestroyed accommodation they could find. Our motorcade consisted of the three troop-carrying lorries with Western journalists on board, together with jeeps, motorbikes and whatever else our escorts could commandeer. And all the time, on the skyline around us, grey and black smoke was going up from bomb explosions, and the thud of anti-aircraft fire could be heard above the grinding noise of our trucks' engines. The Iraqi air force had other targets now.

We stopped in the remains of the town, for no reason that I could see, and were descended upon by soldiers. They were simple men who regarded us as being there out of solidarity, and who were excited and proud of their own achievement. Some were very young indeed, but among them was a man who looked like an Old Testament prophet gone to the bad: his grizzled beard and bald pate, around which was tied a red scarf in most piratical fashion, suggested that he must have been in his late fifties at least. But he was the most warlike figure we saw all day, with two bandoleros stuffed with bullets criss-crossing his chest, and a rifle of antique but threatening aspect – a little like himself, therefore – slung over his shoulder. It would have seemed terrifying to have come across him at dusk on a remote mountain pass; but here he was the foghorn voice of God's victory:

'*Allahu Akbar!* Praise be to God for destroying His enemies! We shall march to Kerbala! We shall liberate the shrines of Hosayn and 'Ali from the hands of the defilers! We shall march on holy Qods itself and capture that in the name of God and the Imam Khomeini! God is great! Khomeini is our leader!'

He was magnificent in his way, the kind of technicolor figure who will look good on any newspaper front page or as the opening shot in a report for television news. He was not, however, a front-line combatant, any more than the teenagers who swarmed about him were. We saw the real combatants a little later: exhausted, grey figures, their uniforms thick with dust, trudging back for other duties after the bombing they had received that morning. But they too raised a cheer for us, and chanted about God and Khomeini. These were the Revolutionary Guards who had swum the Shatt-al-Arab a few days before and captured the Iraqi positions, and were now holding off all the counter-attacks. Not all the bodies of their dead enemies had been buried. Here and there we saw the huddled shapes of men who lay where the bullets or the shells had caught them, singly or in enough numbers to fill a trench, their faces frozen and inhuman, their eyes half-closed, the flies at work on them.

We had already been shown one of the crueller aspects of the war that morning: a bus full of gas casualties. We clambered aboard like tourists, with the encouragement of our 'minders', photographing and filming the appalling state of the men sitting there. Many of them were unable to open their eyes, and were sitting, swaying with the pain and the discomfort. Others were holding medicated cloths to their faces. There was a terrible sound of coughing – the coughing that tears at the lungs and throat. At last someone who was less badly gassed realized that we were there, and began a feeble chant of 'Allahu Akbar!'. Gradually more and more men took it up, chanting the words slowly and weakly, as if they were talking in their sleep. Fists feebly waved in time to the chanting, and then the coughing and the moaning became stronger and the chanting weaker, and the sufferers were left on their own again.

A United Nations team, visiting Iran a week or so later, identified the gas which the Iraqis were using as mustard gas, of a type which revealed its First World War origins in its brand-name: Yperite. It was mostly dropped by bomb from Iraqi planes, and from the moment we landed at Faw I was aware of a faint irritation in the air which made my eyes water a little: it was the almost totally attenuated remainder of mustard gas in the air, a little like the aftermath of a riot where CS gas has been used.

The Iranian soldiers with us said that the white smoke which was still going up from Iraqi bombs as they fell about a mile away from us was mostly gas, and as we looked out from our trucks across the Ypres-like landscape we could see bombs hitting an area not far from where our helicopters had landed. And after we had been shown the captured site of an Iraqi missile-battery and were heading back for the area where the bombing was still going on, we started pulling out our gas masks and working out how they were attached. We sat there, swaying with the motion of the truck, so many anonymous insect-like faces with long protective snouts, when the truck-driver jammed the brakes on and we were out of our seats and diving for the ditch: Iraqi bombers were almost overhead. But they had other targets to attack and ignored us, and when they were safely past we clambered aboard again. It was a little time before I could work out what the Iranians with us thought was so funny about me, until I took my mask off and examined it: the filter had fallen out in the ditch incident. There was nothing between me and the air around us except some unhelpful rubber tubing. I made light of it as best I could, but the thought of the men on the bus with their eyes bulging out and the chemical eruptions on their skin was not a happy one. I sat in my seat with my useless gas mask on my lap, trying not to remember what we had seen.

Back at the landing zone, our tourism finished, there were more immediate problems even than gas: the Iraqis had decided to concentrate on us, and for the next two hours or so we were pinned down, out in the open, waiting for a lull that would be long enough for our helicopters to pick us up. Sometimes twenty minutes or more would pass without any action, and we would be able to stroll around in the open, interviewing people, filming things, and in my case looking out for any useful spare parts for my gas mask.

But the Iraqi bombers always came back, and they always seemed to know where we were – although that is a common delusion of people pinned down by aerial bombing. I would lie on my back at an angle, supported by an eight-foot ramp of bulldozed yellow earth, and watch the little silver crosses high above us in the blue sky. And each time, as the anti-aircraft crews spun about frenetically, trying to get a decent aim, it would occur to me with uncomfortable clarity that the difference of a thousandth of a second in the pilot's timing as he pressed the button to release his load of bombs, would mean the difference between a direct hit and a near miss. My bag and my camera became increasingly mud-stained as I threw myself down each time and began the photographic therapy again.

Eventually someone took the decision: the Iraqis were not going to let our helicopters back in, so we would have to be taken by motor-boat across the Shatt-al-Arab. From there more trucks would pick us up and take us by a long route to an Iranian air base. We loaded ourselves clumsily into the boats during the next lull in the bombing, and headed out fast into the middle of the waterway, with our helpers and guides waving us goodbye from the rickety wooden pier. But not for long. As the last boat was pulling away, the bombers returned. We were still only a couple of hundred yards from the shore, and watched as one bomb in particular threw up its attendant column of débris and white smoke in the place where we had been taking refuge a few minutes before.

We flew back to Tehran, one fewer in number, in an enormous Iranian Hercules because our Fokker Friendship had been requisitioned at the last moment so that a party of government officials and members of the Majlis could visit Ahwaz and Faw. In the relief of having survived a difficult day's experiences it seemed a little absurd of us to believe what our escorts were saying: that we had been the targets of the Iraqi air force raid. The next day we heard what happened to our Fokker Friendship: eighteen miles north-east of Ahwaz, on its return flight to Tehran, it was shot down by two Iraqi fighters. All forty-four people on board were killed.

The war took on a life of its own, as Siegfried Sassoon believed the First World War did. It existed for itself, with neither side being able finally to destroy the other. The balance between the two sides was drawn with a fineness that seemed almost to betray a malign intention: Iraqi weapons and money versus Iranian manpower, the ferocity of Saddam Hussein's determination to root out anyone whose nerve seemed to be failing versus Ayatollah Khomeini's refusal to countenance anything short of victory. In 1986, after six years of fighting, military analysts in Britain and the United States felt that Iran was about to break through the extraordinary barrier of waterways and lakes which Iraq had built to protect the city of Basra, only a dozen miles from the Iranian border. The capture of Basra had become the most tangible of Iran's war aims; suitably enough, perhaps, since the city was founded as a base camp for the Arab invasion of Persia in the seventh century. But shortages of the right kind of weapons prevented Iran from striking the blow that might, at long last, end the war; and there were never enough tanks, missiles or artillery for the Iranians to be able to exploit the breakthroughs which they made. There at least the comparison with World War I was valid: logistics defeated the winning side, time and again, so that no decisive blow could be struck. In World War I victory came only when German resistance collapsed exhausted; at the time of writing it is impossible to say whether that will happen, or whether a political upheaval will render military victory unnecessary.

In the summer of 1987 Iraq managed adroitly to alter the entire focus of the war, from land to sea. By staging a series of attacks against tankers using Iranian ports in the Gulf, Iraq goaded Iran into retaliating against the shipping of other nations, especially those which supported Iraq in the war. Still smarting from the humiliation it had received when a lone Iraqi pilot (later, it is thought, executed after being repatriated) attacked the USS Stark, the United States warned that it would use force, if necessary, to protect itself and its Gulf State friends from attack, and to keep the sea-lanes open. The fact that it was Iraq, and not Iran, which had attacked the Stark and taken the initiative in the war against the tankers was rarely mentioned in the United States; so conditioned had Americans become to the notion that Iran was their natural enemy in the region. The British government, though privately of the opinion that Washington's commitment to 'reflag' Kuwaiti tankers and protect them as if they were American was ill thought-out and unwise, felt obliged nevertheless to sent a quarter of the Royal Navy to the Gulf to join in the exercise as a matter of alliance loyalty. The French, the Italians, the Dutch, the Belgians all joined them. The Russians, for their part, sent a large fleet.

In the early stages of the operation things went embarrassingly wrong. The Iranians used fleet auxiliary vessels and small patrol boats to lay mines of World War II design and manufacture in the sea-lanes of the Gulf, but the United States navy, equipped to deal with the weapons of World War III, had no mine-sweepers on hand to deal with the antique menace. U.S. admirals had, it emerged, always looked down on the art of mine-sweeping as unglamorous because it involved a low standard of technology; as a result the ability to build wooden ships of the right size (wood being required to avoid setting off magnetic mines) had died out in American shipyards. Worse, a 'reflagged' Kuwaiti tanker hit a mine while it was under escort by US navy ships. The government in Tehran made the most of Washington's embarrassment. It denied having planted the mines, insisting that they had been laid by 'hidden hands'; but for a time it looked as though a full-scale war might erupt between Iran and the United States. The Iranians, however, were always careful to prevent that from happening: since the Americans had the capability and probably the desire to inflict heavy losses on what remained of the Iranian air force and navy, Iran's ability to continue fighting its war against Iraq was at stake. And although the attention of the rest of the world was fixed on the Gulf, the Supreme Defence Council which controlled the strategy of the war, and which contained most of the political leaders of the Islamic Republic, were more concerned with the outcome of the land war. Although there were regular provocations against American ships and those of its friends and allies, Iran was careful not to become so heavily embroiled with the United States that it might provoke all-out retaliation.

In August 1987, at the height of the tension in the Gulf, I was again invited to Iran, together with the largest contingent of foreign journalists that had gathered there since the Revolution. We were to be taken to see for ourselves that Iran, far from laying mines as the West believed, was in fact engaged in an elaborate operation to locate mines and render them harmless. It was an uncharacteristically maladroit idea, which had presumably been thought up in order to create an alibi for Iran in case the Americans attacked. We were flown down to the port of Bandar Abbas, from which much of the military and naval hardware seemed to have been withdrawn, and put on board an American-made Sea Stallion helicopter of precisely the kind the US navy was using to search for mines, not far away in the waters of the Gulf. In appalling temperatures we found the small contingent of Iranian naval ships which were supposedly on mine-clearance duties off the coast of the United Arab Emirates, and after circling for half an hour so that the cameramen on board could film everything they needed, we landed on the deck of a support ship. It was a relief to get out into the cool fresh air; the temperature of which was, we later discovered, 119 degrees Fahrenheit.

In the ship's wardroom, an Iranian naval captain and commodore had been delegated to brief us about the operation. They were decent, professional men who had trained in Britain during the Shah's time, and were as awkward about speaking to journalists as most serving officers are in any navy or army. It was, therefore, almost an act of cruelty to interrupt them and ask who had planted the mines they were hunting.

'We don't know who planted them,' said the captain, looking round desperately for the commodore to help him out.

'No, we don't know,' said the commodore. The captain gave a ghastly grin and tried to continue. But the purpose of the exercise had evaporated in the ferocious heat of the wardroom.

There was a great deal of discussion in the United States about the reliability of the sea-going Revolutionary Guards who laid many of the mines and carried out attacks on shipping: were they acting under orders, or were they, as the vogue phrase had it, 'off the wall' – that is, uncontrollable fanatics capable of any insane action? Many American newspapers carried details of an attack by Revolutionary Guards on a ship which proved to be carrying Iranian oil; this was presented as evidence that the attackers were so maddened by zeal that they were capable of crazy acts of destruction. It was in fact a simple error. The ships which use the Gulf tend to bunch together for protection, and in the confused conditions it is not altogether surprising that one tanker should be mistaken for another. However reprehensible the tactic of attacking undefended merchant shipping might be, that was the decision of the Supreme Defence Council in Tehran; there was no evidence that the Revolutionary Guards were doing anything other than obeying the orders they had received. The notion of the off-the-wall fanatic derived from the standard Western view of Iran rather than from any direct observation of the way the Revolutionary Guards behaved.

The human wave tactics of the early part of the war were gradually discredited, and the Iranian generals who advocated them were superseded by men with slightly subtler ideas:

though in the attacks on the immense Iraqi water-filled defences in front of Basra, built to the designs of Soviet military advisers, there was no real alternative to the attempts to storm the canals and lakes by sheer weight of numbers. The failure in front of Basra at the beginning of 1987 led the Iranian Supreme Defence Council to put more effort into alternative theatres of war – the mountains of Kurdistan, in particular, where the Iraqi defences were often thin and the quality of the troops facing the Iranians was lower. The intention was to draw Iraqi forces away from Basra, but the difficulties of the terrain meant that Iran's logistical problems in bringing up the requisite tanks and artillery to exploit a breakthrough on a narrow front were far greater. The Iranian offensives became fewer and farther between, until they seemed to be carried out in much the same fashion as the blows from an immensely heavy hammer wielded by a strong but tiring man: each effort took longer to prepare and its failure took longer to recover from.

During all this time, no voice was raised publicly in Iran to criticize the conduct or purpose of the war, until October 1987 when Grand Ayatollah Qomi, from his base at Mashad, declared that there was no truth in the promise that those who died in the war against Iraq would go to heaven. 'Why should we not try the path of peace?' Ayatollah Qomi asked. It was not a call that anyone felt able to heed while the Imam Khomeini was still alive and politically active. Having declared the war to be holy, he would not compromise until the point where victory came or it proved impossible to fight on. With supple diplomacy, Iran's foreign ministry appeared to go along with the efforts during October and November 1987 by the United Nations secretary-general, Mr Javier Perez de Cuellar, to get a negotiated cease-fire. But there was never any serious doubt that Iran's purpose was purely to gain time for yet another offensive – and to delay a formal UN arms embargo until the necessary weapons had been obtained. For the most part, the West had little interest in the war until Iraq made sure it affected Western interests in the Gulf. It was Iran's purpose to shift the focus back to the land war: which meant more offensives, and more casualties.

The cemetery of Behest-e-Zahra, where Khomeini went on the day he returned to Iran, is nearly twice as large now as it was that February afternoon in 1979. The war has seen to that. As an ugly, graphic reminder of the losses on the battlefield, blood flows here in large quantities every day: the imitation blood that gushes out of the fountain in the middle of the cemetery. The crimson water, unpleasantly realistic, wells out and overflows like a waterfall into the trough below. Sometimes the wind catches it as it jets out, and blows it in the faces of the people who stop to watch.

Nearby are the graves of the leading figures of the Revolution who died in the guerrilla campaign of the People's Mojaheddin. As Tira and I stood beside the grave of Ayatollah Beheshti, several people came and touched the stone, and some, I was surprised to see, were weeping. A young woman in a *chador* stood in front of the grave and, as if she were addressing a living person, said in a loud voice, 'Beheshti, doctor in Islam.' Then, seeing us, she shouted 'Down with Amrika', and walked away quickly. It was one of the very few moments of hostility we experienced on our trip.

There was no hostility from the people who wandered with a kind of aimlessness around the graves in the immense tracts which are set aside for the war dead. The graves themselves are simply small slabs of grey stone set into concrete on the ground, with little grey metal structures like notice-boards over them. Behind the glass of the notice-boards are photographs of the dead man, sometimes as a child as well as in his uniform or wearing a neat suit at some formal occasion. The faces looked out at us seriously, quizzically, sometimes even humorously. Behind the glass might be a little bottle of rose-water to be sprinkled on the grave, or a lamp to signify remembrance. Some graves have been turned into little gardens, with rose-bushes and small, feeble trees planted beside them. But it doesn't make up for the sparseness and barrenness of the place, as the graveyard stretches for mile on mile with its little grey slabs and its grey notice-boards.

From a long way off we could hear a wailing of instruments, and at last a group of mourners emerged into our view: a week's remembrance for a dead Revolutionary Guard. First a small truck, driving at a snail's pace, then the four men playing the instruments – saxophone, clarinet, trumpet, drums – then a detachment of thirty or so men in Guards' uniform, slapping their chests in time to the music and carrying a magnificent banner which showed Khomeini weeping on it: the regimental funeral banner, as it were. A solid black phalanx of a hundred women followed at a suitable distance. The man they had come to remember gazed out at us in a friendly, cheerful fashion from a photograph taped onto the truck window: Seyyed Hussein Hashemi, aged twenty-one, had died of wounds received in the attack on the Faw peninsula. He could have been any one of the dusty, exhausted, still enthusiastic soldiers I saw on my trip

299

there.

'He was wounded four days before he was supposed to be married,' one of the mourners said. Somehow that made it more pointless, rather than more tragic: other people had been drawn into the circle of grief unnecessarily. Someone brought out a box of roses, and the mourners reached in to take them and throw them onto the grave, while a man sprayed rose-water from a bottle over the grave, and some of the drops fell across our faces on this hot, grey afternoon with the coolness of rain. A mullah had started to recite verses from the Koran about the necessity of suffering and the duty to sacrifice oneself, and as his voice grew angrier and louder, cracking on the higher notes, we moved discreetly away: the sorrow of the mourners could quickly have turned to anger against us, as it had with the woman at Beheshti's grave. Little tattered flags fluttered in the dull breeze beside the thousands of notice-boards, and the echo of the loudspeakers around the grave of Seyyed Hussein Hashemi made the sound of the mullah's voice flutter too: '*Allah-ah-ah-ah-ah-u-u-u-u Akbar-ar-ar-ar-ar . . .*'

A little way away, within earshot of the echo, five workmen were sitting round a recent grave, covering the grey earth with grey cement. Beside them, an old woman sat on the tomb of someone else's son, her chin on her hands, watching as her own son was sealed in. Everywhere, black figures were moving down the avenues, finding the graves of their sons and husbands in all this sameness with the certainty with which they would find their own front door. As we were leaving, at 4.30, the Fountain of Blood was switched off and the red water stopped spouting at last. The real flow will not be switched off as easily. When we were at Behesht-e-Zahra, the war graves ended about eighty yards from the road, leaving a wide swathe of rough ground. As I write this, a few months later, that empty space will have been filled with notice-boards, grey slabs, cement, and fluttering little flags, and the black-robed figures of women will be moving among them with equal certainty.

16

A Paradise Full of Luxuries

Let me now lead you into Isfahan, the metropolis of this great kingdom; yea, not inferior to the greatest and best-built city throughout the Orient.

Thomas Herbert, *Travels in Persia*, 1627-9

'HERE,' SAID MAHMOUDI, 'is Isfahan door.'

It was said with a certain proprietorial satisfaction: he was himself an Isfahani, and a concrete and steel fountain in the centre of an intersection, as we passed it, represented the gateway to a different and grander Iran than we had yet seen while we were with him. It also reflected his professional pride, since he had delivered us to our destination at high speed and yet in total safety.

There was, however, no door to Isfahan: just another set of dreary outer suburbs, grey and dusty, dating from the years of enrichment under the Shah. After the dry grandeur of the near-desert in which Isfahan is set, this came as a distinct disappointment. The very names of the suburbs seemed dull and repetitive: Lamjir, Kujan, Marun, Barzan. It wasn't electricity, automobile workshops and tarmacadam we wanted, it was a walled city with domes and minarets; but the walls of Isfahan had long since been pulled down, and although the domes and minarets were there in abundance they had to be viewed through cables and between television aerials. It was like approaching Venice through Mestre: the traveller feels irritable and self-indulgent at such times, and the sight of other people's industrial advancement and material comforts is always a disappointment.

I had been here before with Mahmoudi, when the suburbs were younger and less extensive and the country was waiting for its Revolution. In February 1979 Isfahan had led the way for the rest of the country: the revolutionaries were in control, and we had been welcomed as the first outsiders to see the Islamic Republic in operation. No matter how repellent the reign of the ayatollahs was to become, I always remembered those early days of efficiency and good will and general popular relief which followed the bloodless assumption of power in Isfahan. All revolutions no doubt begin in relief, and many of them end in despair; but we should not altogether forget the beginnings when we deplore the latter days.

In these latter days, Isfahan seemed to have been turned into a military camp. We passed dozens of earth-moving vehicles of Japanese make, painted in military livery and presumably awaiting transport to the front. Everywhere there were young men in military uniforms, marching or idling or sitting by the roadside. One, mistaking us for a local taxi, waved at Mahmoudi to stop and yelled insults at us when he did not. Mahmoudi ignored him with serenity, but he couldn't help glancing in the mirror to see how I had reacted to this display of professional loyalty. I inclined my head, seigneurially, and Mahmoudi seemed satisfied.

The late twentieth century, in laying siege to Isfahan, has penetrated some way into the ancient city, but its front line remains an ugly, system-built hotel, with a portrait of Ayatollah Khomeini at his fiercest painted on its windowless side, his face four storeys high. His beard alone took up a storey, and each of his eyes was the size of a hotel bedroom. We were planning to stay in a very different kind of hotel anyway, but even if that had been full we would not have gone to the Hotel Kowsar: sleeping within the scope of that massive frown would have been altogether too difficult.

European travellers have been coming to Isfahan, ever since Shah Abbas I proclaimed it his capital city in March 1598, and built some of the greatest of its monuments. Among the travellers were, as always, a sizeable number of Englishmen; and none of them has left a more attractive description of what he saw than Thomas Herbert, who visited Persia in the 1620s and added to the pleasures of his account of Isfahan by comparing it continually with the London of his own day:

At the West end of Isfahan is that which is called Nazer-jareeb, a garden deservedly famous. From the Maydan if you go to this garden you pass by Cherbaugh, through an even street near two miles long and as broad as Holborn in London, a great part of the way being garden-walls on either side the street; yet here and there bestrewed with mohols or summer-houses, all planted with broad-spreading chenaer trees, which, besides shade, serve for use and ornament.

In Mahmoudi's battered white taxi we too passed by 'Cherbaugh', or Chahar Bagh ('Four Gardens'), which seemed to me to be a good deal wider than Holborn: a promenade lined with bushes and trees, including many of the *chenar* or plane trees which Herbert had noticed, running down the centre of what is now the busiest road for cars, buses and taxis in Isfahan. Old men sat on the benches beside the shrubs and flowers, and boys rode up and down excitedly on bicycles; but the noise and fumes from the lines of cars on either side had blighted the atmosphere and the trees alike. Plane trees as a rule thrive in twentieth-century cities, but in Isfahan the twentieth century had been too much for them. Their leaves were blotched with the sooty marks of disease, and their trunks were thin and irregularly formed.

I asked Mahmoudi, who had lived the greater part of his life in the city, if he knew where the garden called Nazer-jareeb, which Thomas Herbert had referred to, might be; but although Herbert's ear for Persian names was rather more accurate than that of most of his English contemporaries (George Manwaring called Isfahan 'Aspahaune', William Parry called it 'Hasphane', and Sir Anthony Sherley transcribed the name of the early seventeenth century general Allahvardi Khan as 'Oliver-di-Can') Mahmoudi could not remember any such place, and the western part of the old city, while still tree-lined and containing many gardens, has long since been built over.

We turned off the Chahar Bagh beside the splendid, azure-domed theological school built around 1710 by the last Safavid king, Shah Soltan Hosayn, and into what had been Shah Abbas Avenue. I had promised Tira that we would be staying in one of the most beautiful hotels in the world, but I was conscious, when I saw it after an absence of several years, that its external appearance was something of a let-down. It was no longer called the Shah Abbas Hotel, but the Abbasi; much as every name with the word 'royal' in it was suppressed in France after the Revolution. The front had been badly modernized, probably in the late 1960s, and the glass doors which had been put in then were an offence to the eye. No uniformed porters were on hand to greet us and take our luggage as they had in 1979. But we were not here as tourists, prepared to be offended by every lapse in standards; and few revolutions in human history have led to higher levels of service in a country's hotels.

Inside, the Abbasi was precisely as I remembered it: every

square inch of the walls and ceiling in the immense lobby was inlaid with green, red and gold-coloured glass in patterns which made it seem as though we were viewing them through a kaleidoscope, while the floor was covered with elaborate whorls and curlicues of jaspar and green marble. But I had not remembered the feeling of mild physical unease it all induced: it was, certainly, beautiful in its way, though with the kind of beauty that comes from extraordinary, intricate excess. Nothing in the entire place was plain and unadorned; and what I had thought of as being the marvellous handiwork of the seventeenth century was revealed to me on this second, harder look as the archetypal extravagance of the Shah's years. The style was, unmistakably, late Pahlavi.

When I had last been here, my colleagues and I were the only guests; tourists and travelling salesmen being few in number at times of revolution. But the staff had been charming, if nervous; our bills were waived, on the refreshingly logical grounds that so little money, relatively speaking, would do nothing to solve the hotel's financial problems anyway; and we were each sent off with a present from the hotel gift shop. It wasn't, perhaps, surprising that my eyes were shut by all this generosity and kindness to the occasional vulgarities of the Shah Abbas's décor.

'Cela était autrefois ainsi, mais nous avons changé tout cela'; now there was a man with several days' growth of beard and an unclean shirt behind the counter, who took no notice of us whatever for some time, although there was no one else around. Eventually, after some hard work, I managed to attract his attention.

'What do you want?'

'My wife and I would like a room, please.'

This unexpected request caused a minor crisis: another man had to be summoned from an inner office to look at us and pass judgement. Heads were shaken and dubious words spoken. The problem was not created, however, by any shortage of accommodation: we discovered later that in this immense hotel only four rooms were occupied while we were there; possibly because everyone else had given up at this first hurdle. For the time being, as a concession, I was allowed to fill in some forms.

'Englisi?' he said, peering at my answer to the question of nationality.

I am, of course, but I am just as proud of the Irish passport which I hold, and on which I do all my travelling to more difficult countries. I was also tired of this trial by inattention.

'That's like my asking you if you're Iraqi,' I replied. 'It says

304

"Irish" there.'

Fortunately everyone else – in Iran, crowds gather inside hotels as readily as outside them – thought this was funny. The remark was still being repeated to latecomers some minutes afterwards.

'From Iceland?' he persisted.

'He thinks Irishmen come from Iceland,' I said, and the crowd liked that, too, though they would probably have been hard put to it to know exactly where Irishmen did come from.

At this point Tira handed over her completed form, together with her British passport. Such confusion as had existed before now seemed like a faint evening breeze by comparison.

'Two rooms,' he declared, after top-level consultations had lasted some time.

I was not keen on this; apart from more personal considerations, the rooms at the Abbasi cost 165 dollars, at the official exchange rate. It was only after another twenty minutes' heavy-duty discussion that the holders of two different nationalities were at last allowed to share a single room, and we were given the key.

'Isfahan,' says a Persian proverb, 'is a paradise full of luxuries; there ought, however, to be no Isfahanis in it.' Nevertheless the unshaven one and I parted on remarkably friendly terms, with the encouragement of the now-ebbing crowd; and a moderately polite porter and a delightfully pleasant old woman showed us to our room, the old woman tussling with me to get hold of my suitcase and carry it for me, while making disapproving noises at the porter to show that he ought to be carrying everything anyway.

The room itself, and the view over the gardens, showed me that if I had exaggerated the beauties of the hotel to Tira beforehand, those beauties nevertheless existed. The room had precisely the degree of faded, seedy glory that some of us spend our lives searching for in a hotel; and indeed it was not one room at all, but five: the bedroom, two dressing-rooms, a bathroom, and another room that had no particular function and contained little in the way of furniture, but added to the general impressive tally. The lavatory was equipped with a seat-cover dispenser, made in Milan (*Il Coprisedile Igienico* – *Premere, Presser,* To Press, *Drücken*) but times were hard, and it proved to be empty when the button was *pressé,* pressed or *gedrückt.*

As for the bedroom itself, it was extremely grand, and furnished in mahogany and red plush. The bed was in a large alcove, separated from the rest of the room by a thin gauze curtain which was to mosquito netting what the Abbasi hotel itself was to places like the Hotel Kowsar – the one with the gigantic painting of the Imam all down one side. Its delicate lacework was decorated with cherubs and birds, and it was held in place by ties of red satin. The bed sagged a good deal, and the sheets, though clean and well-ironed, were carefully darned in places. It was like being the guests of a maharajah with a cash-flow problem.

Our apartment was situated in a corner of the hollow square formed by the hotel building, and we opened the elaborately carved cedarwood doors onto a magnificent balcony overlooking the gardens. Fountains played quietly in the late afternoon sun, tea was being served on the terrace, a gentle version of Beethoven's 'Eroica' Symphony floated from the loudspeakers, and tabby cats were tumbling and chasing each other around under the objective eyes of black-headed, grey-bodied crows which had stationed themselves in the higher branches of the trees. Here, indeed, Thomas Herbert's 'chenaers', his plane trees, had come into their own: tall, leafy, cool, 'which besides shade, serve for use and ornament'. It was, all told, as pleasant a sight as I have seen at any hotel anywhere, and we counted ourselves lucky as we stood on our balcony and observed it.

'Let me,' says Herbert, 'lead you into the Maydan . . . without doubt as spacious, as pleasant, and aromatic a market as any in the universe.' The invitation, that warm August evening, was irresistible. Mahmoudi had gone off to spend the night at his father's house, and we wandered out on foot to find the incomparable monuments of Isfahan. We passed through a park entirely filled with pink and white peony-like flowers the height of a man's thigh; and children playing on the pathways that led through the flowers almost disappeared, their heads showing above the surface at intervals like swimmers in a river as they danced along. It was Thursday evening, the start of the Muslim weekend, and entire families were out enjoying the air. People smiled at us and sometimes called out greetings, and posed politely when we took photographs of them. There was something innocent and other-worldly about it all, as though we had strayed not simply to another place but to another time as well.

There was nothing innocent about Karim, however, and his kingdom was very much of this world: and, in particular, the area immediately in front of the Friday Mosque. We had penetrated the pungent alleyways that led under arches and through delicately carved gateways to the magnificent Maidan-i-Shah, a vast open rectangle surrounded by some of the finest buildings erected anywhere during the seventeenth century. But we had no time to look about us. Karim, a fierce old person with a vast girth and a nasty case of skin cancer gathered us up at the very moment we emerged into the Maidan and began, in bad English, to declaim the beauties of the Friday Mosque.

At least, though, he was not ingratiating.

'Shah Abbas One – very old. Four hundred year old. I very old.' He paused to tap me on the breastbone with a friendly finger. 'You very old.'

He herded us, assuring us that we were the first Western tourists he had seen in seven years, through the cloisters and under marble so sensitively worked that it seemed like so many carpets hanging on the walls about us, and past silver doors shone bright by millions of reverent hands. He moved fast for a man so fat, and stopped only when we reached a marvellous arched area behind the main part of the mosque, with four or five stones glinting black in the pavement. A lamp-lighter was wandering around whistling an intricate little tune which I would have liked to listen to more carefully.

Karim took up position on one of the black stones and commenced the exploration of his vast pockets. A little crowd, composed of the lamp-lighter, two cripples and an unknown number of children, gathered round in silence to watch. Tira started to say something, but was silenced with a sign; the performance was in progress. He produced, at length, a box of matches, holding it up with great care between his thumb and fore-finger as though it had special properties of its own which required respect. Then he tapped it gently with the dark brown nail of his other fore-finger: a slight, clear sound. Instantly seven distinct echoes, each louder than the original, sprang out of the brilliant blue, yellow and white tiled dome thirty feet over our heads. The children danced for joy and the cripples banged their bandaged hands together, but because they were not standing on the black stones there was no answering echo. Karim held the match-box up triumphantly, as though the skill lay in it rather than in the abilities of the very old architect.

'*Yek, doh, seh,*' I counted in Farsi, and a little murmur of admiration went round the group at the talents of this *Englisi* linguist; but a much clearer and sharper version from the dome above overtook the murmur, interlaced with it and overmastered it. The lamp-lighter struck a black stone with his wand, grinning, and the seven echoes from that drove us away from the dome altogether. We wandered off with Karim, past two old women who were praying on carpets the general colour and age of the paving-stones they covered. I asked Karim if he would pose for a photograph in what remained of the light, and he hitched up his immense trousers and zipped up the fly which only he had not realized was gaping wide open. He glanced apologetically at Tira as he did so, but she pretended to examine the smooth yellow marble of the walls. The photographs were taken, money changed hands, and the only Western tourists for seven years passed out of Karim's life.

Outside, the darkening Maidan was filled with the surreal echoes of a mullah's voice, hideously distorted by loudspeakers, as he preached a sermon; he should, perhaps, have taken his position on a black stone. Thomas Herbert had stood here, three hundred and sixty years before, and judged the Maidan by eye:

> It is a thousand paces from North to South, and from East to West above two hundred, resembling our Exchange, or the Place-Royal in Paris, but six times larger. The building is of sun-dried brick, and an uninterrupted building. The inside full of shops, each shop filled with wares of sundry sorts; arched above (in cupolas), terrace-wise framed at top, and with blue plaster pargetted . . .

It was a splendid sight; more splendid now, perhaps, than it had ever been. For much of its history a part of it had been set aside as a polo ground, and the rest had been open and weed-strewn. Now it was planted with ornamental trees in lines, and fountains played among the decorative lamp stands. Everywhere people were settling down for evening picnics. Behind us rose the magnificent bulk of the Friday Mosque; to our right was the smaller but more precise and shapely Sheikh Lotfollah Mosque, built by Shah Abbas I and finished in 1619; Sheikh Lotfollah being a Shi'ite scholar from what is now Lebanon, who became Shah Abbas' favourite theologian and died three years after the completion of the mosque which bears his name.

To our left was another superb structure: the Ali Qapu (or 'Magnificent Gate') Palace, where Shah Abbas entertained his noble visitors, and ambassadors like Sir Anthony Sherley. From the balcony, which faces the Sheikh Lotfollah Mosque across the Maidan, Shah Abbas and his guests could watch firework displays or military parades, or polo matches. Sometimes he would join in the game himself:

> . . . after the banquet was ended, the King requested Sir Anthony to look through the window to behold their sports on

308

horseback. Before the house there was a very fair place to the quantity of some ten acres of ground, made very plain; so the King went down, and when he had taken his horse, the drums and trumpets sounded; there was twelve horsemen in all with the King; so they divided themselves six on the one side, and six on the other, having in their hands long rods of wood, about the bigness of a man's finger, and on the end of the rods a piece of wood nailed on like unto a hammer.

After they were divided and turned face to face, there came one into the middle, and did throw a wooden ball between both the companies, and having goals made at either end of the plain, they began their sport, striking the ball with their rods from one to the other, in the fashion of our football play here in England; and ever when the King had gotten the ball before him, the drums and trumpets would play one alarum, and many times the King would come to Sir Anthony to the window, and ask him how he did like the sport.' (George Manwaring, *A True Discourse Of Sir Anthony Sherley's Travel Into Persia*, c. 1600).

Since Sir Anthony Sherley had a well developed sense of self-protection, we can imagine that he said he liked the sport very much indeed. Shah Abbas I, as well as being a patron of the arts and of religion, and a distinguished polo-player, was also ferocious and easily roused. It may be that Abel Pinçon, another of Sherley's travelling companions, was inventing things when he reported that Shah Abbas maintained a troupe of forty cannibals who followed him everywhere and ate his victims, but victims were certainly not in short supply. He killed people as a matter of justice, he killed them as a warning to others, and sometimes (according to the English travellers) he killed them simply because he was bored.

I, too, had once stood on the balcony of the Ali Qapu Palace looking out across Shah Abbas' polo ground; but the vast expanse had then been filled, not with people competing or enjoying themselves, but with worshippers: perhaps, as the organizers claimed, half a million of them. It was in the week immediately before the Revolution, and devotion was at its height.

'What do you think of this?' the chief religious figure in the city, Ayatollah Khademi, had asked me, in words not unlike those of Shah Abbas on a very different kind of occasion.

'Very impressive,' I replied; 'but is it possible to govern a country by prayer meetings?'

Khademi was too wise a man to allow himself the luxury of being annoyed by what I had said.

'You will see,' he answered.

What I did not see at that point, and what he may already have begun to realize, was that as a moderate figure within the overall religious hierarchy of Iran, his powers were strictly limited in comparison with those of the more extreme elements in the new political system. He did not, as far as I could make out, approve whole-heartedly of Ayatollah Khomeini's ferocity of purpose, and he cannot have approved later of the bloodbath in which so many thousands of the régime's political opponents lost their lives. Khademi was by nature a reconciler, in a system which rewarded extremism and violence of political purpose; and that weakened his position seriously.

Now, in the centre of the Maidan where the faithful had prayed in their hundreds of thousands and the Revolution had seemed decent and responsible and full of hope, and where, three hundred and eighty years before that, Shah Abbas I had galloped and scored his goals (helped, no doubt, by the opposing team as much as by his own) Tira and I wandered among the Thursday night holiday-makers. Women in *chadors* were filling their kettles at taps in the pipe which ran the full circumference of the fountains, and settling down with little gas-stoves to make tea. While we watched, two women spread carpets on the paving stones and set out a vacuum-flask of soup and several glass pots filled with various kinds of food, and lit their small portable stove. Three children, one of them scarcely able to walk, frolicked around them while their husbands, who looked like brothers, strolled up and down, talking and laughing, as they picked their way around the other groups of tea-makers.

Elsewhere, a group of four older and more serious children sat playing 'Monopoly', in what looked like the French version. Little horse-drawn *doroshkehs* decorated with green and red battery lights drove past with couples and entire families in them; for a few *rials* they would take you three times round the Maidan. For a few yards in front of the Ali Qapu Palace the reluctant, elderly ponies were persuaded to trot while the younger passengers squealed with delight.

The atmosphere now was rich with the smell of cooking, and the lights from the shops all round the edges of the Maidan illumined the gardens in the centre. Thomas Herbert had noticed them: 'Not far thence are cooks' shops, where men use to feed the helpful belly, after the busy eye and painful feet have sufficiently laboured.' In the cooks' shops now, much the same

310

kind of food was being prepared for the helpful and noticeably large bellies of the customers. In others, men were beating copper into cooking utensils, and in an upstairs room as we passed half a dozen craftsmen were painting scenes from Persian history and literature onto leather, or else hammering tiny coloured slivers of metal and wood to form the decoration on picture frames.

An eight-year-old carrying a blow-up plastic plane in the shape and colours of an Iran Air 747 came running past us, and tripped over a skateboard which flew up and landed on its underside, which was marked 'Thunderbird'. His wailing followed us across the square, as we came across three army volunteers who had lined up and were looking for someone to take their photograph. We were not perhaps quite what they had in mind, but one of them pulled a cheap camera out of a brown paper bag and held it out to Tira.

She made them sit on a low wall, hoisting up her *hejab* in unIslamic fashion in order to get a good shot of them. They lined up close to one another, and tried to keep a straight face as they posed. One of them quickly put on his cap and adjusted it while she was still focussing, and they glowed with embarrassed martial pride, as though they belonged in a photograph from the time of the First World War: three pals from Kitchener's Army, who would be lucky to survive until 1918. They were just about to leave for the front: the lectures they had received about security were too recent in their ears for them to tell us where they were going. A few months later all three could well have been dead, with only a photograph or two surviving as a witness to the fact that they had once sat together on a warm Isfahan evening, looking for a bit of fun.

It was dark by now, and we walked back to our hotel through another public park. Away from everyone else, in the light of a small oil-fired hurricane lamp, an entire family – grandparents, parents, and four children – had just completed their evening meal, and the father of the children was puffing away at his *qalian* or hubble-bubble. Directly they saw us the man held out the mouthpiece of the *qalian* to me, and his mother offered us a plate of cakes, and all the others called out to us to sit down and join them. We took off our shoes and joined them on their blue and red carpets.

The husband was a motor mechanic, and although they were not rich they were reasonably well off.

'We come out here every Thursday night. It's our main form of entertainment. We live over there' he pointed off into the darkness, vaguely, 'and we like to sit and watch people go past, and sometimes we ask them to join us. We are,' he added, 'very honoured that you should be sitting here with us. It is many years since we saw anyone from *Orupa* – Europe – in our beautiful city.'

That, at any rate, is what I think he said; it is certainly the gist of it. As he talked, and as we made what replies we could, we munched on little green savoury cakes and larger flat ones that were yellowish in colour, and drank tea, which was refreshing and very sweet, from small glasses. The grandmother, wrapped in a patterned grey *chador*, kept smiling and peering forward to see how we were getting on with the cakes, and each time we finished one her pretty little grand-daughter was sent along with the plate to offer us another. And when we were finally allowed to refuse any more, the *qalian* was placed in front of me by one of the children.

'I expect they use the *qalian* a great deal in *Englistan*.' It had been established where in Europe we came from by this stage.

I paused for a moment, not wanting to disappoint him but unable to think of anything in England that was remotely connected with hubble-bubbles, with the single exception of the Caterpillar in *Alice in Wonderland*, whom he obscurely resembled.

'It is,' I said cautiously, 'famous in our literature.'

The answer was approved, and passed on to the grandfather, who was hard of hearing. He, too, leaned forward and smiled in a dignified kind of way, as though passing on greetings from one great *qalian*-smoking nation to another, and gripped his bare brown feet with his hands as he sat cross-legged on the carpet.

I took a deep breath, and the hot water boiled up encouragingly in the vessel, weakening and diffusing the effect of the tobacco as it is intended to do. But I am not a smoker, and the harsh taste of it caught in my throat and made me cough, while the family was divided between amusement and consternation. It required another cup of tea to restore me.

'I think,' said our host politely, 'that the *qalian* is not much used in *Englistan* after all.'

'No,' I agreed, when I could. The grandfather laughed a good deal when it was all explained to him, and the wife, who had appeared only occasionally and preferred to stay outside the circle of light on the other side of the group from us, clucked her concern for my throat and refilled my tea-glass with her own hands.

Not long after that we parted with expressions of great mutual esteem and much hand-shaking, even on Tira's part. And when

312

we were a good eighty or a hundred yards away from them we could still see them waving to us, and for some time after that we were able to make out their hurricane lamp gleaming in the surrounding night, like a friendly cottage on a dark moor.

On a chilly winter's afternoon in February 1979, with the light for which Isfahan is famous beginning to fade fast, the camera crew and I, accompanied by the radio broadcaster Harold Briley, had negotiated the traffic in the Chahar Bagh, and worked our way round the edges of yet another protest demonstration which was gathering. In the quieter streets on the western side of the avenue we heard the sound that showed us we were close to the place we were looking for: the characteristic clanging of an English church bell, which seemed as familiar and friendly to us as it was foreign to Isfahan itself. There are places like St. Luke's Episcopal church in every country on earth where the British have exerted an influence – small Victorian simulacra of the parish churches of England, complete with Decorated or Perpendicular window-tracery, gloomy stained glass, and brass plates on the walls; left where they stood by the receding tide of empire.

An elderly, polite convert opened the blue gates with their Anglican cross for us, and we found ourselves in a garden which, even in winter, was recognisably laid out along neat, English lines. After the uncared-for splendour of the rest of Isfahan, it was like finding oneself in an outer suburb of Manchester. Later, we filmed while a congregation of two dozen people, mostly Iranian, sang 'O God Our Help In Ages Past' in Persian, and a young woman worked away to accompany them on a harmonium imported at great cost from England, perhaps in the 1920s. The church itself was quiet and cool and dark. The stained glass was there, and the brass plates with the double-barrelled names, and an altar with a neat white cloth and some winter flowers in a vase.

The Bishop, himself a Persian, looked on approvingly as the familiar yet indefinably eastern notes of the hymn filled the room, and his English wife and their handsome daughters were prominent in the congregation. It was a pleasant sight. But we had come at a difficult time, all the same. Bishop Dehqani-Tafti was deeply worried by the rise of Islamic fundamentalism in Isfahan, knowing that it was likely to be hostile to the presence of Anglican Christians in the city. Under the Shah, religious minorities had been carefully protected, and although the Bishop, like so many others in Iran during the later 70s, had come to disapprove of the Shah's growing autocracy and the power of the secret police, he was anxious now that the imperial protection had been withdrawn. When we interviewed him, he chose his words with almost painful care, anxious not to say anything which might seem like a criticism of the new rulers in the city.

'What I feel,' he volunteered at last, 'is that people want freedom.' Clearly, he meant the freedom of his own small flock to worship as they chose, as well as the wider, political freedom which was being demanded throughout Iran.

Isfahan had never been an easy place for Anglicanism to take root. In the 1880s, when the Church Missionary Society was trying to make headway there, it was too dangerous for Christians to settle in the city itself, and they had instead to live in Julfa, the suburb built for and inhabited by the Armenian Christian community. It was only after the strong, Westernizing, nonsectarian Pahlavi dynasty came to power in the person of Reza Shah that the Anglicans were able to move across the river and establish themselves and their church in Isfahan proper.

But the hostility continued, even though St Luke's and its Bishop – Persia having been constituted a full diocese of the Church of England in 1913 – had imperial protection. There were many converts over the years, even though it is a sin punishable by death for a Muslim to change his religion; and the combination of proselytizing Christianity and the British connexion was enough to give rise to any number of conspiracy theories about the real purpose of St Luke's in the city. Over the years, too, the church spread its activities to other cities, including Shiraz, and established hospitals and schools for the disadvantaged. At St Luke's there was a school for the blind, where Muslim children were educated and trained in various skills. The teachers found that the boys tended to remain Muslims; it was difficult enough being blind, without adding to the handicap by turning Christian. But the girls, who did not usually expect to make their way in the world, often became converts. Wild rumours about the manner in which the conversions were obtained became current in Isfahan; and, wilder still, there were constant accusations that the Bishop and his small flock were in some way British spies. The English Queen had visited the church during her visit to Iran in 1961; the English ambassador had had lunch there; *ergo*, St Luke's was self-evidently a nest of spies.

Having come to know Ayatollah Khademi a little, I believed that all that was required to ensure the safety of St Luke's was to alert him to the Bishop's anxieties, and to act as go-between in setting up a meeting between the two men. Khademi was, I found, sympathetic to the idea: he had little belief, he said, in the rumours about forcible conversion and espionage, and he wanted the Bishop to know that St Luke's was in no danger from the Islamic Revolution. I passed on the message, feeling that something had been achieved, and soon after that we went back to Tehran.

I had misunderstood the nature of the Revolution – of any revolution. When an autocracy is overthrown, two things happen: emotions and ambitions and resentments which have built up over a period of years, of decades even, erupt into the life of the new state and cannot easily be controlled, given the power-vacuum which has been created; and then any number of competing groups and agencies, fuelled by those ambitions and resentments, begin to fill the vacuum. It may be easy enough to identify the topmost leaders of the Revolution, but at the level of daily life any number of self-appointed activists have the scope they need to put their own ideas into practice, on a purely local basis. In Isfahan, I had assumed that because Ayatollah Khademi was the leading religious figure in the city's revolution, he had the power to control the way in which Isfahan was governed. He did not.

In a letter to Ayatollah Khomeini, written from exile in England in September 1980, Bishop Dehqani-Tafti listed the incidents which had followed the Revolution, 'in order', he wrote, 'to show the extent of violence and cruelty against the (Episcopal) church':

19 February 1979: The murder of the Pastor in charge of churches in the Fars Province, in his office in Shiraz.
11 June 1979: Confiscation of the Christian hospital in Isfahan after over a century of service.
12 July 1979: Confiscation of the Christian hospital in Shiraz and intrusion on church property.
12 August 1979: Confiscation of the Christoffel Blind Mission, belonging to the church.
19 August 1979: Raiding the Bishop's House and Diocesan Offices in Isfahan, and the looting and burning of documents and personal effects.
3 October 1979: Illegal confiscation of the farm for the training of the blind in Isfahan, belonging to the church.
8 October 1979: Disregarding the sanctity of the church, and my pointless and humiliating arrest in Isfahan.
26 October 1979: Attacking the Bishop's House in Isfahan, an attempt on my life and the wounding of my wife, in our bedroom.

315

1 May 1980: Savage attack on Miss Jean Waddell, the fifty-eight-year old secretary to the Diocese, and severely wounding her in Tehran.

6 May 1980: The assassination of my only son, twenty-four-year-old Bahram Dehqani-Tafti, on the way back from his college to his mother in Tehran.

5 August 1980: Recalling Miss Jean Waddell from Tehran to Isfahan and her arrest.

9 August 1980: The arrest of Dimitri Bellos, the Diocesan Administrator, in Tehran.

9 August 1980: The expelling of three women in Tehran, who had been responsible for blind work in Isfahan.

10 August 1980: The arrest of Dr and Mrs Coleman in Tehran. (John Coleman was a British medical doctor who had first come to Iran as an Anglican missionary in 1948 with his wife Audrey, and had returned with her in 1977 to run a clinic in Yazd. In October 1979 he had been ordained priest.)

17 August 1980: The arrest of the pastor in charge of St Luke's church in Isfahan.

20 August 1980: The arrest of the pastor in charge of St Andrew's church in Kerman.

It is a shameful list, bringing together the actions of self-appointed thugs and criminals in some cases, and the deliberate policy of the competing organs of the State in others. Under the Islamic Republic, extremism in the defence of religion has a powerful moral validity: and it can be very difficult for moderating influences to make themselves felt. Bishop Dehqani-Tafti never received a reply to his letter. In 1981 the Archbishop of Canterbury's special envoy, Mr Terry Waite, achieved his first successes in the field of releasing political hostages by flying to Tehran and negotiating the freedom of Miss Waddell, the Colemans, and others.

But the one injustice on the Bishop's list which could not be negotiated away was the murder of his son in May 1980. Bahram Dehqani-Tafti was a young man of great promise, who had charmed and impressed all the Western journalists who met him during the period of the Revolution and, later, the seizure of the American hostages. Open, quick-minded and amusing, he had studied at George Washington University and at Oxford. Photographs of him were everywhere in the Bishop's House when we visited it in February 1979, and his father contrived to bring his name into our discussion continually: My son Bahram met him at Oxford. . . . My son Bahram has always maintained. . . . My son

Bahram tells me we must expect more difficulties. . . . The Bishop's English wife Margaret, meanwhile, would sit and listen with pride as the name was dropped into the conversation time and again.

The Bishop had been forced to leave Iran after the incident in which gunmen had broken into their bedroom and fired four bullets at him, narrowly missing him. Margaret Dehqani-Tafti, a brave and resourceful woman, had chased the would-be murderers off, and had been wounded in the hand. She had stayed behind in Iran, and was nursing Jean Waddell after the vicious attack on her several days before when the phone-call came to tell her that her son had been murdered. He had been driving to meet her when he was forced to stop by another car. Two men from it made him move over into the passenger's seat and drove him to a quiet place near Evin Prison. They stopped, and there was a pause during which they talked to him. Then one of them fired several shots into his head.

It was a difficult business to get the necessary permissions to take Bahram's body from Tehran to Isfahan, where his parents wanted him to be buried,and Margaret Dehqani-Tafti had to do it all as best she could, alone. It was five days before the funeral took place. St Luke's, with its red and blue stained glass and its freshly ironed altar-cloth, was packed with people: Muslims as well as Christians. They sang the familiar hymns in Persian, including 'O God, Our Help In Ages Past', to the accompaniment of the harmonium. No one had ever seen the church so full of flowers.

When I returned to Isfahan, Tira and I tried to visit St Luke's. It no longer seemed to be marked on the post-Revolutionary maps of the city, and this time there was no bell to guide me. I recognized the place by the blue gates with their cross, and by the angry flurry of slogans on the walls: 'Death to the nest of spies' being, inevitably, one of them. I pressed the bell, and a man in uniform appeared: the Revolutionary Guards had taken over a part of the compound.

Through the open door I could see what had happened to the place. The garden, which had once been so well cared for, was rough and overgrown, and leaves from the autumns of more than one year lay thick on the pathways. I could see the church building, and the bell, but otherwise everything was quiet.

And yet St Luke's has survived. Every Friday, as before the Revolution, the bell rings, and thirty or forty people assemble for the service. Nowadays, virtually all of them are Iranians. Even during 1980 and 1981, when Bahram was murdered and the

317

leading figures of the diocese were in prison, the church never quite closed down. But the faithful – and in such circumstances the word assumes its fullest meaning – had a difficult and sometimes frightening time in getting past the Revolutionary Guards, and often there were no services as such, merely readings from the Bible. The various families who attended took it in turns to bring food, and the worshippers would sit round a table in the Bishop's House afterwards and eat their supper, taking comfort and pleasure in each other's company.

Gradually, the darkest days lightened. The prisoners were released, and the sense of danger eased a little, though it has by no means gone away altogether. Nowadays the Revolutionary Guards in the rest of the compound are not too difficult, even if they occasionally search the church and the Bishop's House on various pretexts. There is even a new Bishop, consecrated on 11 June 1986, in the presence of four other bishops, one from Pakistan and three from Australia; the fact that they were given visas to enter Iran was the most hopeful sign yet that the régime's attitude was gradually changing. The new wearer of the amethyst ring had been in the church when I had visited it in 1979: a dark, small, peaceful, self-assured man of Jewish ancestry. If anyone had the right, given Bishop Dehqani-Tafti's experiences, to adopt the formula of *nolo episcopari* and reject the offer of elevation, it was he. Instead, he accepted it. The new Bishop is not allowed to leave Iran, but he can at least travel around it, to Kerman where an Anglican clergyman still officiates at the church, and to Tehran, where there is a service most Sundays.

As for the Islamic authorities, they appear to have accepted that the Church has been badly treated, but there is no sign that there will be any compensation for the wrongful arrest of its members, nor for the illegal confiscation of its land and buildings. Different factions within the régime react to St Luke's in different ways: some are sympathetic, some suspicious. No one, however, accuses it of being a nest of spies any longer. If Ayatollah Khademi's powers within the administration of Isfahan had been greater, much of this would probably not have happened; but the history of Isfahan since the Revolution, like that of Iran itself, has been one of rival political groups who have mostly found that extremism succeeds better than moderation. Khademi himself died before the issue of St Luke's had been settled; but long before he died, his voice was disregarded by the ultras.

'The site of Jelphey resembles Pera, which is opposite to Constantinople, or as Southwark is to London, the river Zindarout interposing.' Thomas Herbert, always keen to present things in a way which his readers could readily understand, was straining the comparison a little in this case. Julfa does indeeed lie on the southern bank of the Zayandeh Rud – *rud* meaning river – from Isfahan itself, just as Southwark lies across the Thames from the City of London; but even in 1600 there can have been few other points of similarity.

Shah Abbas I, in creating Isfahan in his own image, needed workmen with the skills to carry out the intricate work that his taste demanded; and although there were many Persians who possessed such skills, he brought in several thousand Christians from Armenia to build the great monuments of Isfahan for him. It may have suited him to have created a community of intelligent, able foreigners on the outskirts of his capital city who were completely dependent on his good will and protection. It is as easy, and sometimes as unenlightening, to make historical comparisons as Thomas Herbert found it to make his topographical ones; but it is hard not to see something of Shah Abbas I, the modernizer and protector of unpopular religious minorities, in Shah Mohammed Reza.

I visited Julfa in 1979, the day after I had said my farewells to Bishop Dehqani-Tafti. The Armenian population, too, was nervous about the possible consequences of the Shah's overthrow; though with less reason than the Anglicans. Although they were always treated with suspicion, and occasionally with outright hostility, the Armenians were accepted even by fundamentalist Muslims as 'People of The Book', whose religion was specifically mentioned with favour in the Holy Koran; and because their particular brand of Christianity was closely associated with their nationality as Armenians, there were few if any converts to it from Islam. The Armenians posed no challenges, therefore, and there were no links with foreign powers, of the kind that made the Anglicans suspect in the eyes of the conspiracy-minded.

There was, however, a very definite anxiety in Julfa at the time of the Revolution. It took a long time for us to establish our *bona fides*, and even longer to get permission to film in the streets of the area. Eventually the Armenian Bishop arrived: a resplendent figure in purple and black, with a magnificent silver cross on his chest. Dr Babian was not yet forty, he was charming and hospitable, and he took the time to show us the marvellous treasures of the Vank Church, which was his cathedral; but he was even less

319

willing to commit himself for television than Bishop Dehqani-Tafti had been. He would consent to being filmed walking with me – but there would be no interview.

As he pointed out the extraordinarily powerful wall-paintings inside the cathedral to us, explaining their significance, his unwillingness to take risks became a little easier to understand. The paintings, which dated from the completion of the Vank in 1664, were a record of the sufferings of the Armenian martyrs for their religion: men and women with superbly naïve expressions of quizzical unconcern meeting death in appalling ways, each of which was recorded with meticulous care. Armenians have survived their own diaspora by keeping the faith, and by keeping quiet at the same time; very sensibly, Bishop Babian was not anxious to add himself or any of his flock to the list of martyrs.

When Tira and I visited Isfahan seven years later, we crossed the Zayandeh on foot by one of the most beautiful bridges on earth, the Khajou, whose twenty-three elegant arches with their upper galleries for pedestrians were built by Shah Abbas II in 1650. It was Friday, and the bridge was full of people picnicking and playing and washing their carpets in the waters of the river: as delightful a sight as one could imagine, and a world away from the cruelties practised against Armenians or Anglicans. On the southern bank of the river we met up with Mahmoudi, who drove us to Julfa.

The domes and towers were visible from some distance away, though other, less attractive suburbs have encroached on Julfa and made it indistinguishable from the rest of southern Isfahan. Once, however, we had turned into the narrow side-streets the character of the place began to assert itself. Immediately, too, we found that the Armenians still had their martyrs, whose pictures were posted up on every wall of the suburb: but they were martyrs of a different kind from the ones Bishop Babian had described to me, seven years earlier. These were Armenian war dead from the conflict with Iraq, and photographs of them appeared on posters of precisely the same kind as we had seen on the walls of Tehran and of Isfahan proper; with the exception that the name and description of the dead man, and the details of the particular operation he had died in, would appear in the delicate Armenian script rather than the Arabic one.

We had made no appointments, believing that it was better not to run the risk of compromising anyone. Instead, Mahmoudi drove us through the narrow streets of Julfa, between the high mud-brick walls, with no clear destination in mind. Although he had grown up in Isfahan, and a growing number of Muslims had settled in Julfa over the years, it was the first time Mahmoudi had entered the place and he knew as little about it as we did. Nowadays there are only about five thousand Armenians in Julfa and the streets were empty for the most part, but the few people we saw upheld the continuing validity of Thomas Herbert's observation: 'The Jelphelyns are habited like the Persians, but differ in aspect, most of these and the Georgians having brighter hair and greyer eyes.'

Having no clear destination, we stopped outside what looked like the door of a church, set in an otherwise blank wall. The handle turned, and the heavy door swung open: but instead of being the entrance to a one particular building it proved to open onto an entire compound, in the middle of which stood a small white-washed church, like the chapel in a Cambridge college. The bright sunlight shafted down onto the polished paving-stones, and the white buildings were dazzling after the shadow of the streets outside.

An old man with one eye – whether greyer than that of most Persians I found it impossible to judge – shuffled out of a room on the edge of the courtyard with a bowl of uncooked vegetables in his hands. The midday meal was on the point of preparation. I negotiated with him about entering the church, and he disappeared inside. Having exchanged the vegetables for an enormous iron key with wards that shone as bright as silver, he walked over the grave-stones that paved the entrance to the church, grey slabs with writing and the outline of figures on them set in an ogee frame that gave them a faint look of the English Middle Ages, with none of the embarrassment I felt about treading on the bones of his ancestors. He unlocked the door for us.

Inside, it was as dark and cool as a cave, and the smell of incense and old wood was overpowering. Silver and brass glimmered in the faint light from the doorway, and then the old man, after fiddling around behind a curtain, turned on all the lights in the place. The effect was extraordinary: the magnificence sprang out at us and captured our senses with reds and golds and greens and the shock of so much decorated space. Even Mahmoudi, the reticent Muslim, muttered some comment, and the old man laughed.

The altar was tiered, with the front part of it covered with an embroidered scarlet cloth and the stages above it cluttered with gold candlesticks and icons, some of which were old when the church was built in the seventeenth century. Every inch of the walls was painted, in a style that was more southern European than oriental. Saints I had never heard of clustered at tables or appeared at the judgement of infidels. Tortures were performed, the blessed were received by angels, and God the Father presided in glory. An anatomically meticulous skeleton in a russet cloak invited kings and emperors to pass along to final Judgment, as the worthies of the time looked on in seventeenth-century dress.

Anxious to take it all in, I was checked by white ribbons tied to the pews, which closed off the aisle.

'Can I get past?' I asked the old man.

He grinned, in a way that fitted him entirely to take his place in the wall-paintings.

'You can do anything if you pay,' he said.

17

Surviving the Revolution

Nevertheless there remain three attributes of the
Persian character which lead me to think that the
people are not yet, as has been asserted, wholly
'played out' . . . There are their irrepressible vitality;
an imitativeness long notorious in the East, and
capable of honorable utilisation; and, in spite of occasional testimony to the contrary, a healthy freedom
from deep-seated prejudice or bigotry. History
suggests that the Persians will insist upon surviving
themselves . . .

George Nathaniel Curzon, *Persia And The Persian
Question*, 1892

WE WERE SITTING in an inevitable traffic jam in the centre of
Tehran. Young boys were working the lines of cars, selling
Marlboro cigarettes, newspapers, and chocolate. It was very hot
and the air was poisonous with exhaust fumes. The line to our
right moved a little, and a battered Hiace pick-up slid into place
beside us. In it was an elderly man, round-faced and with heavy
glasses. He was wearing a dark grey suit despite the heat, but no
tie. His hands shook a little as they rested on the steering-wheel.

There was a sudden noise of recognition from the driving-seat
beside me: a well-to-do North Tehran friend of ours, who was
showing us around some of the places he wanted us to see and
prided himself on knowing everyone who was worth knowing in
the city, had spotted someone who fell into that category. It
seemed unlikely that he would want to know anyone in a Hiace
pick-up, but he did.

'That is one of the biggest dairy farmers in Iran,' he said. 'Once
he had sixty thousand head of cattle.'

'Once?'

'They got taken off him. Now he has to drive around in that.' Our friend was a Mercedes man himself, and found it hard to contemplate driving anything less.

The cattle baron had been caught trying to send money out of the country. It hadn't been some vulgar currency deal: his daughter, who had decided to get out of Iran after the Revolution and was living in Los Angeles, had needed urgent and expensive medical treatment, and he had sent her $50,000 to cover the cost. There was no possibility of sending the money legally, so he had smuggled it out and been caught. It cost him several weeks in prison – hence, perhaps, the shaking hands – and a fine of fifty million *rials*. The episode almost broke him. The cattle had to be sold and the land mortgaged, and everything that was easily saleable went. He might not have been allowed to leave prison otherwise.

'What does he do now?'

'He's still got a few cattle, maybe a couple of dozen. He's got a house around Tehran somewhere, and a little place out in the country.'

The Hiace pick-up moved further ahead of us, and all I could see of the former cattle baron now was his left elbow, sticking through the open window of his cab, together with the arm of a dusty blue suit that must have cost something when it was made for him.

'So what'll happen to him?'

'Oh, nothing now. They leave him alone. There's no reason to do anything else.'

'Does he want to get out?'

'That's the crazy thing – he wants to stay here. He says it's his country and he's not moving. What can you do?' Our friend was in a different position: he wanted to get out, but business happened to be booming at present.

There was a pause. Then, 'He'll be all right, you know. He's got his family and all his connexions still. He'll survive.'

Surviving is a great Iranian tradition. When the Shah, in 1971, celebrated 2,500 years of the founding of the Persian Empire with his ceremony at Persepolis, he was paying homage to his countrymen's extraordinary ability to survive. For more than two and a half millennia, Iran has governed itself within what are still, roughly, the same borders. The Chinese and the Egyptians can make a similar boast, but precious few others. Iran has absorbed changes and conversions and invasions, and has still remained the same. The Shah tried to circumvent the one great historical alteration in his country's status, the Arab invasion and the conversion to Islam, by returning to the earlier political tradition of the Persian Empire. He introduced the imperial calendar which dated back to Cyrus the Great, and followed his father in creating a kind of imperial grandeur which would wipe out the memory of the weakness and frequent humiliations of the late nineteenth and early twentieth centuries – and of the Pahlavis' own short pedigree. Under the Shah it became fashionable to give children names which harked back to the days of the Medes and Persians: Dariush, Cyrus, Jamshid, Shahpour.

None of it lasted. The calendar was dropped in the vain hope of appeasing the angry Muslim clergy. The imperial grandeur was wiped out in a few days of revolution. Children are once again called by plain Arab, Muslim names: Ali, Mohammed, Ahmad. The pendulum had been wrenched too far in one direction, and it swung back with a vengeance. Excesses of all kinds took place: in the early months after the Revolution a group set out from Shiraz with bulldozers to knock down the ruins of Persepolis because of its links with the Shah; fortunately the arguments of conservationists and the sheer difficulty of the task dissuaded them. Another group of zealots headed for the Sassanian ruins at Bishapur to destroy the large rock reliefs there, which were carved in about 250 BC by Roman prisoners; but the reliefs were saved by the quick thinking of a guard, who announced to the crowd that one of the figures who appeared in them was of the man who married the daughter of Hosayn, the Prophet's grandson. Throughout Iran there was vindictiveness and cruelty and a blind implementation of the new rule-book, as there is after every revolution.

But no new dispensation can keep up the fervour of its early years. The intensity slowly fades, and the old pattern of life starts to re-establish itself again. Eight years after the Revolution, there are clear signs that this is happening in Iran. Khomeini's twelve-point declaration at the end of 1982 that people were to be allowed to lead their lives in private as they wished, without interference, as long as they did not break the criminal law, made the change possible. Gradually what one might call the Persian, as opposed to the Islamic, aspects of Iranian life have survived and are surfacing unobtrusively. The family, which is the traditional bulwark in times of difficulty in Iran, helped to protect people from the pressures of the Islamic state; and the state even recognized this in a roundabout way, by pointedly refraining in almost every case from punishing the families of men who were executed for their alleged crimes under the Shah.

Now, many families which were split up at the time of the

Revolution are beginning to coalesce again. Some exiles are trying to make their peace with the Islamic authorities, or taking the first timid steps towards returning, if only for a visit. Thousands have tried it, and found that no one gave them any trouble. The people who cannot return fall broadly into three categories: those who were closely identified with the Shah's rule, those who would be likely to stand accused of corruption, and those who have been involved in opposition politics.

The great majority of people, of course, have stayed in Iran, and conformed during the eight years of holiness. It is impossible to estimate how many have conformed out of conviction, and how many because the state has compelled them to; as a no doubt dangerously broad generalization, Iranians themselves seem to accept that among working-class people in the city and the countryside – seventy per cent of the population – there is greater piety. It is certainly true that attendances at mosques remain significantly higher than before the Revolution: one estimate has put it at twenty per cent higher. But, the generalization continues, among the middle-class minority the early wave of enthusiasm for religion which followed the Revolution has tended to fade. The evidence for this can only be anecdotal, but the anecdotes all tend in the same direction: eight years on, people pray less often and go to the mosque less often than they did.

As for the Westernized upper middle-class, few in number but always more conspicuous, particularly to a visiting foreigner, they have kept their heads down, and because they are Persians, they have developed alternative strategies for survival. The upper middle-class, deprived of the kind of things they had taken for granted under the Shah, have done what they can to make up for them. Alcohol is perhaps the most obvious example. Drinking is a serious offence for a Muslim in Iran, possession of alcohol is worse, and manufacturing it for general sale is a major crime. All three, nevertheless, take place. It is, of course, easiest to come across it in the tiny European community, since Christians are permitted to drink as long as they do so in private. Christians, whether Western or Armenian, are also allowed to make alcohol for their own use. But Armenians are some of the world's most effective businessmen, and the exemption they enjoy has been turned into a considerable source of profit.

The Armenians of Iran make their vodka from raisins. It is sweet, viscous, slightly coloured, and has an attractively nutty after-taste. Called 'Sultanieh', it is best drunk with orange juice or Coca-Cola. In Iran, where admittedly the choice is not great, it is described as being the best in the world, and there are rumours that it is being manufactured, strictly illegally, for export to the Gulf States and elsewhere. Aside from its quality, it has two other important advantages. The first is price stability. A litre costs a thousand *rials*, which is precisely what it cost in 1980, despite the inflation which has affected every other sector of the economy. The second advantage is the distribution network. It is delivered discreetly and anonymously, usually at night-time. Because the penalties are considerable, it is impossible to find out the scale of the trade, but it certainly seems to cover all of North Tehran and a good deal farther afield as well. Transporting it can be difficult, though a Jewish businessman whose car was searched at a motorway checkpoint explained away the bottle of vodka under his seat by saying he needed it to drink the health of the Imam Khomeini.

'On your way,' the Revolutionary Guards told him, 'and make sure you do it.'

The wines of Shiraz, praised by the poet Hafez, were being overtaken in terms of sales and popularity by those of Azerbaijan before the Revolution, Reza'iyeh (white) and Sardasht (red) having the best reputation. Champagne was also produced in Azerbaijan. It is still possible to find Iranian wine, but nowadays it comes from cellars. The manufacture of wine is apparently carried out on a very small scale, not necessarily by the people who once produced it, but it is easier for the *Komitehs* to keep an eye on the owners of vineyards, and the vines which grow spectacularly well along the road to Hamadan, for instance, are nowadays given over to the growing of grapes for raisins. Some of those raisins are no doubt later turned into 'Sultanieh' vodka in the underground distilleries of Tehran.

The night-clubs, restaurants and bars of Tehran were cleansed of their alcohol by groups of well-organized vigilantes early in the revolution. At the InterContinental there were famous scenes as the Revolutionary Guards, in breaking the large stocks of spirits, became seriously affected by the alcoholic fumes and reacted in a variety of ways. Nowadays no one serves alcohol in any public eating-place in Tehran.

We went with a friend to a quiet restaurant which I remembered from my pre-Revolutionary visits in 1978 as an expensive night-club. It was 1.30 in the afternoon. As soon as we walked through the door we knew that things would be difficult: there was a power-cut, and since it was a place which had begun life as a place for quiet assignations late at night, the windows were small and heavily curtained. Now, as then, the only light came from candles; but the bottles behind the bar, as we passed it, contained nothing stronger than Coca-Cola and non-alcoholic Islamic beer.

There had been a piano in one corner, painted white, when I was there last, and a pianist, perhaps from France, had played quiet little Cole Porter and Charles Trenet tunes, almost to himself. Now the piano was gone too; that kind of music is no longer acceptable, and classical music, which is, would not create the right ambience. The Islamic beer-bottles were, I reflected, a rather good image for the place now: it looked more or less like it had been before, but the taste was wrong. Nevertheless the place was filled with people eating poor quality steaks and fried fish, cooked as best the chef could manage in a power-cut, and talking in much the same discreet way they always had, looking round and lowering their voices when difficult words were spoken.

We did the same thing ourselves, and there were plenty of difficult words in our conversation. The man we were with was an old North Tehran figure, impeccably dressed in the old-fashioned grand manner: suit, silver tie, expensive shoes. He was a big industrialist with contacts in the present government, in the Shah's régime, in the opposition: everyone who was useful to him and could do business was his friend – or at least had been involved in an arrangement with him at some time. He knew everyone's price, and maintained that there were plenty of officials in the Islamic Republic who could be bought; such was his main article of faith. Why had he not left? I asked. Because the pickings in Iran seemed to be so good still, was the answer.

He knew everything, it seemed, about getting goods and money out of the country, and into it. Now that the authorities had discovered that people had been smuggling out $100 bills and 10,000 *rial* notes rolled up in cigarettes, he told us what the new method was, in full anatomical detail. He gave us the black-market price for a pair of good quality blue jeans – 15,000 *rials* – and for a torch battery – 3,500. He advised us to be careful about buying the kind of caviare that was on sale inside Iran (though if we had wanted it he was equally prepared to sell us some); caviare had been considerably restricted, he said, but was now available in large quantities because the United States and West German health authorities had determined that the borax which was used in its packing was carcenogenic, and they had refused to sanction its importation.

'I didn't think borax was used in packing caviare,' I said, less because I had any real knowledge of the subject than because I wanted to test him out.

'Ah,' he said.

He told us of problems in Qom between the different generations of ayatollahs, and of arguments within the different
factions of the Islamic Republican Party. He told us of secret links
with the Americans, though with hindsight he seemed to know
nothing about the visit of Robert McFarlane and Lt. Colonel
Oliver North. He told us about Ayatollah Khomeini's state of
health and his likely life-span. He even told us how, if we were
Iranians, we could finance an expensive holiday to Europe.

'It's perfectly easy,' he said; everything seemed to be perfectly
easy to him. 'All you have to do is buy ten large packs of Kellogg's
Cornflakes and bring them back with you.'

'And that pays for the trip?'

'Sure it does. Look. You can get eighty *rials* to the dollar on the
official rate, right? Multiply that by ten to get the black market
rate: that makes eight hundred to the dollar. How much does a
trip to Paris cost? A thousand dollars? OK. 80,000 *rials*, it's going
to cost you. If you pay in dollars you get a discount, say 60,000
rials. Right. You go to Paris. You have a nice holiday. Last thing
you do before you leave, you go to a supermarket, and pick up
ten packets of cornflakes. Big ones. How much that cost you?'

'A dollar each.'

'A dollar each. Right. You bring them back, you take them in to
any grocery store in North Tehran. They're crying out for things
like that here. Know how much they'll pay you for that?'

The only thing to say was 'no', of course.

'They'll pay you 6,000 *rials* a box, and sell them for more. We've
got people here, they can't live without cornflakes. How many
boxes did we say you bring?'

'Ten,' I said, glad to have kept even that figure in my head.

'OK. Ten times 6,000 *rials* makes how much?'

I let him work it out for himself.

'60,000. Exactly. The cost of your trip to Paris.'

'Does a box of Kellogg's Cornflakes really go for 6,000 *rials* in
North Tehran?'

'Check it out for yourself, next time you're up there. See if it's
true.'

We did; it was.

This was the Surviving Persian: no amount of political or
religious upheaval had shaken his conviction that what counted
in life was mental finesse and fancy footwork. I had assumed that
the entire caste of such people had moved to Knightsbridge and
Central Park East and the Boulevard St Germain, but it was not
true. As a result, North Tehran has retained its place as the

conspiracy theory capital of the world. Nothing is what it seems: in places like the *çi-devant* night-club, the British secret service, pulling the Americans by the nose, is still responsible for most of the things that have occurred in Iran, the West has never forgiven the Shah for raising the price of oil in 1973, and the war with Iraq was both imposed by Western interests and is being continued by them through the help the West gives to Iraq.

'I can accept,' Tira said, 'that Western countries are happy to see the stalemate continuing in the war, but why do you say they're helping Iraq?'

'Because they don't want Iran to win. They want to destroy Iran.'

'But if you speak to the State Department in Washington, or to the British or the French, you'll find that they all believe the Iranians are winning, slowly.'

'We won't be allowed to. You see.'

We tried, while we were in Iran, to compile an exhaustive directory of conspiracy theories and rumours, but found they came too thick and fast for such treatment. Here, however, is a short selection:

-When the war enters its seventh (or eighth) year, the United States and the Soviet Union will invoke a secret treaty which allows them to intervene and stop it.
-Conversely, if it looks as though the Iranians will win, the super-powers will intervene to prevent them.
-A new weapon has been developed by the Iranians, but the super-powers will not allow them to use it.
-A new weapon has been developed by the Iraqis, and has caused immense losses, but the Iranian government is hiding the news from the people.
-Iranian and Iraqi deserters have joined forces to attack both armies.
-The sons of various leading ayatollahs have (a) deserted to the Iraqi side, (b) joined the Royalists, (c) been arrested for drugs offences in the United States.
-There are still American diplomats living and working in Iran.
-There are still Israeli diplomats living and working in Iran.
-The Imam Khomeini is an Indian by birth.
-The Imam Khomeini's father was a British employee of the Anglo-Persian Oil Company named Williamson.
-The Imam Khomeini died soon after the Revolution and has been impersonated by an actor ever since.
-A new crisis is about to break because the actor is dying.

No single one of these stories appears to be true, but the attraction of them is not their accuracy or lack of it, but the fact that they feed the common Iranian desire to feel that there are hidden forces at work in almost every aspect of life. The most typical of these rumours are those which deal with things that are literally hidden. After the Revolution the report went round that the museum near the Tomb of Cyrus at Pasargadae had in fact been transformed secretly into a prison and SAVAK torture centre. A Swedish engineering firm was retained to investigate another rumour: that a tunnel had been constructed between the Shah's palace at Niavaran and Evin prison, several miles away, so that political prisoners could be interrogated by the Shah himself.

All this represents the reverse side of the speed of thought and intelligence of the North Tehrani. It is often incomprehensible to the more plodding European mind, and it can be self-defeating. It is common for Iranians who want visas to go to the West to refuse to make an application in the normal way, which involves a wait of between four or six months, preferring to try some supposed back-door method or dubious personal contact which in practice involves an even longer wait. The Persian has little faith in the due processes of the official system, and prefers the greater interest involved in seeking out his own private, hidden way. The least suggestion that some commodity is likely to be short sends people out in large numbers to buy it up.

In July 1986, when the Iraqis attacked the oil refinery at Isfahan, a near-panic set in immediately the news was announced. People left their homes and their offices in order to queue up at petrol stations, and created a shortage where none, in fact, existed. Normal deliveries were unable to keep up with the demand, and the government, knowing the importance Iranians attached to their cars and their freedom of movement, had to send out extra tankers to supply the petrol stations. Since there was in reality no shortage, the problem eventually went away. This kind of thing can happen in any country; but it happens with greater speed, and greater regularity, in Iran than in most other places.

The Tehran Bazaar is the economic heart of Iran: a great block of shops and businesses at the centre of the city where a third of its commerce is carried on. Every year, as Tehran expands, the Bazaar's share of overall trade is a little diminished, but it remains the most important business centre in Iran. When it

331

closed down, in the months before the Revolution, the Shah's hopes of survival closed down with it: losing the confidence of the Bazaar merchants was the equivalent of a massive flight from the currency.

It is a quintessentially Persian institution, in that the most obvious thing about it, the day-to-day selling of goods across the counter, is the least important of its functions. It is the hidden things about the Bazaar that count: the large-scale deals that are done, the loans that are made, the fact that its merchants are in day-to-day, hour-by-hour contact with suppliers, agents, contacts and customers throughout the whole of Iran and farther afield. It is a stock exchange, a banking system and a commodities market, masquerading as a collection of hucksters' stalls.

We chose a bad day to visit the Bazaar: there had been a series of car bombs in the city during the previous few weeks, but our friend from North Tehran in his expensive Mercedes had a cavalier attitude to the problems of parking. After driving round and round for fifteen minutes, he stopped in front of a police station.

'Have you got a bomb on board, then?' asked a sardonic policeman on duty outside.

'No, of course not.'

'Then you can't park here.'

It took us a long time to find somewhere where we could park, and when we did it was necessary to buy our way in. A man who was sitting in his car in a good parking-place signalled to us through his open window, and our friend paid him the going price: 200 *rials*. Having acted as a kind of human parking-meter, he then moved out and drove away, and we edged into the space, which was only just large enough. We found ourselves near the law courts, where official scribes wrote or typed affidavits for witnesses and petitioners and defendants who could not write themselves. Eight years before, when I had been here, the scribes used ball-point pens or aged type-writers which they balanced on the low, flat wall which surrounded the law courts, standing up to write. There was just room for a type-writer between the edge of the wall and the railings which were set into it. Now, though, the scribes' business seemed to have boomed. No one was writing anything by hand now, and the ancient Coronas had mostly given way to smart little portable Italian and Japanese models – though there was still the same limited amount of wall-space in which to operate.

We walked along the narrow streets, past shops that sold white bridal gowns that were indistinguishable from Western ones, and others that specialized in *chadors* and saris, or that sold an extraordinary range of herbs and spices in great open panniers. Banners proclaimed the success of the Revolution and the return to the pure code of Islam. This entire area constitutes the Bazaar, but the core of it is the vast complex of covered alleyways and passages around the street called Bazar-e-Bozorg: the Great Bazaar. The throat-like entrance is draped with decorative coloured lights, and looks the gateway to an ancient city.

We plunged into the interior, like Jonah disappearing into the whale. A constant, restless flow of *chador*ed women and men in open-necked shirts moved through the Great Bazaar, elbowed aside by old men bent completely double under burdens that they carried like donkeys, or making way for goods being pulled along on heavy trolleys by men who whistled loudly to signal their approach. The place was old and very dusty, and although the ground we walked on seemed ancient and was unpaved, the street had obviously been roofed over at some point during the previous seventy years. The sun's rays cut sharply downwards through the holes in the grimy glass panes above us and shone bright enough to make the hoops of neon light which hung everywhere seem pale and weak.

The Bazaar was laid out in a pattern which could only be guessed at by someone who did not know it. Shops selling women's hosiery, the ugly calf-length stockings for use under a *chador*, gave way to shops with headless, armless, and almost bustless mannequins on which were displayed scarves and belts. Further on in the maze of alleyways were the drapers' shops, and the crowlike black forms of women bent over rolls of material, fingering for thickness and texture. Tira, who needed a proper *chador* for a meeting with an ayatollah in Qom – her blue cloak and tunic would not be considered sufficiently decent there – bought the requisite length of black polyester, about three yards, for 5,000 *rials*, and the shopkeeper's twelve year-old son, a serious boy with spectacles and a crew-cut, wrapped it up neatly for her in a parcel of newspaper.

We crossed an unseen frontier into a different area. Here, the shopkeepers were selling plastic goods: a thousand strings of *tasbih*, worry-beads, in green and yellow and red; or tens of thousands of buttons of different sizes and colours; or key-holders of a hundred different designs. But the cheapness and vulgarity of the goods was beside the point. They were usually only a front, an excuse to trade in the Bazaar; the real money here is made in dealing and factoring. The vast majority of merchants in the Bazaar come from Bazaari families, and it is extremely difficult to break into. A stall, if one becomes available, requires a payment of anything up to five million *rials* as entrance money; but it is the telephone that makes it a genuinely going concern, and that costs seven or eight million. With a telephone, you can arrange commodity deals or organize finance; and since the Islamic system prohibits the charging of interest, and the obtaining of loans through the official banking system is difficult and very restricted, the Bazaaris have quietly stepped in to fill the gap which the government has tried to close. There is good business to be done.

The man who sold the key-holders was in his fifties, with an unshaven chin and a high, domed forehead from which his hair was brushed back like Mao Tse-Tung. By the light of a paraffin lamp he showed us his latest and most attractive line: key-holders with little portraits of leading ayatollahs on them. It was irresistible, and Tira and I bought a dozen Montazeris and Rafsanjanis; at which our friend, a great teller of political jokes, pointed to the skimpy moustache and almost smooth chin of Rafsanjani, and told us the one about the new Iraqi peace terms – they would agree to end the war when Rafsanjani grew a beard, and Montazeri found out the name of the United Nations Secretary-General.

We moved on, to find a tailor's shop in a dingy back alley like a courtyard from the London of Dickens, with a little black and yellow bird sitting in a cage and singing in the gloom. The dark shop with its low ceiling was, however, enlivened by three things: the jollity of the workers, male and female, the beauty of one of the girls who were turning out dresses by the dozen every day, and the antics of an ancient messenger who somehow knew several words of German and insisted on repeating them over and over again:

'Gute Morgen, wie geht es Ihnen, sehr gut danke, auf Wiedersehen.' The girls laughed again delightedly as he repeated the mangled phrases and danced a little dance for us, his yellow teeth flashing in a smile. We were given tea, and all business was set aside so that Tira's *chador* could be measured and cut and pinned and hemmed, all in about twenty minutes; and, because this was Persia, the owner refused to take any money for the operation; though he agreed, if ever he was in London, to come and see Tira wearing it. He pretended, to the renewed amusement of the girls (none of whom wore *hejab* in the privacy of the workshop) to be amazed at the news that Western women went around unveiled.

We penetrated after that to the more expensive part of the Bazaar, where gold chains hung in hundreds in the windows of the shops, and where the burdens that the old men carried on their backs, almost as big as themselves, were carpets. Our friend, who had already introduced us to several of the merchants of cheaper goods, seemed to know everyone here as well. A man who was lounging against a pillar and smoking an Iranian cigarette spun the butt away when he saw us, and led us up a flight of steps and along a rickety balcony which overhung the alleyway beneath.

It was a young and rather well-dressed man who met us, and sat us down in the fibrous atmosphere of his shop, and offered us tea and cold drinks and pistachio nuts. After the heat and effort of the morning it was very pleasant. He talked about his business, while at the same time unrolling carpet after carpet to show us, ignoring my protests that we were not interested in buying.

'Just to see,' he said, in the manner of the experienced salesman. Almost all of them were modern, with thick knotting and colours that looked as though they would not last long. Sometimes he half-admitted as much, though the colours were manufactured in the traditional way.

'The reds are from pomegranates, the dark blues are from aubergines, and the yellows they get from saffron. And these reds,' he said obscurely, pointing to one of his older carpets, 'are made from boiling a tree.'

In the years immediately after the Revolution it was impossible to take carpets out of Iran, partly because so many people were taking their money out in that form. But as the war continued and became more and more expensive, and the number of people getting out of Iran dwindled, if only because most of those who wanted to leave had already done so, the government began encouraging the carpet-dealers (though not individual travellers) to export again.

But it is hard to find carpets of good quality in Iran nowadays. Many dealers – I forebore to ask him if he were one of them – treated newly made ones with chemicals, in order to make them look older. For some years the best Persian carpets have been in the shops of Iranian dealers in London, Hamburg and New York. This particular dealer spent several months every year with the tribesmen of the Turkoman country and the Mashad region, buying up the things they made. The European market was particularly good now, he said, but he claimed that the government took five hundred out of every thousand dollars' worth of carpets he sold. Perhaps it did; but sales were holding up and he and his family (his father owned the business) were doing well. He wasn't complaining; or at least he wasn't complaining very

335

much.

Our friend and guide seemed dissatisfied with the carpet-maker, and took us to another merchant, a middle-aged man this time, whose mood suited more with his own.

'This is not a happy country now. No one is happy.' He sat with us in the back of his shop surrounded by valuable objects. There was more tea, and he put the sugar on the front of his tongue, and sucked the tea through it noisily.

'When we had the Revolution we thought something good was going to come. But then we had everything; we didn't have to queue for food or get ration cards. Now look at what's happened. Here in the Bazaar we thought that Islam meant we wouldn't drink. Well, of course, I like alcohol, to be honest, but I accepted that we would have to give it up. And now in the newspaper you read that in Baluchistan they're growing 1,500 kilos of heroin. In an Islamic country! If we had known that this would be what the Revolution would bring us, we would have killed ourselves rather than accepted it, believe me. You can't call this living. We're just waiting for something else to happen now.'

Discontent is an habitual state of mind in Iran. People were discontented with the enormous price rises under the Shah, and the huge growth in corruption; now they are discontented with the shortages and the lack of money. The sharpness of the pendulum's swing brings its own problems. But whatever may happen later, it is safe to say that in 1986 and 1987 there is no sense of a pre-revolutionary build-up, as there was in the last year of the Shah's reign: no powerful cause which can bring people out onto the streets in large numbers and make them forget their personal safety in the desire to force the government to change, through violence if necessary.

No doubt people are scared of standing up and demanding change, especially political change; that kind of behaviour would earn them arrest, imprisonment, ill-treatment. But conditions are not bad enough to goad them into doing that. While the war continues it is impossible to say that things are getting any better, but they are not getting seriously worse. Rationing is introduced for some things, and taken off others; petrol, for example. Iran has reached a plateau – deadening, boring, debilitating, especially for a nation which likes to be entertained and amused. 'You can't call this living.'

In the Bazaar, though, things are not bad; even the gloomy merchant supping tea at the back of his shop accepted that. There are profits to be made, and when the *Komiteh* or the Bazaar's own Islamic Society comes round, collecting money for the war, everybody pays up. The money is there, and at least they are no longer insisting that everyone has to go and fight. The merchant said that Iran wasn't a happy country, and that is certainly right; but it is not as bad as it was during the terror of 1981-3. It is relative improvement, not absolute perfection, that governments have to provide if they are to remain in power.

We emerged at last from the noise and dust and confinement of the covered alleyways, and out into one of the squares which occur at intervals throughout the Bazaar. It was a considerable relief to be out in the open air again, and a fountain splashed pleasantly among the bushes in the centre of the square. We had found our way to the ironmongers' and hardware section of the Bazaar. All around us there were stalls selling electric samovars and tools and keys. There were curious machines, too, which I had never seen before. Our guide explained that they were for putting caps onto bottles. What sort of bottles, Tira asked.

'Think about it. You can't make your own gassy soft drinks in this country; you can't get the ingredients. The only gassy drink you can make at home is beer. No one says so, naturally.'

We examined the ingenious kit which enabled people to offend against the laws of Islam, and then noticed other curious objects, hanging in large bunches nearby. They had short wooden handles, to which were attached a dozen or so lengths of chain, each about a foot long. They looked like immensely, absurdly cumbersome metal fly-whisks, and it was difficult to imagine what they could be for.

'Flails. To beat yourself with, on Ashura. It's coming up soon, and a lot of people do it to make themselves feel better. Look, they're buying them now.'

Indeed they were. Several would-be customers were picking them up and feeling the weight of them, and giving them an experimental shake or two to see how they handled. On Ashura, the tenth day of the month of Muharram, the ceremony of remembrance takes place for the death of Hosayn at the battle of Kerbala. It represents the extreme of religious enthusiasm each year, and has been a part of Persian life for twelve hundred years. 'On that day,' says Edward Granville Browne, who was in Persia on Ashura in 1888, 'bands of men...parade the streets in white garments, which are soon dyed with gore; for each man carries a knife or sword, and, as their excitement increases with cries of '*Ya Hasan! Ya Huseyn!*' and beating of breasts, they inflict deep gashes on their heads till the blood pours forth and streams over their faces and apparel. It is an impressive sight, though somewhat suggestive of Baal-worship.' In 1986, as in 1888 and every other year the crowds of penitents filled the streets, the chains beat down on shoulders, the blood flowed from backs and heads. The Shi'ite clergy have mixed feelings about the parades, approving the element of religious enthusiasm that goes into them, but being mildly suspicious about the sense of excitement and personal exhibitionism which is undoubtedly involved.

You could do it with style, or you could do it cheaply. The shop-keeper told us that the well-made ones with carved handles and brass chain-links cost 5,500 *rials.*

'And these?' I pointed to a utilitarian model, with ordinary steel links and an unadorned handle.

'Four hundred *rials.*'

They were heavy – the chains alone weighed two pounds – but would not themselves do much damage other than bruising: the very thickness of the chains would spread and weaken the effect of the blow. The real enthusiasts prise open some of the links and turn them into hooks, to catch in the flesh and draw blood. It was also possible, at the same stores, to buy little v-shaped pieces of wood to hold against your head when you strike yourself with a sword in the Ashura parades; the idea being that it would catch the blade and stop any really serious damage to the head, while almost certainly permitting the kind of cuts which provide the approved effect: blood pouring down the face in large, impressive quantities.

'Do you expect to sell many of these things this year?' I asked, pointing to the strangely workaday chain flails.

'Not as many as last year,' said the shop-keeper. 'Nowadays, we sell fewer and fewer each year. 1983 was the last really good year.' He said it with a kind of professional mournfulness.

'Do you go in for this kind of thing yourself?'

He laughed. 'What do you think I am? Crazy?'

18

Leaving

Thus ended a journey to which, though fraught with
fatigues and discomforts, and not wholly free from
occasional vexations, I look back with almost unmixed
satisfaction. For such fatigues and discomforts (and
they were far fewer than might reasonably have been
expected) I was amply compensated by an enlarged
knowledge and experience, and a rich store of pleasant memories, which would have been cheaply pur-
chased even at a higher price.

Edward Granville Browne, *A Year Amongst*
The Persians, 1893

By THE END of the week that followed the Revolution in 1979, the
cameraman and sound recordist I was working with, Bill Handford and David Johnson, were getting very tired. So was I. We
had been travelling, filming, and satelliting our reports under
difficult conditions for up to eighteen hours a day ever since
January 25, when we had first arrived at Neauphle-le-Château.
There had been four nights during which we had not slept at all.
We were no different in that respect from the other people from
our organization who were working alongside us and had been
in Iran for longer than we had, or from all the other journalists;
or, for that matter, from the revolutionaries and gunmen and
diplomats whose activities we were reporting on.

In my case, though, there was a difference: my office did not
really want me to be there at all. I was needed back in London. I
resisted for as long as I could, aided by the fact that the airports of
Iran were closed to incoming flights, so that nobody could be
sent in to replace me. But I knew my office would win eventually.
It always did.

In the end, it was decided that we should film the evacuation
which was being organized by the British embassy of British and
Commonwealth citizens in Iran, and fly out with them, first to
Cyprus and then to England. The evacuation was superbly

organized – the British have always been rather good at retreating in style – and a long line of cars and buses brought the evacuees from assembly points all over Tehran up the Shemiran Road to the embassy compound at Gulhak, next door to the British Institute for Persian Studies.

It made good television pictures: the nervous faces looking out of the windows, the children hugging their toys, the escorts which the revolutionary authorities had provided, with their beards and guns and mismatched uniforms, and the British diplomat whom I had seen three months before trying to close the embassy gates in the face of the crowd that burned the chancery building, directing the line of vehicles from a standing position in the lead jeep, rather along the lines of a tank commander at El Alamein.

The crowd of several hundred refugees filled the gardens of the compound, walking aimlessly about, meeting their friends and exchanging stories. Some of them had had a difficult time; several had been shot at, some had been attacked by crowds, and most of them had been threatened in some way. Others were reluctant to leave, but felt obliged to do so for their families' sakes. Three or four large trucks were parked in the driveway, and everybody's belongings, including ours, were loaded onto them. The diplomats had the problem of negotiating with the revolutionary authorities for permission to bring in RAF Hercules transports to take everyone out. Two were to be allowed in, but four more were turned back while they were in the air. With three million people in the country still on strike, and different parts of the city and the administration in the hands of different groups, the confusion was immense.

We had our problems too. The streets were easy enough to get through in big convoys with outriders provided by the revolutionary government, but harder to penetrate if you were on your own. We had to deliver the material we had been shooting that morning to the television station, which was extremely well guarded now after the wild outbreak of shooting that had taken place there a few nights before. That meant getting in without proper passes, finding the right person to give the film to, making sure he or she knew when it had to be satellited to London, and being back at Gulhak in time to film the first group of evacuees being taken to the airport. We had two hours to do it in.

Somehow, at the expense of a great deal of mental and physical effort, we did it; the most difficult part, predictably, was talking our way past the guards at the television station, and the second most difficult part was talking our way back into the British

340

compound at Gulhak where the orders were similar: to admit nobody on any pretext. We got in at last, paid off our taxi-driver (who was not Mahmoudi) and did some more filming. By now people had had a chance to relax and there was less tension. I had decided that there would be no chance of getting these further pictures satellited before we were due to leave, with the first detachment of evacuees, so we too felt able to relax a little.

I was wandering around on my own, looking for people to talk to, when I came across one of the younger diplomats, a particularly urbane figure even in these circumstances.

'I was hoping to find you,' he said affably. 'Your office in London managed to get a phone-call through about an hour ago. It seems they've sent in a new correspondent and crew in a Lear jet, and your people want you to fly back in it. The pilot's been told to wait at the airport till midday for you, and then he'll have to take off.'

I looked at my watch. 'But it's eleven-twenty now.'

'So it is,' said the affable diplomat. 'Oh well.'

I found my colleagues and told them about it, and together we decided that we would try to make it, even though we had no means of transport, our suitcases and equipment would have to be retrieved from the three trucks loaded down with baggage, and it would normally take a good half-hour to get to the airport in normal conditions. Conditions in Teheran that day, as we knew, were not normal. While we were still talking about it, the diplomat sought me out again, this time a little more urgently.

'If you go, would you be able to take someone out with you?'

'Yes, I suppose so, assuming we can make it. Who is it.'

'I'm afraid I am not at liberty to tell you.'

'Well,' I said, 'I don't think I could just –'

'It's someone who has to be got out for his own safety. I can't tell you any more.'

There were executions every day now of military men and government officials who were accused of working for foreign powers, Britain and the United States especially. I didn't want someone's death on my conscience, no matter who they were. I could also see a glimmer of personal advantage.

'If you give us the ambassador's car and driver to get us to the airport, I'll do it.'

There was some diplomatic consultation, and then the answer was passed down to us: it was a deal. The mysterious evacuee would be sent to the airport by a separate route, and would meet up with us at noon. If he were not there by then, we should leave without him. That was the diplomats' suggestion, not mine: I didn't think we would be at the airport by noon ourselves.

There was a certain amount of pessimism about the whole affair by now among my colleagues, who had had time to take in the size of the odds against our making it. For a start, there was the question of the luggage: we couldn't simply leave it, since there was a good deal of valuable television equipment with it. But the three baggage trucks were piled high with a thousand or more suitcases.

'It's no use,' said one of them. 'We'll never make it now.' It was eleven twenty-four.

By now, though, a kind of fury had come over me, a rage to get out. With Bill Handford's help I launched myself up into the most likely of the baggage-trucks and started lifting out cases to see if I could find ours. There must be a rough order to the placing of the luggage, I reasoned, rather along archaeological principles: the earliest layers must be at the bottom. We had been among the first to hand over our bags; *ergo* they must be on the lowest layer, at the back of the truck. I gave a shout of angry triumph: one of Bill's cases was visible, with cases from three later periods laid down on top of it. I pulled it out, and the rest of our cases proved to be buried alongside it. By the time we were fully re-united with our gear, it was eleven-thirty.

The diplomats had, however, been doing their stuff. The ambassadorial Jaguar had been prepared, and the ambassador's chauffeur was already sitting behind the wheel with the engine gunned up to go. This chauffeur was a formidable figure. His quick thinking had saved Sir Anthony Parsons on at least one occasion when his Rolls (in which the American ambassador William Sullivan was also a passenger) was being chased down the street by a gang of men wielding clubs. The chauffeur headed into the car-park of a bank, and the gates were firmly locked behind them. He was a Pakistani, tall, rangey, and with a fiercely hooked nose. He was, I suppose, in his fifties.

Mildly intimidated by this splendid figure, I said something about needing to hurry. He took no notice, having already received his orders. He drove the Jaguar at speed through the gates and out into the Shemiran Road without pausing, and began one of the most alarming car journeys of my life. There was a good deal of traffic about, but the chauffeur spurned it as dust beneath his heel. When there was no room for us on the wrong side of the road he simply mounted the pavement and drove along that. Shoppers threw themselves in fear out of his path.

This grand vehicle raced through the streets of Tehran like a liner through pleasure-boats. My memory tells me, quite erroneously, that there was a Union Jack fluttering on one of the car wings, but although there was not I came to think of that journey as one of the last imperial acts of the British in Persia. At the time, however, I was merely frightened. We passed through the last of the road-blocks at the airport, and for the first time I felt able to take my eyes off the road ahead and look at my watch. It was two minutes to twelve.

The airport was almost deserted. No scheduled flights had been landing or taking off there for days, and the administration had been purged several times by different groups of armed men. I had been here on two occasions since the Revolution had taken place, a week before, trying to ship our film out of the country, and the man I had dealt with previously had, someone said, been shot. Today the fact that there was no one around was a distinct advantage. It meant that the lone figure standing outside the main terminal building, wearing a peaked hat and looking anxiously at his watch, was almost certainly waiting for us. He saw the Jaguar and waved.

'My name's Martin,' he said, and shook hands with us.

There was no sign of the person whom we had agreed to take with us. I told Captain Martin that there might be another passenger who was travelling independently to the airport. He raised an eyebrow slightly, but asked no questions. We agreed that we would wait until twelve-thirty, if the airport authorities allowed him to keep the Lear jet on the ground that long, and that if the other man had not turned up by then we would leave without him. It was half an hour longer than the arrangement I had made with the British embassy, but I was reluctant to run the risk that he might turn up a few minutes late and find us gone.

We said goodbye to the magnificent figure of the ambassador's chauffeur, and I stood outside the terminal building alone, watching the Jaguar head off a little more slowly, while the others took the gear through the customs hall and loaded it onto the plane. The road was empty as far as the eye could see. The silence remained unbroken.

'It's twenty to one,' said a quiet, tactful voice.

'I know,' I said.

'We're cleared for take-off.'

I stared as hard as I could down the road to Tehran: whoever it was, he wasn't going to come now.

Leaving Iran seven years later was a great deal better planned, but not without its stresses. Our flight was due to leave at 9.40 am but that, we knew, bore little relationship to the time it would leave, and none at all to the time we should arrive at the airport. We had a good many difficult articles with us: cassettes of Iranian television pictures we had bought from the Islamic Republic of Iran Broadcasting Corporation, together with those which the IRIB cameraman we hired had shot for us, plus our own rolls of stills and the sound tapes Tira had recorded for her radio outlets – not to mention the two Ashura flails I'd bought. There seemed no possible chance that we could get all that through the various check-points without at least a little trouble.

Working it all out, we decided to leave by 3.15 a.m. It was too early, as it turned out, but it made us feel happier. To avoid any problems Mahmoudi volunteered to sleep at the British Institute, having driven us back from the countryside outside Tehran at nine o'clock the previous night. He selected a couch in the table-tennis room, surrounded by the shelves that carried Martin Charlesworth's science fiction paperbacks.

Even at that time of night, with the roads virtually empty, it took us ten minutes longer to drive the same route to the airport than it had in 1979 in the ambassador's Jaguar; but Mahmoudi was in no great hurry. For the last time we drove down the steep hill of the Shemiran Road, past the shops where we had bought our supplies of pistachio nuts and our glasses of grape-juice, and the restaurants where we had eaten our *chelo kebabs*, and down towards the centre of the city. It was familiar territory. We debouched onto what had once been Shah Reza Avenue and was now Revolution Avenue, and on towards the buildings of Tehran University.

In the peaceful dark, it was impossible to imagine the streets filled with hundreds of thousands of people, attacking and burning anything that was anti-Islamic or connected with the royal family. We passed the end of Kuche Porofesor Brown, the street which was still named after Edward Granville Browne, and along what had once been Eisenhower Avenue. Ahead of us lay Freedom Arch, built by the Shah as a memorial to the endurance of his own system, and the airport itself.

'Welcome to the scene of the battle between righteousness and wickedness', said a sign outside the terminal building which I had not seen before. Mahmoudi parked his ancient Paykan as close to the entrance as he could and insisted on carrying most of the luggage over for us. I was depressed at the thought of saying goodbye to him, and we scarcely spoke. We established a base camp with our bags at approximately the point where I had met

344

Captain Martin, the pilot who had flown us out seven years previously. Mahmoudi suggested waiting, but Tira and I felt that was unfair on him. We shook hands, and gripped each other's arms, and I handed him a tight and not ungenerous wad of notes as a farewell offering. He placed his hand over his heart, bowed, and walked away, turning every now and then to wave. It did not lower my opinion of him in the slightest that I should have noticed him surreptitiously counting the notes as he reached his car: quite the contrary, indeed.

We had the place almost entirely to ourselves. Only one other small group of four people had been pessimistic enough to come this early. The terminal was closed, and there were a couple of sleepy guards on the door to prevent our entering. Under the Shah, Mehrabad Airport was an appalling place, swarming with noisy, demonstrative, importunate people day and night. Nowadays they dealt with that by stopping anybody except passengers from going in, and even they could enter only at a specific time before their flight. We stood outside in the quiet warmth of the pre-dawn, the crescent moon and a star making the Arabic letter 'n' over the Elburz Mountains. The call to prayer started up from the village of Jey nearby a little after four o'clock, and the queue had grown to about a dozen.

By five o'clock, there were more than a hundred of us, and it was starting to get light. There were sounds of doors being opened, and the queue began to shuffle forwards, with us in the vanguard. I was allowed through, but Tira was told, quite roughly, to go in through the next door, which was for women. It was the start of an experience which reminded us that people who want to travel to the West are not regarded with favour by the authorities. For us, the luggage check was little more than a formality, but for the Iranians who were starting to come through it was a strict and unpleasant business. And whereas it took a woman to check Tira's ticket at a separate entrance from the men, a man, both bored and amused, searched her luggage, riffling through her underwear or anything else he chose. But he wasn't interested: the flails, our various cassettes and books all escaped examination. We gathered our things together, the first people to be allowed through the luggage check, and made it over to the check-in desk by 5.40. The flight was still four hours away, and we seemed to have beaten the system.

It was not to be as easy as that. For a start, we discovered, after making our way through the entire system, past the passport checks and the money counters, that we had omitted to pay our airport tax; we had to go all the way down and start again. The desk where the tax was to be paid turned out to be completely unmarked. I noticed that the man who had been ahead of us in the queue to enter the terminal was still at the customs desk having his bags searched. He must have been there for fifty minutes or more, and his things were lying on the tables and the floor about him while two men were going through every tube and box and pocket and hem that his luggage contained. As for us, we worked our way through the system again, managing to by-pass the passport check, for which there was a queue of thirty or more people. We handed over our receipts for the airport tax and were allowed in to the departure lounge.

The restaurant area had been cleaned up rather well since the previous time I had passed through, and we were able to drink our tea and eat English cake for the last time while sitting at a decent table with a decent table-cloth. The caviare shop was closed but there was a stall which gave away improving literature with titles like *Eternal Life* and *What Is Prayer?*, and even the *Protocols of the Elders of Zion*, reprinted with a violently expressed preface by an agency of the Iranian government.

Once again everything seemed to be going smoothly, and once again there was a hitch. As we presented ourselves for the final security check the immigration official noticed that our passports had not been properly stamped the first time we went through; so we had to go back again. This time the queue was shorter, but the man behind the desk couldn't read the words of the extension which had been written into our original visas. The fact that we had different passports upset him too. He took them away while the queue piled up behind us, and then came back and slammed them down irritably on the desk in front of me. So that was all right.

At first, the security examination went well. The Bartók and Shostakovich, and the books I was carrying were glanced at and found acceptable – since I was leaving the country it is hard to see why they wouldn't be – but the trouble came with the bag of video cassettes from the IRIB which I had with me. They were sealed and stamped and taped up by a senior IRIB official, who had sent a letter with them explaining that everything had been done correctly and that the tapes were my property. The security man read the letter and took it to his superior, who came and looked at me and the cassettes and the letter, and took them to his superior, who did the same things in the same order.

'You cannot take these things out,' he said in excellent English. 'You need permission from the Ministry of Islamic Guidance.'

'But the Ministry of Islamic Guidance told me that all I needed was a letter from the IRIB.'

'You'll have to wait until someone from the Ministry of Islamic Guidance comes.'

'When will that be?'

'Around ten o'clock.'

'But my plane leaves at 9.40.'

There was nothing he could do, he said, and went and did something else in a marked kind of way. I stalked up and down in rage, and made unspecific threats.

Five minutes later, a balding, weasel-faced individual appeared.

'I am from the Ministry of Islamic Guidance,' he announced.

All my troubles seemed to be over. I switched from rage to an explanatory mode.

'Ah, I cannot help you, I'm afraid. You need clearance from the Ministry of Islamic Guidance.'

'But you are from the Ministry of Islamic Guidance.'

'Maybe tomorrow,' he replied obscurely.

More rage. Then the security chief went off, taking my cassettes with him. The man at the check-in point, who has seen me pass four times now, flashed me an apologetic smile.

'Tomorrow,' he murmured.

There was the sound of a quickened tread behind me on the black marble floor. I turned round and saw the senior official's face beaming as he came towards me. He held out the tapes in one hand and with the other he flourished the IRIB letter. Whatever its inadequacies had been before, they were inadequacies no longer. The other glowering faces around me turned friendly, and the security searcher who had originally created the difficulty became positively jovial.

'Paper money, gentleman?' he asked, with fractured politeness. I showed him the dollar and pounds I was carrying.

He laughed, patiently. 'No – paper, money.'

'Oh, you mean the form for changing money.'

There was laughter all around. We were great friends now, all in this together. He searched me, with great emphasis on the lower regions, and I was free to go through.

Tira, however, had been having a far more difficult time because she was a woman. The searchers on the women's side of the barrier were large and brutish, and their actions had had a vindictive quality to them. When the tape recorder she had used for her radio reporting was discovered, the searcher told her she would not be allowed to take it out of the country. This was quite common: the searchers regarded it as their duty to prevent

women from taking valuable items, their personal jewelry especially, out of the country, presumably to prevent their selling
them. The items were not confiscated from them, though, and it
was established practice to ensure that some friend or relation
accompanied you to the airport to take charge of embargoed
articles.

Tira, however, did not conform to the pattern.

'Keep it, then, if you want it,' she said. 'It belongs to an
American company. They can claim for it on insurance. It's too
damned heavy anyway. I make you a present of it.' There was
anger and annoyance then, but Tira stayed aloof from it all, as
though it were merely a dispute between the Islamic Republic of
Iran and the National Broadcasting Corporation of America. Two
other passengers, who had problems of their own with the
searchers and might have been expected to keep quiet for their
own sakes, rallied round to translate and mediate: yet another
example of the Persian habit of doing acts of kindness to
complete strangers, because they are regarded as guests in the
country; and guests are to be treated well, whatever the
circumstances.

This was not, apparently, a philosophy shared by the
searchers, who dismissed Tira roughly and turned their renewed
attentions to the women who had tried to help. The methods of
searching women are usually hostile and sometimes approach a
more brutal level; one girl of 17 told us that on a previous trip to
London she had been obliged to take out her Tampax to prove
that she was not smuggling anything. In Tira's case, though, just
as the curtains of the examination booth were opened to let her
pass, one of the officials came out and handed her the disputed
tape recorder, without saying a word. The bureaucratic problems
of keeping an object as awkward as that had presumably turned
out to be insurmountable.

I had been waiting in the departure lounge for twenty minutes
while this was going on, being kept informed by other women
who were emerging from the examination area of the progress of
the case. In the end, Tira emerged herself, brandishing NBC's
rescued property. It was a splendid moment. I looked around the
departure lounge and quoted D.H. Lawrence to her: 'Look! We
have come through!' The passengers were sitting there in attitudes of relief and relaxation, having gone through the worst part
of the entire trip. Not even the searching on arrival at Tehran is as
unpleasant as the searching on leaving it. The man who had
originally been ahead of us in the queue outside the terminal
building, five hours before, and had had a rough time of it since

then, was still in trouble: his wife had not yet been allowed through, and he was having to cope with a screaming baby. In his open-necked blue shirt, and carrying an umbrella and a leather brief-case, he was kneeling in front of the child as though begging it to stop crying. The method did not seem to be effective.

I went to the desk where our seats were allocated, and asked to travel in the upper cabin of the 747 plane. The Iran Air official was apologetic.

'I'm afraid that isn't possible.'

'But I can see that it's still half-empty.' I pointed to the map of the aircraft which lay in front of him, with stickers representing seat numbers on it.

'It's not that, sir; it's for male passengers only. In case of emergency.' He gave a sheepish little smile, knowing what I was going to say next.

I didn't say it; now that our trip was almost over, there seemed no point.

Late-comers continued to board the plane for a good half-hour after we had settled down in our non-emergency seating. Several of the women and little girls were in tears, having presumably had a rough time of it during the search. But soon they, too, settled down: a holiday lay ahead, and a chance for those who were not particularly enthusiastic Muslims to sample the pleasures of a Western society for a few weeks or months.

Why should they go back, if they find life difficult or repressive there? Because they are Iranians, first and foremost: their families are there, and the habits and customs of Persian life are strong and persistent, and difficult to leave. They can live better there than anywhere else. Secondly, it is hard to settle in the West now; immigration officers in most Western countries want to see clear evidence that would-be refugees do indeed have a well-founded fear of persecution if they return. Thirdly, Iran is not Eastern Europe: it is not particularly difficult to leave the country, unless you are a man of military age and seem to be trying to evade service in the armed forces. Leaving or staying are not, therefore, major decisions on which the future of one's life depends; it is simply a question of whether one can afford to go, given the financial obstacles the authorities place in the way of people who want to travel.

Our plane trundled towards the runway, an hour late in taking off. A sign on the airside of the terminal building, alarming at first to the holder of an Irish passport, read 'IRA Down With USA.' But it did not refer to the Irish Republican Army; the 'n' had fallen off 'Iran'. We rose steeply in the air, and I was able to take a last look at Tehran, already hot and dust-laden below us, and the mountains rising clean and cool behind it. It was impossible, at such a moment, not to speculate on the future of the experiment in holiness which had been going on for eight years there.

Things can change fast in Iran, as the Shah found: he began 1978 in full and undisputed control of the country, and ended it with his authority and his régime in ruins. But there was real anger and an organized opposition to his government long before 1978, and a focus of alternative leadership in Ayatollah Khomeini. As things stand in 1987, those conditions do not exist within Iran. Instead of anger there is a feeling of lassitude. People are waiting for something to happen next; though what it might be, few seem able to agree.

J. M. Balfour wrote in *Recent Happenings in Persia,* in 1921: 'There are apparently three possibilities. That things will continue much as at present, that another revolution will take place, or that a general break-up will occur.'

Not, perhaps, a very startling range of possibilities, but accurate enough. Reza Shah had just led his coup, and proceeded to build a dynasty which lasted until the Revolution of 1979. In other words, things continued 'much as at present'.

Nowadays there is a good deal of speculation about what is likely to happen after Khomeini's death. Once again the possibilities are threefold: things will stay the same, there will be another revolution, or a general break-up will occur.

No one can know, of course: the circumstances of the moment will decide what happens. It is perfectly possible that Khomeini's death will be followed by serious faction fighting, or by an attempted *coup;* though the Islamic Republic has established an almost Soviet system with its *Komitehs* in every suburb, town and village; and it has established, in the Revolutionary Guards, a parallel army which is strong enough to deter any attempts by the regular armed forces at a military coup.

In that case the régime, given strong underpinning, will survive under one of the present clerical leaders, but will be obliged to change its orientation slowly: beginning with an end to the Gulf War, if that has not yet already taken place, and moving on to a mild liberalization of the system. Almost certainly, the peculiarly virulent hardness of the Khomeini years will go out with him.

But it has to be said that the Islamic Republic, however firmly based it may be, does not have a final, settled feel to it; at least in its present form. Until the Imam dies and the war with Iraq is

350

ended, the main feeling will be of a country watching and waiting, and trying to get on with everyday life in the meantime.

Tira, annoyed by the treatment she had received at the hands of the airport searchers, ignored the presence of the two Revolutionary Guards in seats near us (one was reading a magazine, his lips moving slowly) and went into the lavatories to change out of her tunic and headscarf. Everybody's eyes were on her as she walked back to her seat, bare-armed, made-up, and with her hair free on her shoulders. No one said anything. The Revolutionary Guard stopped reading and watched as she passed, but he picked up his magazine again and forgot about her. We speculated about the reaction of the stern-faced sterwardess in her severe black *hejab:* would she, perhaps, refuse to serve this deviant her lunch? The trolley came towards us and stopped; the plastic tray was placed carefully on Tira's table. We looked carefully at the stewardess: she was wearing eye make-up.

Quietly, slowly, the severity of the Iranian system is relaxing; the level of the first few years after the Revolution has proved too difficult to maintain. Human nature has reasserted itself, and obliged the system to compromise a little.

At Terminal Three at Heathrow, Tira and I, weighed down with the hand-baggage which had cost us so much effort to bring through the airport at Tehran, stood on the travelator that was taking us to the passport control and the baggage hall. In front of us was an attractive woman in her mid-thirties, with a daughter of about twelve, a son of seven and a baby in a push-chair. She took off her black cloak, and folded it away carefully, revealing an expensive silk dress underneath. Then, at last, as a kind of ceremony, she took off her black headscarf.

'*Ouf,*' she said, as though a weight had been lifted off her. In George Nathaniel Curzon's words, history suggests that the Persians will insist upon surviving themselves.

19

Valedictory

> He [Edward Granville Browne] so loved his Persians
> that he forgave everything, and only stayed to praise
> and admire.
>
> Sir E. Dennison Ross, Introduction to *A Year Amongst*
> *The Persians*, 1926 edition

I RETURNED TO Iran for ten brief days in August 1987, when the bulk of this book had already been written. Things had changed in the year I had been away: there was more supervision of foreign journalists by the Ministry of Islamic Guidance, as a result of a fierce campaign by religious hardliners which had been fought out (as political campaigns within the government usually are in Iran) in the pages of the newspapers. More people than before came up to me in streets, hotels and offices to say that things were getting worse and to ask that this fact should be properly reported in the West. The cost of living had risen considerably, and it was more difficult for a middle-class man to pay his family's way without taking on a second job; and so I met school teachers who doubled as taxi drivers at night and during the holidays, and office workers who worked as night porters in other people's office blocks. There was plenty of food in the shops, and prices were pegged by the government, but the strategy seemed unlikely to succeed for long.

The war in the Gulf had been taken to new lengths by the Iraqis, who had resumed the bombing of tankers carrying Iranian oil. Iran for its part was threatening to attack Kuwaiti and other ships which flew, for the sake of convenience, the American flag and were escorted by ships of the United States navy. Iran was once again completely isolated as far as world opinion went, and was engaged in some typically Persian diplomacy to avoid having to agree to a permanent cease-fire in the war with Iraq. There was talk of another major offensive. In other words, nothing had changed radically, but everything had continued a little farther along the same lines.

The leadership of the Islamic Revolution seemed as firmly entrenched as ever, protected from insurrection by the *Komitehs* and from a military coup by the Revolutionary Guards. Even the assumption, generally made in the West, that everything would be thrown into the melting-pot by the death of the Imam Khomeini, seemed less likely inside Iran itself; and since Khomeini's elder brother, also a mullah, lived to the age of 96, not even death was necessarily certain to intervene in Iranian politics in the short run.

To the outside world, Iran under its Islamic Republic seemed a dangerous and uncontrollable place; and the fact that most of the small number of Westerners who remained there liked it despite its difficulties and restrictions was largely unknown. People have a positive desire for horror stories about countries like Iran; but the prosaic truth is that Iran is neither Cambodia in Year Zero nor Uganda under Idi Amin; it is in the grip of an ideology, but in most respects it is run like other countries, and more efficiently and logically than most.

And it remains profoundly Persian. During my visit in 1987 I was driving up a road in North Tehran with two colleagues: Peter Matthews, the cameraman who had filmed my interview with Ayatollah Khomeini at Neauphle-le-Château eight years before, and the sound recordist Roy Benford, who had qualified for the curious title of 'living martyr' after being injured by Iraqi poison gas three years earlier. I noticed a building belonging to the Revolutionary Guards by the side of the road, and asked the driver to stop. (It was not, alas, Mahmoudi, but a less prepossessing and much more timid man who could never work out how to address me, and settled finally on 'Simpson', which had an imperious ring to it.) On the wall of the building was a vivid portrait of Khomeini, and I thought I might persuade the Revolutionary Guards standing outside to allow me to have my photograph taken for the dust-jacket of this book alongside them and the portrait.

Peter Matthews and I climbed out and went to talk to them. They were pleasant, but reluctant to agree on the grounds that the paint on the portrait was starting to peel, and it might seem disrespectful. While I was arguing about that someone broke in to say that we would anyway have to get the permission of the commanding officer. After a pause he came out: a man of about thirty with a gentle, smiling face. He listened for a while to my request.

'I am afraid it would not really be possible. I am sorry.'

'But if it's a question of covering up the peeling paint . . .'

'It's not that, it's something else. I can give you a list of other Revolutionary Guards buildings where you can have your photograph taken if you want, but not here.'

'Why not?'

He was embarrassed. 'Because this is a special place.'

'Special?'

'A kind of prison.'

'What kind of prison?'

'A prison where we . . . we ask people questions.'

'You mean it's an interrogation centre?'

'Something like that, yes. I am very sorry not to be able to help you. If there is anything else I can do. . . .' He scribbled down an address and gave it to me. 'You understand, it's difficult here.'

I understood; especially since a vanload of new prisoners was brought in, looking frightened, their hands tied. The commanding officer shook hands with us in the most affectionate way: as pleasant and thoughtful a man as ever ordered electrodes to be attached to a suspect. As I walked away, I reflected that there were many things which had remained unchanged since the first Englishmen had visited Persia four centuries before.

During my trip I met a number of old friends, including Mahmoudi, who had been demoted from his place at the Laleh Hotel for some unspecified offence which had brought a complaint from a customer. I found it difficult to think that the complaint could have been justified, and tended to the view that Mahmoudi had been intrigued against. We met in the hotel lobby and exchanged three enthusiastic kisses in the Persian fashion; his three days' stubble gave me beard-rash. Later he presented me with an enormous box of pistachio nuts to take home to Tira.

When I left Iran, it was with a genuine sadness. The authorities in Tehran have a particular dislike for books about the country, and will certainly disapprove of this one. I am much afraid that once it is published I shall not be permitted to return: a kind of exile, in a way. If that happens, I shall miss a good many people, though I will be able to meet some of them outside Iran from time to time. What I shall miss more, if anything, is the country itself – the mud-brick walls and blue domes of the towns and cities, the mountains, the rivers, the deserts, the endless grassy steppes. It would at least be something I would have in common with the two great nineteenth-century travellers in Persia, Edward Granville Browne and George Nathaniel Curzon, neither of whom returned to Persia after the visit on which they based their famous books. Browne taught Persian literature at Cambridge and remained a passionate supporter of Persia; as for Curzon, he

354

went on to become the greatest Foreign Secretary, perhaps, in British history. But he never forgot Persia; and his biographer Harold Nicolson explained the hold which the country kept on him:

He was for ever haunted by those plains of amber, those peaks of amethyst, the dignity of that crumbled magnificence, that silence of two thousand years.

Bibliography

Acheson, Dean, *Present at the Creation: My Years in the State Department*, New York 1969

Afshar, Haleh (Editor), *Iran: A Revolution in Turmoil*, The Macmillan Press Ltd., London 1985.

Bakhash, Shaul, *The Reign of the Ayatollahs*, I.B. Tauris & Co. Ltd., London.

Bernard, Cheryl & Khalilzad, Zalmay, *The Government of God: Iran's Islamic Republic*, Columbia University, New York 1984.

Browne, Edward Granville, *A Year Amongst the Persians*, A & C Black Ltd., London 1893. Republished Century Publishing Co. Ltd., London 1984.

Carter, Jimmy, *Keeping Faith: Memoirs of a President*, Bantam Books, New York 1982.

Cordesman, Anthony H, *The Iran-Iraq War and Western Security 1984-87: Strategic Implications and Policy Options*, Jane's Publishing   Co., Ltd., London 1987.

Curzon, George Nathaniel, *Persia and the Persian Question*, London 1892.

Dehqani-Tafti, Bishop H.B, *The Hard Awakening*, Triangle, London 1981.

Graham, Robert, *Iran: The Illusion of Power*, New York 1979.

Halliday, Fred, *Iran: Dictatorship & Development*, Penguin Books Ltd., London 1979.

Heikal, Mohamed, *The Return of the Ayatollah*, André Deutsch Ltd., London 1981.

Hiro, Dilip, *Iran Under the Ayatollahs*, Routledge & Kegan Paul plc., London 1985.

Hobson, Sarah, *Through Persia in Disguise*, Murray, London 1973.

Hoveyda, Fereydoun, *The Fall of the Shah*, Weidenfeld & Nicolson, London 1980.

Kapuscinski, Ryszard, *Shah of Shahs*, Quartet Books Ltd., London 1985.

Keddie, Nikki R. & Abrahamian, *Iran Between Two Revolutions*, Princeton University Press, 1982.

Keddie, Nikki R. (Editor), *Religion and Politics in Iran*, Yale University Press, 1983.

Kissinger, Henry, *White House Years*, Boston 1979.

Lewis, Bernard, *The Assassins*, Weidenfeld & Nicolson, London 1967.

Morier, James, *The Adventures of Hajji Baba of Ispahan*, George G. Harrap & Co. Ltd., London 1948.

Mottahedeh, Roy, *The Mantle of the Prophet*, Chatto & Windus Ltd., London 1985.

Naipaul, V.S, *Among the Believers: An Islamic Journey*, André Deutsch Ltd., London 1981.

Pahlavi, Mohammad Reza, *Mission for My Country*, Hutchinson & Co. Ltd., London 1961.

Pahlavi, Mohammad Reza, *Answer to History*, Stein and Day, New York 1980.

Parsons, Sir Anthony, *The Pride & The Fall*, Jonathan Cape, London 1984.

Radji, Parviz C, *In the Service of the Peacock Throne*, Hamish Hamilton, London 1983.

Roosevelt, Kermit, *Countercoup: The Struggle for the Control of Iran*, McGraw-Hill, New York 1979.

Ross, Sir E. Denison (Editor), *Sir Anthony Sherley and His Persian Adventure*, George Routledge & Sons, Ltd., London 1933.

Rubin, Barry, *Paved With Good Intentions: The American Experience in Iran*, Oxford University Press, Inc. 1980.

Ryan, Paul B, *The Iranian Rescue Mission: Why it Failed*, Naval Institute Press, Maryland 1985.

Salinger, Pierre, *American Held Hostage: The Secret Negotiations*, Doubleday, New York 1981.

Sick, Gary, *All Fall Down; America's Fateful Encounter with Iran*, I.B. Tauris & Co. Ltd., London 1985.

Stark, Freya, *The Valleys of the Assassins: And Other Persian Travels*, John Murray, London 1936.

Sullivan, William H, *Mission to Iran*, W.W. Norton & Company, New York 1981.

Taheri, Amir, *The Spirit of Allah: Khomeini and the Islamic Revolution*, Hutchinson & Co. Ltd., London 1985.

The Tower Commission Report, Bantam Books, Inc, New York 1987.

Willis, C.J. *Persia As It Is: Sketches of Modern Persian Life and Character*, Sampson Low, Marston, Searle & Rivington. London 1887.

Wright, Sir Denis, *The English Amongst the Persians*, I.B. Tauris & Co. Ltd., London.

Wright, Robin, *Sacred Rage*. André Deutsch Ltd., London 1986.

Spark, Gisela. *The Number of the Nouveau And Other Science Articles.*
Published by...London 1976.

Sutcliffe, William H. *A Sailor in Space.* V.W. Norton & Company
New York 1965.

Talbot, Annie. *The Theory of ... Women and the Human Revolution.*
Hutchinson & Co. Ltd., London 1985.

The Social Contract and Representation. Prentice-Hall, Inc. New York
1977.

Webster, J.H. Parsons. *H.G.B. Shadow of Atom.* Princeton University and
London Cambridge On Mission Science Educational, London
1965.

Wright, Sarah Davis. *Growth.* ... under the Population Laboratory &
Co. Ltd. London.

Wright, Robin. *Sacred Rage: Angry Arabs Fighting.* Ltd. London 1986.

250

Index